SECOND EDITION

READING
DIAGNOSIS
·FOR·
TEACHERS

• An Instructional Approach •

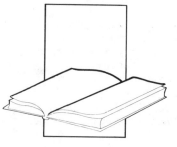

Rebecca Barr
National College of Education

Marilyn W. Sadow
Chicago State University

Camille L. Z. Blachowicz
National College of Education

Longman
New York & London

Dedicated to
MARILYN W. SADOW
A valued friend and colleague
(1925–1987)

Reading Diagnosis for Teachers, second edition

Copyright © 1990 and 1985 by Longman, a division
of Addison-Wesley Publishing Co., Inc.

Longman 95 Church Street, White Plains, N.Y. 10601
A division of Addison-Wesley Publishing Co., Inc.

Associated companies:
Longman Group Ltd., London
Longman Cheshire Pty., Melbourne
Longman Paul Pty., Auckland
Copp Clark Pitman, Toronto

Executive editor: Naomi Silverman
Prduction editor: Marie-Josée Anna Schorp
Text design adaptation: Kevin C. Kall
Cover design and illustration: Kevin C. Kall
Text art: K & S Graphics and Susan J. Moore
Production supervisor: Kathleen M. Ryan

Library of Congress Cataloging-in-Publication Data

Barr, Rebecca.
    Reading diagnosis for teachers.
    Bibliography: p.
    Includes index.
    1. Reading—Ability testing. I. Sadow,
Marilyn W., 1925–1987. II. Blachowicz, Camille L. Z. III. Title.
LB1050.46.B37 1990   372.4′076   89-8313
ISBN 0-8013-0290-0

ABCDEFGHIJ-DO-99   98   97   96   95   94   93   92   91   90   89

Contents

Preface *vii*

Chapter 1 Model for Reading Diagnosis and Instructional Planning 1

Goals of Reading Instruction 1
History of Reading Diagnosis 2
Reading Diagnosis as Part of Classroom Instruction 3
About This Book 5
Model for Reading Diagnosis 8
Case 1: John 12
Case 2: Mary 12
Case 3: Larry 13
Case 4: Tom 13
Subsequent Diagnosis 18

Chapter 2 The Development of Awareness of Printed Words 19

Stages of Understanding Print 19
Development of Print Awareness 20
Diagnosis of Print Awareness 25
Case 1: Jody's Understanding of Storybook Reading 27
Case 2: Jody's Understanding of Writing 30
Instruction to Support Print Awareness 33
Summary 38

iii

Chapter 3 Knowledge of Print   39

Development of Print Knowledge   39
Diagnosis of Print Knowledge   47
Case 1: Diagnosis of Ken's Sight Vocabulary   49
Case 2: Alex's Reading of a Graded Word List   51
Case 3: Ken's Spelling   55
Case 4: Alex's Skill in Word Identification   57
Instruction in Print Knowledge   58
Summary   64

Chapter 4 Reading Integration and Fluency   65

Development of Integration and Fluency   65
Diagnosis of Integration and Fluency   68
Case 1: Eva—Diagnosis   84
Instruction to Support Integration and Fluency   89
Case 2: Eva—Instruction   89
Case 3: Stan   94
Summary   98

Chapter 5 Vocabulary Knowledge: Development, Diagnosis,
               and Instruction   99

Development: Words, Meanings, and Concepts   100
Diagnosis of Vocabulary Knowledge Difficulty   116
Case 1: Raymond   119
Case 2: Tanya   128
Instructional Techniques   136
Summary   142

Chapter 6 Comprehension: Its Nature and Development   143

The Nature of Comprehension: What Good Readers Do   144
What Influences Comprehension?   145
Questions and the Development of Comprehension   156
Summary   171

Chapter 7 Reading Comprehension: Diagnosis and Instruction   173

Instructional Level   174
Diagnosis of Comprehension Difficulty   176
Case 1: Paul—Questioning   183
Case 2: Andrea—A Retelling   190
Case 3: Jake—Think-Aloud   192
Comprehension Instruction   194
Summary   204

Chapter 8 Diagnosis Based on an Instructional Passage 207

Diagnostic Procedures 210
Case Study Application 216
Case 1: Sharon 216
Case 2: Patricia 225
Summary 230

Chapter 9 Diagnosis with Standardized IRIs 231

Administration 231
Case 1: Chuck 233
Interpretation of Results 237
Case Study Applications 239
Case 2: Sara 240
Case 3: James 244
Summary 250

Chapter 10 Organizing Students for Instruction and Interpreting
Standardized Test Results 253

Beginning-of-the-Year Assessment and Grouping 253
Standardized Testing 261
Using Standardized Test Information 266
Summary 271
Conclusion 272

Appendix A: Dolch Basic Sight Vocabulary 275

Appendix B: Blachowicz Informal Phonics Survey 277

Appendix C: Complete Records of Performance on an IRI: James 281

References *305*

Index *319*

Preface

The goal of this book is to help classroom teachers acquire the knowledge and skill that is necessary for classroom-based reading diagnosis and instructional planning. In planning a text to accomplish this purpose, we have been influenced by many considerations. Most important among these are our views on the nature of reading and learning and the role of assessment within classroom instruction.

Reading is an active process in which readers interact with text to reconstruct the message of the author. Research in recent years emphasizes the extent to which reading depends on the background knowledge of readers. Printed symbols are signs which lead an active mind to reflect on alternatives during the process of constructing knowledge.

Learning to read must similarly be an interactive process in which students and teacher examine the alternative ways in which they make sense of text. Some constructions, however, may be limited because children have difficulty dealing with printed words; others may reflect inadequate knowledge of concepts that are central to the message of an author; still others may have structured the message in plausible ways which differ from the original intent of the author.

The role of teachers in this process is extremely complicated. For those students who are unable to make use of the signs provided by authors because of inadequate knowledge of print, teachers must find ways to develop this knowledge. Similarly, for students who lack basic concepts, this knowledge must be developed through experience, discussion, and explanation. Finally, some students with good knowledge of print and underlying concepts need help to weave the meaning of authors from sentence to sentence and across paragraphs.

We believe that teachers must know certain things in order to help students develop the background, skills, and strategies for effective reading. First, teachers must understand the nature of reading development. They must know how students develop knowledge of print, vocabulary concepts, and reading comprehension strategies. Second, they must be able to determine the nature of student problems when they encounter difficulty. Teachers must become good observers who also know how to make sense of what they observe. Third, and finally, they must know what to do to help students when they identify problems. They must know how to plan instruction that will help students solve their problems with reading. In other words, teachers must know about reading development, diagnosis, and instructional planning. Accordingly, we have organized our chapters in this text around these three major topics.

Just as we believe that learning is an active process for students, we also believe that it should be an active process for teachers. Thus we have planned a series of activities to promote thinking and problem solving. We have done this in several ways. First, we believe that an understanding of reading disability, diagnosis, and instruction, can be achieved only through consideration of a variety of cases exemplifying different sorts of problems. Accordingly, most chapters in the book include several cases which are the focus of study and instructional planning. We have also been guided by our belief that skill can be acquired only through guided practice. Thus we have included procedures to help teachers develop basic observational skills and a sequence of tasks of increasing complexity that involve practice of previously acquired skills.

This is a time when many in the field of reading are inquiring about the nature and function of reading assessment (see, for example, *The Reading Teacher,* April 1987). For classroom teachers, we believe that diagnosis and other forms of assessment should occur as a part of ongoing instruction, that it should be based on normally occurring instructional assignments, and that it should serve as the basis for developing appropriate instruction. Accordingly, for this textbook we have selected diagnostic and instructional procedures that are appropriate for classroom use. While many of the suggested procedures will need to be practiced with individual students initially, once they are well learned, they will be incorporated into a teacher's repertoire to be used more informally during the active give and take of instruction.

Like all projects that involve the development of ideas over an extended period of time, this one has depended on the support and critical insight of many people. We owe a great debt to a number of students in the Graduate School at National College of Education, the Reading Department at Chicago State University, and the Department of Education at the University of Chicago. These students contributed the case studies that we have modified for inclusion in the text, provided important insights into the diagnostic process, and helped us evaluate the manuscript in its many stages. Some students went beyond these requirements of the courses we taught in order to provide us with additional case materials and help us refine the text; we are especially indebted to Pam Guastafeste, Katherine Morsbach, Nancy Lamia, Bobbie Johnson, Carol Cain, Alice Heiman, Kenneth Bryant, and Diana Kent. We also gratefully acknowledge the help of Naomi Silverman and Marie-Josée Schorp from Longman.

Our efforts were encouraged by our colleagues at National College of Education, Chicago State University, and those in the reading education community. In particular, Darrell Morris, Laurie Nelson, Diane Sullivan, Nikki Zarefsky, Pam Guastafeste, and Noreen Winningham provided instructive comments on earlier drafts. In addition we benefited from the clinical experiences and insights that Judith Daskal shared with us, as well as from the many comments and suggestions of James Cunningham, Peter DeWitz, Linda Gambrell, Catherine Hatcher, Peter Johnston, and Michael Kibby.

CHAPTER 1

Model for Reading Diagnosis and Instructional Planning

GOALS OF READING INSTRUCTION

Reading enables us to enrich our lives. All of us have experienced the thrill of reading a good story and the satisfaction of locating needed information. As teachers, we are committed to helping our students use and appreciate the experiences afforded through reading. Our goals must be to support children as they develop skill in reading and to instill in them a love for reading.

Achieving these goals is easy with some children. They learn to read easily, and the satisfaction they experience leads them to read often and to love reading. Unfortunately, there are other children who experience considerable difficulty reading. As a consequence, they see reading as unpleasant and grow to dislike it. These are children whom teachers worry about a great deal. It is the purpose of this book to provide teachers with the understandings needed to help these children. We believe that if teachers understand the needs of their students, they can help them to avoid extremely frustrating experiences while learning how to read. In turn, as these children acquire greater proficiency in reading, they will begin to appreciate the power reading gives them to enrich their own lives.

What do teachers need to know in order to diagnose the nature of these children's reading difficulty and to provide appropriate instructional support? This is not an easy question. Much is known about reading difficulty that would be useful to teachers in meeting the needs of their students. Yet we argue that this knowledge needs to be presented in such a way that it can be used by teachers during the active give-and-take of everyday instruction. Thus we have examined the body of knowledge about reading difficulties, derived mainly from clinical studies, and translated this knowledge into a format that we believe is useful to teachers. In the remainder of this chapter, we will briefly discuss what is known about reading diagnosis and the treatment of reading difficulties from a historical perspective, then consider how this knowledge must be framed to be directly useful to teachers, and finally describe a model for reading diagnosis and instructional planning in classrooms.

HISTORY OF READING DIAGNOSIS

Much of what we know about reading disability and its diagnosis comes from clinical studies of the 1920s and 1930s. Although earlier studies by physicians had described certain extreme cases (Fisher, 1905; Jackson, 1906; Morgan, 1896; Thomas, 1905), two developments in the field of education converged to support the scientific study of reading disability: (1) investigations into the psychological processes of reading (Dearborn, 1906; Dodge, 1905, 1907; Huey, 1898, 1900, 1908; Quantz, 1897) and (2) advancements in psychometric theory, which laid the foundation for the development of instruments to measure human traits.

Considerable testing of school populations had occurred between 1910 and 1915. In 1916, Uhl published a report describing the use of test results to diagnose the reading needs of individuals (see also Zirbes, 1918). It may surprise some readers to find that the earliest diagnostic work was conducted in the school setting by teachers and other school personnel. The first professional book on reading diagnosis, *Deficiencies in Reading Ability: Their Diagnosis and Remedies,* written by Clarence T. Gray in 1922, relied in large part on what had been learned from school-based studies of reading difficulty.

Concurrently, it became apparent to educators that more detailed study of students experiencing difficulty with reading would provide insight into reading processes and how they become disrupted. Further, detailed case studies would promote the design of appropriate testing procedures and the development of effective remedial instruction. Special educational laboratories and reading clinics were established, mainly in university settings (Clowes, 1930; Dougherty, 1929; Fernald & Keller, 1926; Monroe, 1928, 1932). In order to appreciate the knowledge acquired during this early period, the reader should examine the classic study conducted by William S. Gray and his associates at the University of Chicago Educational Laboratory (Gray, Kibbe, Lucas, & Miller, 1922). The purpose of the investigation was threefold: to diagnose the nature and causes of reading difficulty, to classify types of poor readers, and to test experimentally the efficacy of remedies.

Other research in the 1920s and 1930s served to expand and develop the knowledge gained through clinical case studies. Pelosi (1977) notes several developments during this period that contributed to the refinement of reading diagnosis. First, case study investigation, which continued to be the dominant method of research, became more elaborate and sophisticated (see, e.g., Baer,

1926; Gates, 1927; Hincks, 1926; Monroe, 1928, 1932). Second, precise diagnostic instruments and procedures were developed (see, e.g., Betts, 1934; Dolch, 1936; Durrell, 1936; Ford, 1928; Gates, 1926, 1935; Monroe, 1932). Finally, there was an ever-increasing interest in the nature of reading processes and the causes of reading disability (see, e.g., Bond, 1935; Dearborn, 1933; Jastak, 1934; Orton, 1928; Robinson, 1937, 1946; Tinker, 1934).

During this period researchers in such related fields as medicine and psychology popularized the term *dyslexia* when referring to children with reading difficulties. This term is confusing to some teachers, who wonder what it really means. Literally translated, it means a dysfunction with words (the Latin prefix *dys* means "difficult" or "faulty" and the Greek root *lexia* refers to "words"). Thus the term is simply descriptive; it does not address the underlying nature of the difficulty. We therefore believe that such labeling is not particularly useful, especially since it often carries with it the connotation of a central functioning impairment. Currently, the use and definition of this term are being reconsidered by professionals in reading and related fields. Similarly, we believe that other forms of labeling such as "visual learner," "left-brain dominant," and "perceptually handicapped" are of little help to teachers in planning appropriate instruction, and they may be misleading in that they imply simplistic approaches. As will be shown in the following sections of this chapter, we prefer to identify the nature of the reading difficulty in a way that anticipates appropriate instruction.

READING DIAGNOSIS AS PART OF CLASSROOM INSTRUCTION

In our consideration of what teachers need to know in order to diagnose students' reading problems, several major influences have shaped our thinking. First, we believe that diagnosis undertaken by teachers and by reading specialists in classroom settings should differ in several important respects from the diagnostic procedures developed by clinicians in reading clinics.

Classroom conditions make it difficult for a reading specialist or teacher to undertake certain diagnostic procedures. For example, both extensive work with individual students and the use of testlike tasks are often impractical. Perhaps more important, useful alternative procedures are available. We emphasize the basic differences between the conditions or constraints under which reading clinicians and classroom teachers work because we believe these differences have profound implications for *how* the procedures of reading diagnosis, which were developed originally in the clinical setting, should be modified for use in the classroom.

A clinician typically sees a student for a limited period of time for the specific purpose of evaluating his or her reading skill and identifying appropriate instruction. The evaluation is based on a variety of standardized and informal tests of aptitude and achievement. In order to judge whether a reading problem exists, the clinician compares the reading achievement of the student with his or her expected level of achievement, the latter based (usually) on measures of verbal and nonverbal ability, with years of schooling and age sometimes taken into account. The clinician then identifies specific areas of reading difficulty by analyzing the student's performance on standardized and informal measures of reading and language skills. Instructional recommendations are generally based on the clinician's tutorial experience with students who experienced similar reading difficulties.

However, it is difficult for a teacher to incorporate these procedures into his or her repertoire of skills. One reason is that formal testing represents a departure from the typical instructional activities and is difficult to undertake on an individual basis along with the responsibilities of managing a class. But more to the point, whereas standardized tests are essential for the clinician because they provide a normative frame of reference, they are much less important for the classroom teacher, who has the performances of other children in the class available as a normative standard.

Further, standardized tests are unnecessary because teachers have access to a wealth of evidence about the reading and language development of their students on a daily basis. They listen to children read orally, note their answers to comprehension questions, and observe how they think and talk about a variety of topics. Nevertheless, teachers' observations tend to be haphazard, partly because they are constantly faced with the job of managing the class as well as instructing students—but also partly because they have had little training in how to observe and interpret students' responses. Most teachers have not been taught to design informal "probe" questions or oral reading tasks in order to clarify the nature of a student's misunderstanding. Typically, teachers are trained to diagnose reading difficulties by interpreting scores and reading behaviors on standardized and informal reading tests. They must then generalize from the results of these tests back to the student's performance on classroom materials. We believe that a more sensible approach is to help teachers acquire the observational and interpretive skills that will enable them to use the wealth of evidence that is available on an ongoing basis in the classroom.

Teachers usually see their students over an entire school year. By contrast, a clinician usually sees a student for a limited number of diagnostic sessions. Accordingly, the clinician is under considerable time pressure to make an accurate diagnosis and does so by the administration of multiple tests. Because teachers work with students for an extended period, "working hypotheses" rather than diagnostic conclusions would seem to be a better goal for classroom diagnosis. That is, teachers have the opportunity to revise and modify their understanding of their students' reading skills on the basis of successive observations interlaced with instructional intervention. This time advantage needs to be capitalized on in the development of an effective diagnostic strategy.

Teachers possess information about their students' current instructional program and response to it and they are in a position to evaluate their physical and social well-being. Thus teachers can set goals and expectations that are consistent with the classroom program. The aim of the teacher is to help students who encounter some reading difficulty to acquire the skills necessary to reenter the mainstream of class instruction. By contrast, in the clinical setting, the student's verbal and sometimes nonverbal abilities constitute the main basis for establishing an expected level of reading. As a result, some very able and relatively good readers are identified as disabled reader simply because there is a discrepancy between their reading and their (high) verbal development. Similarly, students with low verbal ability and commensurately low reading skill may be viewed as having no reading problem even though they are unable to cope with the reading materials used by the class.

We recommend that the expected reading level of students—and whether or not they are considered to have reading problems—be established in terms of the levels of materials used by the class or by a subgroup thereof. Accordingly, some children who read in accord with their mental ability but are unable to cope with material read by their reading group will be identified as having reading problems. Further, some proficient readers reading below their verbal ability will not be identified as having reading problems. The comparison for delineating reading problems used in this text lies not within the child's performance per se (reading skill versus verbal ability) but rather in the interaction between student reading proficiency and classroom reading demands. We believe that this recommendation reflects the reality of instructional alternatives in classrooms and the objectives teachers are expected to help their classes achieve. We are not arguing that it is wrong to use aptitude or verbal ability as a standard against which to evaluate reading achievement but, rather, that such measurements are simply less useful in the classroom setting than in the clinic.

In sum, we believe that classroom diagnosis and instructional planning should be based on students' performance with classroom instructional materials, that the existence of a reading problem should be determined on the basis of a discrepancy between a student's reading level and that needed in order for him or her to learn from class materials, that both diagnosis and instruction should be modified on an ongoing basis, and that instructional plans should be formed with the conditions of the classroom and school in mind.

ABOUT THIS BOOK

Goals

The goal of the book is to help reading and classroom teachers acquire the knowledge and skill necessary for reading diagnosis and instructional planning. What must be learned falls into three main categories. First, teachers must acquire a systematic framework for diagnosis—one that identifies the major decisions that have to be made as well as the evidence that is needed in order to make them. Second, teachers must develop observational skills in the areas of listening to children read and answer questions. Finally, they must learn how to translate diagnostic findings into a plan for instructional support that is realistic in view of the student's needs and the school's resources.

Organization and Content

In writing this book, we were influenced by our belief that teachers need a model to organize their thinking about the problems students encounter as they learn to read, and to guide them as they explore the nature of these difficulties.

Beyond this we believe that skill in reading diagnosis and instruction can best be acquired through guided practice. Thus we provide training procedures for developing skill in observation and also provide a sequence of tasks of increasing complexity for practicing previously acquired skills.

Finally, we believe that an understanding of reading difficulty and its diagnosis and treatment can be achieved only through a consideration of a variety of cases exemplifying different types of problems. Accordingly, most of the chapters include cases, which are the focus of study and instructional planning. The 23 cases presented provide a useful basis from which to derive some understanding of the various forms of reading disability and appropriate instruction.

This book is organized into four main sections. The first one, Chapter 1, discusses the perspective and goals of the book and also presents a framework or model for diagnosis, a model that is used as the organizing perspective in subsequent chapters. The model focuses on three components of reading: skill with print, vocabulary meaning, and reading comprehension.

The second section elaborates on each of these components. Chapters 2, 3, and 4 develop a theoretical perspective about the development of skill with print. Chapter 2 examines how children first develop an awareness of print and describes tasks that teachers can use in classrooms to further explore and support the development of this awareness. Chapter 3 examines how children develop underlying kowledge about print as evidenced in their sight vocabulary and word identification skill. Teachers may wish to use some of the informal tasks to delineate further the nature of reading problems observed during contextual reading. Instructional approaches to help students develop a sight vocabulary and word identification skill are described. Chapter 4 details methods teachers can use to observe children's oral reading of selections, to pinpoint areas of difficulty, and to interpret the results. Instructional procedures for the development of reading integration and fluency are also described.

Chapter 5 discusses vocabulary knowledge and its role in comprehension and then shows how this knowledge may be assessed and the results interpreted. Instructional procedures for the development of vocabulary knowledge are discussed. Chapters 6 and 7 provide an overview of the nature of comprehension, introduce procedures for developing comprehension questions that pertain to the text as a whole, and describe useful diagnostic procedures. These two chapters also describe useful instructional procedures for enhancing comprehension and present a framework for choosing among them.

In the third section, Chapter 8, knowledge and skill acquired in the preceding chapters are combined in a comprehensive diagnosis of different types of reading disability. Although necessarily systematic and compressed, the case studies are intended to develop diagnostic, observational, and interpretive skills that the teacher can then use in a more flexible fashion during classroom instruction.

In the final section, the model and way of thinking about student's reading difficulties are applied to standardized assessment procedures. Chapter 9 shows how diagnostic strategies can be used with informal reading inventories to delineate in comprehensive fashion the reading problems that students encounter. Chapter 10 discusses the nature and design of standardized reading tests and shows how they may be used diagnostically to reveal the nature of student reading difficulty.

Characteristics of the Book

Several characteristics distinguish this book from other books on reading diagnosis. As was mentioned, this book discusses many case studies of students with reading problems. Each case study is presented so as to require active teacher participation in some aspect of observation, analysis, and interpretation. Because reading diagnosis is a complex process, we have broken it into component skills for ease of study and practice; at the same time, we have retained the integrity of each case. As a result, teachers become aware of how component processes fit within the whole. In the final chapters, teachers must deal with all phases of the diagnostic process.

Each time a case is considered, the diagnostic model developed later in this chapter is used as an organizing framework. Our interest is not only in developing observational and analytic skills, but in enabling teachers to make comparisons across areas of a student's reading and language functioning in order to identify strengths and weaknesses and, on this basis, to set instructional priorities. Too often teachers learn to interpret results from single standardized or criterion-referenced tests without obtaining a comprehensive view. Because this text repeatedly looks at cases within the framework of the diagnostic model, it facilitates the development of comprehensive diagnostic thinking.

Our case presentations reflect our belief that diagnosis must lead directly to instructional planning. An elaborate diagnosis is unnecessary if few instructional alternatives exist; the purpose of diagnosis is to provide the basis for deciding among instructional alternatives. Accordingly, case presentations include discussion of how reading evidence is transformed into an instructional plan.

These strengths of a systematic training program have resulted in the omission of many topics that are often developed in traditional texts on reading diagnosis. For example, this book contains no systematic treatment of intelligence testing or perceptual testing, a limited discussion of the nature of standardized tests, and no discussion of school-based remedial reading programs. The omission of these topics stems from the decision to cover a limited number of topics in considerable depth. Moreover, these topics are already amply covered in existing textbooks on reading diagnosis.

MODEL FOR READING DIAGNOSIS

Our view of reading diagnosis and instructional planning assumes that students are active problem solvers. Therefore, the manner in which they develop reading skill is influenced by the instructional tasks they confront from grade to grade. For example, if students are instructed with a systematic phonics program, they learn to solve a somewhat different set of problems than if they are instructed with an eclectic program that emphasizes comprehension and a core vocabulary of reading words. Similarly, if students are given considerable experience reading and answering questions on expository materials, they develop different comprehension skills than if they read mainly narrative materials.

Two implications follow from this view. First, diagnosis must consider how students currently approach the task of reading in relation to the reading tasks they have encountered in the past. Second, subsequent instruction must build on this foundation. Thus, diagnosis by a teacher who is familiar with the instructional history of students and who tests their response to current instructional materials provides an optimal basis for instructional planning.

What must a teacher know in order to diagnose the nature of a student's reading difficulty? A diagnostician is much more than someone who knows how to administer tests. The diagnostician is like an active explorer whose search is guided by a carefully developed conceptual scheme. This scheme identifies the major decision points in the diagnostic process and then, once a particular decision is made, certain subsidiary decision points. Through this sequential decision-making procedure, plausible explanations for the difficulty are progressively evaluated.

Major Diagnostic Decisions

In the basic model of reading diagnosis shown in Figure 1.1, the central and most important process in reading is comprehension, the ability to reconstruct meaning from printed text. Within the classroom setting, the goal of reading is to accomplish the normal reading tasks that are part of instruction. Certain underlying processes such as print skill and vocabulary knowledge are viewed as supporting effective comprehension. These underlying areas become important if a student is experiencing difficulty with comprehension. In sum, within our thinking in this book, the main goal of reading diagnosis and reading instruction is to help all students develop effective strategies for comprehension.

A first decision that teachers must make is determining whether or not their students comprehend the textual materials that are part of instruction; if not, it can be concluded that a student is experiencing problems in reading. We believe that a student's expected reading level—and whether or not a reading problem exists—should be established in terms of the level of materials used by the class or a subgroup thereof. If a student is able to read and comprehend classroom material, then, within our scheme, we conclude that no reading problem exists. The student can be assigned the appropriate materials and given suitable instruction during the daily reading lesson. However, when there is evidence that a student cannot adequately understand the materials used for regular class instruction, a reading problem is considered to exist and further diagnosis is warranted.

When there is evidence of a reading problem, the second decision point involves identification of the general nature of the problem. The goal of reading is the comprehension of text. Deficiencies in three general areas may interfere with comprehension: (1) inadequately developed print skill, (2) inadequate vocabulary knowledge pertaining to the phenomena described

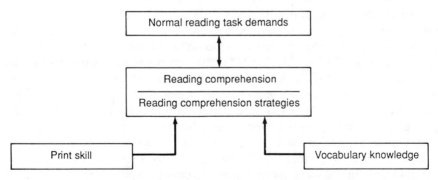

Figure 1.1   Basic model of reading diagnosis.

in a passage, and (3) inadequately developed strategies for understanding text (see Figure 1.1).

Print skill refers to the ability of readers to efficiently translate printed symbols into spoken language or meaning. This area includes not only skill with phonics, structural analysis, and syllabication, which permit a student to identify previously unknown words, but also the acquisition of a set of words that are recognized instantaneously. It includes the proficient integration of word recognition and word identification with contextual information as a student responds to prose.

Most children acquire basic print skill in the course of their early reading instruction, and this skill becomes integrated and automatic through elementary school reading experiences. It should be noted that the emphasis of early instruction can have a profound influence on the particular print concepts that students learn. Further, students who have difficulty acquiring print concepts that are taught explicitly also have difficulty inferring those that are not explicitly taught. For example, some reading programs emphasize the development of phonic concepts but do not teach the process of blending and the application of phonic knowledge in context. For those students who do not spontaneously infer how to blend phonic values, good knowledge of phonics may be of little value in identifying unknown words. Print skill is more fully described in the next three chapters.

Vocabulary knowledge refers to knowledge not only of the key words contained in particular reading selections but also of the encompassing concepts that are being conveyed and the ways in which word meaning is revealed by context. For example, to understand a passage about the discoveries of Copernicus and Galileo, students must be familiar with the meanings of such words as *planet* and *telescope,* but beyond these, the encompassing concept of "movement" is central to an understanding of how the solar system works. Students differ in the extent to which they can comprehend a passage without adequate knowledge of the concepts presumed to be known. Vocabulary knowledge is more fully considered in Chapter 5.

In addition to experiencing problems in print skill and/or vocabulary knowledge, students may experience problems in their *comprehension strategies.* That is, a student may have no difficulty with print translation and may be familiar with the meanings of the words and concepts that are central to understanding a passage but may still fail to comprehend. This failure stems from difficulty with the integration of information across a text. Whereas a writer begins with a conception of the important message to be conveyed in a passage and then confronts the problem of how the message may be parceled into words, sentences, and paragraphs, the reader must reconstruct the author's message by processing these units and recombining them into one or several arguments or descriptions. Some readers experience difficulty unique to this integration process, as well as to the monitoring and fix-up strategies necessary to recognize and address these problems. For example, readers often encounter pronouns, nouns, or phrases that refer back to a previously identified person or topic, and they must realize that a new topic is not being introduced but, rather, that more information is being provided about the same topic or person. Then they must understand what to look for and how to reread and connect the information they missed on first reading. Comprehension strategies are considered in Chapters 6 and 7.

The second step in the first stage of diagnosis is, then, to determine whether a student is experiencing difficulty with print skill, vocabulary knowledge, and/or comprehension strategies. While these three areas are part of an integrated process, it is useful to consider them separately for several reasons. To begin with, each requires different sorts of information and assessment procedures to determine its status. Print skill is typically assessed by having students read passages, words, or word parts aloud, whereas discourse processing is typically assessed by having the reader "retell" the passage content or respond to comprehension questions based on a selection that has been read. Vocabulary knowledge assessment does not necessarily involve reading; rather, it uses questions to elicit a student's understanding of selected terms. The three areas are also different in terms of the sorts of instructional procedures that enhance their development. For example, the instruction that is useful for helping a student to develop word identification strategies is quite different from that which is effective in facilitating discourse comprehension.

The model for diagnosis shown in Figure 1.1 assumes not only that these three areas can be considered separately, but also that two of them, print skill and vocabulary knowledge, represent conditions that are necessary in order for the third, comprehension strategies, to be effectively employed. Accordingly, if a student fails to comprehend a passage, it is important to examine the student's print strategies and vocabulary knowledge in order to determine whether problems exist. Problems in either of these areas could account for the observed difficulty in comprehension. Thus, it is difficult in such cases to ascertain whether the student is experiencing problems in comprehension over and above those that stem from deficiencies in print skill or vocabulary knowledge. Comprehension strategies constitute a central category within the model: problems are assumed to occur in this area when comprehension is weak *and* both vocabulary concepts and print skill are adequately developed.

In order to begin thinking in terms of the diagnostic scheme, let us consider the strengths and difficulties of four students (Cases 1–4) who have encountered problems reading classroom materials. The reader is encouraged to consider the evidence and determine each student's relative strength in the areas specified by the diagnostic model. On this basis, it should be possible to specify the area(s) in need of further diagnosis.

CASE 1: John

John is 11 years and 2 months old and is in the sixth grade. His teacher has found that he has considerable difficulty understanding not only his social studies and science textbooks, but also the stories in the fifth-grade-level reading book used by her slowest-paced group. His oral reading, however, is flawless and he even reads the social studies and science passages with considerable fluency. His teacher first noticed that he has extremely vague concepts pertaining to biological terms and then pursued his understanding of more common terms. She found that he knew only superficially or not at all words from his reading book such as *revenge*, *comrade, foundation,* and *craftsmen.*

The reader should pause for a moment to consider John's case. In terms of the diagnostic scheme, which are the areas of this boy's strength and difficulty?

Diagnosis. The oral reading evidence indicates strength in the area of print skill. John's inability to answer the questions posed by his teacher is therefore attributable to inadequate vocabulary knowledge and/or poor comprehension strategies. This possibility that vocabulary knowledge is an area of difficulty is suggested by his lack of knowledge about terms known by his classmates. Thus, we tentatively conclude that vocabulary knowledge is John's major problem area. It is possible that comprehension difficulties also exist, but this remains to be determined by having him read a passage for which his vocabulary knowledge is sufficiently well developed. Vocabulary knowledge, then, should be the first area of focus.

CASE 2: Mary

Mary is 7½ years old and in the second grade. She is currently in the middle reading group, which uses second-grade-level materials. When she reads aloud during reading instruction, she does so fluently, making few errors. However, many of her answers to postreading questions show that she has not understood major events within the story. Questions about important terms within the story reveal that she has a good command of English and is more knowledgeable than other students in the group.

The reader should consider the following questions. Does Mary have any problems in reading and, if so, in what area(s)? What evidence supports these conclusions?

Diagnosis. Obviously, Mary's reading difficulty is not associated with inadequately developed print skill or vocabulary knowledge. Her inability to comprehend what she reads may therefore derive from discourse-level inadequacies. Accordingly, comprehension strategies merit further exploration.

CASE 3: Larry

Larry is 10 years old and in fourth grade. He is in the slowest-paced group in the class, which reads from third-grade materials. Larry's teacher had almost immediately noted his difficulty in reading aloud. Although Larry had developed familiarity with some common words, he would wait for the teacher to assist him on many other words, particularly those that were multisyllabic. His comprehension of stories that he read silently was extremely low; however, he comprehended well when the others in his group read aloud. He also demonstrated good understanding of key words in the reading selections; indeed, he was one of the most knowledgeable class members when it came to science activities and social studies discussions.

Again, it is important to consider the nature of Larry's reading. The reader should derive a tentative diagnosis of his reading strengths and difficulties.

Diagnosis.   Larry experiences difficulty in the area of print skill but also in comprehension of materials that he has read. He is strong in vocabulary knowledge. Therefore, we conclude that his comprehension difficulty reflects his poorly developed print skill. There is evidence to support this conclusion, namely, his good comprehension when he listens to others read. Once he acquires skill with print, he should become a proficient reader, given his well-developed vocabulary knowledge. The task at hand is further diagnosis of his print skill in order to learn how to facilitate his development in this area.

CASE 4: Tom

Tom is 7 years and 9 months old and in the third grade. In second grade he was with the middle reading group, and his third-grade teacher has continued that placement. His answers to comprehension questions indicate excellent understanding of what he reads, whether silently or aloud. Further, informal questioning about key vocabulary words indicates a breadth of vocabulary knowledge and fluency of expression. However, his oral reading is characterized by frequent substitutions of words. He seems to have developed extremely careless reading procedures.

Again, the reader should consider how we might make sense of these reading characteristics. Does Tom have a reading problem and, if so, what is its nature?

Diagnosis.   It is clear that Tom's strengths are his good vocabulary knowledge and his adequate comprehension. Nevertheless, his print skill appears to be inadequately developed and should be explored further. Note that in terms of the model, Tom's pattern of reading strengths and weaknesses is one that is unlikely to occur. The model suggests that adequately developed print skill is a prerequisite for adequate comprehension, and typically this is true. Exceptions occur, however, among students with extremely well-developed vocabulary knowledge. Such students, on the basis of this knowledge and minimal information from print, are able to make sense of a story or passage. While we may conclude that Tom has no reading problem at the present time, his print skill will become inadequate to the demands of reading as the materials become more technical and precise in their informational content. Therefore, it is appropriate to treat Tom as having a reading problem in the area of print skill and to diagnose further the nature of his difficulty.

Diagnostic Patterns

These cases show how the diagnostic model may be used to determine whether a reading problem exists and to identify the areas in need of further diagnostic exploration. In a more systematic fashion, Table 1.1 shows the number of different patterns of reading skill that are possible when comprehension, print skill, and vocabulary knowledge are considered. For example, John, the first case we considered with poor comprehension and vocabulary knowledge but good print skill, conforms to Pattern 3. The second case, Mary, with adequate print skill and vocabulary knowledge but inadequate comprehension, conforms to Pattern 2. The third case, Larry, represents Pattern 5, with poor print skill and comprehension but good vocabulary knowledge. Finally, Tom conforms to the relatively uncommon Pattern 6, with good comprehension and vocabulary knowledge but inadequate print skill.

In Pattern 1, reading comprehension and underlying print skill and vocabulary knowledge are all sufficient for the student to cope with the reading tasks normally given him or her. Because there appears to be no reading difficulty, further diagnosis is unnecessary.

Pattern 2 consists of adequate print skill and vocabulary knowledge but inadequate reading comprehension: clearly, the potential for adequate comprehension is strong, but the student has not yet acquired some skills or organizing concepts for processing text. Further diagnosis in the area of comprehension is needed to determine the nature of the problem.

Pattern 3 is that of the student often identified as a "word caller"—the student who possesses adequate print skill but inadequate vocabulary knowledge and reading comprehension. Where we see this pattern, we assume that limited vocabulary and concepts interfere with reading comprehension: the student's limited experiences set a ceiling on what he or she can comprehend through print. Further exploration of the student's language functioning is appropriate. For example, a student may have experienced certain situations or events but failed to acquire the pertinent verbal labels. The instruction recommended for this student would be very different from that recommended for a student who also lacked the experiential base.

In Pattern 4, reading comprehension and both sets of underlying skills are inadequately developed. Further exploration of the student's vocabulary knowledge and print skill is appropriate.

Pattern 5 characterizes the student who has difficulty in translating print

TABLE 1.1. DIAGNOSTIC PATTERNS OF PRINT SKILL, VOCABULARY KNOWLEDGE, AND READING COMPREHENSION STRATEGIES

Skill area	Common patterns					Uncommon patterns		
	1	2	3	4	5	6	7	8
Reading comprehension	+	0	0	0	0	+	+	+
Print skill	+	+	+	0	0	0	+	0
Vocabulary knowledge	+	+	0	0	+	+	0	0
Further diagnostic exploration[a]	Discontinue diagnosis	Explore comprehension strategies	Explore vocabulary knowledge		Explore print skill			

[a] In Patterns 3, 4, and 5, comprehension strategies might also be an area of weakness. However, this area is directly explored only when vocabulary knowledge and print skill have been eliminated as major factors in reading difficulty.

into familiar language. Here we assume that poor print skill accounts for poor reading comprehension. The student has the strength of good language development, as indicated by strong vocabulary knowledge. Further diagnosis should focus on how the student identifies and recognizes words.

Because reading comprehension typically depends on the development of print skill and vocabulary knowledge, the remaining three patterns, in which comprehension is good while print skill and/or vocabulary knowledge are poor, occur infrequently. Pattern 8, in fact, probably does not occur; or, if observed, it probably reflects invalid measurement in one of the three areas. Pattern 6, as we have seen, occurs mainly for extremely able students with well-developed verbal skills. These students are able to compensate for rather poorly developed print skill by using a combination of contextual cues, minimal print cues, and past experience; as a result, they score at an adequate level in reading comprehension. For this pattern, further examination of print skill is recommended. Although the student will often tolerate the frustration of the reading task when working with the teacher on an individual basis, he or she may avoid reading tasks when left to work alone. And although it may be possible to compensate for skill deficiencies at this stage, these may later interfere with comprehension of more difficult reading material.

Finally, Pattern 7 rarely occurs. If it is observed, it probably reflects a kind of "production deficiency." That is, a student, although able to summarize a passage or respond to questions based on it, may have difficulty generating definitions of terms or demonstrating their use.

The purpose of the first stage of the diagnosis is to examine each of the three aspects of reading and to determine its relative status. This procedure ensures that major problem areas will not be overlooked and that areas for more intensive exploration are identified.

Developmental Flexibility of the Model

The diagnostic model is applicable to all levels of skill, from initial reading acquisition to mature reading proficiency. That is, it is useful for understanding the strengths and difficulties of a beginning reader as well as of a college student. The flexibility of this diagnostic approach follows from conceptualizing reading as having the three component areas. Each area can be seen as having a different pattern of development, in accordance with the different problems posed by the reading materials that students are expected to understand at successive levels. (See Chall, 1983, for a more comprehensive but somewhat different treatment of developmental stages in reading). These changing demands of reading materials, considered here briefly, are treated more comprehensively in subsequent chapters.

The first two years of reading instruction usually emphasize the development of skill for translating print to speech or meaning. Some reading programs focus on the development of phonic concepts, others on the development of a sight vocabulary. Most current programs work on both types of concepts, through a skills sequence and extensive reading of contextual materials. These contextual materials are generally narrative in form, with the characters (people or animals) performing acts and speaking thoughts that are familiar to young children. Accordingly, most children already possess the relevant vocabulary knowledge and have acquired the necessary comprehension strategies through listening to stories read to them. However, when this is not the case, these aspects of reading must become areas of instructional focus along with print skill.

Students refine and integrate their print skill during subsequent years in several ways. They become able to tackle longer and more complex words, some of which they have never heard before. They become so familiar with the characteristics of print that processing becomes almost automatic for "easy" materials. As a consequence, reading rate improves dramatically.

As print skill is refined, however, new problems arise. Beginning with third grade, typically, students encounter new forms of printed materials. They are expected to read texts other than the basal readers—texts that are often characterized by a markedly different paragraph structure. In subject areas such as science and social studies, paragraphs are often organized around a major topic plus examples of supporting information or organized in terms of temporal, spatial, logical, or cause-and-effect relationships. Such a structure differs not only from that of narrative materials but also, of course, from the oral language forms with which students are familiar. Once students encounter expository materials, they must acquire many new skills for processing information.

Simultaneous with these new discourse-processing problems, new demands are being made on vocabulary knowledge. In sharp contrast to the primary materials, science, social studies, math, and more advanced forms of literature introduce vocabulary and underlying concepts and text structures that go beyond the students' prior experiences and vocabulary knowledge. Thus, students must learn how to obtain new knowledge from text.

The problems posed in elementary school continue throughout school and college because students are assigned reading materials that make increasingly difficult conceptual and organizational demands. Further, students must become more independent readers in order to accomplish homework assignments. The increasing amount of reading required demands increasingly efficient print processing. And information from a variety of sources must be evaluated, compared, and integrated in ever more sophisticated reports and projects. This brief discussion indicates some of the ways in which reading demands change over time. And the point to which we return is that despite the changing nature of reading acquisition, the diagnostic model is able to account for reading difficulties at all levels.

SUBSEQUENT DIAGNOSIS

The first stage of reading diagnosis involves assessing the relative strength of a student's print skill, vocabulary knowledge, and comprehension in response to the demands of reading materials typically used in his or her class. The second stage is somewhat more complex, for it involves more detailed diagnostic exploration of the areas of reading in which a student is experiencing difficulty. In the next six chapters, we will examine the nature of and the diagnostic strategies for assessing print skill, vocabulary knowledge, and reading comprehension. The third stage of diagnosis, that of developing an instructional plan responsive to the difficulties that a student encounters, is discussed in general terms in each chapter and more specifically with each set of cases presented.

CHAPTER 2

The Development of Awareness of Printed Words

STAGES OF UNDERSTANDING PRINT

Learning to read is a complex process in which children solve many different problems. This and the next two chapters focus on the problems that children must solve and the stages they pass through in understanding how print relates to speech and meaning. Different researchers think about the development of literacy in different ways. Chall (1983), for example, identifies five major stages through which students progress as they develop reading proficiency. Following a prereading stage, these are (1) initial reading or decoding (grades 1–2), (2) confirmation and fluency (grades 2–3), (3) learning the new from a single perspective (grades 4–8?), (4) learning the new from multiple viewpoints (high school), and (5) comprehending from a world view (college). From somewhat different perspectives, Heath (1983), Cochran-Smith (1984), and Taylor and Dorsey-Gaines (1988) and argue that purposeful reading in which children are concerned with meaning occurs from the earliest periods of learning to read.

While we agree that meaning and function of reading and writing should be clear to children in the beginning stages of reading as well as later, we also believe that it is useful for teachers to understand changes that occur in the awareness and knowledge that children possess about printed text. Accordingly, we have delineated three major stages through which they progress as they learn about the nature and functions of print. We refer to the first as the development of *print awareness*. During this stage, children begin to notice print and to speculate about its meaning; some even begin to understand that print is related to speech and meaning in complicated ways.

During the second stage, the development of *knowledge of print,* they acquire systematic knowledge about the nature of words and letters. When children first try to remember words, they may do so on the basis of one or a combination of characteristics, including the initial letter, word length, an unusual letter, or a smudge on a card bearing the printed word. As they learn more about words, they attend to word features in a more systematic fashion, noting initial and final consonants as letter sound cues, medial letters, and a greater number of features in combination. This learning is often referred to as the dual development of a sight vocabulary and phonics knowledge. During this stage, children are also solving the problem of how speech, in particular, and meaning, in general, relate to print.

The third stage is the development of *reading fluency,* in which knowledge of print is consolidated and words are recognized rapidly and automatically, permitting undivided attention toward comprehending the meaning. Reading fluency depends on well-developed knowledge about print as well as the integration of print knowledge with information derived from context.

In this chapter we will consider children's emerging awareness of print during their preschool years. In Chapter 3 we will focus on their growing knowledge of printed words and letters. In Chapter 4 we will consider the development of fluent and effective reading strategies that come from consolidation of word knowledge and the integration of information from different sources during contextual reading. Within the chapters for each of these developmental periods, we will describe what children know about print (*development*), will discuss diagnostic procedures that provide windows into their thinking (*diagnosis*), and will describe instructional strategies that have been found useful in supporting the reading development of children (*instruction*).

DEVELOPMENT OF PRINT AWARENESS

Printed words are a common part of our culture. Walking down streets, we notice street signs, advertisements, T-shirt slogans, and printed directions. Inside homes we see magazines, letters, labels, and trademarks. Even when we watch television, we frequently see printed words. Because of the number of printed messages in our environment, almost all children encounter printed words and see people reading and writing. Some become aware of print at a very early age (Taylor, 1983). In this sense, learning to "read" print begins long before children engage in formal reading instruction.

Many children come to understand why people read and write by participating in acts of reading and writing. If they are read stories, they come to see that reading provides entertainment. If they participate in reading recipes, they see that reading provides information. If they help in writing lists, they come to see the value of writing as an aid to memory. Some children, however, are not direct participants in reading and writing. They observe adults doing so but develop only vague notions of why people read and write. Active participation in and observation of literacy activities are important because once children view these activities as pleasurable, useful, and informative, this experience forms the basis for their wanting to learn to read.

More difficult then inferring the reasons for reading and writing is understanding what people actually do when they read. It is not outwardly apparent what goes on in the minds of adults and older children when they look at print as they read or write. Children must guess about what is read or written and how the process works. Recent studies of young children inform us about some of the hunches children have about reading and writing and how these change over time (Harste, Woodward, & Burke, 1984).

From being read stories, children learn about the conventions for writing English and other languages. Learning about the arrangement of text involves knowing where a book begins, where to begin on a page, in what direction to move, what to do at the end of a line, and what to do at the end of a page. Further, it involves learning that printed words—and not just pictures—are reliable cues to speech and meaning.

For some children, learning about books and print begins long before school instruction. At home and in preschool, they have been read to from books, and they examine books themselves, sometimes with the help of a friend or older sibling. They ask questions about reading, try to mimic reading, and sometimes ask a reader to demonstrate reading by pointing to words as the story progresses. Knowledge about the arrangement of print develops through a variety of experiences extended over time. Some children, however, come to school without the advantage of these experiences, and, accordingly, lack much of the knowledge about print that has been acquired by their more fortunate peers. Studies reveal that children differ considerably in their knowledge about print (Clay, 1975; 1979). Thus, teachers must know how to examine these differences so as to be able to provide appropriate instruction.

Young children also grow in their understanding about the nature of story reading. Sulzby (1985), for example, had preschool and kindergarten children read their favorite stories to her. Predictably, she found that children could be divided into two main groups: those who depended mainly on such cues as pictures and their memory of a story as the basis for their storytelling, and those who relied on the print as the basis for reading. Further, she found that children in the first group differed in the extent to which their stories were well formed and the extent to which they reflected oral versus written language patterns. Some children mainly labeled or commented on the pictures, while others retold the actions in the story. Some told stories in a fashion similar to the way they talked, while others sounded as if they were reading (although their story showed little conformity to the story as printed in the book).

There were also differences among children who were aware that print in storybooks serves as the basis for reading. Such awareness was indicated by some children in their refusal to read because of not knowing the "words"; others focused on a limited number of known letters or words; and still others demonstrated varying degrees of reading proficiency. Studies such as this show that children vary in their understanding of the nature of stories and what it means to read.

One of the earliest problems to be solved by children concerns the nature of print. Children must come to realize that print is more than a series of marks. Failure to appreciate the representational nature of writing is common for very young children (Ferreiro & Teberosky, 1982). For example, Ferreiro (1984) reports that when asked, "What could be read here?" (pointing to the text), a 3-year-old responded, "Letters." When asked further, "What does it say in the letters?" he responded, "Letters." This and other evidence suggested that the child was not yet aware that letters were more than letters; he had not discerned the symbolic function of writing. In other words, print was seen as being no different from other marks or designs. Thus a major development toward literacy is achieved when children understand that writing represents meaning.

Young children must learn what it is that is read and written. They frequently believe that pictures as well as print are read. For example, Hiebert (1981) found that many 3-year-olds and some older preschoolers pointed to pictures when they were asked what readers should look at in books containing both pictures and print. Later, even when children distinguished pictures from print, they continued to identify numbers as letters. Gradually, they formed a concept of what it is that people read and write.

As part of this process, children must determine where writing goes in relation to pictures. On the basis of responses of preschoolers, Ferreiro (1984) speculates that children believe that writing must be inserted into drawings or abutted next to them to have meaning. Only later do they learn that the position of writing on a page can change in relation to the picture without changing the meaning of the text.

Somewhat later, children experiment with the number of letters that should be used to represent words. For example, Ferreiro (1984) reports that Fernando at 4 years, 11 months, represented "one corncob" with a single letter and "three corncobs" with three. Four months later he represented both "one child" and "five children" with three letters. He had progressed from believing that each letter corresponded to each object to the concept of words as composed of a fixed number of letters. Ferreiro also found that some children at a later stage represented longer spoken words with more letters than shorter words, one for each syllable. Her research also shows that different children approach the problem in different ways and develop somewhat different hypotheses.

Children during this period of early print awareness also learn to "read" words in context. That is, they can recognize labels and other signs that regularly occur in the same contexts, such as "stop" on an octagonal red sign at the street corner or "PEPSI" within a red-white-and-blue design. Careful studies show, however, that when the words are taken out of context, children do not always recognize them; further, when the writing itself is altered ("XEPSI" instead of "PEPSI"), the change is not detected (Masonheimer, Drum, & Ehri, 1984; see also Mason, 1980). This means that children identifying words in this manner have not yet entered the stage of word learning when they depend solely on the letters and other print-related features to recognize printed words.

Each of these studies helps us to gain insight into the problems that young children must solve as they grow in their understanding of printed messages. In order to gain even greater appreciation of the complexity of the task, consider the ways in which children's knowledge about their language must be related to the printed words they see. When they first become aware of print, they already possess a well-formed language system. Nevertheless, they have not learned to think about their language in an objective fashion. For linguists, language is a complex, hierarchical system, in which smaller units of language are nested within larger ones. For example, large units of discourse can be divided into sentences, and sentences into words or morphemes. Words are themselves composed of smaller units, syllables, which in turn are composed of sounds (phonemes and phones). Although students do not need to acquire the sophisticated perspective of a linguist in order to learn to read, they must become more aware of the nature of their language in order to understand the various ways in which spoken language corresponds to writing.

The correspondence between speech and writing is complicated because relationships occur on a number of levels and are by no means always obvious. At the most general level, the message of written exposition relates to a spoken counterpart. At a lower level, a printed sentence will also correspond to a spoken sentence. But whereas a capital letter and a period indicate the boundaries of the printed sentence, inflectional characteristics may indicate the boundaries of the spoken sentence. Spoken words also relate to printed words; but whereas printed words are marked by spaces, spoken words are not delineated from each other. Indeed, children may begin reading with little awareness of how speech becomes partitioned into word units. As children learn to read and spell, they acquire a visual representational system that allows them to see what they say and hear. Thus, word learning as a part of reading instruction involves not only learning about the nature of printed words, but also discovering how language may be segmented into units that correspond to printed words.

Below the level of meaningful words, spoken phonemes and syllables correspond to letters (graphemes) and series of letters. Establishing the relations between phonemes and letters is complicated for several reasons. First, just as children are not aware of word units in their spoken language, so they are not aware of the phonemes that compose spoken words. In fact, it has been argued that it is experience with letters that sensitizes children to the phonemes of words (Ehri, 1983). Second, although there are only 26 letters, some are easily confused because they are mirror images (*b* and *d*) or rotations (*n* and *u*) of each other. Finally, in English it is not always the case that one letter is used to represent one phoneme. For example, the pairs *sh, th,* and *ch* each represent a single phoneme. Further, particularly for vowels, the correspondence is more complex. A letter may stand for several different phonemes, and a phoneme may be represented by several different letters and/or combinations thereof.

In sum, children learn to understand language in an objective fashion on four main levels. At the level of stories and other textual messages, they develop *pragmatic awareness,* or the ability to relate sentences and messages to each other within the larger context in which they occur. This form of metacognitive awareness is discussed in Chapter 6 with regard to comprehension. At the level of sentences, they develop *syntactic awareness* about how the words in sentences relate to each other. For example, often children reading a sentence anticipate the part of speech that should occur next in the sentence. At the level of words, they develop *word awareness,* or the understanding of how language is segmented into printed word units. Finally, at the level of word elements, children develop *phonemic awareness,* or the ability to hear and manipulate subunits of words.

Recent research supports the importance of children being able to develop their ability to hear and objectify subunits of language. In particular, phonemic awareness has been identified as critical in the development of reading skill (Bradley & Bryant, 1983; Ehri, 1979). While there is some evidence that this awareness can occur through instructional tasks that help children hear the sound units in words without seeing how words are written (Lundberg, Frost, & Petersen, 1988), we believe that this ability is most naturally developed in classrooms in the context of reading and writing tasks.

In particular, we have selected diagnostic and instructional approaches that can be used easily with groups of children in classrooms. However, we believe it is important for teachers to understand how to diagnose the stages at which children are in their development of word and phonemic awareness. For example, children give evidence of word awareness when their storybook reading closely conforms to the text. The methods for developing "concept of word" in the section on instruction later in this chapter represent ways in which teachers can help their students to develop word awareness.

We believe that writing tasks represent a natural way for teachers to examine their students' phonemic awareness. Further, as we will suggest in the section on writing instruction, teachers can help students to hear sounds in words as they write language experience stories and as they help their students to write.

During their early years, children become aware of the nature of print and its relation to speech and meaning in many ways. Children differ greatly in the understanding they have achieved at the time they enter school. Some, in spite of extensive story reading and exposure to print, fail to make connections about the nature of storybook reading and writing. Others experience a less rich print environment and many are read stories infrequently. Often these children have not had the opportunities or encouragement to begin exploring the nature of print. Teachers must be able to assess their students' awareness of print and language in order to plan appropriate instructional activities. In the following section, procedures are described that can be used to explore the awareness that children have developed about reading and writing.

DIAGNOSIS OF PRINT AWARENESS

Teachers, particularly those in preschools and kindergarten, frequently encounter children who show little interest in reading and writing. Before beginning formal reading instruction, it is important to assess their knowledge about reading and writing. We have selected two major approaches that will help teachers gain insight into the awareness that children have of reading and writing. The first involves storybook reading and the second entails having children read what they have "written."

Storybook Reading

One effective way to explore children's understanding of reading and writing is to use the procedures developed by Sulzby (1985) in which a child reads a "favorite" storybook. To begin this informal diagnostic process, the teacher asks the child to select a favorite book from the class library. The teacher then takes the child to a quiet corner of the room and places the book sideways, cover down on the table and then asks the child to "Read me your book." If the child hesitates or refuses, the teacher should encourage him or her by saying, "Well, pretend you can. Pretend-read it to me."

While the child reads or pretends to read the story, the teacher must draw conclusions about how well the child understands the conventions of writing and whether the reading is based on pictures in the book or on the text. The form shown in Figure 2.1 can be used to summarize the teacher's observations during the assessment of a child's storybook reading.

With respect to the conventions of writing, the teacher should note whether the child:

- knows how to hold the book right side up
- begins at the beginning of the story
- begins reading at the top of the left hand page
- reads across the page from left to right

Figure 2.1   Form for summarizing results from storybook reading.

SUMMARY FORM—STORYBOOK READING CHECKLIST

Date

Conventions of Writing
Little knowledge ——————————————————————
Some knowledge ——————————————————————
Complete knowledge ——————————————————————

Picture-Based Reading
Labeling and commenting ——————————————————
Well-formed story in the form of oral language ——————————
Well-formed story in the form of written language ——————————

Text-Based Reading
Refusal—doesn't know the words ——————————————
Identifies a limited number of words/letters ——————————
Reads known words with substitutions for unknown words ————————
Reads word by word ——————————————————————
Reads fluently ——————————————————————

Comments:

While the child reads, the teacher needs to judge whether the reading is based on pictures or text. If what the child reads does not match with the text, the teacher needs to determine whether the "story" consists of a series of comments or a well-formed story. If the story is well formed, the teacher must listen to the intonation: Is it similar to the way the child speaks or is it in the form of written language?

If the reading corresponds to the text, it is important for the teacher to determine whether the child watches the print or is "reading" on the basis of memory. When a child responds to the print, the teacher can then determine the extent of knowledge: Can he or she identify some letters or words, read some words substituting responses for unknown words, read word by word, or read fluently?

Sometimes there will be a mixture of reading and storytelling. Other times the child may refuse to read because he or she doesn't know the words. This refusal shows that the child is aware that what is read must be text based.

In order to demonstrate these diagnostic procedures in greater detail, we have selected the case of Jody, an immature girl in the second month of kindergarten.

CASE 1: Jody's Understanding of Storybook Reading

Jody's teacher wanted to learn more about her understanding of storybook reading. She asked her to bring her favorite storybook to school. After placing the storybook sideways, cover down on the table, her teacher began the storybook reading in the following way:

> T: What's the name of your book?
>
> J: *Baby Come Out* (by Fran Manushkin)
>
> T: And your Mom's having a baby so you must really like to read that!
>
> J: Yeah.
>
> T: Okay. Please read me your book.
>
> J: I don't know how to read it.
>
> T: That's fine, pretend you can. Pretend-read it to me.
>
> J: If I make a mistake it's okay. I can do it over again, right?
>
> T: Sure, it's okay.
>
> J: This mother was having a baby and every day she felt her tummy and she said, "Baby do you like your breakfast?" And the baby said "Ahhhh." (Aside to teacher: 'cause she couldn't say 'Ummmm' yet.)
>
> T: Not yet. . .
>
> J: So she said, "Ahhhh." (giggle)
>
> T: The next morning she went into the painting room to paint a picture and she said to her baby, "Baby, do you like the picture that I'm making for you?" And she said, "Ahhhh." (giggle)

Jody continued reading the storybook in this fashion. Her teacher observed that she began reading at the beginning of the book and turned the pages one by one as she reenacted the story. She looked at the right-hand page first as she read and often did not even look at the left-hand page. She reconstructed the story through the pictures, often pointing at them for her own benefit or to show the teacher something. At no time did she point at the words or attend to the print.

The intonations and inflections she used reflected the use of both oral and written language. Although she began the story in an oral language mode ("This mother was having a baby and everyday she feeled her tummy"), she quickly shifted into dialogue-characteristic intonational patterns of written language ("She said, 'Baby do you like your breakfast?' And the baby said, 'Ahhhhh.'") This mixture of oral and written language styles continued during the remainder of the story.

The reader should think about Jody's response. According to this evidence, at what stage of development is Jody in terms of her storybook reading? First, what does the she know about the conventions of writing? Second, what is the basis for her reading? Given the evidence provided, is Jody's reading based on pictures or on text? How should the form in Figure 2.1 be completed?

Her teacher noted that Jody started at the beginning of the book and continued through the book in a page-by-page fashion. Jody clearly has some knowledge of the conventions of writing. At the same time, she did not attend to the print and she focused first and sometimes only on the right-hand page. This indicates that she does not yet have complete understanding of the conventions of print. Thus, in completing the Print Awareness Summary Form, her teacher recorded the date next to "Some knowledge" to show that on October 15, 1987, Jody had some knowledge of the conventions of writing.

The teacher further observed that Jody was reading the pictures and that she did not attend to the printed words. Indeed, there was little correspondence between the text as printed in the storybook and Jody's reconstruction of the story. Thus it is appropriate to classify her reading as picture-based. But she certainly went beyond labeling and commenting on pictures, to retell the action of the story in a well-formed fashion. What was the language like that she used to tell the story? Did it approximate oral language or written language? Since both forms were represented, it is appropriate to record the date in both places. The fact that some of the story was related in the form of written language shows that Jody is developing awareness of the nature of written language. She has not yet developed an understanding that spoken words must correspond to the text, or the awareness of how language can be segmented into word units so as to match printed words.

Later in the winter or spring Jody's teacher may have her read another favorite storybook in order to observe her growth in awareness about the nature of stories. At this later time, her teacher will use the same summary form to record new dates to show Jody's progress during the year.

In order to learn how to assess children's print awareness through storybook reading, it is necessary for a teacher to complete this activity several different times with children at different stages of development. By carefully observing the storybook reading of several children in a systematic fashion, teachers develop the observational and interpretive skills that enable them to monitor the progress of their students in a more informal way.

Writing

A second important way in which teachers can gain insight into the understanding that their students have of print is to examine how they write.

Diagnosis of print awareness through writing occurs most easily in classrooms where print is being used for a variety of purposes. Printed messages embedded in situational contexts and accompanied by oral language enable children to "read" before they have acquired control of mechanical skills. For example, labels are placed on the block bin, the snack closet, and the bathroom door. When children are making decisions about where to go on a field trip or what to name a class pet, the suggestions are written in list form and reviewed. Notes to parents or children reminding them of important events and deadlines can be posted in conspicuous places. When children have drawn pictures, they are helped to label them. Moreover, when teachers write language experience stories, they have the opportunity to model writing.

In order for a teacher to obtain a sample of a child's writing, the child should simply be asked to write. The teacher should help the child to think through what he or she wants to write. Perhaps the child will want to draw a picture first and than label it or describe it in some way. When children respond that they cannot write, they should be encouraged "to do it their own way" or "pretend-write"; they should be assured that it doesn't have to be like "grown-up" writing.

After the child has finished writing, in order for the teacher to interpret the writing accurately, it is important to ask the child to read what he or she has written. After the child has read the writing once, the child should be asked to point to the writing as he or she reads it, and the teacher should notice the degree of correspondence between what is written and what is read.

Diagnosis occurs in two stages. First, the symbols used by the child are examined. Are scribbles, letters, or numbers written? If there is a picture on the page, where is the writing placed in relation to the picture? If letters are used, are they grouped to form wordlike images? Does the writing proceed from left to right and from top to bottom?

Second, the nature of the correspondence between what was written and how it is read by the child is considered. How many symbols are used to represent each spoken word? Is there a direct correspondence between the number of symbol groupings and the number of spoken words? If so, what is the nature of the correspondence? That is, are words typically represented with one or more symbols? Are some words represented by letters that relate systematically to the word (e.g., an initial consonant)? If so, what is the nature of the correspondence?

The form in Figure 2.2 can be used to summarize the observations that a teacher makes during the assessment of a child's writing. The results can be updated periodically on the same form.

To illustrate these procedures, we present the case of Jody. In addition to having her read her favorite storybook, her teacher also had her write.

Figure 2.2   Form for summarizing results from writing task.

SUMMARY FORM—WRITING CHECKLIST

Date

Scribbles not related to meaning _____
Scribbles related to meaning _____
Letterlike sequences related to meaning _____
Letters related to words _____
Letter sequences related to words _____
Letter-sound correspondence _____

Comments:

CASE 2:   Jody's Understanding of Writing

In order to obtain further information about Jody's awareness of print, her teacher asked her to write a story. This was not the first writing done by Jody. Her teacher had recorded her stories and she had participated with the rest of the class in writing a story. In addition, when her teacher invited her to write on her pictures, she frequently did. Jody and her teacher began the activity in the following way:

T: Do you have something you'd like to write about?

J: Yeah, at day camp we played outside.

T: You did?

J: We played kickball and . . . and kickball and (long pause).

T: Were there other kids there?

J: Yeah.

T: Did you play something else besides kickball?

J: Yeah, I'm thinking of what we played . . . Of what it's called. Some kind of ball . . . it was when you kick the ball and, um, you have to roll the ball and you have to try to catch someone. Was it . . . (long pause)

T: Dodgeball?

J: Oh, yeah. We had fun playing dodgeball.

T: All right, that sounds like a good idea for a story. Here's a pencil and here's some paper. Okay, now take a few minutes to write.

J: How do you spell "we"? (This was the first word Jody was attempting to write.)

T: Do it your way—it doesn't have to be like "grown-up."

While Jody wrote, her concentration was intense. Although she wrote her name from left to right, she started the story on the right side of the page and proceeded across the line to the left. Unlike many young writers, she did not say the words softly to herself in elongated fashion as she wrote them. Although she labored over some parts of her writing, she executed other parts more rapidly. Jody worked intensely for about four minutes and then announced that she was done with her story. Her writing is shown in Figure 2.3.

When Jody was finished, her teacher continued the activity as follows:

T: Okay, now I'd like you to read it to me.

J: "We played kickball and . . . dodgeball at camp."

T: Okay. That's a good story. Do you want to add more?

J: No.

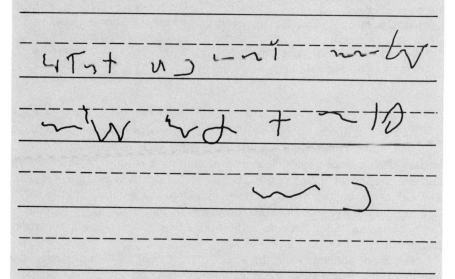

Figure 2.3 Sample of Jody's Writing.

T: Okay. Now what I'd like you to do is read it back to me and point to what you're reading as you read it.

J: "We played kickball and . . . dodgeball at camp."

T: Okay. That's it! Thank you very much. It's a terrific story.

When asked to read what she had written, she did so with "written language" intonation. On both readings, she seemed to have difficulty remembering the word "dodgeball." On the second reading, when asked to point to what she was reading, she began on the right side of the page; she pointed several times to some sequences and skipped over others.

The reader should stop for a moment and consider the evidence. Given Jody's writing and her reading of it, what do we know about her awareness of print? Look closely at the nature of her symbols. Are they scribbles, letters, or numbers? What is the nature of the correspondence between what she wrote and how it was read? How should her understanding be noted on the form in Figure 2.2?

Her teacher observed that some of her writing looked very letterlike, while some must be classified as scribbles. The forms, however, seem to be grouped into clusters that resemble words. The writing did not proceed from left to right, although the second line of writing indicates a top to bottom progression.

With respect to the nature of the correspondence between what she wrote and how it was read, her teacher concluded that Jody is aware that writing represents meaning, as indicated by her intent to write a story and her ability to read what she had written. However, spoken words are not yet paired in any systematic way with print, as indicated by her failure to point to what she had written in a regular way. Though the initial "W" is suggestive and may be used to represent "We," and the "C" may represent "camp," there are no other examples of words being represented by letters that relate systematically to the word. Jody is at the stage in writing in which letterlike sequences relate in a general way to meaning. Thus her teacher, in completing the "writing checklist," recorded the date next to "Letterlike sequences related to meaning" to show that on October 15, 1987, Jody had some knowledge of the nature of writing and its relation to meaning (see Figure 2.2).

As was true for the storybook reading, it is important for teachers to work with individual children to acquire diagnostic skill in assessing children's writing. This includes learning to record children's reading of their writing, and interpreting the nature of the relationship to infer their awareness of print. Through observing the writing of several children in a systematic fashion, they develop the observational and interpretive skills that enable them to monitor the progress of their students in a more informal way during classroom instruction.

As part of understanding the reading and writing of their students, it is important for teachers to be mindful that physical conditions can also influence children's success in learning to read. The following section discusses these conditions.

TABLE 2.1. SYMPTOMS THAT MAY INDICATE PROBLEMS IN VISUAL OR AUDITORY ACUITY

Visual acuity
1. Does the student experience frequent eye infections or pain?
2. Does the student rub his or her eyes or evidence other signs of visual discomfort, particularly when reading?
3. Does the student finger-point or use a marker while reading long after other students have discontinued such practices?
4. Does the student hold books in atypical positions or at unusual distances from his or her eyes?
5. Does the student frequently skip words or lines when reading?

Auditory acuity
1. Does the student experience frequent ear infections or pain?
2. Is the student's speech unusual in any way (slurred, monotonic, inarticulate, or loud)?
3. Is the student frequently inattentive?
4. Does the student often either fail to follow directions or ask to have them repeated?
3. Does the student fail to pronounce new words and names correctly?

Physical Conditions Interfering with Reading Development

With regard to all areas of reading development, but particularly in the development of print skill, the teacher should keep in mind that certain physical problems may interfere with reading progress. While inadequate nutrition or rest may result in inattention, other physical problems may also lead to inattention and cause reading difficulty. Most important, the teacher should be aware that inadequate visual or auditory *acuity* may cause extreme discomfort in the beginning stages of reading, as well as later, if uncorrected. Table 2.1 lists some questions that should be asked in order to identify students with problems in visual or auditory acuity. If a student shows any of these symptoms over some period of time, he or she should be referred to the appropriate specialist for a thorough examination.

INSTRUCTION TO SUPPORT PRINT AWARENESS

Diagnosis is of little value unless it helps a teacher to identify the activities and instructional support that will help children to further develop reading and writing skill. Although diagnosis necessarily focuses on the needs of children one at a time, the teacher typically organizes instruction for groups of children. Thus it is necessary for the teacher to consider the special needs of all children in a group and to provide a composite form of instruction that will meet the needs of all group members. For example, Jody may be a member of a small group of children in kindergarten. When planning instruction, the teacher must not only consider Jody's special needs but also those of the other children in the group.

Instructional planning consists of two main steps: (1) identifying the needs and appropriate instruction for individual children; (2) considering the range of needs and instructional possibilities for a group of children and selecting those instructional approaches that will further the development of all children.

The instructional approaches that we describe in this section are broad-gauged in that they permit children to engage in them on a variety of levels. Those who are less mature, such as Jody, will profit from the instructional experience in a somewhat different way than those with more advanced understandings of reading. Generally, young children who show few signs of print awareness need to be provided with experiences that provide such knowledge. The two types of experiences that we recommend here, story reading and writing, are particularly useful in classrooms because they allow children at different stages of development to participate at the level of their existing knowledge. They can be used with the whole class or with small heterogeneous groups.

Story Reading

Story reading in classrooms should occur in a variety of ways. Certainly, teachers should read good literature written for children to their classes and encourage discussion of the stories. The form of story reading most effective in developing print awareness is shared reading of stories. Children need to see the print as it is being written or read in order to understand how print is arranged and related to speech.

One form of storybook reading involves large-sized "big" books which let students see the print and participate in the reading (Holdaway, 1979). The teacher should talk about where the story begins and demonstrate with a hand motion the portion of the text that is currently being read. Similarly, concepts pertaining to positions ("top," "end"), print ("word," "letter"), and punctuation can be explained and demonstrated. In this form of supported reading, the teacher may read the story aloud several times on different occasions. Once children are familiar with the story, they may wish to engage in choral reading or take turns reading sentences with teacher support.

A second approach, the Language Experience Activity (Stauffer, 1970), encourages children, with the support of the teacher, to write a story about a shared experience. The story must be written sufficiently large on a large sheet of paper or the blackboard so that all the children can see it as it is being composed and reread. The steps to follow in undertaking a LEA are the following:

1. Children are encouraged by the teacher to discuss an experience or a topic. Usually, topics based on common experiences (field trips, a storybook reading, raising pets in class) are more effective because they are familiar and all children can contribute.
2. Following a period of initial discussion, children dictate the story while the teacher records it. As part of the authoring, there may be revisions, additions, and deletions. The teacher guides the process by asking questions such as, "And then what happened?" and "Is this what you want to say?" The teacher records the story in the natural language of the students.
3. The teacher and the students reread the story in unison, making any needed changes (clarifying ambiguous sentences, adding or omitting sentences).
4. Reading and rereading the story should occur in a variety of ways. Although use of word or phrase cards to develop a sight vocabulary and cloze activities to encourage guessing on the basis of context are typically prescribed as part of the method, we recommend a somewhat modified presentation of these procedures as described below.

The procedure for demonstrating and assessing "concept of word" developed by Morris (1980) can be used as an effective instructional procedure with language experience stories, big books, and familiar poems and songs. The activities include the following:

1. The teacher reads the first line of the selection aloud to students, pointing to words as she reads. She continues modeling the "finger-point reading" procedures as she reads the remainder of the selection.
2. Next, children are encouraged to participate in choral reading of the entire selection while the teacher reads and points to the words read.
3. The teacher then marks off the first line and asks if there is a child who would be willing to read it while pointing to the words read. Other children are given the opportunity to finger-point read the remaining lines.
4. She then asks if any child can point to a word she names in the sentence. She continues by asking other children if they can locate other words in the first and remaining sentences.

This set of procedures can be used flexibly. The teacher may begin with the choral reading and repeat this step until the children are familiar with the selection. The final step may be omitted altogether. The procedure is extremely useful because it models the relation between printed and spoken words for children who are in the beginning stages of print awareness, and it lets more advanced children demonstrate their knowledge of print. Their accuracy in finger-point reading and locating words directly reflects the extent to which they have solved the problem of how printed and spoken words relate to each other, which is to say, the extent to which they have formed a "concept of word." One interesting observation made by Morris was the tendency of children to point more than once for words of several syllables. That is, on the second syllable of a longer spoken word they would point to the next printed word on the line. This indicated that they had not yet completely solved the problem of how spoken words relate to print.

These instructional procedures have been incorporated into a three-day cycle of activities (Morris, 1986) as follows:

Day 1: The teacher leads the children in a discussion of a shared experience: for example, making popcorn, making valentine cards, watching snowflakes fall, visiting the school library or cafeteria, planting a seed, retelling the story of Columbus's voyage, and so on. Following the oral discussion, the children dictate two or three sentences describing the experience, and the teacher records these few sentences in manuscript print on a large sheet of chart paper.

Making Popcorn

> We made popcorn.
> We made it in a popcorn popper.
> We put butter and salt on the popcorn.

Next, the teacher models a reading of the completed experience story, pointing to each word as she reads. Finally, the children join in choral-reading the story several times, with the teacher continuing to point to the words on the chart paper as the group reads.

Day 2: The Day 1 story is brought out and choral-read several times, with the teacher again modeling finger-point reading. Next, some informal questions can be asked and games played with the now familiar story. For example:

- Who can come up to the chart and show me where we start reading? Where we end? Where do we go when we reach the end of a line?
- These little dots in our story are called "periods." What do they tell us?
- Who knows this word (teacher points to 'popcorn')? Good! Can someone else find the same word at another place in the story?
- What is the first letter in this word (teacher points to the *p* in *put*)? Can you find another word in our story that begins with a *p?*

Day 3: On Day 3 the teacher works at a table with groups of seven to eight children at a time. The "popcorn" story has been transferred from the large chart paper to the bottom of an 8½ × 11 piece of paper, and each child at the table has a copy. The teacher reads the story several times and the children attempt to follow along on their own copy. Next, the teacher instructs the children to illustrate the popcorn story on the top half of the paper. As the children begin drawing, the teacher moves around to each child and asks him or her to finger-point read the three-line story. (Note: Early in the year the teacher may have to use an echo-reading strategy. That is, the teacher reads one or two lines and then the child attempts to echo-read these lines while pointing to the words on the page.) If the child is successful in finger-point reading the story—that is, matching spoken words to written words in an appropriate manner—the teacher can afterwards point randomly to individual words in the text and see if the child can identify them, immediately or by using context.[1]

Kindergarten children will differ considerably in their ability to finger-point read a short, familiar text like "Making Popcorn." Therefore, the Day 3 procedure described above, aside from its instructional value, is important diagnostically. It allows the teacher to observe carefully the reading development of individual children at a low cost in time, one to two minutes spent with each child (Morris, 1986, pp. 5–6).

Writing

The best way to encourage young children to write is to create an environment in which reading and writing are clearly functional (Calkins, 1986; Sulzby & Teale, 1987; Temple, Nathan, Burris & Temple, 1988). Cochran-Smith (1984) describes a preschool class in which a variety of literacy activities were routinely interwoven as part of everyday situations. Printed notes were sometimes used as substitutes for oral conversation; for example, notes to parents were posted on the front door to remind them of special trips or of tuition due; parents included notes to children in their lunches. Print was used as a source of information; for example, in the classroom, labels marked the snack cupboard; outside the classroom, street signs, posters, and advertisements were noted. Printed words clarified the status of objects and pictures: who owned them (child's name on an object), and what they were about (a picture labeled "my dog."). Writing was also used to help the class solve problems such as naming the guinea pig; listing names helped children remember and select an appropriate name. More traditional literacy activities also occurred such as writing stories to recall trips and other experiences. The purpose of such writing activities in naturally occurring contexts was not to develop knowledge of the formal characteristics of print, but rather to develop awareness of the functions that print serves in our society.

Teachers can also help children develop knowledge about print through more traditional writing activities. For example, while writing a language experience after a field trip or some other experience, the teacher pronounces longer words syllable by syllable as she writes them to model the division of

---

[1] From *Teaching reading in kindergarten: A language-experience approach* (Occasional Paper No. 13, pp. 4–6) by D. Morris (1986). Evanston, IL: The Reading Center, National College of Education. Reprinted by permission.

words into parts. At a later time, she can solicit help from the class in dividing words into syllables. When she writes words on the blackboard, she can ask students to listen for the sound at the beginning of the word. Later during the year she can say words slowly to see if children hear their phonemic components. These experiences which develop phoneme awareness can also be undertaken with individual students as teachers assist children during seatwork. Such experiences help children to develop awareness of print that later supports them as they learn to read and write in less contextually supported situations.

SUMMARY

This chapter has considered the complex learnings that are involved in becoming aware of the nature of print and how it functions. Two diagnostic strategies for examining print awareness, storybook reading and writing assessment, were described, and their use was demonstrated in the case of Jody. Broad-gauged instructional procedures for developing print awareness were described in the final section of the chapter. Some children come to school with well-developed awareness of print; many, however, need supportive instruction with stories and writing to help them develop greater familiarity and security with printed messages. These experiences prepare children to learn printed words and the relations that hold between letters and sound within words. The next chapter examines children's knowledge of print, its development, diagnosis, and instruction.

CHAPTER 3

Knowledge of Print

DEVELOPMENT OF PRINT KNOWLEDGE

The discussion in Chapter 2 shows how children develop a growing understanding of print and its relation to speech and meaning through their participation in reading and writing activities. Through story reading, they learn how stories are arranged in books and come to understand that printed words are meaningful. When children write, they explore the nature of writing and how it relates to spoken words. At some point in their development, they realize that printed words are individual nameable objects. Once children become aware of this correspondence, they are able to learn words and to explore the relationships that hold within words between letters and sounds.

At the same time, some knowledge of letter names or sounds helps children to develop a stable concept of word (Ehri, 1980; Morris, 1988). As Ehri (1980) argues, knowledge of letter–sound associations constitutes the "glue" that holds word images in memory. The development would seem to be reciprocal in that some knowledge of letter sounds makes new words more familiar; at the same time, a sense of printed word boundaries in relation to speech allows children to infer additional knowledge about letter–sound correspondences.

Ehri (1980) describes this process of word learning in the following way:

> Since beginners already know how words are pronounced, their task is to assimilate the word's printed form to its phonological (speech sound) structure. They do this by matching at least some of the letters to phonetic or phonemic segments detected in the word. These segments serve as "slots" in

lexical memory which are filled by images of letters seen in the word's spelling (p. 313).

In other words, children form mental images of printed words that are stored in memory with the spoken (phonological) identity of the word and its meaning. The image when first stored may be fragmentary, but upon repeated reading of the words and increased ability to segment words phonemically, the image will become more complete.

Within this developmental view, the ability to learn words is closely interwoven with the ability to learn the sound components of words. Recent research (Bradley & Bryant, 1983; Lundberg, Frost, & Petersen, 1988; Tunmer, Herriman, & Nesdale, 1988) suggests that the development of phoneme awareness is a critical achievement in the process of learning to read. In the following sections we will consider the nature of word awareness and learning first, and then the development of phoneme awareness and word identification strategies. While we treat these two aspects of learning to read separately, it must be remembered that the two develop concurrently and are interconnected.

Word Awareness and Learning

One of the most important achievements in reading is learning to recognize printed words instantaneously. In word learning, beginning readers must confront two problems. The first is learning to segment oral language into parts that correspond to printed words (word awareness). The second is learning to discriminate among the printed words.

Word Awareness. It is difficult for literate adults to imagine that young children may listen to sentences without being aware of the specific words that compose them. Yet, evidence from research indicates that this is true. Perhaps the study that has most influenced our thinking about the development of word awareness is that conducted by Karpova (1955, as described in Slobin, 1966). Karpova found that the word consciousness of children develops in three stages. In the first, at 3–4 years of age, children understand sentences as semantic units, without distinguishing individual words. For example, they report that a sentence such as *Galyla and Vova went walking* contains two words: Galyla-went-walking and Vova-went-walking. During the next stage, prereaders become able to separate sentences into subject and predicate. Finally, during the third stage, children learn to identify the words that compose sentences, although they experience difficulty with compound and multisyllabic words and fail to distinguish some function words as separate units. They must also learn the conventions of English that pertain to wordness—for example, that *not happy* and *full spoon* are represented by two words in English, whereas *unhappy* and *spoonful* are represented by one.

Failure to develop word awareness during the initial stages of reading is manifest in oral reading that bears little or no correspondence to the printed words being read. The development of such awareness is evident in Clay's (1967) description of the stages through which beginning readers instructed by a sentence method progressed:

> As [the children] developed skill in matching behavior, fingers were used to point to those parts of the text that were supposed to correspond to the vocal responses. Fluency gave way to word by word reading. At this point the child's reading became staccato as he over-emphasized the breaks between words. He could be thought of as "reading the spaces" or "voice pointing" at the words [p. 16].

Thus, pointing to words during the initial stages of reading indicates the development of awareness of words and of the correspondence between spoken and written language. Voice pointing and, subsequently, natural phrasing reflect increasing familiarity with and control over print. Both finger and voice pointing should be interpreted as signs of progress, and as Clay notes, they are not behaviors to be "hurriedly trained out." Nevertheless, continued use of finger pointing may also indicate difficulty in visual coordination or acuity.

Most children do not encounter difficulty in becoming aware of words and learning them. However, there are some who require explicit instruction before they attend carefully to printed words and understand the nature of the correspondence between print and language. The instructional methods developed by Morris (1986), which are described in Chapter 2, show how teachers can help children to develop concept of word and the word awareness that underlies it.

Printed Word Discrimination. Most children in the United States learn to read from basal programs in which words are introduced gradually into stories and repeated in subsequent stories (e.g., Houghton Mifflin, Harcourt Brace Jovanovich, Heath). One sign of such control is the existence of a list of words at the back of readers or in the teacher's guide indicating the new words introduced in each story. Given this design of instructional materials, learning words is not simply a matter of memorizing sequences of letters and their aural counterparts, one at a time. Instead, word learning involves comparing new words with previously learned words in order to identify features that are useful for distinguishing among them. For example, in learning the words *red, blue, yellow, green,* and *orange,* children need only attend to the initial letter of each word in order to discriminate among them and give a correct response. If, however, the word *brown* is added to the set, the children will need to consider more than the initial consonant to discriminate correctly, since *blue* and *brown* begin with the same letter.

Thus, a problem with the discrimination learning of printed words is that as the set of words learned becomes larger, features that were initially useful in discriminating among words are no longer sufficient and students must attend to other features. Primary teachers observe this problem most often in the failure of students to distinguish among words with similar beginning and ending letters but different medial vowels (e.g., *but, bat,* and *bit*). Most children eventually learn to attend to enough word features so that words are rarely confused. In addition, they learn to use other sources of information, such as phonics and contextual cues, to facilitate rapid word recognition.

Not all basal programs, however, control words in stories. Some (e.g., Open Court, Economy, Distar) control the introduction of letter–sound associations. As part of the instruction, children are taught letter–sound associations and how to blend them into words. Such "synthetic phonics" programs have children read stories composed of words that can be identified with the knowledge that they are acquiring about letter–sound associations (Beck & McCaslin, 1978; Meyer, Greer, & Crummey, 1987). Linguistic readers (e.g., SRA, Miami), in contrast, control the introduction of word patterns. For example, such similarly patterned words as *cat, hat, fat, mat,* and *rat* may be combined with other sets of patterned words to form stories. Whether letter–sound associations or word patterns are controlled, the contextual selections in the beginning-level materials in synthetic phonics or linguistic readers tend to contain many short, similarly patterned words; however, beyond the beginning-level materials, it is difficult to distinguish these selections from those of other basal programs.

The nature of the reading program and the stories children read affect how they learn words. Children who are instructed with materials in which word introduction is controlled make different types of reading mistakes than those learning from materials in which word patterns or letter–sound associations are controlled (see, for example, Barr, 1975; Elder, 1971; Juel & Roper/Schneider, 1985). Consider how two disabled readers read the sentence *Now he does not try to take his dog* (Spache, 1972). Kay, 8 years of age, who had been instructed with a phonics program, read the sentence, "Now *his dose* not *tray* to take his dog." Bill, 10 years of age and exposed to eclectic materials, read ". . . . he *did* not *take* to take his dog." The errors that these two students made on words presented in isolation are similar to those they made in reading text. For example, Kay substituted "erv" for the printed word *every,* "doan" for *done,* "road" for *round,* and "those" for *these.* Bill's responses to the same words were "very" for *every,* "did" for *done,* "about" for *round,* and "what" for *these.* While Kay's responses match the printed words more closely than Bill's, some of them are nonsense words and her errors in textual reading tend to make less sense than do Bill's.

Bill was taught to read with basal stories in which words were controlled, while Kay was taught with a synthetic phonics program in which letter–sound associations were controlled. Children instructed with reading materials in which words are controlled tend to depend on visual and/or phonic cues, mainly from the initial and final portions of words, in conjunction with contextual information (Biemiller, 1970), whereas those who are instructed with synthetic phonics materials are likely to develop greater sensitivity to phonic cues from medial as well as extreme portions of words and to depend less on purely visual or on contextual information for word discrimination (Cohen, 1974–75; see also Allington, 1983; Barr, 1972, 1974).

Some reading materials control neither words nor letter–sound patterns. Instead, stories with natural language structures are drawn from children's literature. Such reading programs are in widespread use in other countries; for example, Clay (1967) describes how children in New Zealand learn to read with such materials. Materials designed in this fashion were introduced in the United States by Scott Foresman in the mid-1970s. Although they were not widely accepted at that time, developers of basal programs have recently eased the extent to which they control the introduction of words (see, for example, the current program by Scott Foresman published in 1986).

We do not know yet how materials designed in this fashion influence the learning of words. Some evidence suggests, however, that when children are encouraged to rely on both contextual and graphic (print) information from the earliest stages of reading, later integration and reading fluency may be facilitated (Clay, 1979).

In general, however, most beginning readers in this country learn to read from programs in which the set of words introduced in the first-level stories are limited. Whatever words are included in beginning reading materials, in addition to influencing how children learn words, they markedly influence the set of words that they learn as sight words (Barr & Dreeben, 1983; McKinnon, 1959). That is, most children learn many of the words they encounter repeatedly in contextual materials; while preficient readers soon progress beyond this set of words, less proficient readers often do not read many stories beyond those included in instruction and they therefore learn to read mainly those words that are introduced through instruction (Bennett, 1942). Accordingly, the content of the basal programs is a significant force in the development of an initial sight word vocabulary.

As was discussed earlier, most children who learn words through basal instruction are simultaneously taught phonics concepts. Becoming aware of the elements of words and how they represent phonemes is critical to word learning and the ability to decode words. In the next section we will consider how students accomplish this learning.

Knowledge of Word Elements

Knowledge about words and their elements develops over time as words are learned. By *word element* we mean the knowledge that children have of English orthography (spelling) that enables them to identify words they have not seen before. Knowledge of word elements includes that pertaining to letter–sound associations and the structural components of words, such as root words and affixes (e.g., *-ing, -ed, re-, un-*), as well as procedural knowledge about word elements (e.g., how to blend word elements to form a word, how to analogize from a known to an unknown word as in using the ending of *sat* to help in identifying *mat*). Underlying the development of knowledge of word elements is phoneme awareness. We will consider the development of phoneme awareness first and then will discuss the development of knowledge of word elements.

Phoneme Awareness. Children first learning to speak discern differences at the phonemic level within words; that is, they are able to distinguish between words that differ in only one sound (e.g., *cat* and *bat*). At the same time, they have little conscious control over phonemes as distinctive units; they are unable to treat them in an objective fashion. Various research strategies suggest that becoming aware of phonemes develops only gradually. For example, children below the age of 7 experience considerable difficulty reporting the word that remains when a phoneme is deleted (i.e., when /h/ is deleted from *hill* or /d/ from *card;* Bruce, 1964; Rosner & Simon, 1971). Liberman, Shankweiler, Fischer, and Carter (1974) report that none of a preschool group and only 17 percent of a kindergarten group were able to segment words into their phonemic components, whereas 70 percent of a first-grade group were successful.

That the development of phoneme awareness and reading are highly correlated is well established, but there is debate over whether phonemic awareness is a prerequisite or facilitator of reading development, whether it develops concurrently with reading, or whether reading leads to phoneme awareness (Ehri, 1979). Although it has been shown that instruction to develop phoneme awareness enhances later reading achievement (Bradley & Bryant, 1983; Lundberg, Frost, & Petersen, 1988), it has also been demonstrated that reading influences the way children perceive phonemes (Ehri, 1983). For our purposes here, teachers need to be conscious that many children profit from instruction that encourages them to hear phonemes in words. Rather than intensive instruction in phoneme awareness followed by instruction in letter–sound associations, we believe that the two should occur together as part of reading and writing activities.

The problem of distinguishing phonemes within words is complicated by the fact that each phoneme has several sound variants, and these are treated as equivalent in the writing system. This situation makes it difficult to explain and illustrate the concept of phonemes.

The phonemes of English correspond (more or less well) to graphemes, and these correspondences are referred to as *phonic concepts.* Almost all beginning reading programs now in common use introduce phonic concepts. Where programs with a heavy emphasis on phonics are used, students' reading progress is heavily dependent on their mastery of phonic concepts. However, in many of the phonic programs, phonemes are introduced in isolated form and students bypass the important learning that words can be segmented into phonemes. Accordingly, students learn phonic correspondences on an item-by-item basis and fail to acquire a general procedure by which to relate word forms and phonemes.

Word Identification. Most children learn to read from programs that include instruction in phonics and other word elements. The instructional program and the portion children cover greatly influence their knowledge of word elements (Barr & Dreeben, 1983). Further, children who are taught to read with synthetic phonics and linguistic programs develop greater understanding of word elements than those instructed with other programs including contextual selections in which letter–sound associations or patterns are not controlled (Bond & Dykstra, 1967; Chall, 1967; Lesgold & Resnick, 1982).

Yet while some children may demonstrate knowledge of word elements, unless this knowledge becomes organized systematically to support word identification and spelling, it is of little functional value. Children's early writing, which differs in systematic ways from standard spelling, has been shown to provide a window into their knowledge (Read, 1971). The early spelling responses of children can be classified developmentally according to stages (Henderson, 1981, 1985). In the first stage, as shown in Figure 3.1, words are represented by letters and numbers; the spellings bear no resemblance to correct spellings. Such responses indicate that children understand that words are represented by a series of letters, but they have not yet solved the problem of how elements within spoken words are represented.

In the second stage, alphabetic writing occurs in which children represent some sounds of words in a systematic way, particularly those at the

Figure 3.1 Spelling strategy classifications for five children.

Tim Kindergarten Stage 1	Anne Kindergarten Stage 2	Jonathan 1st Grade Stage 2	Silvia 2d Grade Stage 3	Jane 2d Grade Correct
AMINƆ	J	CHIRP	CHIRP	CHIRP
EM3321	SB	SAP	STAMP	STAMP
SEMAꟻS	AT	EDE	EIGHTEEY	EIGHTY
19ИHM	J	GAGIN	DRAGUN	DRAGON
SAMH	P	PRD	PURD	PURRED
MENENA	TP	TIP	TIPE	TYPE
ENIMM	T	CHUBRL	TRUBAL	TROUBLE

(From *Teaching Spelling* [Fig. 2.5, p. 47] by Edmund Henderson. Copyright © 1985 by Houghton Mifflin. Used with permission.)

beginnings of words (see Figure 3.1). This second stage can be divided into two substages: the first, which we refer to as "initial consonant," in which only initial consonants are represented, and the second, which we refer to as "consonant frame," in which both initial and final consonants are represented. In the third stage, children represent within-word patterns more completely; in particular, letters representing vowels and those that mark the pronunciation of vowels (e.g., final-*e* pattern) are included. Nevertheless, as is shown in Figure 3.1, the spellings still depart in systematic ways from standard spelling for some words. Finally, children learn to spell words in standard form (Henderson & Beers, 1980).

What this development in spelling reflects is growth in the underlying knowledge that children have about words and the elements that compose them. To think of this development in terms described earlier by Ehri (1980), the images of words that children store in memory become more complete. Her research shows that children spell words not simply on the basis of letter–sound knowledge but also on the basis of their stored images of words, because silent as well as voiced letters are represented in their spellings.

Children progress through similar stages in their ability to identify unknown words. By having students attempt to identify unfamiliar words or syllables, we can infer their underlying knowledge of word elements, including letter–sound associations, the structural components of words, and procedural knowledge about how to use knowledge of word elements (e.g., ability to blend sounds and ability to chunk words into syllables).

Summary

What do we as teachers need to know about children's developing knowledge of print? First we must understand how word learning occurs—that it represents the culmination of a long sequence of exploration on the part of children about how speech and print are related. Word learning occurs when children become aware of spoken words as units and realize that each relates in a systematic fashion to a series of letters bounded by spaces. The nature of the systematic relation may not be fully understood by children when they begin to learn words, but awareness of phonemes within words and some understanding of initial consonants seem to permit the development of a stable concept of word. This understanding of what a word is, in turn, permits further word study and the discernment of systematic relations at the ends of words and in the medial portions of words. We as teachers need to understand how this developmental progression occurs.

We also need to understand that we can help children progress in this understanding through the instructional support we provide. We need to be able to diagnose how well a child understands printed words so as to encourage progress to the next level of understanding. If, for example, a child is experiencing difficulty in the initial stages of word learning (developing a sight vocabulary), we must explore the child's understanding of concept of word and the child's knowledge of phonemes, letter names, and letter–sound relations. If such knowledge is lacking, it should be taught around the set of words being introduced. If the child has already developed the beginnings of a stable sight vocabulary but is not aware of the relations that hold in the middles of words, we must further examine her or his knowledge of short and long vowel associations. In the following section we will describe ways in which teachers can obtain further information about a child's knowledge of print. The purpose of this diagnosis is to determine the focus of instruction.

DIAGNOSIS OF PRINT KNOWLEDGE

In this section we will describe three useful procedures that can be used by teachers to assess children's knowledge of print. Each of these procedures involves attention to words and word parts. In other words, these techniques reveal what children know about print based on graphic information. For a complete picture, students' knowledge about print must also be examined as they read contextual selections. Indeed, we believe that the heart of diagnosis of print skill should examine contextual reading proficiency. Once a problem in print skill is identified, it is often useful to explore the nature of the difficulty further by examining children's ability to identify words and word parts. We will consider diagnostic procedures with words and word parts first because they seem to be easier for teachers to learn. In the next chapter we will describe diagnosis with contextual materials. It is important to remember that diagnosis of a student's print skill normally begins with contextual reading, followed by exploration of words and word parts. In other words, the tasks described in this chapter should not be administered to all students in a class. Rather, they can be used to further specify the knowledge of children after their contextual reading indicates problems.

The first of the three procedures described in this chapter permits teachers to assess the development of a student's quick recognition sight vocabulary, using samples of words drawn either from the basal program or from more formal lists of words. The other two procedures enable teachers to examine a student's knowledge of word elements. One, the *Developmental Spelling Test* (Ferroli & Shanahan, 1987; Morris & Perney, 1984), permits us to assess the underlying knowledge that children have about print, particularly in the early stages of reading (kindergarten to grade 2). The second, an informal "probe" procedure which can be used with any set of words, is useful in assessing student knowledge of word elements at all grade levels.

In learning how to use these procedures, it is important to begin with only one or two. The grade level of the children should determine which procedures the teacher learns first. Teachers working with children in the beginning stages of formal reading instruction should learn to administer a sight word test composed of basal words and the *Developmental Spelling Test.* Teachers of older readers should begin with a graded word list (see, for example, the Word Lists of the *Analytical Reading Inventory* by Woods and Moe on page 283) and the informal probe of word elements. Each of these pairs of tests yields information about sight word development and knowledge of word elements.

Word Learning

Basal Program Words. During the first years of reading, children develop a sight vocabulary—words that can be recognized immediately on exposure. One way to examine how well a beginning reader is learning the words encountered during reading instruction is to form a list of the words introduced and repeated in the basal readers or other reading selections. Some programs list these words at the end of each reader or in the teacher's guide. A sample of approximately 10 to 20 words should be written on cards or in list form on a page. When the child reads these words, it should be noted if recognition is immediate or delayed (one-half second or more). Immediate recognition of the majority of words shows that the child is developing command of the vocabulary that is being introduced and reinforced in the reading program.

If mastery of the basal vocabulary is less than 50 percent, steps should be taken by the teacher to determine whether the child has developed an understanding of how spoken words relate to printed words, using the "finger-point reading" procedures developed by Morris (1980, see page 35). If the child has not mastered this "concept of word," then language experience and big book activities described for storybook reading in Chapter 2 should be undertaken. If the child demonstrates ability to point to words as they are read (concept of word) but still has difficulty remembering them, the child's word learning should be reinforced through word writing and spelling and through repeated reading (see specific recommendations in the following section on instruction).

Delayed recognition usually indicates the potential of the child to identify words that have not yet entered the child's quick recognition sight vocabulary. If the child recognizes many more words during the delayed than the instantaneous presentation, this usually means that the child needs more contextual (rereading and new reading) practice to consolidate the set of words that can be identified into his or her quick recognition sight vocabulary.

Occasionally teachers are unfamiliar with the basal program from which a student has learned to read; therefore, it is not possible to sample words from the basal text. As an alternative, a "basic" sight words list may be used. Words introduced in the stories and other selections of reading programs include nouns, as well as verbs, adjectives, and structure words that are referred to as a "basic" sight vocabulary. The list developed by Dolch (1936), who was among the first to develop such a list, is in Appendix A. These words not only occur frequently in early reading materials, they also account for about 70 percent of running text in general. The Dolch list or other comparable basic sight word lists (e.g., Harris & Jacobson, 1982) are an efficient means for assessing the sight word knowledge of a child when the basal program is unknown or when a more general measure of sight word knowledge is needed. Procedures similar to those outlined for testing of the words presented in basal materials should be followed. That is, the words should be written on cards or in list form and presented one at a time, the teacher noting whether recognition is immediate or delayed. In interpreting the results, the teacher should consider whether or not the child has had an opportunity to learn any of the words that were not known. When the child has had the opportunity to learn the word, the interpretation is the same as that for the basal sight words. In order to demonstrate these procedures, we will consider the case of Ken.

CASE 1: Diagnosis of Ken's Sight Vocabulary

Ken's parents contacted his first-grade teacher at the beginning of April, concerned about his "slow" progress in learning to read. They wondered if he had a learning disability and whether he should attend summer school. Ken was a member of the low reading group, which had completed the preprimer-level books and was beginning the primer-level book. Although Ken had had difficulty attending to the reading tasks the preceding fall, from about Christmas on his teacher felt that he was making good progress. When he reread stories from the basal, he did so with few errors, but in a word-by-word fashion. He had more difficulty reading stories that were unfamiliar, particularly when they were not from his basal reader. In order to confirm her impressions, his teacher decided to have him read a set of words that she selected from the basal reader.

In order to select the set of basal words, his teacher found the basal list showing the new words that were introduced in stories and repeated in subsequent stories. From this list, she sampled every third word; she also added to the end of the list some words from stories that Ken had not yet read. She printed the list on a sheet of paper and then asked Ken to read them, saying: "Here are some words. Some you know and some you may not have had yet. Do the best you can with them." As Ken read the words, she noted whether he recognized them immediately or after studying them. She also wrote what he said when he did not know a word. The results are shown in Figure 3.2.

The reader should pause for a moment to examine these results. What are Ken's strengths and difficulties with sight word development? As can be seen, he recognized immediately all the words he had been taught. When he encountered words that had not yet been introduced to him in the basal reader, he had some

Figure 3.2 Ken's recognition of basal sight words.

Basal Word	Immediate Recognition	Delay Recognition	Response
get	✓		
stop	✓		
not	✓		
you	✓		
me	✓		
it	✓		
see	✓		
little	✓		
swim	✓		
rabbit	✓		
duck	✓		
said	✓		
at	✓		
look	✓		
can	✓		
*what			want
*don't			duck
*hop		✓	
*fast			fat
*letter			little

(* These basal words had not yet been introduced to Ken's group.)

difficulty, although he was able to identify one of the new words, *hop* by realizing that the ending was similar to *stop*. When he attempted the other three new words, he correctly identified initial consonants and some ending consonants.

What do his responses indicate about his reading? First, he is mastering well what he has been taught, as shown by the fact that he quickly recognizes the basal words. This strength is also reflected in his reading basal stories; he is one of the stronger members of the low group. His attempts to identify unfamiliar basal words, however, show that he is not yet able independently to identify most new words but that he is developing some knowledge of word elements, particularly beginning consonants.

Graded Word Lists. Other available lists, such as those that accompany informal reading inventories, are often more useful for students beyond the beginning stages of reading. These lists include words graded according to their difficulty. The primary and first-grade word lists provide measures similar to the basic sight word lists. More advanced lists show how well students are incorporating other words into their store of quickly recognized words. Elementary grade students expand their set of sight words beyond the basal reader set to include most other words they encounter frequently during contextual reading. Proficient readers are in command of a large store of sight words. An example of lists of this type are in Appendix C.

We recommend that teachers have their students read these lists of sight words under two conditions: a *flash presentation* that measures the instantaneous sight vocabulary of the student, and an *untimed presentation* that measures a student's ability to identify words under less pressured conditions. The procedures for flash administration consist of using two rectangular cards, one placed just above the word to be flashed and the other covering the word. When the student is ready, the teacher quickly moves the bottom card down, exposing the word. After a half second exposure, the top card is moved down to cover the word. Correct responses are marked on the student record form with a check ($\checkmark$) whereas incorrect responses are recorded phonetically. When the student fails to respond, this is recorded as "NR" (no response), "DK" (don't know) or "x." Words that are not recognized during the flash presentation are reexposed immediately, with no time limitation, in order to see if the student can identify the word.

To demonstrate these procedures, we will consider the case of Alex, a fifth grader, who transferred to a new school in January. His records, including reading test scores, suggested that he was reading at the high third- or fourth-grade level. His new teacher wanted to know more about his reading development in order to decide what level materials to have him read. In addition to seeing how well he read selections from the basal readers currently being read by her students, she checked his sight vocabulary and his skill in word identification skill on a graded word list.

CASE 2:   Alex's Reading of a Graded Word List

To check his word reading, Alex's teacher administered the word lists from the *Basic Reading Inventory* (Johns, 1978). The word lists measure quick recognition sight vocabulary (flash presentation) and word identification skills (untimed presentation). They range from basic sight words on the preprimer list up through difficult content words on the intermediate and middle grade lists. In order to provide immediate success, she had Alex begin by reading the easiest list. She first exposed the words on the list for about one half second using the flash procedure described earlier and then reexposed any words that Alex did not immediately recognize to give him time to study them. She presented successively more difficult lists until he scored below 75 percent correct on the untimed administration. The results are summarized in Figure 3.3.

Again, the reader should pause to study the results and consider what we have learned about Alex's word recognition. He recognized immediately all but one word on the first-grade lists. On the second- and third-grade lists, most words were familiar sight words; however, with extended time he was unable to identify one word on each list. He encountered difficulty on the flash presentations of the fourth- and fifth-grade lists, and only on the fourth-grade list was he able to achieve higher than the 75 percent criterion with extended time.

His responses on the fourth-grade list are shown in Figure 3.4. Study the responses

Figure 3.3 Alex's reading of the standardized word list.

| Level | Word Recognition Test | |
	Flash (%)	Untimed (%)
Preprimer	100	—
Primer	95	100
First	100	—
Second	90	95
Third	85	95
Fourth	55	85
Fifth	45	60
Sixth		
Seventh		
Eighth		
Ninth		

Figure 3.4 Alex's responses to the fourth-grade level words.

Level 4	Flash	Untimed
double	✓	
swoop	✓	
automobile	ŏuto	✓
balanced	blanced	blanced
platform	bat-l-for	✓
metal	✓	
level	lĕv ✓	
serious	✓	
falsehood	falshŏd	✓
harbor	✓	
observing	n.r.	obszing
capture	✓	
language	laugh	✓
vanishing	vancing	vancing
predict	protection	
force	✓	
island	✓	
ought	✓	
target	targest	✓
impossible	✓	

to see patterns emerge. Does he have more difficulty with longer than shorter words or with words that begin with consonant blends or other clusters?

One- and two-syllable words seem to be easier for him than longer words. He correctly identified nine of fifteen such words on flash exposure. The two-syllable words he did not identify correctly were *balanced* (ending with a final suffix), *platform* and *predict* (beginning with consonant blends), *falsehood* (a compound word) and *target* (a regularly patterned word). All but the first of these were recognized when Alex was provided extended time. Of the five words of three or more syllables, two were recognized on flash exposure: *serious* and *impossible*. Two of the other three words were not recognized even with extended time: *observing* and *vanishing*. These patterns suggest that Alex has some difficulty with multisyllabic words, particularly those of more than two syllables. At the same time, the results indicate good knowledge of word elements and some skill in identifying unknown words. A large difference between words that are immediately recognized and those that can be identified with more time often reflects limited reading practice.

While the reading of word lists yields some information about a student's ability to identify words, it is often important to assess knowledge of word elements more systematically. In the next section we will describe a spelling task and an informal word probe. Both of these permit a teacher to obtain knowledge about how well a student can apply knowledge of word elements.

Knowledge of Word Elements

Spelling Task. One of the best ways to assess children's knowledge of word elements is to ask them to write a series of words. As was discussed earlier, how children spell words reveals their underlying knowledge about word elements and their developmental stage in understanding English spelling (Henderson, 1985). Although many different lists of one-syllable sight words are useful for this purpose, the *Developmental Spelling Test* which we describe here (Ferroli & Shanahan, 1987; Morris & Perney, 1984) is particularly useful because it includes words of various complexity and it is sensitive to changes that occur in the beginning stages of spelling (see Figure 3.5). The spelling task has been used with kindergarteners (Ferroli & Shanahan, 1987) and first graders (Morris & Perney, 1984) and found to be a good predictor of later first-grade achievement.

The list is composed of twelve words as shown in Figure 3.5. Before administering the list, the teacher must prepare children through a demonstration of spelling. First they should be asked to listen for the letter names they

Figure 3.5 Developmental spelling test items and illustrative spellings at each stage.

Correct	Preliterate	Initial Consonant	Consonant Frame	Phonetic	Transitional
BACK	RE	BET	BC	BAK	[a]
SINK	E	C	SE	SEK	SINCK
MAIL	A	MM	MOL	MAL	MAEL
DRESS	S	DN	JS	GAS	DRES
LAKE	AH	L	LAE	LAK	LACE
PEEKED	TTT	PF	PT	PECT	PEKED
LIGHT	IEIX	LSIE	LAT	LIT	LIET
DRAGON	ATJA	JK	GAN	DAGN	DRAGIN
STICK	F	S	STC	SEK	STIK
SIDE	TC	ST	CI	SID	CIDE
FEET	V	F	FT	FET	[a]
TEST	ABT	TS	TST	TAST	TEEST

([a] No transitional spellings were produced by the subjects for these words.) L. Ferroli and T. Shanahan, 1987. Kindergarten spelling: Explaining its Relation to First-rate Reading. In J. E. Readance and R. S. Baldwin (Eds.) *Research in Literacy: Merging Perspectives.* Thirty-Sixth Yearbook of the National Reading Conference. Rochester, NY: National Reading Conference. Based on D. Norris and J. Perney, 1984. Developmental Spelling as a Predictor of First-rate Reading Achievement. *Elementary School Journal, 84.* Copyright © 1984 by the University of Chicago Press. Reprinted by permission.

hear in a few sample words not found on the list such as *mat* and *dip;* the teacher should then write these letters on the blackboard, supplying unknown letters if the children offer only a partial spelling. For example, if the children hear only the *m* and *t* in *mat,* the teacher might say "Good," write M __ T on the board, and say "and there's an 'A' in the middle." Following this modeling, children should be encouraged to spell the list words "as best they can" by writing the letter names they hear. It is important to praise them for whatever spellings they produce. The list should be given in a fashion similar to a spelling test.

Figure 3.5 also includes typical spellings generated for these words by children at different stages of development. On the basis of these spelling responses, the teacher can determine whether the majority of a child's responses are preliterate, initial consonant, consonant frame, phonetic, transitional, or correct. As will be discussed further in the next section, instruction in word elements should be geared to the child's stage of development. For example, for a child in the preliterate stage, knowledge of letter names should be checked to determine which, if any, need to be taught; similarly, for a child in the consonant frame stage, further testing of consonants and consonant blends in final positions and short vowels is appropriate to determine what word elements need to be taught.

To demonstrate this procedure, we return to the case of Ken, whose parents had been concerned about his progress in reading. Before drawing any conclusions, his first-grade teacher wanted to have more information on his knowledge of word elements.

CASE 3: Ken's Spelling

In order to describe this knowledge more precisely, his teacher administered the *Developmental Spelling Test.* She began the test by demonstrating how to spell two basal words: *mat* and *dip.* She first had him listen to *mat* to see what sounds he could hear. He heard the phoneme corresponding to *m* at the beginning and that for *t* at the end. His teacher encouraged him to write the letters associated with these sounds. Then she had him first say *dip* slowly to himself and then write the letters he heard. Then she presented the test words, encouraging him "to write them as best he could." The results are shown in Figure 3.6.

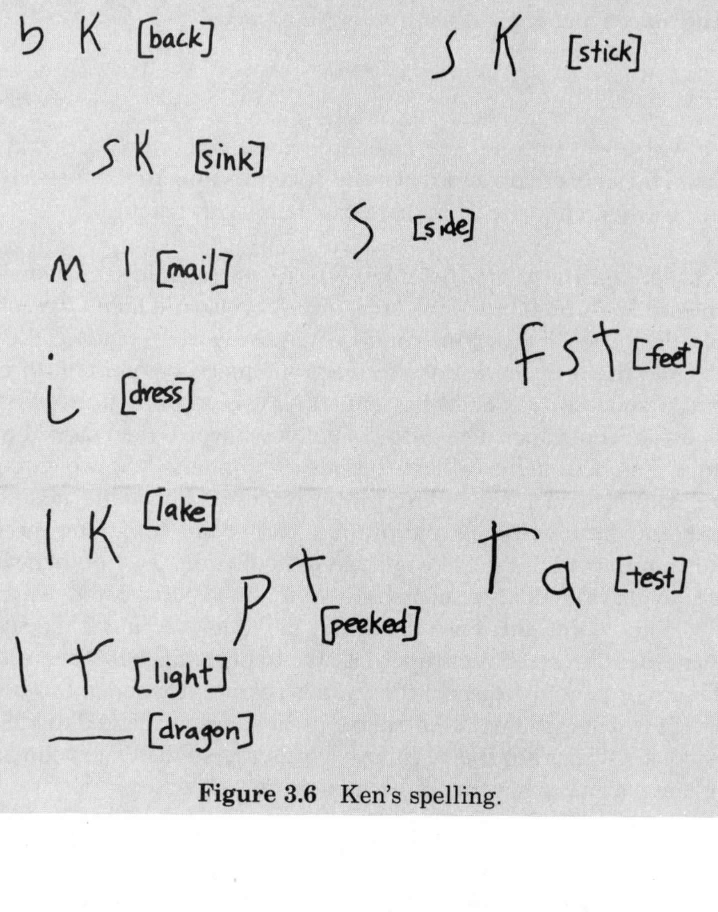

Figure 3.6   Ken's spelling.

The reader should study the results. At what stage is Ken in in terms of developing knowledge about English orthography? An analysis of the results shows that he has good command of consonants in the beginning and endings of words but that he is not yet able to represent consonant blends and vowels. In terms of his underlying knowledge about words, he is in command of the consonant frame of words.

The administration of the spelling test, as well as the basal sight word task, helped Ken's teacher confirm her impressions about his sight vocabulary and his knowledge of print. The results show that he is learning the set of words that are formally introduced through instruction and practiced during story reading. Yet he has not yet generalized much beyond this set of words. Thus, in her conversation with Ken's parents, she encouraged them to read and reread books with him at home and to let him participate through echo reading (see p. 37) when he wished. His solid mastery of the basal vocabulary made her realize that he probably could proceed at a faster rate through the basal program than other low group members; hence she decided to have him join the middle group while at the same time continuing as a member of the low group. His strength in word identification and his underlying knowledge of word elements confirmed that he should be able to participate in many activities currently being undertaken by her middle group. At the same time, work in the low group would introduce some new phonics concepts and serve to consolidate his reading through easy practice.

We will now consider one final procedure with word lists that can be used easily by teachers on a formal basis. It can also be used informally during instruction when children encounter problems with reading.

Informal Diagnostic Probe. One way to assess children's knowledge of word elements is to focus on words that they have difficulty reading. For example, during small group instruction or individual oral reading, the teacher may observe that certain words are mispronounced or omitted. In order to learn more about why a child has difficulty, it is appropriate to write these words on a sheet of paper. The probe of unknown words then takes the form of assisting the student in his or her attempts to pronounce the words correctly. A more complicated form of the probe is described in the next chapter. However, for the time being, the probe consists, first, of asking the child to pronounce the word. If the child still has difficulty, the teacher then simplifies the task by having the student respond to only part of the word. For a single-syllable word, the teacher covers all but the initial consonant or consonant blend to see if the student is able to pronounce it. Then she covers all but the word ending to see if the child is able to pronounce this portion. If the student is successful with both parts, he or she is then asked to identify the whole word. Otherwise, the teacher records the student's pronunciation of word elements and proceeds to the next word on the list.

For words of more than one syllable, the teacher first sees if the child can pronounce the word. If the child experiences difficulty, the teacher encourages him or her to cover all but the first pronounceable chunk or syllable and to identify it. If the child is successful, he or she is encouraged to identify the next pronounceable chunk, continuing to the end of the word. If unsuccessful with any syllable, the procedures described for single-syllable words should be followed. From this informal probe, the teacher is able to determine (1) whether a child lacks knowledge of letter sounds or (2) whether the child has such knowledge but has difficulty applying it to identify unknown words.

In order to provide assistance during the informal probe, a teacher must have knowledge about which elements of print are easier and are usually learned first (consonants in beginning and final positions, vowel phonograms), which are more difficult (consonant blends and digraphs, short and long vowels), and which are most difficult and are usually learned later (vowel digraphs, controlled vowels). For further definition of these elements and the order in which they are typically introduced in basal programs, see the *Blachowicz Informal Phonics Survey* in Appendix B. The Blachowicz Survey may also be used to examine a student's knowledge of phonics in a more systematic fashion.

Although the informal probe is more difficult to learn than more structured inventories such as the Blachowicz Survey, once mastered, it is an easy procedure to use informally in the classroom. We return to the case of Alex in order to demonstrate this procedure.

CASE 4:   Alex's Skill in Word Identification

In order to learn more about Alex's skill with longer multisyllabic words, his teacher undertook an informal diagnostic probe of the three words that he failed to identify on the graded word list with extended time. She first printed *balanced* on a sheet and asked Alex how he might divide the word into pronounceable chunks or syllables. He responded that it didn't need to be divided. His teacher then segmented off the initial syllable *bal;* Alex correctly identified this syllable. She then covered *bal,* exposing the remainder of the word, which Alex pronounced immediately. His teacher then asked him to say the word, which he did, saying, "Oh! balanced." She then printed *observing* on the sheet and asked Alex to divide it into chunks that he could pronounce. He divided it as follows: *ob/ser/ving* and then correctly identified it. Finally, she printed *vanishing,* which he divided as *van/is/hing.* He pronounced each syllable "van" "is" "hing" but was unable to identify the word. His teacher explained that certain consonant pairs, such as *sh, ch,* and *th* usually function as units and thus they should not be divided. He redivided the word as *van/ish/ing* and correctly pronounced it. From this probe, his teacher learned that he has some sense of what constitutes a syllable but that he needs more supervised practice dividing and pronouncing longer multisyllabic words.

We cannot fully understand Alex's reading until we also examine his contextual reading strategies (Chapter 4), his vocabulary development (Chapter 5), and his comprehension strategies (Chapters 6 and 7). In particular, to determine an appropriate reading group placement, his teacher needs to identify the level of material that he can read with acceptable comprehension (Chapters 6 and 7) and relatively few oral reading errors (Chapter 4). The results from this detailed study of Alex's knowledge of print provide one major focus for instructional support; diagnosis of vocabulary concepts and comprehension may reveal other areas in which instruction is needed.

On the basis of this analysis, Alex's teacher would group him with other students who need support to identify multisyllabic words and to apply their knowledge of print. Such instruction is described in the following section. Typically, such instruction can occur before students read a new selection by the teacher's placing mutlisyllabic words on the blackboard and having the *group* determine how they should be divided into pronounceable chunks (or syllables). Once words are divided, group members typically have little difficulty applying their knowledge. They need support, however, in applying this procedure when they encounter longer words during their silent reading of selections.

Summary

In order to learn to use diagnostic strategies, a teacher must study them and then use them with children on an individual basis. Later, once she is familiar with the procedures, she can use them more informally in the classroom while children work on seatwork activities or during small group instruction. The teacher's knowledge about what particular children know about words and word elements will become more precise over time.

INSTRUCTION IN PRINT KNOWLEDGE

Instruction to Develop Knowledge of Words

It is not our intention in this section to describe procedures that are introduced in most reading methods courses. We will, however, describe supplementary procedures that can be used with reading groups in order to reinforce learning. New sight words to be taught to the student should be drawn from the contextual materials used by the teacher. Instruction should never involve development only of words in isolation. Rather, contextual reading should be a part of every instructional session so that it serves to reinforce the learning of sight words. The number of new sight words introduced each day should depend on the student's mastery. For example, if five new words are introduced but only two mastered, the teacher should reduce the number to two or three at the next session.

The degree of instructional reinforcement should be adjusted to what is needed by the student for retention. Word-sort activities, writing, and spelling can all be used to reinforce the initial learning of sight words.

1. *Word banks.* The use of word banks is an outgrowth of the language experience approach, in which various reinforcement activities serve to help students learn and remember words (Stauffer, 1970). The word bank consists of words that a student is learning through contextual reading (basal materials or language experience materials) and other words that are of interest to the student. When a new word is encountered or identified, it is printed on a 3 × 5 card. Since the ability of some beginning readers to write evenly and accurately is limited, it is sometimes better for the teacher to print the words in a form similar to print in books. The student can use the back of the card to draw a picture or write a sentence that will cue him or her to the identity of the word. As new words are encountered, the stack of cards accumulates. A box and rubber bands should be provided to help students keep and organize the word cards.

The cards may be used for a variety of reinforcement activities. They may be reviewed by children working individually or in pairs. They may be used to form sentences, as a small-group or individual activity.

One of the most productive activities involves sorting the words into various classes on the basis of alternative features (see Gillet & Temple, 1982, for a more detailed description of procedures to be followed during *word sorts*). During small group instruction, children may be asked to go through their cards to find those that exemplify a certain characteristic. For example, they may be asked to select words that begin or end like the word *balloon,* that name an animal, or that are three syllables in length. Alternatively, students may be invited to identify words that conform to a criterion of their choosing. Once they have identified and displayed a group of four to six words to their classmates, they can see if the other students can determine the characteristic that the selected words share.

2. *Writing and spelling.* Beginning readers who have difficulty learning words are often helped to remember them by being encouraged to spell and write words that have been introduced in their reading materials. These activities seem to prompt children to scrutinize words, particularly the medial portions, and to become more aware of the phonemic correlates of the words. Further, once they have learned to write basic sight words, they often draw on these high-frequency words during their other writing activities. Thus, writing is made easier and basic sight words are reinforced.

3. *Contextual reading practice.* One of the best ways to consolidate sight vocabulary is through extensive contextual reading. Many basal programs are designed to provide practice on words that have been introduced by including them in subsequent stories. However, such practice may be insufficient for students who have great difficulty remembering words. Thus, it is important for the teacher to devise ways to give students more practice on the words they are learning. Easy-to-read books such as the "Frog and Toad" series by Arnold Lobel are appropriate. Also, some basal series provide supplementary materials for this purpose. Alternatively, students may reread stories that they have previously read. For example, once a book is completed, the teacher may ask students to identify their favorite stories from the book and then have students take turns reading them. The teacher may pose a new question about a previously read story and have children read the story silently to identify information relevant to the question. Some teachers find that a prior edition of a basal series provides a "new" set of stories that includes many of the words introduced in the newer edition. These texts may therefore be useful as supplementary reading for students having difficulty learning words.

One reason that teachers fail to provide supplementary reading is that students in the most slowly paced group proceed at a very slow rate as it is. To take time for additional contextual practice would result in an even slower pace. Thus, in order to provide additional practice, it may be necessary to plan extra small-group instructional time. For example, it may be necessary to meet with the most slowly paced group twice a day (morning and afternoon) rather than once.

Instruction to Develop Knowledge of Word Elements

In considering instruction in the area of word identification, we need to distinguish between students who have difficulty identifying single-syllable words and those that have difficulty mainly with words of two or more syllables. The first group of students need to be taught basic letter–sound associations and/or how to apply such knowledge when identifying single-syllable words. The second group needs to learn how to divide words into pronounceable "chunks" so as to be able to identify these units with the knowledge they possess.

Single-Syllable Words. Some students have acquired extensive knowledge of word elements (consonants, consonant blends, vowels, vowel markers, word endings) but fail to apply this knowledge when identifying unknown words, particularly during contextual reading. Other students lack basic knowledge of word elements and these must be taught.

Word Elements. In teaching phonic associations, the instructional materials used in the class should be examined to determine the sequence in which the word elements unknown by the student are introduced. For example, some programs introduce long vowels before short, others short before long. Learning to hear the phonemes (sounds) in a word is the first step in learning phonics associations. Some students may need to develop phoneme awareness by listening to words of two or three phonemes to identify the number of different sounds they hear. During this process, children should be encouraged to say the words in segmented fashion, as they do when attempting to spell the word. Sometimes drawing a series of connected boxes corresponding to the number of phonemes in a word helps children to hear the sounds (Elkonin, 1963). The teacher should write the letters corresponding to phonemes as the children says them; she can supply any unknown elements.

Each phonics association to be taught should be introduced through a series of words in which the phoneme occurs in initial position. If students have difficulty remembering the phoneme, a key word (which contains the phoneme at the beginning) should be introduced in printed form. Whenever students encounter words beginning with the newly learned phonics association, they should be encouraged to pronounce that portion of the word. This activity teaches them that phonics associations provide valuable cues for word identification. Finally, students should be encouraged to use phonics knowledge in conjunction with contextual information during contextual reading.

In teaching phonics associations, it is often necessary to introduce the concept of *markers* (see Venezky, 1970, for discussion of this concept). In certain contexts, vowel letters generally and some consonant letters as well "mark" the pronunciation of another letter in that context (e.g., the e or i following a c marks the pronunciation of c as /s/). Students need to learn, for example, that the second of two vowels or a final e often marks the pronunciation of a preceding vowel. This concept should not be taught as a rule but rather by presenting examples from which students can infer the generalization. The teacher should begin with the final e concept (*can–cane, mat–mate, tap–tape*) and then move to vowel combinations (*pad–paid, ran–rain, bat–bait, man–main*). Though most students pick up this concept rather easily, they sometimes have problems applying it during contextual reading.

Some students who have acquired a large sight vocabulary encounter difficulty reading multisyllabic words in the intermediate grades because of their limited knowledge of word elements. Some of these experience extreme difficulty learning phonics associations. They can, however, sometimes learn to pronounce syllables using an alternative strategy.

Once words are divided into syllables, these students need instruction in analogizing in order to see how known words and word parts can be used to identify unknown syllables. Students are encouraged to think of a word that ends the same as the first syllable of the unknown multisyllabic word and then to use a consonant-substitution method to identify the syllable. For example, in identifying the word *barter,* students are first encouraged to split the word into two units (*bar–ter*). Then the teacher asks them to think of a word that ends the same as *bar,* such as *car.* If the students have difficulty thinking of an appropriate word, the teacher should supply one. Finally, the cue word is written on top of the first syllable and students are encouraged to identify the syllable by substituting initial consonants. The procedure continues for the remaining syllable. To begin with, only multisyllabic words with obvious sight word analogies should be selected. Once the procedure is mastered, words without obvious analogies should be attempted under the guidance of the teacher. Often the step of dividing mutlisyllabic words into units is sufficient to permit their identification.

For students who have considerable difficulty thinking of appropriate cue words, the systematic training procedure described by Cunningham (1978; see also 1975–76, 1979) may be effective. In this approach, students are made aware that they are familiar with a large number of sight words that can be used to identify unknown words. In the first step, students write the words *he, went, her, can,* and *car* on index cards. Then they are asked to select two of the cards that match parts of such unknown words as *banter, ferment, meter, barber, percent,* and *garment.* Additional sight words are added during the second and third steps and further matching practice is provided. In the fourth step, students are encouraged to use "the whole store of words in their heads as words to match to unfamiliar [two-syllable] words" (pp. 610–11). In the fifth and final step, the procedures are applied to words of three or more syllables.

Application and Blending. Many students with knowledge of word elements fail to apply this knowledge because they have developed a habit of hastily guessing at words, particularly those in context, on the basis of partial information. They need to be taught a new procedure for dealing with unknown single-syllable words. This procedure consists of five steps:

1. Pause (instead of guess).
2. Look at the initial part of the word and pronounce it.
3. Look at the remainder of the word and pronounce it.
4. Blend the word parts together into a word.
5. Check to see if the word makes sense in context.

After applying this procedure slowly and systematically, students will become able to scan words more rapidly and pronounce them accurately given their print knowledge.

Some students, however, have difficulty with the fourth step of the procedure: blending word elements together. To teach blending skill, the following procedures can be used, either with individual students or with groups. Instruction should begin with the blending of syllables (*but–ter, wag–on, ti–ger*). If this is difficult for the students, compound words such as *football, doghouse,* and *cowboy* should be presented along with pictures corresponding to the component words; the students should identify the picture that corresponds to the "word-syllable" being pronounced. When students can blend compound words, other two-syllable words should be attempted. Next, phoneme blending should be developed. First a vowel unit should be blended into a final consonant (*ca–t, bo–x, de–sk*), then a consonant into an ending (*f–oot, h–and, p–en*), and finally, three units should be blended (*r–a–t, f–a–ce, p–a–ge*). Many students are helped by seeing the sequence of letters while they hear the teacher pronounce the sounds and by imitating the way the teacher separates and blends sounds within words. Blending should be practiced for short periods every day for several weeks.

Multisyllabic Words. Students who experience difficulty mainly with longer words and relatively little difficulty with single-syllable words need to be taught how to "chunk" or divide mutlisyllabic words into pronounceable units. To learn the concept of syllable, students should listen to the teacher pronounce two-, three-, and even four-syllable words and tap the number of syllables they hear. Next, they should examine the syllables of two-syllable words that are regular in pattern (*butter, rabbit, window, pencil, erase, apron, table, open,* and *paper*) to see if they can figure out what constitutes a syllable (that it contains at least one vowel) and determine typical syllable patterns. (These patterns are consonant–vowel–consonant, consonant–vowel, vowel–consonant, and vowel, where a consonant may be either a single consonant, a consonant blend, or a consonant digraph, and where a vowel may be either a single vowel, a vowel digraph, or a vowel plus vowel marker.)

Students should be advised to pronounce vowels in mutlisyllabic words as they would in one-syllable words and then to blend the syllables into a word that makes sense. The concept of "open" syllable (e.g., *be*) suggesting a long vowel pronunciation and a "closed" syllable (e.g. *bet*) indicating a short vowel pronunciation is difficult for some students to learn. The most effective procedure for developing the concept involves word comparisons or word sorts (for further discussion, see Henderson, 1985). To begin with, two-syllable words familiar to the students should be selected. The first set should include words such as *hopped* and *hoped, dinner* and *diner.* The students should focus on the first syllable and be guided to see that the nature of the syllable (open or closed) influences vowel pronunciation. Then words within the same initial vowel can be compared: *hopped, potter, hoped, hotel, cotton.* Students should be able to give a reason for sorting certain words together. Finally, the words compared or sorted can include several different vowels: *butter, paper, rabbit, window, favor.*

Some students have extreme difficulty with syllable pronunciation because syllables are *nonsense.* One way to help students deal with this problem is to use a word family approach: students should identify several known words first, then related syllables (*bat, cat—lat, tat*), next a real word followed by a syllable (*bed–med, rod–fod, cab–pab*), and finally a list of nonsense syllables.

Once students understand how to divide longer words into syllables and to identify the syllables, it is important that they be provided with regular practice doing this as part of their reading instruction. When stories or expository selections are assigned, the teacher should identify approximately three to five multisyllabic words that may pose a problem for the students and write these words on the blackboard. The teacher should ask the students how the first word can be divided into syllables. Sometimes there will be disagreement among group members. Students should then be encouraged to pronounce the syllables, identify the word, and draw a conclusion about the best way to divide the word. Once the words are identified, the teacher should check to see that the meanings are familiar to all students in the group. The concepts underlying any unfamiliar words should be discussed using procedures described in Chapter 5.

SUMMARY

In this chapter we considered the knowledge that students have about print and how it contributes to the development of a sight vocabulary and word identification skill. We described three diagnostic strategies for examining sight word recognition, knowledge of word elements, and word identification strategies and demonstrated their use through the cases of Ken and Alex. Particularly in the area of print knowledge, ongoing diagnosis provides the basis for effective instruction. Finally, we described some of these instructional procedures. In the next chapter, where we focus on contextual reading assessment, we will continue to discuss the development of print knowledge and consider how it underlies the development of reading integration and fluency.

CHAPTER 4

Reading Integration and Fluency

Chapters 2 and 3 considered the stages through which children progress as they develop awareness and knowledge of printed words; in this chapter we will focus on contextual reading and reading fluency. By "fluency" we mean reading unfamiliar as well as familiar selections with appropriate intonaiton, phrasing, and rate. It is possible for children to demonstrate fluent reading with familiar stories they have read many times, but unless this same fluency is demonstrated with unfamiliar selection, we cannot conclude that they are fluent readers. The capability to read fluently depends on two conditions: (1) instantaneous recognition of an extensive set of printed words and (2) considerable practice reading contextual selections. Some skillful young readers achieve fluency in their first year of reading. Many, however, require several years of reading experience before they acquire sufficient word knowledge and contextual practice to read unfamiliar material fluently. The focus of this chapter is on determining whether children have achieved fluency when reading unfamiliar selections and delineating the reading experiences they need to further the development of fluency.

DEVELOPMENT OF INTEGRATION AND FLUENCY

Biemillier (1970) describes three stages of development in beginning reading skill. In the first stage, beginning readers when reading contextual selections attend mainly to contextual information; that is, when they come to words they do not know, the words they substitute are words they have guessed on the basis of context. For example, in the sentence *The red wagon rolled down the hill* might be read as "The red wagon *sped* down the hill." The substitution of *sped* for *rolled* suggests that the child, failing to recognize the word *rolled,* used the contextual meaning of the sentence to determine an appropriate substitute.

In the second stage, children appear to focus much more on the print in that when they encounter an unknown word, their substitutions tend to match some part of the unknown word. For example, a child at this stage reading the sentence *The red wagon rolled down the hill* might substiture the nonsense word *railed* for *rolled* if he or she did not know the word *rolled.* Children at this stage are beginning to attend much more closely to the features of printed words.

In the final stage, they integrate information from print and context when identifying unknown words. Biemiller found that errors they made tended to be appropriate both to the context of the sentence and the graphic features of the word. For example, the student in reading the same sentence might substitute the word *raced* for *rolled.* The substitution makes sense in terms of the meaning of the sentence and it matches some of the features of the printed word. It is during this stage that readers learn to integrate information from context and print to aid them in identifying unknown words.

All readers in the process of becoming proficient readers learn to orchestrate information from a variety of sources while reading. This integration of information can be seen most clearly in the case of beginning readers. In the early stages, they seem to be able to consider only one source of information (context or print) at a time; later when they confront unknown words, their substitutions indicate use of information from several sources (Biemiller, 1970; Weber, 1968).

An issue of considerable importance is whether the ability to integrate information from a variety of sources underlies fluent reading, or whether fluent reading comes about in some other way. In essence, the debate focuses on whether fluent reading is achieved through coordination of print and contentual information, with decreased attention to print in favor of meaning, or whether knowledge of words and word identification proficiency are solely or mainly responsible for fluent reading (Stanovich, 1986).

On one side, many reading experts argue that fluent reading arises from the complex orchestration of information sources (Bussis, Chittenden, Amarel, & Klausner, 1985; Clay, 1979). For example, Goodman (1976) asserts, "Skill in reading involves not greater precision, but more accurate first guesses based on better sampling techniques, greater control over language structure, broadened experiences and increased conceptual development" (p. 504). Indeed, expressed as part of this position is the assumption that heavy dependence on print causes poor reading. For example, Smith (1971) argues, "The more difficulty a reader has with reading, the more he relies on visual information; this statement applies to both the fluent reader and the beginner" (p. 221).

The opposing position has been articulated in recent years. Among the first to focus on the development of fluency or automaticity, LaBerge and Samuels (1974) proposed that instantaneous processing of print evolves as component skills of word identification become automatic through practice. They suggest that practice facilitates two different developments. First, it results in the consolidation of separate processes. At a basic level, for example, phonic associations and blending are consolidated within word identification. That is, children learn to blend letter–sound associations to identify previously unknown words. At a more advanced level, visual recognition leads immediately to semantic awareness with or without phonological mediation. Readers are no longer aware of the visual forms or sound of words they read but are aware only of their meaning. This consolidation is revealed when children no longer hesitate in recognizing words. Second, practice permits the reorganization of perception into larger units, allowing the reader to go, for example, from word-by-word reading to reading word groups or phrases. This reorganization is sometimes manifested in an increase in reading rate.

What is interesting about the initial version of the automaticity formulation is that fluency was seen as developing through automaticity of word knowledge; the role of context was not considered (see Samuels, 1979, for later versions that consider the role of contextual facilitation in the development of fluency). Other researchers have attempted to clarify the nature of the role of context in fluent reading. For example, Perfetti (1985) has shown that there is a linear relation between isolated word recognition time and contextual facilitation. That is, the more difficult a word is to recognize (because a reader lacks word knowledge or because a word has been degraded), the more important is context in contributing information.

Stanovich (1980, 1986) develops this position further by distinguishing between two forms of contextual support: an automatic contextual facilitation that occurs outside of conscious control, and a consciously controlled process. The automatic process is viewed as operating in memory without reader awareness; the topic under consideration triggers or activates related concepts, thereby making them easier for a reader to retrieve. The conscious process is seen as directed by the purpose of the reader, with his or her full attention. Stanovich argues that this conscious use of context occurs when readers encounter problems recognizing words; one negative consequence is, however, that the resulting focus of attention on word recognition detracts from comprehension. Good readers, who have developed automaticity in word knowledge, encounter few problems with word identification when reading and therefore can direct all their attention toward meaning. Poor readers who encounter many problems with print are forced to use context to aid word identification, and this division of attention between print and meaning leads not only to poorer comprehension but also to less adequate contextual information to support word identification.

In this book we take the position that the goal of reading is comprehension and that adequate comprehension depends on the orchestration of knowledge from different sources, including the reader's background knowledge on a topic, the developing understanding of an author's message, knowledge of language structures, and knowledge or print. At the same time, we believe that fluent processing of print depends on automaticity of word knowledge, the quick recognition of words without effort devoted to analysis. We agree with Stanovich that when readers encounter few problem in word identification, they are able to focus more completely on reconstructing the messages of authors. There is, however, a stage before fluent reading when most readers profit from learning to integrate information from print and context to aid their word identification.

DIAGNOSIS OF INTEGRATION AND FLUENCY

Areas of Reading Assessed

By listening to students read contextual selections, a teacher can identify problems that exist in three areas: (1) knowledge of print, (2) integration of knowledge sources, and (3) reading fluency. In this section we will describe the areas of reading that are assessed through oral reading of contextual selections. Following this we will describe the specific procedures that teachers should follow in order to learn how to assess oral reading competently.

Knowledge of Print. Problems may exist in two areas of print knowledge: knowledge of sight words (commonly occurring words that should be instantaneously recognized) and knowledge about word identification. Strategies for assessing knowledge of words presented in isolation and word parts were described in Chapter 3; in this chapter we examine knowledge of print demonstrated through contextual reading. Both forms of evidence are necessary and complementary. Many students possess well-developed knowledge of sight words and word identification when tested on isolated words and word parts, but they fail to apply this knowledge when reading contextual selections. For other students, the problem goes beyond that of application: they have not developed adequate word knowledge in the first place.

Both sight word knowledge and word identification are examined through an assessment of the ways in which students' oral reading deviates from the text. For an evaluation of sight word development, those words that occur frequently in about 70 percent of running text are considered. This diagnosis focuses on how quickly and accurately students recognize these basic sight words. For an evaluation of word identification, content words that are mispronounced during contextual reading are considered. This diagnosis focuses on whether portions of words are correctly read and whether students can deal with multisyllabic words. In both cases, the way the oral reading response deviates from the text is considered.

Integration. Students frequently encounter words that they do not know. The diagnostic procedures described in Chapter 3 focused on word identification and its improvement through the development of knowledge about words and word elements. Assessment of students' oral reading of contextual selections allows us to consider word knowledge, but in addition it permits us to examine how well students combine their knowledge of print with information from other sources in identifying unknown words. For example, picture cues, story themes, prior sentence context, reader knowledge of syntax, and reader experience with a topic are all useful sources of information that may aid a student in identifying unknown words. Students who have not developed balanced strategies for words identification need to be shown how to use information from a variety of sources for more efficient and effective word identification.

Students' oral reading responses can be analyzed in terms of *how* as well as *whether* they match responses that are expected on the basis of the text (Goodman, 1965, 1967, 1969). Some incorrect responses, or "miscues," as Goodman perfers to call them, may reflect use of information about print; others may be influenced by prior sentence context, that is, they may make sense in terms of contextual meaning derived from the story topic, pictures, or the previously read portion of the sentence. Furthermore, some responses may reflect both these factors, whereas others may show the influence of neither. Some children, for example, in the beginning stages of reading rely on context or picture cues to the neglect of print cues; others produce nonwords that are cued by print but show no influence of context. An analysis of how oral reading responses match with expected responses permits teachers to learn about the strategies students have available when they encounter unfamiliar words. If most miscues show the influence of contextual information, it can be concluded that the reader used this source of information and is trying to make sense of what has been read.

The number and type of miscues that readers attempt to correct also shed light on their ability to integrate contextual and print information and to monitor their reading. Several categories of correction behavior in oral reading have been identified (Page & Barr, 1975). When a reader corrects a response, he or she gives evidence of dissatisfaction with the original response. Conversely, failure to attempt a correction indicates a lack of dissatisfaction or insufficient knowledge on which to base a correction. Consider an oral reading response that is semantically and syntactically acceptable but differs in letter–sound correspondence from the expected response, as in *Tim ran down the* road for *Tim ran down the lane.* If the reader does not attempt to correct the miscue, a reasonable assumption is that semantic and grammatical cues from the context permitted him or her to verify the response and feel satisfied with it. We can also assume that, to some degree, the phonic discrepancy did not cause the reader to feel dissatisfied.

If no pauses or other miscues immediately precede or follow the response, the assumption concerning a lack of influence from phonics cues is strengthened. If *road* and *lane* are used interchangeably by the reader in a semantically acceptable way throughout the passage, the assumption is further strengthened. If, on the other hand, the reader attempts to correct his or her substitution of *road* for *lane,* we must assume that the phonics cues are operating at this point, because the original response caused the reader some dissatisfaction. The attempt to correct may be successful or unsuccessful. If it is successful, we may assume that phonics cues are influencing the reader's processing.

The production of a semantically and grammatically unacceptable response, such as *Tim ran down the* lone, would warrant an inverse sort of interpretation in terms of corrections. Once again, failure to attempt a correction would suggest that semantic, grammatical, and phonics information was inadequately processed. If an attempt yields a vowel change such as *lean* for *lane,* we can assume that phonics cues are generating the correction attempt. On the other hand, a correction attempt with *line* for *lane* suggests all sources of information may be involved. In any event, a careful look at what elicits a correction response and what miscues go uncorrected can yield a great deal of information about the reading process.

It is also important for teachers to ask students how they were able to identify unfamiliar words. Often students are able to describe the bases for their readings in ways that provide teachers with ideas for further instruction.

Reading Fluency. Fluency or lack thereof is evident when one listens to the oral reading of students. The reading of those who have not yet mastered the component skills of print processing is characterized by substitution errors, long pauses, frequent repetitions, and inappropriate phrasing. In other words, problems exist in word knowledge tht make it impossible for a student to demonstrate fluent reading.

Oral reading analysis sometimes reveals no major problems—few substitutions, pauses, and repetitions—but phrasing that is inappropriate to the syntax and meaning of the selection. Reading occurs word-by-word or in clusters of words with brief pauses between them. It is as if print knowledge has not become sufficiently automatic to permit attention to phrasing during the oral rendering or recoding of the message.

Often, when students experience difficulty with reading fluency, the cause lies in other problems, such as sight word knowledge and word identification. Yet this is not necessarily the case. One can distinguish a primary fluency problem from one that is secondary to other reading problems by having the student read text that is extremely easy for him or her. If the characteristics of nonfluent reading—poor intonation, inappropriate phrasing, long pauses, and word-by-word reading—persist, then it can be concluded that the problem is primarily one of fluency. Some readers become extremely anxious when asked to read aloud, and their oral reading is disrupted, not necessarily because they lack fluency, but because of their anxiety. In such cases, it is not possible to assess reading fluency accurately by having the students read aloud. As will be discussed in the following paragraph, one can gain some understanding of their fluency by noting their rate of silent reading.

From approximately third grade level and beyond, a reading rate in the average range can be used to infer adequate reading fluency. When this information is combined with oral reading evidence, a teacher can draw useful conclusions about the development of print knowledge and reading fluency. Once students no longer experience problems with word identification, it is appropriate for teachers to help them develop their reading rate.

As is illustrated in Table 4.1, the reading rates of students improve dramatically from first to second grade and thereafter show steady but more moderate increases. Although a comparison of the average reading rates of students on various reading tests shows wide variation (Harris & Sipay, 1980, p. 556), this variability in part reflects variations in the difficulty of the test material. Some tests consist of extremely easy passages, while others include more technical material. The rates shown in Table 4.1 are based on passages that are appropriate in difficulty to the grade of the students tested; accordingly, these ranges provide a useful standard against which to compare the reading of students at different grade levels. Silent reading rates are somewhat higher than the ranges shown for oral reading, particularly for the intermediate grades and beyond (Carver, 1983; S. E. Taylor, 1965). Reading rates below the ranges shown in Table 4.1 indicate lack of fluency.

TABLE 4.1. AVERAGE READING RATES ON THE GILMORE ORAL READING TEST

Grade level	Average range[a] words per minute
1.8	30–54
2.8	66–104
3.8	86–124
4.8	95–130
5.8	108–140
6.8	112–145
7.8	122–155
8.8	136–167

[a] The average range includes approximately 54% of students, those in stanines 4, 5, and 6 and in the 23–76 percentile band. *(Source: After Table 3, Manual of Directions, Gilmore Oral Reading Test. Copyright © 1968 by Harcourt Brace Jovanovich, Inc. Reproduced by permision. All rights reserved.)*

In sum, oral reading of a selection enables the teacher to judge the fluency of students, both in terms of phrasing and intonation and in terms of reading rate. Conclusions about fluency, in combination with those concerning word knowledge, provide the basis for planning appropriate instruction. The goal of the diagnosis is not only to determine whether the reading is fluent, but also to determine the level of material where the reader encounters few problems with print. If reading is not fluent, it is important to provide instruction to build knowledge about print and to encourage extensive practice on problem-free materials in order to promote reading fluency.

Procedures for Oral Reading Assessment

In order to learn how to listen to students as they read aloud, it is important for teachers to practice oral reading assessment following systematic procedures. Many complex decisions are involved in selecting an appropriate story or expository passage, learning to record oral reading responses, analyzing the responses, gaining further needed information, and finally, interpreting the results. It is necessary for teachers to practice oral reading assessment with children individually before they become sufficiently proficient to undertake such assessment informally during the rapid give-and-take of classroom instruction.

The procedures for oral reading response analysis will be described here in considerable detail. Those teachers for whom oral reading analysis is a new skill should follow each recommended step. As always occurs with a new skill, the first attempts to use these procedures will be difficult and time consuming. However, with practice the appropriate skills and knowledge will become automatic so that oral reading responses analysis can be undertaken with ease. Indeed, after listening and interpretive skills have been developed, many teachers can perform a useful diagnosis by simply listening to students' oral reading. The procedures involve six main steps. First, some *preparation* is necessary before the teacher listens to a student read. Following this preparation, the teacher *administers* the passage and records the student's oral reading. Third, the teacher *analyzes* the response patterns. With this third step, the first stage of the diagnosis is completed. Then a second work session may be needed in order to *probe* selected aspects of reading; this fourth step may provide evidence that modifies or supports the tentative conclusions reached. Fifth, the teacher *interprets* the response patterns and integrates the results from the probes with the results from the initial diagnosis. Finally, the teacher translates the diagnosis into an *instructional plan.*

Preparation

Normally the teacher will select a passage from instructional materials being used in the classroom. The teacher should make a judgement as to the level at which the student is able to read. A trial run with several short selections may be necessary. Oral reading may be from any appropriate book including the student's basal reader. For each selection, a double-spaced typewritten version or photocopy should be prepared. The portion used for analysis should be 50–100 words in length for beginning readers and 100–200 words or more for more advanced readers. The total length should approximate that which students typically read at any one time in the classroom.

As was discussed previously, the oral reading responses of any student can be recorded and analyzed to determine how he or she translates print into meaning (see Hood, 1976; Wixson, 1979, for further discussion of oral reading analysis). Figure 4.1 provides one set of recording symbols for teachers to use as they record how a student's oral reading departs from the responses expected on the basis of the text. For example, substituted words are recorded by crossing out the mispronounced word and writing the student's pronunciation over the miscued word. Similarly, pauses (breaks in phrasing) are recorded with a single slash. A teacher learning to diagnose students' reading problems should be familiar with this system or some similar scheme. It is recommended that the student's oral reading be tape-recorded as well, so that it will be possible to check the accuracy of the recording. The reason for the diagnosis should be discussed with the student.

Administration

The teacher should make sure that the student is comfortable and sufficiently relaxed. If the oral reading will be tape-recorded, the student's permission should be obtained. It is important to provide an orienting statement to help

Figure 4.1 Symbols for recording oral reading responses.

Omissions. Circle the word, group of words, or part of a word omitted.	Danny ran up to the door.
Insertions. Write in the word or word part inserted. Indicate its position with a carat.	He rode his bicycle. *(on inserted)*
Substitutions or mispronunciations. Identify the mispronounced word(s) by crossing out or underlining it (them). Write in the substituted word(s).	He bicycled around the block. *(bic / black)*
Repetitions. Underline repeated words using a line and arrow or a wiggly line.	He rode around the block. *(black)*
Corrections. Indicate corrected responses by a c inside a circle.	He rode around the block. *(© black)*
Pauses. Indicate pauses by a single slash. Pauses that exceed 2 seconds should be recorded by a double slash.	He got a // glass / of milk.
Punctuation. Indicate failure to pause for a comma or period by circling.	The milk tasted funny⊙ Danny thought it might be too warm.

the student relate to the content and theme of the selection (see Beck, Omanson, & McKeown, 1982, for procedural suggestions). It is also important to explain to the student what he or she should do. For example, the following may be said:

> This is a story in which . . . [theme-related preparatory statement]. Please read this story aloud for me. If you come to a word you don't know, try to figure it out, guess at it, or skip it. I will not be able to help you, so do the best you can. After you finish, I'll ask you some questions.

The teacher should record the student's responses on a photocopy or typed version of the story. Responses should be recorded by the teacher even if the oral reading is tape-recorded. The time that the student begins and finishes reading the passage should also be noted.

If the reader becomes frustrated at some point, the teacher should reiterate that it is all right to guess at a word or skip it. If the reader continues to pause and becomes upset, the word causing difficulty should be provided. If the reading passage proves generally too frustrating, the diagnosis should be discontinued and an easier passage read at some later time.

Analysis

The oral reading record should be examined in order to determine whether the passage is of appropriate difficulty and to assess the student's sight word recognition, word identification strategies, and reading integration and fluency.

Passage Difficulty. This analysis pertains to the level of materials that would be appropriate for various purposes (such as, for reading instruction as opposed to independent reading) and is based on the student's overall accuracy and fluency of word recognition. The criteria for judging whether a passage is appropriate, summarized in Table 4.2, derive from those originally recommended by Betts (1954). Betts suggests that more than 1 error for every 10 words read indicates that the material is too difficult for the student. That is, when less than 90 percent of a passage is read correctly, the material is at the

TABLE 4.2. CRITERIA FOR DETERMINING
READING LEVELS

Level	Oral reading accuracy (%)
Independent	98–100
Instructional	95–97
Borderline	90–94
Frustration	Below 90

student's frustration level. Betts recommends further that students should make no more than 1 error per 20 words on materials that are read as part of instruction. That is, when instructional support is provided, students should be able to read passages with 95 percent accuracy or greater. There is, thus, a borderline range of 90 to 94 percent accuracy. What should a teacher do when students perform in this region? Typically, students are asked to read diagnostic passages with little or no instructional support. Therefore, when students perform in the borderline range, the teacher should study the kinds of problems that are encountered to determine whether instructional support might be developed to bring the student's oral reading accuracy into the acceptable instructional range (95 percent accuracy or greater).

Betts recommends that materials intended for independent reading should pose very few problems for students. Specifically, he recommends that there be no more than 1 problem per 100 words read. However, this standard is based on testing wherein students read a passage silently before they read it aloud. Thus, we recommend a slightly lower standard for oral reading on sight: no more than 2 errors per 100 words. Perhaps more important than the number of errors is evidence concerning the student's fluency. The material that a student reads independently should be sufficiently easy so that he or she reads with good intonation and phrasing.

Powell's research (Powell, 1970; Powell & Dunkeld, 1971) suggests more lenient oral reading standards for primary grade readers than those noted above. However, subsequent research (Ekwall, 1976; Pikulski, 1974) shows some inconsistency with Powell's findings. Given this inconsistency and our own clinical experience, we suggest standards that are generally in line with those originally suggested by Betts. We also caution the reader, however, that these standards should not be used mindlessly. In addition to counting the number of errors, it is also extremely important to consider the quality of the errors (Biemiller, 1979; Kibby, 1979; Whaley & Kibby, 1981). Some, for example, may indicate serious problems with print while others may suggest carelessness.

These criteria pertain to oral reading accuracy. Obviously, in judging the appropriateness of materials, comprehension must be considered as well. In Chapter 7, criteria for evaluating comprehension are discussed.

In determining whether a passage is of appropriate difficulty, the teacher should study the entire passage for dialect influence and for repeated errors (i.e., where a character name or word is mispronounced more than twice). It should be noted whether the student ever solves the identification of the word, especially when it is a key word. All but the first two instances of any repeated error and all dialect-influenced responses should be disregarded in further analysis.

The teacher should note the proportion of omissions, insertions, and substitutions (including mispronunciations, and responses that were later corrected) in relation to the total number of words in the passage. The total number of miscues should be divided by the total number of words to get a percentage figure. For example, if a student makes 7 miscues on a passage of 140 words, the proportion of miscues is 5 percent. If we then subtract the proportion of miscues from 100, we determine the proportion of the passage that was error free—in this case, 95 percent. The criterion scores shown in Table 4.2 should be used for judging oral reading performance. The results from this assessment of passage difficulty should be recorded on the oral reading summary form shown in Figure 4.2 in the space provided under A.

Sight Word Recognition. The teacher should separate the sight word errors from the miscues made in response to unfamiliar content words. For miscues in response to sight words, the following questions should be considered:

1. What is the proportion of sight word errors in relation to the total number of words in the passage?
2. Is the reading fluent and do these miscues distort the author's meaning?
3. Are these miscues corrected by the reader?

On the basis of this evidence, the teacher should determine whether sight word errors pose a problem and decide whether word recognition should be checked further during the follow-up probe. Sight word errors should be recorded under B, on the left side of the form. If further testing is necessary, the Evaluation section on the right side of the form should not be completed until this is accomplished.

Word Identification. In order to study the student's word identification strategies, the teacher should record unfamiliar word miscues in section C of the form in the following way. First, single-syllable words should be separated from multiple-syllable words. Errors on single-syllable words should then be sorted into two groups: (1) those that deviate from the printed word in more than one element and (2) those that deviate from the printed word in one element only. Errors on multisyllabic words should also be separated into two groups: (1) those involving structural elements (i.e., common prefixes and suffixes) and (2) those involving other elements. Classification of miscues in this fashion makes it easier to identify patterns in a student's approach to word identification and hence facilitates further probe of word identification skills.

After the word and miscues are recorded, the teacher should examine them to identify patterns. The following questions should be considered:

1. To what extent do the errors resemble the expected response graphically? Is the reader in command of the following phonics associations: consonants, consonant blends and digraphs, vowels, and vowel digraphs? Is the function of markers understood?

Figure 4.2 Oral reading response analysis form.

ORAL READING ANALYSIS

Name_____ Grade____ Date____

Book/Page_____ Level____

A. DIFFICULTY

____/____ _____% Correct

Level: Independent   Instructional
       Borderline   Frustration

B. WORD LEARNING: Sight Word Errors

Printed Word	Oral Response	Probe	Evaluation
_____	_____	_____	
_____	_____	_____	
_____	_____	_____	
_____	_____	_____	
_____	_____	_____	
_____	_____	_____	
_____	_____	_____	
_____	_____	_____	

C. WORD IDENTIFICATION: Content Word Errors

Printed Word	Oral Response	Probe	Evaluation
_____	_____	_____	
_____	_____	_____	
_____	_____	_____	
_____	_____	_____	
_____	_____	_____	
_____	_____	_____	
_____	_____	_____	
_____	_____	_____	
_____	_____	_____	
_____	_____	_____	
_____	_____	_____	
_____	_____	_____	
_____	_____	_____	

D. INTEGRATION – FLUENCY

Integration: _____

Fluency: Rate ____/____ = ____wpm Evaluation_____
         Phrasing_____

2. Are miscues corrected by the reader and, if so, on what basis?
3. What does the evidence reveal about the reader's ability to identify affixes and syllables?

On the basis of this evidence, the teacher should decide whether the student has difficulty in any area of word identification and whether skill in selected areas should be explored further in the follow-up probe. When further testing is indicated, the Evaluation section should not be completed until the probe has been undertaken.

Integration and Fluency. The teacher should determine whether the student's miscues evidence use of contextual information. For example, are more than half the errors contextually appropriate and does the student have and use contextually based correction strategies? The teacher should also describe the student's reading fluency and calculate his or her reading rate. Rate is calculated by dividing the number of seconds that the student took to read the passage by 60, to get the number of minutes involved, and then dividing the number of words in the passage by the number of minutes to get a words-per-minute rate. This information should be recorded in section D of the form.

Probe: Further Testing

Often, following the oral reading analysis, questions about the strengths and weaknesses of a student's print skills remain. Some of these questions can be answered by working with the student during a second session, using probe techniques.

Basic Probe. The probe of sight words is fairly straightforward: The student should be asked to pronounce the words miscued during oral reading after they have been rewritten in list form, and the teacher should note how accurately and rapidly the student is able to respond. If the student does not recognize a word, the teacher may then treat the word as an unknown word and use the probe procedures described for content words.

The first step of the probe of content words is to determine whether the student can pronounce the words that were miscued during contextual reading when they are presented in isolation. Correct reading of any of these words suggests that the student knows more about word identification than he or she is able to apply in context. Failure to use this knowledge during contextual reading sometimes results from a strategy that is highly dependent on contextual information to the neglect of graphic information. Other times it suggests that the student has become overwhelmed with the task of contextual reading. When a student identifies words in isolation that he or she is unable to recognize in context, the reading problem is one of application. That is, the student possesses the necessary knowledge but has not yet integrated this knowledge into his or her strategy for contextual reading.

Advanced Probe. More often, however, words that are not identified in context are also not identified in isolation. The probe of unknown content words in order to assess the student's skill in word identification then takes the form of assisting the student in his or her attempts to pronounce the tested words correctly. Basically, the procedures involve isolating parts of words in order to facilitate the student's analysis of them, varying the unit or word-part that is isolated to probe different aspects of reading skill. Using such procedures, knowledge of phonic principles, word-structure elements, blending skill, and syllabication can each be examined as necessary.

The advanced probe is quite complicated and should not be attempted until the procedures of the oral reading analysis and the basic probe are mastered. Nevertheless, the reader should study the following material to learn more about how error types should be interpreted and for a general overview of procedures that can be acquired at some later time.

The advanced probe procedures differ for (1) errors involving multiple elements in one-syllable words, (2) errors involving a single element in one-syllable words, (3) errors involving structural elements, and (4) errors involving elements in multisyllabic words.

Errors Involving Multiple Elements in One-Syllable Words. Every oral reading response corresponds to the printed word in some way. Occasionally the match is only in length but usually, at the very least, the response matches the text in both length and the initial or final consonant (e.g., "day" for *deep,* "true" for *towed*). When such errors occur frequently, it is likely that word identification skills are very limited. Even when the response has more than the initial letter in common with the text (e.g., "chase" for *catch,* "snow" for *swam,* "coat" for *crowd*), if the shared letters are not in the same sequence, then word identification must still be considered quite weak. That is, when miscues of this type predominate, it is likely that they reflect a whole-word strategy—a tendency to process words as single units—rather than a letter–sound analysis. This tendency is not unexpected with younger children (first and second grades) whose instruction has emphasized whole-word learning, and in such cases it should be regarded as a developmental stage in reading acquisition rather than a weakness. With older students, however, these errors suggest an overdependence on whole-word strategies and failure to use word identification as a supplemental or alternative technique. In either case, the teacher should explore the possibility that the student actually knows many letter–sound associations as a result of specific instruction but cannot make a letter-by-letter analysis.

The general procedure to be used in exploring the knowledge a student has about letter–sound associations is as follows. The teacher directs the student's attention to a consonant that was mispronounced, then asks the student if he or she knows what sound it stands for. If the student responds correctly to a sample of 8 to 10 consonants, then his or her knowledge of letter–sound associations represents a strength that is clearly not yet functional in reading tasks. Consonant digraphs and consonant blends can be tested in the same way.

For many students who are learning to read, knowledge of letter–sound associations develops into functional reading skill through a process of consonant substitution. When a student has command of a number of letter–sound associations, even though the letter-by-letter correspondence between his or her oral responses and the printed words may be quite limited, the teacher should explore the student's skill or readiness to profit from instruction in this technique. Selecting a mispronounced word that contains a common phonogram (e.g., *-ill, -an, -op*), the teacher covers the first consonant and asks if the student knows a word that looks like the remaining part of the word. In the event that the student responds appropriately (with a rhyming word), the initial letter is uncovered and the student is encouraged to pronounce the word. If the student is unsuccessful, the teacher may then assist by directing attention to the sound of the initial consonant. In the event that the student does not recognize the phonogram as part of a familiar word, the teacher should pronounce it for him or her, uncover the initial letter, and ask the student to try to pronounce the word.

If the student succeeds in identifying the word in either of these situations, he or she has demonstrated the capacity to blend an initial consonant with a final phonogram; and to the extent that the student recognizes phonograms, he or she is prepared to develop the technique of consonant substitution through practice. On the other hand, if the student proves unable to identify the word after he or she (or the teacher) has identified the phonogram, the teacher should model the blending technique. The teacher pronounces first the initial consonant, then the phonogram, and finally the word itself (e.g., *f–all, fall*). Then the teacher writes another word with the same phonogram (*t–all*) on a sheet of paper and encourages the student to imitate the blending process. If the student is successful, he or she can easily be prepared for the consonant substitution technique; if not, more intensive instruction in blending will be needed.

Errors Involving a Single Element in One-Syllable Words. When most errors involve only a single element in one-syllable words, greater strength in word identification is demonstrated. In such cases, the teacher should explore the student's mastery of letter–sound associations and phonics principles as distinct from his or her skill in using those associations and principles during contextual reading. A gap between the two may simply be a matter of practice and experience or may represent a more serious difficulty requiring individualized instruction.

- *Consonants and consonant digraphs.* When errors involve only a single consonant or consonant digraph (*beat—beak, shop—chop*), it is a simple matter to explore the student's knowledge of letter–sound associations. The teacher covers the word, leaving exposed only the element that is in error, then asks the student, "What sound does this letter stand for?" If the student gives the correct sound, the teacher prompts him or her to attempt the word again, saying, "What sound should this word end [or begin] with?" . . . "What is the word?" If the student succeeds in identifying the word and can repeat the success with a few other words, the teacher may conclude that the student has strength in knowledge of letter–sound associations but is weak in his or her application of that knowledge. This is particularly likely to be the case when consonants are in error in final position but not in initial position. However, there is usually no such position bias with consonant digraph errors.
- *Consonant blends.* The procedure is similar to that outlined above. The teacher covers the word except for the blend and asks, "What sounds do these letters stand for?" If the student answers correctly, the teacher prompts him or her to try the word again. If the student cannot answer correctly, the teacher exposes only the first letter of the blend, then only the second letter, and so forth, asking each time for the sound the letter stands for. If the student knows the individual sounds, the teacher asks him or her to say them together; if the student succeeds, the teacher prompts him or her to attempt the word again.
- *Vowels.* When errors involve only vowels, the teacher must explore the student's knowledge of vowel markers as well as his or her knowledge of vowel letter sounds. The examination of vowel letter sounds follows the general procedure described above. If the errors are such that the short sounds of the different vowels are confused with one another (*cat—cut, fell—fill*), then the sounds most commonly associated with each vowel may not be firmly fixed in the student's mind. The teacher probes this possibility by isolating the vowel letter (covering the letters surrounding it) and asking if the student knows a sound it stands for. If the student answers correctly, giving the vowel's short sound, the teacher then prompts him or her to make another attempt at pronouncing the word. If the student gives the long sound of the vowel—which many students do, because it coincides with the vowel name—the teacher should ask if he or she knows another sound for that letter. If the student does, he or she is encouraged to try the word again.

  On the other hand, if the errors are such that each vowel is consistently associated with its short sound even in the presence of a long vowel marker (e.g., a vowel digraph such as *ai* or *oa* or a final *-e* in the pattern of CV*Ce*), then the student may know only one sound for each vowel. The teacher probes this possibility with the same general procedure as outlined for short vowel confusions.

- *Markers.* If vowel errors are such that both the long and short sounds associated with each vowel are used at times but not used appropriately with vowel markers (final -*e,* vowel digraphs, *r*-controller), then the student may be confused about the situations in which one or the other sound is appropriate. On the other hand, the student may have knowledge of certain vowel markers but have difficulty monitoring for their presence while alternating with ease and fluency among the different sounds associated with each vowel letter. (Students often become habituated to the short sound for each vowel and have difficulty making the variable response function in reading tasks). Each type of marker should be examined separately. The general procedure is, as above, to isolate or point to the vowel and ask for the sound it represents. To test specific knowledge, the teacher than calls the student's attention to the marker and asks if he or she knows what function it performs. Finally, the teacher encourages the student to say the word and notes the fluency with which he or she alternates the sounds as the marker is changed. If the student is not familiar with the vowel marker as such, the teacher should explain it briefly, with examples, to determine the student's readiness to receive such instruction.

- *C and G markers.* When a student fails to associate the letter *c* with its alternate sound correspondent (/s/) when appropriate (i.e., when *c* is followed by the letters *e, i,* or *y*), the teacher explores, first, whether the student knows that *c* has an alternate pronunciation and, second, whether he or she understands that the presence of *e, i,* or *y* is the governing condition. The teacher points to the letter *c* and asks the student to give the sound it stands for. If the student gives the phoneme /k/, the teacher asks if he or she knows another sound for the letter *c.* If the student recalls that the letter *c* sometimes stands for the *s* sound, the teacher may demonstrate and explain the principle and then ask the student to apply it to a few appropriate words, in an effort to assess how readily he or she can learn to make this new response. Errors involving the alternative sound of the letter *g* (/j/) should be dealt with in the same way.

Errors Involving Structural Elements. A structural error involves the substitution of one affix for another or the omission of the affix while the base word is correctly identified (*brings—bringing, shipping—ship*). Only when such errors occur repeatedly should they be of concern. The teacher tries to determine whether they are caused by a lack of familiarity with particular affixes or by a failure to monitor affixes carefully while reading difficult words. The teacher covers the base word and asks the student to identify the affix. If the student recognizes the affix, the teacher suggests that he or she correct the error, although this may be done spontaneously in many cases. If the student does not recognize the affix, the teacher identifies it and asks him or her to try the word again.

Errors Involving Elements in Multisyllabic Words. Examples of such errors include "country" for *century,* "cherry" for *chimney,* "conferation" for *conversation,* "invention" for *invitation,* "coming" for *company,* and "downcade" for *decade.* The identification of multisyllabic words is greatly facilitated when they are broken down into smaller or even one-syllable units (provided, of course, that the student is skilled in identifying these smaller units). When errors involving multisyllabic words occurs, the teacher first explores whether the student is able to divide words into pronounceable units. As a second step, to determine whether the student can pronounce syllables, the teacher covers all but the first syllable of the word. If the student identifies it, the second syllable is exposed, and so on. Finally, the student is encouraged to put the syllabic parts together to form the word.

If the student is unable to divide words into pronounceable units and the teacher's aid enables the student to succeed in identifying a number of words, then it is likely that he or she will profit from instruction in syllabication techniques. If the student lacks sufficient skill to identify the first syllable, the teacher should explore his or her mastery of letter–sound associations just as was described for one-syllable words and his or her ability to analogize from a known word to identify an unknown syllable. The division of words into syllabic units is perhaps one of the most useful features in the diagnostic probe, as it often serves to teach the skill as well as to test it.

Finally, it should be emphasized that if the informal diagnostic probe is to be of value, care and good judgment must be used. The teacher should keep within the limits of the student's patience and endurance and should avoid pursuing specific skills once it is clear that they are too difficult for the student. Only a few problem areas should be probed, with the aim of identifying where instructional focus is needed. The informal probe is *not* designed to be an inventory of known and unknown blends, diagraphs, and so forth; such an inventory can be taken another time (see Appendix B). The major purpose of the informal probe will be served if the teacher becomes aware of particular skills the student needs to develop, understands the way in which the student organizes printed words, and can judge wisely where the student can profit from carefully chosen practice exercises and where he or she needs more intensive personal instruction.

Interpretation

Evidence on print-processing skill must be used together with evidence on comprehension and vocabulary knowledge in order to determine whether the student has a reading problem and, if so, in what major area(s). Oral reading response evidence alone can be interpreted to answer the following questions:

A. Does the passage represent an appropriate level of difficulty in terms of the reader's print skill?

B. Is the reader developing a sight vocabulary or are there problems in this area?

C. Has the reader evolved a successful strategy for identifying unknown words or is further development needed?

D. Has the reader evolved a strategy that is based on the integrated processing of graphic and contextual information?
[When few print processing problems exist, it is appropriate to pursue the final question.] Is the reader's rate of reading in accord with that of his or her classmates or are there problems of reading fluency that need correction?

Instructional Recommendations

Recommendations for instruction follow directly from the interpretation of the reading response evidence. They involve both an evaluation of the appropriateness of the current reading materials and the identification of any areas in need of instructional support. The focus of instruction should be specified along with appropriate methods and materials for the initial stages of instruction. We now present a case study in considerable detail in order to demonstrate the procedures for assessing oral reading.

CASE 1:   Eva—Diagnosis

Eva's teacher was concerned about her lack of interest in classwork and wanted to know how she could help Eva improve her reading. For this reason, the teacher decided to analyze Eva's oral reading. Eva was 9 years, 5 months old at the time and in the second month of fifth grade. She had changed schools four times in the previous four years and there was little in her record to help the teacher understand her achievement problems. It should be noted that although Eva is fluent in English, Spanish is sometimes spoken in her home.

PREPARATION
Eva was tested on a passage from *Discovering Treasure*, a third-grade reader in The New Open Highways series (Scott Foresman). This book was being read by the lowest reading group in the class, the group to which Eva belonged. The story selected was "The Picnic Mystery." Although Eva read the entire story, only a representative portion is analyzed here. Eva was told that the story was about a boy and his uncle who was a detective. She was asked to read the story to see if she could solve the picnic mystery. Eva's oral reading, which was both tape-recorded and recorded by the teacher on a typed double-spaced copy of the story, is shown in Figure 4.3.

Figure 4.3   Record of oral reading: Eva.

The Picnic Mystery

Lee(s) uncle was a (famous) detective. During the ride Lee asked him ~~2~~ 1 [10] *

(dozens) of questions about his work. At last the detective laughed, "You ask 1

more questions than I do during a police ~~ease~~ [care]," he said. "Let's stop and rest 1

for a while."

He drove until he came to a ~~group~~ [grape] of ~~shade~~ [several] trees in a ~~field~~ [forest]. As he parked 3

the car, he saw something ~~strange~~ [sparkling].   1

Spread under one of the trees was a white paper tablecloth. Picnic food

was set out on the cloth. But there was no one in sight.

"~~Where~~ [© When] is ~~everyone~~ [© anyone]?" asked Lee. "I don't see a place where anyone 2

could hide. Why ~~would~~ [© was] people go off and leave their picnic?"

* Dialect-based miscues were not counted.

(Passage from *Discovering Treasure*, pp. 46–50, in *The New Open Highways*, published by Scott, Foresman, 1973. Story entitled "The Abandoned Picnic," from *The Second Baffle Book* by Lassiter Wren and Randle McKay. Copyright 1929 by Doubleday & Company, Inc. Copyright 1929 by Clues, Inc. Reprinted by permission of Doubleday & Company, Inc.)

ORAL READING ANALYSIS

After recording a student's oral reading and checking the accuracy of the record, the first task is always to determine whether any errors reflect dialect. In Eva's case, one error is suspicious: She tends to drop the final *s* during conversation, and here has misprounounced *Lee's* as "Lee." This was therefore not counted as a miscue. In order for an error to be counted as one of repetition, it must occur more than twice. No such errors occurred in the segment analyzed. The numbers at the right of each line in Figure 4.3 indicate the number of miscues per line. It should be noted that miscues that are subsequently corrected are nonetheless counted as errors, the reason being that they are indications of difficulty. That they were subsequently corrected is noted by a © on the oral reading analysis sheet, and these corrections are considered a sign of strength.

Difficulty.   In all, Eva committed 10 miscues whild reading this portion of the story. The length of the selection is 115 words. If we divide 10 by 115 (and multiply by 100), we find the percentage of miscues, which is 9 percent. Accordingly, 91 percent of the passage is read correctly. When we compare this level of accuracy with the criteria levels in Table 4.2 we find that it falls below an acceptable instructional level, in the borderline range. We can now complete section A of the oral reading analysis form (the section pertaining to passage difficulty), as shown in Figure 4.4.

Word Learning.   The next step is to record the miscues in response to sight words in the first two columns of section B of the form. (The Probe and Evaluation columns are completed later.) As is shown in Figure 4.4, three of the miscues are in response to high-frequency words. (The Dolch Basic Sight Vocabulary, contained in Appendix A, may be used as an aid in identifying sight words.) All three miscues were corrected, apparently on the basis of subsequent contextual information. The fact that they were corrected is indicated by a © in the second column under B.

Although most of the sight words in the passage were read correctly, the three errors represent about 2 percent of the total passage (3/115). Because the sight word errors are few in number and because they were corrected spontaneously during contextual reading, we conclude that there is no major problem in this area. However, the fact that such errors were made at all suggests that Eva has not consolidated her sight vocabulary.

Word Identification.   The next step is to record in section C miscues in response to unfamiliar content words. We begin first with miscues that deviate from single-syllable printed words in several elements, followed by those that deviate in a single element, then with errors that reflect a problem in affixation, and finally with miscues in response to multisyllabic words. Errors of omission are then listed following the substitution errors, as shown in Figure 4.4. In contrast to sight word recognition, Eva makes no successful corrections of unfamiliar context words.

Three of the seven miscues deviate from the printed word in more than one element and involve substitution of multisyllable for single-syllable words. The next two miscues, which show a close correspondence, are also in response to single-syllable words. Finally, Eva omits rather than attempts two words that are two syllables in length. This pattern of response suggests that Eva has serious difficulty in word identification.

Although almost all Eva's miscues show an initial consonant match, she erred on two of three initial consonant blends and digraphs. Vowels in miscued words are more often mispronounced than not, and she seems to have no knowledge of vowel digraphs and markers. Affixed words were, however, an area of strength, with *laughed, during, asked,* and *parked* all correctly pronounced. Overall, the evidence suggests little skill in word identification. This possibility should be explored through a follow-up probe with the miscued words.

Integration and Fluency.   Eva is lacking in integration, in that she relies heavily on context in identifying unknown context words. With few exceptions, her substitutions in response to content words are plausible with respect to prior sentence context, but they show low correspondence with print. Although Eva

Figure 4.4   Analysis of Oral Reading Responses: Eva.

ORAL READING ANALYSIS

Name *Eva W.* Grade *5* Date *4/15/83*

Book/Page *Discovering Treasure* Level *gr. 3*

A. DIFFICULTY

10 / *115*   *91*   % Correct

Level: Independent   Instructional
(Borderline)   Frustration

B. WORD LEARNING: Sight Word Errors

Printed Word	Oral Response	Probe	Evaluation
where	when ©	✓	*Sight word errors are few in number*
everyone	anyone ©	anyone ©	*and were corrected during contextual*
would	was ©	✓	*reading. Thus, no major problem*
			exists. However, the miscues
			seemed to interfere with obtaining
			the author's meaning. Eva needs
			to consolidate her sight
			vocabulary.

C. WORD IDENTIFICATION: Content Word Errors

Printed Word	Oral Response	Probe	Evaluation
shade	several	should	*On one syllable words, she*
field	forest	fill	*uses initial consonants - but*
strange	sparkling	NR *	*word middles and endings do*
case	care	care	*not always correspond. Her*
group	grape	grape	*Knowledge of initial*
famous	[omitted]	NR	*consonants is limited. On a*
dozens	[omitted]	NR	*probe of word elements, she*
			produced a word rather than a
			sound in response to initial
			consonants. She seems to
			recognize words on the basis
			of visual cues and context.
			She does not attempt unknown
			multisyllabic words.

* NR = no response

D. INTEGRATION – FLUENCY

Integration: *Overreliance on prior context; most miscues violate author meaning. Effective use of repetitions and pauses to correct errors.*

Fluency: Rate *115* / *1.8* = *64* wpm   Evaluation *Slow - even for a second grader*

Phrasing *Rapid reading interspersed with long pauses for word recognition* shows an effective use of repetition to correct sight word errors, she is unable to correct her content word miscues.

Her reading is not fluent, as it is characterized by many pauses before unfamiliar words. She read this portion of the story in 108 seconds. By dividing the number of seconds by 60, we get a time of 1.8 minutes, as shown in Figure 4.4. By then dividing the number of words in the passage—namely, 115—by 1.8, we determine Eva's reading rate—64 words per minute.

This rate is extremely slow; it is even below the average range for second graders shown in Table 4.1. We would expect, however, that Eva's rate would be faster on easier materials that posed fewer word identification problems for her. Because word identification difficulties are seriously interfering with her reading fluency, we will not make further exploration of this aspect of her reading at this time. Rather, the probe will focus on the development of her sight vocabulary and her word identification skills.

PROBE AND INTERPRETATION

Sight Words.   Eva's response to the three sight words that she missed during contextual reading was rapid. Further, all but one of the sight words was pronounced correctly (indicated by a check in the third column of B), and when she was asked to look at *everyone* again, she was able to recognize it.

The results from the probe suggest that Eva knows most basic sight words, even if she at times confuses certain similar sight words. These results support the hypothesis that Eva's main problem in word learning is not in knowing the words but, rather, in being able to recognize them quickly when under the pressure of difficult contextual reading. Eva needs to consolidate her existing set of sight words through contextual reading of easy materials as summarized under "Evaluation" in B.

Word Identification.   Most of the probe focused on Eva's ability to deal with unfamiliar context words. As is shown in Figure 4.4, when words that were miscued during contextual reading were presented in isolation, Eva was still unable to recognize them.

During the probe that followed, she was first asked to respond to initial consonants, in order to confirm their apparent effectiveness as a cue system. Surprisingly, she experienced extreme difficulty producing the sounds that corresponded to the initial consonant letters identified. This finding suggests that she uses initial consonants as effective visual cues to search for known words in her memory but not as elements that cue an appropriate initial sound.

Because of her extreme difficulty with initial consonants, no further probe was undertaken at this time to assess her knowledge of other letter–sound associations. That will come later, once initial consonants become an explicit part of her knowledge about print. Further probing did reveal that with support, Eva is able to segment off the initial phoneme of a known word. This is probably the point from which instruction should begin.

Assessment of Eva's knowledge of the structural characteristics of words revealed that she is familiar with most common word endings (e.g., *-ing, -ed, -er, -est*). She has no knowledge about how to segment multisyllabic words into pronounceable units. However, when some of the words were divided for her, she was able to pronounce a few syllables correctly because they resembled known words. This facility suggests that Eva may be able to use her relatively well-developed sight vocabulary to help her identify syllables through an analogizing procedure.

Summary

The oral reading analysis and probe provide detailed evidence about Eva's knowledge of print and her oral reading strategies. However, unless the understanding gained from diagnosis leads to instructional intervention, it is of little use.

INSTRUCTION TO SUPPORT INTEGRATION AND FLUENCY

In the final section of this chapter we will consider instructional issues. First we will consider the instruction that would be appropriate for Eva and then we will consider, in a more general way, instructional approaches that are appropriate for the development of reading integration and fluency.

CASE 2: Eva—Instruction

The instruction developed by a teacher must follow from the understanding developed through ongoing diagnosis. In Eva's case, her teacher must determine whether she can profit from the instruction appropriate for her low group members and/or whether she should receive individualized instruction. Because Eva lacks knowledge in the area of word identification, instruction must be designed to develop her underlying knowledge of word elements. The initial plan of the teacher (to be modified with new evidence) was as follows:

Reading Materials.   Eva should be reading from materials at two levels of difficulty. First, in order for her to consolidate her sight vocabulary, material should be at a level that poses few word identification problems. Whether second-grade-level materials would be appropriate for this purpose needs to be established. Second, Eva's teacher should experiment with instructional support prior to and during the reading of basal stories in order to determine whether the current (third-grade) materials can be used. It is important to keep Eva involved in ongoing class activities if at all possible. However, if the third-grade basal materials are still too difficult with instructional support, the teacher will need to establish an individual reading program for Eva with somewhat easier materials.

Sight Vocabulary.   Eva's sight vocabulary is quite well developed, as indicated by the large number of sight words she recognized during contextual reading and the fact that she was able to recognize all miscued sight words correctly when they were presented in isolation. However, the fact that she miscues on sight words during contextual reading means that they are not yet learned to the level of immediate and automatic recognition. In order to consolidate her sight vocabulary, Eva should be encouraged to read easy, highly interesting materials. Charts should be kept to let Eva see her reading progress.

Word Identification.   Eva's teacher will focus on three objectives in the area of word identification: (1) making explicit Eva's knowledge of initial consonant associations, (2) developing procedures for helping Eva divide multisyllabic words into pronounceable chunks, and (3) developing strategies for pronouncing syllables. The teacher will work with Eva individually to achieve the first goal, since all other members of Eva's reading group already possess this knowledge. The other two ojectives will be worked on as part of small-group reading instruction in conjunction with the introduction of unfamiliar words.

As a first step in helping Eva acquire explicit knowledge of consonant correspondences, her teacher will pronounce words and have her listen to them and identify their component sounds. Once Eva is aware of the phonemic composition of words, the teacher will present known sight words, all beginning with the same consonant, in order to have Eva identify the initial consonant correspondent. If Eva has difficulty remembering the consonant association, it might be helpful to have her select a key word as a means to retrieve the phoneme. For example, if she has difficulty remembering the phoneme corresponding to *d,* she might use the key word of *dance.* Whenever she sees a *d,* she can think of *dance* and abstract the initial sound. Typically, this sort of memory aid is not needed for many consonants and, where needed, is not needed for long.

Teaching syllabication and syllable pronunciation can easily be incorporated into small-group reading instruction. After introducing a new story but before reading it, the teacher should present any unfamiliar content words. Using certain of these words, the teacher can conduct the following two-part exercise. The words are written on the board, one at a time. After a word is written, students should speculate about how it might be divided into "chunks" that can be pronounced. A line should be drawn after each chunk and the teacher should proceed to the right until the word has been completely divided. Even when the final product does not conform exactly to what is specified by rules for syllabication, the teacher should proceed to the task of pronouncing the syllables. If students wish to revise their prior decisions, they should be allowed to do so.

The second part of this exercise consists of teaching analogizing. After examining the first chunk, the students are asked if it looks like any word they know. This word should then be written above the syllable to see if students can use it to identify the syllable. If they are unable to think of a word, the teacher should supply one or provide the phonogram with which the syllable ends as an alternative. The students should then use a consonant substitution (word family) approach to identify the syllable. Correct and incorrect attempts should be presented to the group for their evaluation.

This procedure can be used for three or four of the multisyllabic words appearing in the story or as long as the attention of the group is sustained. Other unfamiliar words should simply be pronounced by the teacher, as part of a discussion of the meaning of all unfamiliar words and how they pertain to the theme of the story.

Integration. Eva's overreliance on contextual information indicates that integration is a problem for her. Her difficulty stems from the lack of a proper balance between the use of contextual information and attention to graphic information. Therefore, integration should be reexamined as she develops greater proficiency with word identification.

Fluency. As part of her program, it is important for Eva to experience "problem-free" reading, that is, reading selections that pose few word identification problems for her. Not only will this easy reading help to consolidate her sight vocabulary, it will give her the opportunity to focus on meaning free from word identification distractions. It is on material at this level that the teacher may wish to incorporate some of the instructional approaches designed to promote integration and fluency which are described in the following section.

Instruction to Promote Integration

Students frequently encounter words that they do not know. Those who have not developed balanced strategies for words identification need to be shown how using information from a variety of sources leads to more efficient and effective word identification.

Cloze Tasks. If few oral reading miscues are contextually appropriate, further exploration must be made, through tasks such as the cloze test, to determine whether the student is able to use context to anticipate words (see, e.g., Blachowicz, 1977; Bortnick & Lopardo, 1973). In a modified cloze approach, words that students were unable to pronounce during contextual oral reading are identified and students are instructed to read the sentences in which they occurred, saying "blank" for the unknown words. After they have read the sentence with the "blank," they are encouraged to think of words that might make sense in the blank. If they are able to produce words that are semantically acceptable within the sentence, we conclude that they are able to make use of context for word identification. It should be noted, however, that some sentence contexts provide little relevant information to aid word identification; such sentences should not be used for this activity.

Application. If students are able to complete a cloze blank correctly but show little use of contextual information during oral reading, we can conclude that the problem is one of application. The students know how to use contextual information but have developed a reading strategy that usually does not draw on context as a source of information for anticipating responses and for correction. This type of strategy development is not unusual for some students who have been instructed with a synthetic phonics approach. Students who are able to complete cloze blanks, once alerted to context as a source of information and encouraged to use it, usually learn to use contextual information during passage reading quite easily.

Additional Cloze Instruction. Relatively few students have difficulty using context to fill in a blank once the procedure has been demonstrated as a class guessing game. These few require more systematic practice completing sentences in which a single word has been omitted. To begin with, nouns should be deleted from the final part of a sentence whose initial part contains an explicit clue—for example, *He hit a home run with his new* _____ . In such activities, any response that makes sense in context should be accepted as correct. Subsequently, deletions other than nouns from sentences with explicit clues should be practiced.

Finally, during activities where students read aloud, it is appropriate for the teacher to ask students who pronounce difficult words correctly how they identified the word. It is also appropriate after cloze procedures have been introduced to ask students whether a response "makes sense." Once students have received instruction focusing on the division of words into syllables and syllable identification, it is useful to ask them to identify the first syllable of an unknown word and then attempt to identify the word on the basis of context and the first syllable.

Instruction to Develop Fluency

Reading Practice. Contextual reading practice is the most effective means for developing fluency. Many disabled readers fail to achieve fluency because they are continually asked to read materials that are too difficult. They have little opportunity to experience the pleasure of problem-free reading and to develop reading fluency (Allington, 1983). Thus, for practice to improve fluency, the material read *must* be easy for the reader. That is, it should pose almost no word identification problems and no comprehension problems.

Having students reread selections can be used as a means for eliminating many problems posed by a selection. After a first reading, the student is familiar with the context and can recognize most difficult words. Thus, he or she is more able to focus directly on meaning and to read at a faster rate. The method of repeated readings can also be used more formally (Chomsky, 1976; Lopardo & Sadow, 1982; Nelson & Morris, 1988; Samuels, 1979). First the teacher identifies a segment to be read orally and has the student read it aloud, noting the errors and the reading speed. The student then rereads the same selection and the number of errors and reading speed for the second reading are compared with those of the first. The procedure can be continued one or two more times.

Typically, reluctant readers need tangible forms of reinforcement to encourage them to practice reading. Charts showing the number of pages read per day or week within a certain period of time (e.g., 15 to 30 minutes) provide a tangible record for students to see the amount of reading accomplished and any increase in the number of pages read within the time period (reading rate). Similarly, records of repeated reading can be used to show improvement in reading accuracy and speed over a period of weeks. Sometimes it is useful for students to receive tangible rewards (e.g., toys, books, food) for completion of books, or to receive support and encouragement from peers through paired repeated reading (Koskinen & Blum, 1986).

Modeling Fluent Reading. It is sometimes useful for a teacher or an older student who is a proficient reader to read to a student in order to demonstrate the nature of fluent reading. One method effective for disfluent readers is to model phrase reading (Walker, 1988). First the teacher tapes the student reading a short selection that is of appropriate difficulty (instructional level). Then the teacher reads a sentence with brief pauses between phrases of the sentence. The student reads the same sentence with similar phrasing. Once the student demonstrates adequate phrasing, the teacher reads more than one sentence, followed by the student's doing so. Finally, the student reads the remainder of the selection independently or with the teacher. The teacher then tapes the student reading the entire selection and compares the phrasing and general fluency on the final reading with that of the first reading.

An alternative method consists of having a student read with a fluent reader (or a tape recording) or slightly after the proficient reader. The model reads slightly ahead and somewhat louder than the student, finger-pointing to the line of print as it is read. Once the student reads fluently, the teacher or student model can relinquish control to the student by reading more softly and somewhat behind the student. In general, the purpose of providing a model of fluent reading is to show clearly the nature of fluent reading and to get the student to compare his or her earlier reading with reading that is fluent.

Reading Rate Improvement. Teachers are well aware of differences in reading speeds among their students. Although there has been little emphasis placed on increasing the reading rates of students, it is not inappropriate to encourage them to improve their rates once they have developed a sight vocabulary, word identification strategies, and reading fluency. In order to read material at a faster rate, they must often change old habits of word-by-word reading and focus instead on silent reading of phrases.

Two types of reading selections should be used: easy, independent-level materials that the student is interested in reading (a novel, biography, science fiction, etc.) and expository selections followed by comprehension questions (it is also useful if a word count is included). The student first reads the easy materials for a specified time period (approximately 15 minutes) and counts the number of pages read or, alternatively, reads a specified number of pages and records the time taken. He or she then reads the expository selection and responds to the comprehension question. Finally, the student determines his or her reading speed on the easy material (the average number of words per page times the number of pages read divided by the number of minutes), the reading speed on the expository selection, and the percentage of comprehension questions correctly answered.

This information is recorded on a chart and compared with that from the prior reading session. The student should be encouraged to increase reading speed on the easy material while maintaining adequate comprehension on the expository material. As reading rate on the easy material increases, a corresponding speed increase on the study-type materials is typically observed. If no check is made of the comprehension of study-type materials, the student may develop skimming procedures that sacrifice comprehension.

To end this chapter, we present another case. As you read the case, actively interpret the evidence to see if you draw conclusions similar to those presented. Attempt to determine whether Stan has any problems in the development of print skill and, if so, the nature of the problems he is experiencing.

CASE 3: Stan

Stan is an eighth-grade student who lives in an affluent suburb. He achieves well below average in his school, and usually students in his academic situation suffer greatly in this achievement-oriented community. At various times during his schooling he has received remedial help in reading. Unfortunately, there has been little evidence of application of newly learned strategies. Stan's reading teacher has decided to examine his reading in order to see whether he is applying the skills that they have been working on and to determine whether a new set of materials is appropriate for Stan's subsequent reading instruction.

PREPARATION
Stan read a selection entitled "Two American Girls in a Turkish Jail," from *Topics for the Restless* (Jamestown Publishers). According to the Raygor Readability Measure, this selection is of ninth-grade-level difficulty. A portion of the record of Stan's oral reading is shown in Figure 4.5. His oral reading was frequently unsteady and his voice often lacked expression. The reader should examine the record in order to draw tentative conclusions about the difficulty level of the passage and the development of Stan's sight vocabulary, word identification strategies, and fluency.

Figure 4.5 Record of oral reading: Stan.

Two American Girls in a Turkish Jail

12

At first the girls were ~~confident~~, even ~~cavalier~~, pressing close to the   2
(confinedent ②) (confined ①) (cal–) (©)

barred window of their cell to smile for a guard who wanted to take their   1
(© s)

picture. Then came the shock of the verdict: the young tourists from Amer-

ica, Kathy Zenz and JoAnn ~~McDaniel~~, were found guilty last December of   1
(McDayel)

smuggling ~~hashish~~ into Turkey. Their penalty: death, later commuted to life   1
(hashes)

imprisonment.

Kathy and JoAnn are among the 1,000 or more Americans—largely

~~youthful~~ white and middle class/— currently being held ~~in~~ jails overseas on   2
(young ful) (the)

various drug charges. There are fifteen others in Turkey alone. Most are

serving relatively short terms of five or ten years, but Kathy and JoAnn ~~had~~   2
(© have ② / are ①)

the misfortune to be arrested shortly after the United States had brought

pressure to bear on the Turkish government to crack down on ~~that~~ country's   1
(the)

~~opium~~ trade, one of its principal cash crops. The Turkish courts were in no   1
(opinyum)

mood to be ~~lenient~~ toward Americans.   1
(© lenent)

(Passage from *Topics for the Restless* (Brown) series), by Edward Spargo (Ed.) pp. 73–75. Providence, R. I.: Jamestown Publishers, 1974. [Originally published in *People* Magazine, 1974, Time Inc.])

ORAL READING ANALYSIS, PROBE, AND INTERPRETATION

Before proceeding, the reader should compare his or her analysis with the summary of the results from the analysis shown in Figure 4.6. As can be seen, Stan had difficulty with only two types of words: a small number of sight words and multisyllabic words.

Difficulty. While oral reading affords the opportunity to observe how well Stan translates print, his nervousness may have increased the number of errors that he made. Thus, while the analysis may accurately reflect the strengths of his print processing, it may underestimate his general proficiency. However, on the basis of this oral reading sample, this selection seems to be of borderline difficulty. Clearly, the material is too difficult for him to read without initial preparation.

Figure 4.6 Analysis of oral reading responses: Stan.

ORAL READING ANALYSIS

Name _Stan G_ Grade _8_ Date _2/15/83_
Book/Page _Topics for the_ Level _9 (?)_
Restless, p. 73

A. DIFFICULTY

_12_/_157_ _92_ % Correct

Level: Independent Instructional
(Borderline) Frustration

B. WORD LEARNING: Sight Word Errors

Printed Word	Oral Response	Probe	Evaluation
in	the		Although an occasional sight
had	are/have Ⓒ	Not tested	word miscue is not contextually
that	the		appropriate, sight word errors
			are few in number and tend
			not to interfere with meaning.
			Thus, sight words do not
			pose a problem.

C. WORD IDENTIFICATION: Content Word Errors

Printed Word	Oral Response	Probe	Evaluation
window	windows Ⓒ	✓	Stan has
youthful	youngful	✓	well-developed word
relatively	relative	✓	identification strategies
confident	confined / confinedent	Con-fi'-dent	particularly with isolated
cavalier	cal - Ⓒ	✓	words. May need
McDaniel	McDayel	McDayneel	practice applying this
hashish	hashes	✓	knowledge during
opium	opinyum	opinyum	contextual reading.
lenient	lenent Ⓒ	✓	

D. INTEGRATION – FLUENCY

Integration: _Many nonsense word miscues; most other miscues are_
contextually appropriate. Many repetitions - to make corrections and to
get meaning.
Fluency: Rate _157_ / _1.92_ = _82_ wpm Evaluation _Slow - caused by pauses for_
word indent
Phrasing _Not fluent - poor intonation and phrasing_

Sight Words. Stan missed three sight words or slightly less than 2 percent of the words in the portion of the selection analyzed. Two of the three did not distort the author's meaning and the third was corrected. On the basis of this evidence it is concluded that sight word learning and recognition of sight words in context do not pose problems for Stan. Accordingly, no further probe of this area is necessary.

Word Identification. As was noted earlier, Stan had no difficulty with one-syllable words. Three of nine miscues of multisyllabic words involved affixed words. In one ("windows" for *window)* an affix was added and then corrected; in a second ("relative" for *relatively)* the ending was omitted; and in the third, ("youngful" for *youthful)* the root word was miscued. It is surprising that the second and third were not corrected, on the basis of contextual information *(relatively)* or vocabulary knowledge *(youthful).*

The remaining six miscues of multisyllabic words represent minor deviations from the printed words, and two of these were corrected *(cavalier, lenient).* The degree of correspondence suggests well-developed word identification skills. Nevertheless, in order to confirm this assumption, Stan was asked to identify the nine words in isolation. He correctly identified six of them and, in the process, demonstrated a highly refined application of his print-processing strategies. Two of the words he failed to identify—*McDaniel* and *opium*—were words that were unfamiliar to him. The fact that *opium* is not a familiar term suggests that vocabulary knowledge may be a more general problem and one that interferes with his word identification. While he derives a close phonemic approximation, because many words are only vaguely familiar to him he may have difficulty making a match— particularly under the pressure of contextual reading.

The analysis of Stan's word identification skill reveals well-developed knowledge of phonics and structural analysis. However, he is less proficient in the application of this knowledge. This difficulty may simply reflect lack of practice; more likely, it also reflects inadequate vocabulary knowledge. Such a deficit could pose a problem not only in the identification of specific words, but also in the general comprehension of a selection (see Chapters 5, 6, and 7).

Integration and Fluency. The analysis indicates that many of Stan's miscues are not contextually appropriate (many are nonwords) and that in spite of this, he only rarely corrects miscues. He reads extremely slowly, with many short pauses and repetitions. While the function of these may be for word identification, they also seem to reflect an attempt to clarify the meaning of phrases. Evidence on comprehension and vocabulary knowledge is particularly crucial for determining the basis for Stan's lack of fluency. If comprehension is adequate, then the fluency problem would appear to result from lack of reading practice. On the other hand, if comprehension is inadequate because of limited vocabulary knowledge, then further assessment of Stan's reading integration and fluency should be undertaken with easier materials.

Further testing using procedures described in the next three chapters did reveal that Stan's knowledge of vocabulary contained in the selection was inadequate, as was his comprehension. Nevertheless, even on materials (eighth-grade level) that posed no vocabulary difficulties, Stan's oral reading showed many of the same pause and repetition characteristics and his rate of silent reading, though somewhat faster, was normal for fourth- or fifth-grade readers. Thus, we may conclude that Stan's reading fluency needs to be improved through extensive practice with easier material.

INSTRUCTIONAL PLAN

Stan's immediate instruction should focus on two objectives: (1) the development of reading integration and fluency, and (2) the development of vocabulary knowledge to facilitate comprehension.

Difficulty. Stan's reading materials should be on two levels of difficulty: extremely interesting materials on the sixth- or seventh-grade level and materials on the eighth- or ninth-grade level (such as that used for the initial testing) for the development of word knowledge.

Fluency. It is particularly important to find materials that match with Stan's interests and that are easy enough so as not to pose any print-processing problems. Stan should be encouraged to keep his attention on the meaning of the story or article and increase his reading rate. Techniques for directing students' attention to the meaning are described in Chapter 7. The teacher should use procedures described earlier to develop fluency.

Vocabulary Knowledge. Procedures for the development of vocabulary knowledge are described in the next chapter.

SUMMARY

Since this chapter contains a great deal of information, it should be referred to and read closely until the procedures become well learned. In order to master these procedures, it will be necessary to reread sections while diagnosing the reading problems of individual students. The case presentation of Stan clearly shows the difficulty involved in trying to assess print skill without at the same time examining vocabulary knowledge and comprehension. In the next chapters, we will consider these important topics.

CHAPTER 5

Vocabulary Knowledge: Development, Diagnosis, and Instruction

The structure of this chapter will closely parallel that of those preceding it. In the context of our overall concern with the growth of vocabulary knowledge, the first section will introduce some of the essential issues that undergird an investigation of the question, "How do vocabularies grow?" In doing so, it will introduce relevant vocabulary and will consider some of the distinctions between the terms *words, meanings,* and *concepts.* It will also examine two other important issues: that words can mean more than one thing and that words have extended and figurative meanings. The first section ends with a brief discussion of how words are learned and surveys some of the relevant research as to how this learning takes place in schools.

The second section focuses on analyzing word knowledge problems and presents a six part diagnostic procedure with two exemplar cases in which such diagnosis is relevant. The last section focuses on instructional techniques consistent with some of the theoretical underpinnings provided earlier in the chapter.

What unifies these three parts of the chapter is the assumption that words are the basic units of meaning in language. It seems evident, therefore, that understanding a message that is made up of words should require some degree of familiarity with those words. And, in fact, when we examine the relationship between vocabulary knowledge and reading comprehension, we typically find a very high correlation (Davis, 1968; Thorndike, 1973). Yet recent attempts to demonstrate a simple causal relation between knowledge of specific words and the comprehension of texts containing those words have not been uniformly successful. Markedly increasing the number of difficult words in a text leads to poorer comprehension, just as decreasing the number of difficult words leads to better comprehension (Wittrock, Marks, & Doctorow, 1975), but teaching students the difficult words before reading does not necessarily result in comprehension gains (Jenkins, Pany, & Schreck, 1978; Tuinman & Brady, 1974). One explanation of this latter result is that knowing words well enough to select appropriate synonyms on a multiple-choice vocabulary test is not necessarily sufficient for the comprehension of discourse. The reader must also be somewhat familiar with the cultural context or domain of knowledge in which the words occur. For example, a high school student may know that a geologist studies the history of the earth through its rock formations, but this student will have difficulty comprehending the function of a geologist on a deep-sea expedition unless he or she is also aware of recent technological advances that make it possible to study the earth beneath the ocean floor. Thus it is important to recognize a distinction between word knowledge as traditionally conceived (and measured) and the cultural or general knowledge that may be necessary for understanding a given text. This distinction is somewhat analogous to the difference between a dictionary and an encyclopedia, between a definition and a full-fledged concept. Nevertheless, it is through words that readers gain access to their relevant stores of knowledge—their mental encyclopedias as well as their mental dictionaries—and through them that we assess that knowledge in diagnosing comprehension difficulties.

When a student fails to show good comprehension of a diagnostic passage and print skill is not the primary source of difficulty, the problem can often be traced to lack of familiarity with a particular word or words. In this chapter we will discuss and illustrate some procedures for investigating this possibility. First we will offer some general insights into the nature of words and meanings and provide an overview of the "state of the art" teaching word meanings.

DEVELOPMENT: WORDS, MEANINGS, AND CONCEPTS

The words of a language comprise its *lexicon.* Different languages have different lexicons in the sense that they use different sequences of *sounds* (phonemes) to express the same *meanings.* But languages also differ in the meanings or concepts, the aspects of experience, and have words which reflect the different concerns and interests of the communities that speak them. For this reason, the lexicon of a language is never static. Words are constantly being added to express new thoughts and conditions; and some words fall into disuse while others undergo changes in primary meaning or intent. In a very real sense, the lexicon is an inventory of the concepts available to a language community, a map of the categories into which reality has been segmented and organized. For, though words are the names we give to objects and actions, events and experiences, and so on, this naming activity involves, in the first place, the construction of concepts that determine the way in which the environment is subdivided into parts and the parts grouped into categories. For example, in English we divide the color spectrum in such a way that the colors blue and green are placed into separate categories designated by the words *blue* and *green*. Some languages, however, do not have different words for the colors blue and green but use a single word to designate this portion of the color spectrum. To take another example, some languages have words for individual kinds of trees but lack a general term for the entire class analogous to the English term *tree* (Langacker, 1973). These differences are not just linguistic curiosities. They reflect differences in the categorization of experience and illustrate the important principle that the categories of objects, actions, and properties labeled by words are not "given" by the nature of things but rather reflect our desire to organize our experiences.

Words and Meanings

What does it mean to know a word in the lexicon? It means, first of all, knowing how the word sounds when it is spoken and, in the case of literate speakers, how it looks in printed or written form. Proficient readers occasionally have the latter knowledge but not the former. We have all had the experience of discovering, upon hearing a word for the first time after years of encountering it in print, that it is pronounced quite differently from what we had thought. This is most evident when we first encounter "loan words," which come into English from another language. If someone pronounces *détente* to rhyme with *repent-y,* it is a fair inference that the word was learned from print, not from hearing the word used in everyday speech. Both the spoken and printed forms of a word can provide direct access to the listener's/reader's stored knowledge of its meaning; that is, either can provide a virtually instantaneous pairing of word with meaning.

Second, knowing a word means knowing the aspect of reality to which it refers—which entities in the universe of entities it serves as a verbal label for. In the case of a noun, this means knowing the objects or ideas, persons, and places to which it refers. In the case of a verb, it means knowing the actions it denotes. And, in the case of adjectives and adverbs, it means knowing the qualities of objects and actions which these words designate. When we tell students that a *snare* is a trap or that a *squabble* is a quarrel, we are identifying the real-world referents of these words, the known objects or ideas they name (on the assumption that traps and quarrels are familiar as real-world entities).

Yet, it should be clear that words are not simply verbal labels for particular experiences or individual segments of reality. They are, rather, labels for *categories* of things. The child who believes that the word *dog* refers only to the family pet does not know the meaning of the word, for that entails understanding that the word applies to all other animals of a similar kind.

To be sure, we use words to refer to specific things—the *car* we drive, the *meal* we ate, the *anger* we feel. That is their central function, enabling us to talk of things in their absence, of events in the past or future, of thoughts and feelings that cannot be seen. But the meaning of a word is not so much embodied in its referents as in the attributes of its referents that are criterial in distinguishing them from the referents of other words. That is, it consists of the properties that determine whether something is or is not an instance of a category. The meaning of the word *story,* for example, does not begin and end with any particular story, or type of story, or even all the stories in the world. It consists, rather, of what a thing must be like in order to be considered a story, as distinguished, for example, from a poem or essay.

There is a sense, then, in which words are verbal labels for specific entities. This is their referential, or *extensive,* meaning. And there is a sense in which words stand for the defining attributes of classes of things. This is their *intensive* meaning (Anglin, 1977). But, of course, the one implies the other. When we use a word to refer to a specific thing (its extensive meaning), we identify that thing as a member of a category and so attribute to it the properties common to all members of that category (its intensive meaning). When we refer to an object as a *chair,* we mean that it is like all other chairs in certain essential respects. When we refer to that same object as an *armchair,* we give it some additional characteristics not shared by all chairs. And when we refer to it as *furniture,* we exclude those qualities that distinguish it from tables, beds, and so forth. We could even refer to it as *junk*, giving it an entirely different set of attributes.

Because words have both intensive and extensive meanings, the act of using them to name things is more than a matter of convenience in talking about things. It provides a shorthand for communicating information. This was illustrated above in the possibility of referring to a chair as *junk*. Similarly, in telling a child that a certain strange-looking animal is a *dog,* we make available much information that is not immediately apparent—for example, that it barks, chases cats, and chews on bones. By the same token, if someone tells us that an object we are unfamiliar with is a *fruit*, we immediately know that it is edible and grows on plants (Anglin, 1977).

The notion of words as designating categories of referents is relatively clear-cut in the case of common nouns. We are accustomed to organizing "persons, places, and things" into hierarchical systems according to their shared properties (e.g., animal → human → adult—child). But a moment's reflection makes it evident that verbs are also category labels. The verb *build,* for example, may refer to a baby in relation to blocks, a bricklayer in relation to a wall, an entrepreneur in relation to customer goodwill, and so on. It is a generic term for actions that are different in many ways but alike in terms of the meaning of *build*, to construct something from elementary parts. To illustrate with a less obvious example, even the simple act of walking differs from time to time for each individual and from one individual to another, so that the verb *walk* actually designates a range of locomotive behavior.

Adjectives also refer to categories. The *red* of one apple is different from that of others; oranges and apples are two different forms of *round;* and a *happy* coincidence and a *happy* child are different varieties of *happy.* In the process of segmenting reality into manipulable parts and naming them, we necessarily ignore much detail. Otherwise, the number of words needed to map reality would become unmanageable. More important, words could cease to serve an important function of naming, which is to establish the equivalence among items in a class (Bolinger, 1968).

What we have described thus far as the meaning of a word may be seen as closely akin to what dictionaries attempt to record. The typical dictionary definition gives the essential properties of a category of objects, actions, or qualities, which may be used to identify word referents, or instances of that category. And it does this in a most economical way, by naming the extensive, or superordinate, category to which the word referents belong and then setting forth the special characteristics that distinguish them within this more extensive category. This system eliminates the need for specifying for each word the properties of the extensive category to which it belongs.

That word meanings and (dictionary-type) definitions are more or less coterminous, at least in common parlance, is nowhere more evident than in the responses people make to questions about meaning. When adults are asked "What does ——— mean?" or "What is (a) ———?" they most commonly use the dictionary format—that is, they name the superordinate and the differentiating features, or give a word with similar meaning (a synonym). Students aged 9 or 10 also use this definitional form more often than any other (and this tendency increases with age). Younger children, on the other hand, are most likely to define words in terms of function or salient physical characteristics. Thus, an adult will say that *straw* is "dried grass," *gown* is a "long dress," and *orange* is "a fruit," whereas a young child will say of *straw,* "It's yellow"; of a *gown,* "You wear it, what you sleep in"; and of an *orange,* "You eat it." Similarly, a young child will say that *puddle* is "what you step in," while an older child will say that it is a "small pool of water" or "water that gathers after a rain." An explanation type of response (e.g., *skill* is "being able to do something"; *priceless* means "worth a lot of money") is infrequent among younger children but occurs at age 11 or 12 as the second most frequent response though still considerably less frequent than the superordinate or synonym response (Feifel & Lorge, 1950).

It has long been believed that these age-related differences in definitional form reflect the developmental changes in conceptual processes. Accordingly, "functional" definitions, which seem to be more personal and less generalized then explanations, superordinates, and synonyms, are considered less mature. However, Anglin (1977) points out that adults and older children often include use, or function, in their definitions, "the difference being that children mention only use whereas adults mention a superordinate category as well [p. 21]." Nelson (1974) has also argued that function is an important aspect of word meaning for adults as well as children. Moreover, all types of definitions are found at all ages, and the shift from predominantly functional to categorical meanings is a gradual one (Wolman & Barker, 1965). If the form in which children defined words were primarily a manifestation of their "stage" of cognitive development, each stage being qualitatively different from the preceding one, we would expect the transition from one form to another to be more sudden. It may be that children's definitions gradually become more like those of adults mainly as a reflection of their gradually increasing knowledge about the nature and origin of things. In other words, as children gain in knowledge of where things come from and how they are made, their definitions are likely to include such information. After all, one must know that straw *is* dried grass in order to define it that way.

An alternative explanation for the fact that children do not typically give superordinate terms when asked to define a word is that many superordinate terms are not frequently used and are therefore not known to them (Cocks, 1974). Thus, when asked to defined such words as *robin, apple,* and *dog,* a large majority of children are likely to give "mature" definitions (e.g., "A robin is a bird"), because the superordinate terms for these objects are well-known. In contrast, when defining words with low-frequency superordinate terms (e.g., *pencil, umbrella, cup*), children are likely to use "semantically empty" superordinates, such as *something* (e.g., "A pencil is something to write with"). Cocks argues that definitions that take this latter form reflect a high level of understanding of the requirements of the definitional task.

Meanings and Concepts

We tend to think of concepts as precisely formulated ideas concerning the essential attributes of classes of things. This tendency stems in part from the close association between concepts and scientific thought and also from a long tradition in psychological research. In this tradition, concepts are generally considered to involve a limited set of stable features (e.g., red geometric figures that have four sides and are surrounded by dots). However, it is mainly scientific concepts that are so well defined. Most "natural" concepts—the ones we use in everyday thought and action—do not have clear-cut boundaries. Is a wooden shoe "clothing?" Is coffee "food"?

A further complication is that the various members of a category are not necessarily considered equivalent: some members seem to be much more central or dominant than others. For instance, people are much more likely to name a sparrow or a robin as an example of a bird than they are to name a penguin or a duck. Similarly, it is easier to verify statements of category membership for central instances or "good examples" of a cateory than for peripheral instances. That is, it takes less time to verify that a doll or a ball is a toy then to verify that a swing or a skate is one. These phenomena are not merely artifacts of word frequency or familiarity—*doll* and *swing* occur with equal frequency in the language. They appear, rather, to reflect a general awareness of differences in the extent to which individual members of a category exemplify that category. Thus, when college students in an experiment were asked to rank the degree to which various objects were "good examples" of a category, they not only found the task meaningful (i.e., they could respond to it without confusion or wonder) but tended to agree with one another as to the "best" and "worst" examples of the various categories used. For instance, almost 100 percent of the 117 subjects gave chemistry, football, and carrot the highest rating as examples of a science, a sport, and a vegetable, respectively, while history, weight lifting, and pickle, respectively, were given low ratings in these same three categories by a majority of subjects (Rosch, 1973).

It appears that the pattern in which children develop knowledge of categories is also from central to peripheral. When 9–11-year-old children were asked to verify category membership by answering "yes" or "no" to statements like "A chicken is a bird," they made no errors on the items that were rated as "central" by adults, whereas 25 percent of their responses were incorrect on the items rated peripheral (Rosch, 1973). In a somewhat similar study (Anglin, 1977), it was found that even very young children—preschoolers—tended to include the "good examples" as members of a category and exclude the less exemplary ones. What is particularly interesting about Anglin's results is that the good examples did not have to be familiar to the children in order to be classified correctly: pictures of a wombat, an aardvark, and an anteater were identified as animals just as frequently as pictures of a cow, a horse, and a cat. Anglin interprets this as evidence of the "inferential or generative nature of the child's concepts, for they will consistently include in concepts various kinds of instances which they have never seen before, provided they are central instances [p. 156]." On the other hand, familiar items were sometimes misclassified (though not by the majority of children) if they were peripheral. For example, an ant, a butterfly, and a starfish were not considered animals by a few children. This tendency seemed to be related to the fact that the children had another name for familiar objects such as these—they would say, "That's a tree, not a plant"; "That's a butterfly, not an animal."

What these studies suggest is that concepts are much more than definitional. They include (at least when reasonably well developed) not only the attributes necessary for category membership (i.e., the criteria for determining what is or is not a category member) but also what is *characteristic* of most members—information about the people and places, objects and actions, with which they are commonly associated as well as information about origins, internal constituents, and functions of category members. Thus, an adult's concept of flowers is not limited to the idea that they are the part of a plant in which seeds are formed. Rather, it includes the knowledge that flowers wilt, are considered pretty, are likely to be seen at funerals as well as weddings and parties, and much more.

In sum, words are the names we give to categories of objects, actions, and the qualities of objects and actions, and their meanings lie in the set of properties that distinguish one category from another. A statement of these properties constitutes a definition, and the things to which a word applies by virtue of having these properties are its word referents. Thus, words are terms of reference for specific objects as well as units of the language with intrinsic meaning. But, as we have seen, the properties that define a category are only part of what an individual knows about that category, only part of his or her word-knowledge. Underlying each word in an individual's lexicon is a concept, and this may be thought of as comprising all of the significant knowledge an individual possesses in association with that word (including its definition). *Vocabulary knowledge, then, involves the meaning of words in the strict sense and in the broader sense of the concepts underlying words.* It is the sum total of knowledge associated with words. We can also refer to this as "verbal knowledge."

Finally, it is conceptual or vocabulary knowledge, and not definitional knowledge alone, that is implicated in the comprehension of discourse. For we do not use words merely· to refer to things or identify their category of membership. We use words in sentences to describe situations—that is, the relations between objects and actions and the qualities of objects and actions. Even a simple sentence such as *John pulled Mary's hair* involves a series of relationships, between *John* and *pull,* between *hair* and *pull,* and between *Mary* and *hair.* More importantly, sentences are used in discourse, so that the situations they describe become part of a larger complex. It is here that conceptual knowledge is likely to play a role. One cannot understand the following vignette:

> John pulled Mary's hair. She ran home crying, and he was sent to the principal's office.

unless one's concept of hair includes the fact that it is painful to have it pulled.

Multiple Meanings

Many words in the English language have more than one meaning. In fact, there are relatively few words that do not. This situation normally causes little difficulty in communication, however, since the reader or listener can usually tell which meaning is intended from the immediate context or the topic of discourse. For example, the word *cell* is almost sure to refer to the cells of the human body in a biology text and to a small room or apartment in a treatise on monasteries. In a book on reading, the word *passage* will generally refer to a portion of printed text rather than to a hallway. However, it is only true, of course, that words with several meanings pose no special problem if the intended meaning is known and readily accessible in memory. If the word *passage* has never before been encountered in reference to written material, a "reading passage" might be construed as a "hallway in which to read." Thus, a word with several meanings is more likely to cause confusion and misunderstanding if one of its meanings is known but this is not the intended one than if the word is completely unfamiliar. In the former case, unware of his or her ignorance, the reader will be tempted into an erroneous interpretation. In the latter case, the reader simply faces the ordinary problem of an unknown word.

Extended Meanings and Metaphor

The several meanings of a word sometimes have little in common. *Bat* is an example. The fact that two entirely different entities—a small rodent and an item of equipment used in baseball—have the same verbal label seems to be purely coincidental. The word *fair* in the sense of "just," and *fair* in the sense of "light colored, blond" is another example.

On the other hand, what we think of as the several meanings of a word can often be seen, upon closer examination, to be closely related. Think of the word *sharp*. In *sharp mind,* it means "quick, intelligent"; in *sharp picture,* it means "not blurry"; a *sharp outfit* is "stylish"; and a *sharp knife* is one that "cuts well." Yet, all of these senses seem to share a common core of meaning.

> On purely intuitive grounds, one could maintain that *sharp* in the sense of 'having an edge that cuts well' is somehow basic and that the other versions of *sharp* are secondary, being derived from it as essentially metaphorical creations. A mind is sharp in that it cuts with ease through difficult problems; a picture is in sharp focus when the lines are thin and well defined, like the blade of a keen knife; a sharp outfit is one that stands out in sharp focus against the background of mediocrity [Langacker, 1973, p. 86].

Such extensions of meaning are extremely frequent in the language. They are closely related to metaphor in the sense that they involve attribution of a quality commonly associated with one kind of thing to another, completely different kind of thing. That is, comparisons are drawn across different realms of experience. If it is common to speak of *pure* water, *pure* food, *pure* air, and so forth, then we can also, by extension, speak of a *pure* heart or mind. And we can have *strong* evidence as well as *strong* muscles. The difference is that in extension the quality we wish to impute is specified, whereas in true metaphor we merely liken one thing to another and the reader must infer which property (or properties) of the one is shared by the other. When Romeo says Juliet is "the sun," we must understand that he is referring to the sun's warmth, brilliance, and life-sustaining qualities (and not to its shape or color).

Research on the comprehension of metaphor is not extensive, but a few interesting observations have been made. For example, many adjectives describing physical sensations are also used to describe psychological characteristics (e.g., *sweet, warm, cold, rough, hard* and *loud*). In one study, children ranging in age from 3 to 12 were first asked about the literal meanings of some of these dual-function words (to verify mastery at this level), and then they were asked about their figurative meanings (e.g., "Are people cold? What do they say or do when they are cold?"). It was not until the age of 7 or 8 that children showed some understanding of the psychological meaning of these terms. Even then they were unaware of the connection between psychological and physical meanings, believing the words to be entirely unrelated. By 9 and 10, children were more sensitive to this connection; and 11- and 12-year-olds were often actually able to explain the connection (e.g., "hard things and hard people are both unmanageable"; Asch & Nerlove, 1960, cited in Gardner, Winner, Bechhofer, & Wolf, 1978, p. 8). To summarize, the physical or concrete meanings of dual-function adjectives are generally understood even by preschool children; the psychological meanings are mastered during the early years of schooling; and recognition of the metaphoric connection emerges during preadolescence (Gardner et al., 1978).

This pattern of development holds true for metaphoric comprehension in general. That is, children of 8 or 9 can understand the meaning conveyed by a metaphor, but only on an intuitive basis: they can match a picture to the statement "He has a very heavy heart" but cannot easily paraphrase the statement. This limitation may be related to the fact that children of this age tend to avoid figurative usage in their own speech and, perhaps because of their concern with dictionary definitions, tend to prefer ordinary, established meanings and comparisons, occasionally protesting that figurative expressions are "silly": "A tie can't be loud"; "A person can't be a rock." This may be a necessary stage of development; one must understand what words usually (and literally) mean before one can appreciate the departures and extensions of metaphoric comparisons (Gardner et al., 1978).

This point was recently demonstrated, to some extent, in a study of instruction in the comprehension of metaphors and similes (Readence, Baldwin, & Rickelman, 1983). The investigators hypothesized that the key to comprehension of these expressions is vocabulary knowledge. More specifically, they pointed out that one must be sufficiently familiar with the "vehicle" term to know which of its features is being predicated to the "topic," the thing being described. For example, in *his hands were sandpaper, hands* is the topic and *sandpaper* the vehicle; that is, *sandpaper* is the means for conveying the idea that his hands were rough. In order to understand this metaphor, one must be familiar enough with sandpaper to know that roughness is its most significant characteristic. To cite another example, *The smoke from the forest was pea soup* can be understood only if one knows that pea soup is thick; knowing that it is green or edible provides no help. The investigators found that when fifth- and sixth-grade students misinterpreted metaphors and similes, it usually turned out that they did not associate the necessary attribute with the vehicle term. For example, they might not think of pea soup as thick. However, when these students were given lists of attributes (including the one being predicated of the topic) for the vehicle terms of the metaphorical statements they had misinterpreted, they were able to correct 77 percent of their misinterpretations (Baldwin, Luce, & Readence, 1982).

Similar results were obtained in a related study of similes (cited in Readence et al., 1983). In this study, one control group simply practiced interpreting similes; a second control group studied paragraphs that described the vehicle terms in the experimental materials, but that did *not* include the specific attributes necessary for their interpretation. The experimental group read descriptions of the vehicle term that included the necessary attribute. As was expected, subsequent performance on the test of simile interpretation was considerably superior for the experimental group.

These studies suggest that failure to understand metaphorical language is not primarily due to lack of the necessary reasoning powers or inability to recognize the type of comparison involved. Consequently, "drill exercises in discriminating between literal and metaphorical statements or matching interpretations with metaphors and similes may have little effect [Readence et al. 1983, p. 111]." Rather, direct instruction in the critical attributes of word referents seems more appropriate.

Nevertheless, the difficulty of understanding figurative language must not be underestimated. Familiarity with the terms used is certainly essential, but it is not sufficient. In order to determine which of the possibile attributes of a metaphoric vehicle is the intended one, the reader must understand the situational context. We understand what Romeo means when he says Juliet is "the sun" because we know from what has gone before how he feels about her.

The following teacher–student dialogue exemplifies the difficulty that students may have in identifying the intended metaphorical attribute:

> TEXT: "When he lands, he alternately tugs on vent lines and burner throttle to waft the balloon at heights of only 10 or 20 feet right over slight ridges, up gully inclines, and across ponds to the dime he has in mind. An error or a few feet could butt the basket against a rock or put it in the water ["A Love of Flight," in *Chicago Tribune*, 11/18/83]."
>
> TEACHER: What does the pilot do to land the balloon?
>
> STUDENT: Tug on the lines and burner throttle.
>
> TEACHER: What is difficult about this landing?
>
> STUDENT: He could hit a rock or fall into the water.
>
> TEACHER: Yes. And why is it difficult to avoid the rocks and water?
>
> STUDENT: You have to steer it.
>
> TEACHER: Yes, he has to steer very carefully. But why?
>
> STUDENT: (No response.)
>
> TEACHER: What is meant by "the *dime* he has in mind"?

STUDENT: The place he wants to land . . . open spot.

TEACHER: What about the dime? What does that tell you about the open spot?

STUDENT: . . . it's round?

TEACHER: What other quality of a dime would relate to this situation? For example, compare a dime to a quarter.

STUDENT: It's less.

TEACHER: Think of another quality.

STUDENT: It's smaller.

Thus, although a dime is an extremely familiar object, its small size was not immediately recognized as the relevant attribute, in part, it seems, because the student had little grasp of the fact that the size of the landing area might be important.

By the time students reach the age of 10 and 11, they can paraphrase as well as understand metaphors. Evidently, their conceptual and lexical knowledge is sufficiently consolidated that they do not resist or protest against comparisons between animate and inanimate objects, physical and psychological properties, and so on. However, it is not until adolescence that students are likely to fully appreciate the nature of metaphor, to recognize the links between sensory, physical, and psychological realms and perceive the significance of comparisons drawn across them (Gardner et al., 1978).

How Are Words Learned?

An eminent psycholinguist, George Miller (1977), recently observed that young children seem to learn the words that name colors before they learn to match those words to specific color stimuli. That is, they will answer "red," "blue," "green," (or some other color word) in response to the question, "What color is this?" even though the color they name is not the correct one. And when asked to point to all the blue things in any array of objects, they may point to all the tan ones, showing that they can distinguish between colors without knowing which color-name to apply. The same phenomenon has been observed with respect to time words: children will give time units in response to questions about time, but the numbers they give are often quite bizarre in relation to the questions (e.g., in answer to the question, "When was your daddy little?" a 3-year-old will respond, "Last week").

These observations led Miller to reflect on his own vocabulary knowledge, and he recognized that he, too, knew many words whose specific referents he could not identify or did not understand. For example, he knew that the words *camellia, nasturtium,* and *marigold* were the names of flowers but he did not know what these flowers looked like. Many adults are probably in a similar position with regard to tree names like *sassafrass* and *cottonwood* or animal names like *wombat* and *aardvark.*

What these observations suggest is that both children and adults often learn the general domain of knowledge or experience to which a word belongs before they understand its precise meaning. It should not surprise us, therefore, when students can give only the most general of information about certain words—that *anxiety* means "feeling"; *soliloquy* is "a statement"; *penance* means "punishment" (Drum, 1983). This probably represents a first stage in the process of learning words. With further experiences in a variety of contexts, word meanings become more differentiated.

The phenomenon of overgeneralization of word meaning is well documented among very young children (Clark, 1973). They commonly use the term *dog* as a label for other animals (horses, cows, sheep), *baby* for young children, *tick-tock* for instruments with round dials (gas meter, bathroom scale), *ball* for spherical objects (marbles, balloons), *Christmas tree* for all evergreens, and so on. One child used *open* for both untying of shoes and the peeling of fruit! We can understand these overextensions as stemming from the perceptual similarity of "correct" and "incorrect" word referents. And, to some extent, it may be that the child is aware of the difference between babies and children, a clock and other dialed instruments, and so on, but has not yet acquired the appropriate verbal labels. This would also explain the child's use of the terms *big* and *little* to cover all dimensions of size—long and short, wide and narrow, thick and thin, high and low. In other words, some overgeneralizations undoubtedly stem from the fact that children must use the terms that are available to them to refer to new objects and ideas.

More difficult to explain is the common confusion between antonym pairs such as *more* and *less, before* and *after, same* and *different.* One theory (the Semantic Feature Hypothesis) is that the meanings of words can be broken down into smaller units or elementary components of meaning (semantic features) and words that share many features are likely to be confused. More specifically, the meaning of one word in an antonym pair is likely, at first, to be extended to cover the meaning of the other as well because the contrastive feature of the second word has not yet entered the child's "mental dictionary." In other words, the meaning of *less, after,* or *different* has not yet been differentiated from (respectively) *more, before,* or *same;* the lexical entry for these words is incomplete (Clark, 1973). Perhaps this same notion of incomplete entry accounts for the confusion, found even among adults, between *affect* and *effect, imply* and *infer.*

The Semantic Feature Hypothesis represents just one attempt to understand the development of word meaning, and much can be said about its limitations (cf. Anglin, 1977; Nelson, 1974). From our point of view, one serious limitation is that it is based on observations of preschool children. Nevertheless, we believe it is sometimes useful to think of words as "bundles" of semantic features and to understand students' partial or vague knowledge of words in these terms.

Possibly more frequent than overgeneralizations of word meanings are undergeneralizations. These tend to go unnoticed in spontaneous speech (upon which much of the research on child language is based) because they do not result in erroneous verbal labels—the child merely applies a word to a more restricted range of objects than is necessary. Consequently, under-generalizations have been relatively neglected in the study of word meaning. They are, however, much in evidence when observations are based on comprehension tasks (Anglin, 1977). Whether a word is overgeneralized or undergeneralized appears to depend somewhat on its level of generality. The reason for this is that perceptual similarity plays an important role in children's categorizing behavior. General terms tend to refer to an assortment of dissimilar items and therefore to be undergeneralized. Thus, Anglin found that with the general terms *food, plant,* and *animal,* atypical instances such as ketchup, trees, and insects, respectively, were excluded. Rarely were these terms overgeneralized. Specific terms, on the other hand, were often over-generalized to perceptually similar items—*apple* to tomato, *flower* to other plants (cacti, philodendron). In general, then, children's acquisition of word labels cannot be said to progress either from specific to general or from general to specific. Rather, "vocabulary development is characterized by the complementary trends of differentiation and of hierarchic integration [Anglin, 1977, p. 237.]."

In conclusion, we have argued that underlying the meaning a student attaches to a word is a concept. This includes, even for young children, knowledge of what instances of the concept look like, smell like, taste like, and so on, where they are found, the uses to which they can be put, and what they can do. With development, a concept comes to include knowledge of the relations of instances to other things, their internal constituents, and their origins (Anglin, 1977). But it should be clear that there can be concepts without words just as there can be words without conceptual underpinnings. The distinction between words and concepts is an important one for vocabulary instruction; it implies that teaching definitions is not the same as teaching concepts. The teaching of definitions (or synonyms) makes sense when words pertain to well-developed concepts. Even then, new words must be practiced in a variety of verbal contexts if they are to be useful in comprehending discourse. But when the concepts underlying words are somewhat unfamiliar, definitions will be inadequate; instruction must also provide the verbal and nonverbal experiences necessary for concept development. In the following section we will review recent research on vocabulary instruction and describe some innovative instructional practices.

The Influence of Instruction

It was noted earlier that the high correlation between vocabulary and comprehension is not well understood. There is currently some controversy over whether word knowledge is directly "instrumental" in understanding text or is itself a reflection of "deeper and broader knowledge of the culture [Anderson & Freebody, 1981, p. 81]." That is, on the one hand, students who score high on a vocabulary test may simply "know more of the words in most texts they encounter"; on the other hand, it may be that "possessing a certain word meaning is only a sign that the individual may possess the knowledge needed to understand a text [p. 81]." The second position assumes that students who select the right responses on a multiple-choice test know more about words than their definitions (though that is all that is demonstrated on the test). This position is consistent with the view of verbal knowledge that we have proposed.

Unfortunately, as Anderson and Freebody (1981) point out, there is little besides logic and intuition to support the view that vocabulary scores reflect primarily conceptual or background knowledge. The tendency among reading researchers has been to study background knowledge as separate and distinct from vocabulary. However, there is a kind of support for the vocabulary-as-background-knowledge view, by default, in the finding that simply teaching definitions does *not* tend to improve comprehension. Out of eight studies recently reviewed by Mezynski (1983), four resulted in comprehension gains due to vocabulary instruction and four did not. In each of the four that proved unsuccessful, students were taught simple definitions or synonyms, accompanied in some cases by illustrative sentences. By contrast, in each of the successful studies, instruction went beyond this narrow type of drill.

In one of the successful studies, the additional instruction amounted to little more than answering two questions about each word. For example, in addition to learning that *altercations* are "fights," students answered these questions: "Do you have altercations with your teacher? Do you have altercations with a tree? [Kameenui, Carnine, & Freschi, 1982]." One wonders why this should make the difference between success and failure. Perhaps the questions helped students associate the new word with an underlying concept—meaningful experiences or knowledge—rather than with a rote definition. In any case, since this study is possibly unique in effecting gains in passage comprehension through short-term instruction in difficult passage words, further research is necessary before we can have full confidence in the efficacy of its instructional method.

Whereas Kameenui et al. (1982) taught a small number of words (six) and used a short experimental passage incorporating these words to assess the effect of instruction on comprehension, the other successful studies involved large numbers of words taught over a period of many months and assessed the effects of instruction through standardized comprehension tests. Thus, there is evidence in favor of instruction that is geared toward improving students' *general* vocabulary as well as support for direct instruction in difficult passage words. More significantly, in the general vocabulary studies, words not only were taught (i.e., defined, illustrated, explained, and discussed), but were also presented in rich contexts. The Draper and Moeller (1971) study constituted a veritable "barrage" of new words—1,800 in all—presented in the context of fables, folktales, and Greek and Roman myths. The Lieberman study (cited in Mezynski, 1983) used a social studies and English curriculum materials as the context for new words. A slightly different approach was taken by Beck, Perfetti, and McKeown (1982). Instead of providing narrative or expository contexts for newly learned words, they designed activities in which the meanings of words were explored and refined. For example, students completed sentences or answered multiple-choice questions about the situations, behaviors, or events in which word referents might be involved. To illustrate, for the word *accomplice,* students were asked, "Would an accomplice be more likely to (a) squeal to the police in return for not having to go to jail? (b) rob a bank by himself? (c) enjoy babysitting? [p. 510]." Also, the words taught in the Beck, Perfetti, and McKeown study were grouped into semantically related sets, eight to nine words per set, and some questions were designed to probe the overlap among words in a set. For example, *accomplice, novice,* and *hermit* were in the "people" set of words, and the questions asked were: "Could an accomplice be a novice? Would a hermit likely be an accomplice? [p. 510]."

If there is any lesson to be learned from this body of research, it would seem to be that instruction in definitions alone does not adequately prepare students for the task of comprehending discourse. It has also become increasingly clear that contextual learning is a powerful force in the vocabulary development of the school-age child (Nagy and Herman, 1987; Sternberg, 1987). Though the exact size and growth rate of children's vocabularies are arguable, it is clear that instruction cannot account for a major part of our word learning. In a recent meta-analysis of vocabulary research, Stahl and Fairbanks (1986) conclude that a combination of definitional and contextual learning is more effective than either alternative alone. A broad, rich range of experiences seem to be necessary before newly learned words can be understood in novel contexts. Such experiences can evidently be provided through exploratory questions as well as through contextual exercises which engage the learner in discussing, using, analyzing, and playing with new words. These experiences make definitions "come alive": They enable students to connect words with real-world events, situations, and behaviors—with existing conceptual knowledge.

Many suggested guidelines have been given for vocabulary programs in the classroom (Blachowicz, 1985; Carr and Wixson, 1986) and some can also be drawn from meta-analyses of instructional programs mentioned above. The process of word learning should be an active one for learners with the goal of connecting the new words to what they already know.

The goal should be to augment both the breadth and depth of existing word knowledge and to build independent word learning habits (Nagy, 1988). For maximum effect, this development takes place within the context of content learning or, at a minimum, in concert with textual reading instruction and should incorporate the following, though not necessarily in this order:

1. *Assessing what students already know.* Briefly worded explanations, synonyms, associations, or hypotheses about the word's meaning should be elicited from the student, if possible, and elaborated upon by the teacher. When the word is connected to a well-established concept, the dictionary can be consulted (Parker, 1984). For variation, the teacher might present sentences from which target words have been omitted but that contain clear clues to the words' meaning so that students can supply synonyms to match a new word's meaning (Blachowicz, 1977). If defining is the first instructional step, whatever defining characteristics are proposed should be viewed as tentative and reevaluated after more experience is given with the word.

2. *Active discussion.* The concepts underlying words should be developed through discussion of illustrative situations; meanings should be expanded and clarified through associations with familiar people, places, objects, and actions. Students' own experiences are of course elicited wherever possible. However, when students' experiences are limited, the teacher should invent appropriate scenarios.

3. *Application.* Concepts should be reinforced and refined through further interaction with illustrative contexts. This activity can take the form of exploratory questions similar to those used by Kameenui, Carnine, and Freschi (1982) and by Beck, Perfetti, and McKeown (1982), or it can involve instructional materials regularly used in reading or content area instruction. In addition, when time permits, students may be given writing assignments in which they generate sentences and paragraphs around the newly-learned words.

4. *Use and practice.* Reading in context is essential for vocabulary development (Nagy & Herman, 1987), as is hearing the new words used in oral language, storytelling, and story reading (Eller, Pappas, & Brown, 1988). To further make a word one's own, using it in writing is an excellent, and traditional, way to cement a new meaning. Further, word games and word play provide both practice and motivation for word learning which is so essential for growth.

One final issue should be mentioned before we conclude this discussion of instructional research. It concerns the special importance of vocabulary instruction for less able readers who generally exhibit poor performance on vocabulary assessment measures. Though research continues to emphasize that contextual reading is essential for growth in word knowledge, it may not be sufficient for these readers who begin school knowing fewer school-type words than their more able counterparts (Becker, Dixon, & Inman-Anderson, 1980). These are the readers who are frequently unmotivated or unable to do the amount of contextual reading that would close the gap with their age mates. Further, McKeown (1985) found that disabled readers lagged behind able readers in the use of strategies that allow readers to gain new word meaning from context: knowing that one needs to use context; generating possible meanings for an unknown word; using the prior and subsequent context to choose among generated alternatives.

Roser and Juel (1982) looked at readers' performance on word learning tasks in regular reading classrooms. They selected children in first through fifth grades who were either average or poor readers (i.e., who were reading either at or one year below grade level). Each group read stories from their classroom reader, one with vocabulary instruction and one without. The words taught were those identified in the teacher's manual as "new words," and the instructional method emphasized the relationship of each new word to the children's lives. Specifically, new words were presented along with sentences in which blanks were substituted for the new words, and the teacher guided the group in selecting the appropriate word for each sentence, centering the discussion on students' knowledge and previous experiences. The results showed a marked increase in passage comprehension after vocabulary instruction only for the poorer readers in third, fourth, and fifth grades. The average readers in all grades performed just about as well without instruction as with it. In first and second grades, not only did instruction have no effect, but the poorer readers performed as well as the average readers. These results are not unexpected, given the fact that beginning reading materials make fewer demands on students' vocabulary knowledge. A noteworthy feature of this experiment was the use of instructional-level materials in regular reading lessons conducted by the classroom teacher. Therefore, an appropriate instructional program for disabled readers with poor vocabularies would include motivation and time for wide reading but would also provide prereading instruction of key concept vocabulary and strategy development for effective context use.

DIAGNOSIS OF VOCABULARY KNOWLEDGE DIFFICULTY

We have seen, from the review of experimental research above, that knowing the definitions of words in a passage does not always lead to increased comprehension. By the same token, *not* knowing word meanings does not necessarily interfere with comprehension. Why should this be so? Clearly, much depends on how many unknown words there are and on how important they are to the central content (Freebody & Anderson, 1983a). The influence of these factors on comprehension will depend, in turn, on the familiarity of the content (cf. Freebody & Anderson, 1983b). A large number of unknown words may present no obstacle to comprehension in a highly predictable context. For example, a simple 100-word fairy-tale-style story was readily understood by a fifth-grade group of average readers even though 10 of the words were taken from an eighth-grade list and, moreover, an average of 7 of those words were marked incorrectly by the experimental group on a multiple-choice test given after instruction (Stahl, 1983). On the other hand, even a few unknown words can severely disrupt comprehension if they represent key concepts in an expository passage on an unfamiliar topic.

In the usual case, however, unknown words tend to result in losses or misinterpretations of information that are more limited in scope. By way of illustration, a child who did not know the meaning of *snare* and *clipped* read a story that began as follows: "A miller laid a snare, and a baby eagle flew into it. The miller tied him to a pole and clipped his wings. [Hughes, Bernier, & Gurren, 1979, p. 19]." The unknown words prevented her from answering questions about the *causes* of the bird's predicament; but the *facts* of its predicament—captivity and inability to fly—were clearly understood from ensuing events. In general, students appear to tolerate unknown words as long as other, compensatory sources of information are available to them, either from the passage itself, in the form of redundant information, or from their own store of knowledge.

In the following section we will present two case studies illustrating the way in which word knowledge and topic familiarity influence comprehension. The first case represents the moderate loss in comprehension likely to be observed when passages are not overly demanding relative to the reader's conceptual knowledge. The second shows a more severe loss, due to a more demanding (relative to the reader) passage. The presentation of these cases will, in addition, demonstrate the diagnostic procedures useful in assessing word knowledge and evaluating its effect on comprehension.

Diagnostic Procedures

The general procedure for reading diagnosis, as is discussed in Chapter 4, involves the preparation of materials, test administration, a preliminary analysis of test results, an informal probe, an interpretation, and finally, an instructional plan. It is during the preparation stage that words are selected from the passage for the assessment of word knowledge. Comprehension questions are also constructed at this time (specific procedures are discussed in the next chapter). Then, after a preliminary analysis of the results, additional words may be selected and presented during the probe. The purpose is to determine whether vocabulary knowledge is a major source of difficulty in reading—more specifically, whether uncommon words could have interfered with comprehension and whether unknown words represent unknown concepts as well.

Step 1: Preparation: Selection of Words. Three to eight words (depending on passage length) are selected for an initial appraisal of vocabulary knowledge. The words should be important to the passage that is chosen from instructional material—that is, they should convey information pertaining to the main ideas and essential details. Figurative expressions and phrases of a technical nature should also be selected, since they too represent possible obstacles to comprehension. Basic to this step, then, is a careful reading of the passage to identify its central content. The teacher must also be alert to the occurrence of common words used in uncommon or metaphorical senses. In selecting words for presentation, it is helpful to distinguish between those explained by the context of the passage and those without such illuminating contexts. The former can be used to probe for context use strategies, whereas the latter words are more appropriate for estimating the difficulty of a particular material for student use.

Step 2: Administration: Presentation of Words. The words selected are presented to the student in isolation after the comprehension questions have been asked. The teacher simply asks, "What does ——— mean?" or "What is a ———?" In the case of words with multiple meanings, the context in which the word occurred may also be provided. If the student cannot formulate a definition, or the response leaves some doubt as to the accuracy or fullness of the student's vocabulary knowledge, the teacher probes further, asking for an exemplary object or situation to which the word would apply or requesting that the student use the word in a sentence. Examples as well as sentences often have to be explored still further. For example, Raymond (Case Study 1 below) suggested that the word *sophisticated* could be applied to a truck. Although this is potentially correct, further questioning indicated that he thought it was motion (rather than modern design or engineering) that made a truck sophisticated.

Step 3: Preliminary Analysis of Results. In this step the teacher notes the degree of success achieved in defining the words presented in Step 2. If as many as half the words presented are unknown, the teacher should consider vocabulary knowledge an area of general weakness. The diagnosis does not end there, however. The teacher must also determine the extent to which unknown words constituted a specific impediment to comprehension. Doing this involves scrutiny of incorrect responses to comprehension questions. In particular, the teacher must determine, for each question that was answered incorrectly, whether the information needed to answer it was unavailable to the student because of an unknown word. If this is true for a majority of incorrect responses, then reading difficulty can be attributed to inadequate vocabulary knowledge.

Obviously, the words and ideas that will cause confusion and misunderstanding cannot always be anticipated during the initial selection of words; often the student's responses to questions reveal difficulties that were entirely unexpected. In Case Study 1, for example, the word *crude* was not recognized as a possible source of difficulty in the teacher's first analysis of the passage and was not, therefore, included in the initial set of words presented. In such cases, the additional words are selected for presentation to the student during the next step, the probe.

Performance on the comprehension questions is also examined at this point for evidence that the student lacked the conceptual knowledge or specific information necessary for general comprehension of the passage. If such evidence exists, questions to explore this possibility are formulated and then presented during the probe. This procedure is particularly important when overall comprehension is poor—say, 50 percent or less—and specific words do not seem to be directly implicated.

Step 4: Probe. The additional words identified in Step 3 as potential obstacles to comprehension are presented to the student as in Step 2. The results enable the teacher to complete the determination, begun in Step 3, as to whether particular questions were answered incorrectly because the meanings of certain words were unknown. The questions devised to explore conceptual knowledge and information are also administered. Further, discussing the words explained by context and letting students refer back to the text can provide a window from which to evaluate the student's context use strategy. These results provide further insight into the source of comprehension difficulty.

Steps 5 and 6: Interpretation and Instructional Plan. The results of Steps 3 and 4 combined serve as the basis for final evaluation of the role of vocabulary knowledge in the student's reading difficulties. If questions about the passage cannot be answered for lack of vocabulary knowledge, then vocabulary knowledge represents an area of weakness in reading and warrants instructional emphasis. Whether the passage should be considered too difficult for instructional purposes on account of vocabulary knowledge will depend on the severity of the comprehension loss. If the loss is limited in scope, as in Case Study 1, then passages of equivalent difficulty will probably be suitable for instruction as long as important words are taught before reading. On the other hand, if the loss in comprehension is widespread, extending to information not specifically related to unknown words, as in Case Study 2, then the student should be assigned an easier level of materials.

CASE 1: Raymond

Raymond is a seventh grader whose work in school is generally above average. But he is ambitious and expresses some concern about his reading ability. The diagnosis was undertaken in an attempt to identify areas of performance that might be strengthened through specific instruction.

PREPARATION
An expository passage from his seventh-grade reader, entitled "Kinds of Housing" (275 words in length), was selected for Raymond to read. It is shown in Figure 5.1. Using the procedures that have been described, the reader should examine the

Figure 5.1   Diagnostic reading passage: Raymond.

Kinds of Housing

With a few exceptions, environment determines the kinds of shelter people choose. So, houses are usually built from materials that are most readily available in the surrounding area.

The temporary dwelling, as its name suggests, is not built to last. Nomads, people who are always on the move, build temporary dwellings. For example, Native Americans of the plains developed the tepee made of buffalo hides. When buffalo were plentiful, they were an important food source. To avoid waste, Native Americans found a practical use for the hides of the animals. When the tribe moved on, the tepees were left behind.

The grass lean-to is favored by the Bush people of the Kalahari Desert. It is made from grasses and sticks found in the area in which they live.

There are two kinds of permanent housing: crude and sophisticated. Igloos, log cabins, and adobe huts are crude permanent housing. They are built to last. The surfaces, however, are rough and unfinished.

The igloo is a dome made of blocks of hard-packed snow. The snow acts as an insulator. It makes the igloo surprisingly warm.

Log cabins were common during America's westward expansion. As settlers headed west, the thick forests provided timber for housing.

Adobe is sun-dried mud. Adobe huts are found in warm, dry areas, such as parts of Mexico and the American Southwest.

Sophisticated permanent housing can be made from many materials. Homes with concrete foundations are built to last from owner to owner. Very often, these houses have a framework of wood, iron, or steel. The location of steel mills and ironworks often determines the areas where this housing is found.

(From *Exploring Paths: Reading Skills Workbook,* HBJ Bookmark Reading Program, by Margaret Early, Donald Gallo, and Gwendolyn Kerr. Copyright © 1979 by Harcourt Brace Jovanovich, Inc. Reprinted by permission of the publisher.)

passage to identify key vocabulary items that would interfere with Raymond's understanding of the passage if they were unknown to him.

The reader should then compare his or her selections with those made by Raymond's teacher. She selected six words. The first, *environment,* is important for understanding the thesis of the passage. The second word, *determines,* was included because it is central in understanding the main idea of the passage, that environmental conditions influence the nature of housing. The third, *available,* is a general vocabulary word that is important for understanding why kinds of housing vary according to the locale. The fourth, fifth, and sixth words—*temporary, permanent,* and *sophisticated*—represent major concepts that distinguish major types of housing. The word *insulator* was not included because the insulating property of snow was deemed incidental to the main point of the passage. Futhermore, the meaning of *insulator* was explained in the sentence following the one in which it was introduced. This is an example of the type of word that can be used to probe contextual strategies. As with *adobe, igloo,* and *nomads,* also well explained by the context of the selection, the teacher can ask the student to locate clues to the word's meaning in the passage during the comprehension probe if vocabulary knowledge appears to be a problem.

The preparation stage involved not only the selection of key vocabulary items but also the development of comprehension questions (to be discussed in the next two chapters). These are shown, together with the vocabulary items, in Figure 5.2; the expected answers are in parentheses. The first nine questions can be answered from information either stated or implied in the text; the remaining three require interpretation or application of text information.

ADMINISTRATION

Raymond read the passage aloud while the teacher recorded his errors and noted the amount of time he took to read it. The comprehension and vocabulary knowledge questions were administered immediately thereafter. Raymond's responses are shown in Figures 5.3 and 5.4 The reader should study his answers in order to make a tentative judgment about the adequacy of his comprehension and vocabulary knowledge.

PRELIMINARY ANALYSIS

Print Skill.   Raymond had difficulty with only three words, or fewer than 1 percent of the words in the passage. Two miscues involved inserted and omitted sight words that did not alter the meaning of the passage. The third was potentially more serious; it involved the mispronunciation of the word *determines,* with the third syllable pronounced like the word *mines.* Raymond read the passage in 2 minutes and 12 seconds, at a rate of 125 words per minute. This is within the average range for seventh graders. On the basis of this evidence, it is possible to conclude that Raymond's print-processing strategies represent an area of strength.

Comprehension.   Of the nine questions that pertained to text information, Raymond answered five correctly and two incorrectly (Items 6 and 8). His answers were only partially correct on the remaining two questions (Items 1 and 9). The partially correct answers involved use of examples rather than the more general formulations called for by the questions. Thus, Raymond's comprehension score (6 out of 9) was below 75 percent. Is there a possibility that his incorrect (or incomplete) answers were due to unknown words? We believe it will be useful for the reader to consider this issue before reading on; in particular, it is important to examine the way in which information pertinent to the questions Raymond missed was presented in the passage.

Raymond's incorrect responses to the comprehension questions suggested confusion over the terms *crude* and *sophisticated.* In response to the question of the difference between these two types of housing (Item 6), he replied that "crude is built to stay longer and sophisticated is not that long." In addition, he could not

Figure 5.2 Comprehension and vocabulary knowledge questions: Raymond.

Comprehension

1. a. What determines the kind of shelter people choose? (environment; available materials)

   b. Where do we usually get the materials we build houses from? (environment; surrounding area)

2. What is a temporary dwelling? (one that is not built to last)

3. What are the people called who build temporary dwellings? (nomads)

4. Why do some people build temporary dwellings? (they are always on the move)

5. What are the two types of permanent housing? (crude and sophisticated)

6. What is the difference between crude and sophisticated permanent housing? (crude are rough and unfinished; sophisticated are made from modern materials)

7. Name some types of crude permanent housing. (igloo, adobe, log cabin)

8. What are some materials sophisticated permanent housing is made of? (wood, iron, steel)

9. What determines where sophisticated permanent houses are built? (location of materials)

*10. If you had the choice between living in an igloo, a log cabin, or an adobe hut, which would you choose and why? (discuss climate and comfort)

*11. Of all the types of housing mentioned in the passage — temporary and permanent, crude permanent and sophisticated permanent — which type do you live in? (permanent sophisticated)

*12. Do climate and environment still govern what materials we use to build houses today? (discuss role of climate and environment and today's construction)

   * Beyond-text question

Vocabulary Knowledge

Key Concept Words

1. environment
2. determines
3. available
4. temporary
5. permanent
6. sophisticated

Contextually Explained

7. insulator
8. adobe
9. igloo
10. nomads

Figure 5.3 Responses to comprehension questions: Raymond.

½ **1.** a. ½ What determines the kind of shelter people choose? (environment; available materials)

RESPONSE: It can be the grounds, maybe grass or sand; and like if it's cold or sunny.

b. ½ Where do we usually get the materials we build houses from? (environment; surrounding area)

RESPONSE: Sometimes we can make it. Like the log cabins, you could get it from the trees around you. The igloos you could pack the snow yourself.

✓ **2.** What is a temporary dwelling? (one that is not built to last)

RESPONSE: It's not built to stay long.

✓ **3.** What are the people called who build temporary dwellings? (nomads)

RESPONSE: Nomads.

✓ **4.** Why do some people build temporary dwellings? (they are always on the move)

RESPONSE: They are always moving around.

✓ **5.** What are the two types of permanent housing? (crude and sophisticated)

RESPONSE: Crude and sophisticated.

✗ **6.** What is the difference between crude and sophisticated permanent housing? (crude are rough and unfinished; sophisticated are made from modern materials)

RESPONSE: Not sure—crude are built to stay longer and sophisticated is not that long.

✓ **7.** Name some types of crude permanent housing. (igloo, adobe, log cabin)

RESPONSE: Log cabin, adobe hut, igloo.

✗ **8.** What are some materials sophisticated permanent housing is made of? (wood, iron, steel)

RESPONSE: I think one of the houses are igloos made out of snow—or I think wood. [Anything else?] Steel.

½ **9.** What determines where sophisticated permanent houses are built? (location of materials)

RESPONSE: Well, if they were wood, they would be by a forest.

½ *10. If you had the choice between living in an igloo, a log cabin, or an adobe hut, which would you choose and why? (discuss climate and comfort)

RESPONSE: Igloo, or log cabin. . . . Well, I would choose an igloo because it keeps you warm. Maybe a log cabin; it was built like a house—and that's what we mostly live in, like in cabins in the woods. [So which would you choose?] Log cabin 'cause it's built like a house.

Figure 5.3 (*continued*)

✓ *11. Of all the types of housing mentioned in the passage — temporary and permanent, crude permanent and sophisticated permanent — which type do you live in? (permanent sophisticated)
RESPONSE: I think sophisticated. [Is it permanent or temporary?] Permanent.

✗ *12. Do climate and environment still govern what materials we use to build houses today? (discuss climate, environment, today's construction)
RESPONSE: Not sure. [Do you think people can build any kind of house no matter what the climate is?] Well, not exactly — don't know how to explain it.

* Beyond-text question

Figure 5.4 Responses to vocabulary knowledge questions: Raymond.

✓ 1. *environment*
RESPONSE: The things around you.

✗ 2. *determines*
RESPONSE: They . . . say it, they predict.
TEACHER: Can you use the word *determines* in a sentence?
RESPONSE: He determined that the number was gonna be five.

✓ 3. *available*
RESPONSE: That it's . . . I can't explain it.
TEACHER: Then use it in a sentence.
RESPONSE: This pen is available for anybody that wants to use it.

✓ 4. *temporary*
RESPONSE: It's not built to stay long.

✓ 5. *permanent*
RESPONSE: That it stays there . . . the house stays up longer.

✗ 6. *sophisticated*
RESPONSE: I don't know the meaning of that word from the other thing, but I think I know another meaning.
TEACHER: O.K. Tell me the meaning you know.
RESPONSE: Well, I don't know how to explain it.
TEACHER: Could you put it in a sentence?
RESPONSE: This is a sophisticated truck.
TEACHER: What does that mean about the truck?
RESPONSE: That it's in a kind of motion or something. A kind of way.

remember the kinds of materials used in sophisticated housing (Item 8), a plausible consequence of unfamiliarity with this term. Again, to gain experience with the diagnostic process, the reader should examine Raymond's responses on the vocabulary knowledge assessment at this point. Is there corroborating evidence that vocabulary knowledge interfered with comprehension?

Vocabulary Knowledge.   Of the six words selected for assessment, there were only two that Raymond could not define—*sophisticated* and *determines.* For *sophisticated,* he thought that he knew "another meaning" for it—other than the one intended in the passage—but the meaning he gave ("a kind of motion") was incorrect. Note that the passage characterizes *crude* permanent housing (as in igloos, log cabins, and adobe huts) as "rough and unfinished" and later states that *sophisticated* houses have concrete foundations and frameworks made of wood, iron, or steel. Thus, the meaning of *sophisticated* in the sense of smooth, finished, and involving advanced technology is not given; this must be inferred from the contrast with *crude.* Raymond was evidently unable to make this inference; possibily he did not know what *crude* meant.

Because Raymond's difficulties on the comprehension questions seemed to be caused by his limited understanding of such terms as *determines, crude,* and *sophisticated,* his teacher decided to focus the subsequent probe on his vocabulary knowledge. In addition to determining his understanding of *crude* and further specifying his knowledge of *determines,* she planned to explore his understanding of the words *plentiful, readily,* and *insulator.*

PROBE

The next day, after having Raymond reread the passage, the teacher asked what *crude* meant. He replied that *crude* "was a kind of housing" (as stated in the text) and he recalled the three examples that were given in the passage. Further questioning revealed that he had never before heard the word used nor could he use it in a sentence himself. It now seemed reasonable to consider Raymond's difficulty with Item 6 on the comprehension test as stemming primarily from the unfamiliarity of *crude* and *sophisticated.* Without prior knowledge of these two words, Raymond could only assume that the difference in the materials used in these two types of housing made for a difference in degree of permanence. Although the terms *rough* and *unfinished* were used in the passage to describe crude housing, he evidently failed to relate these words to the meaning of *crude.* Consequently, he could not, in turn, grasp the idea that *sophisticated* was the opposite of rough and unfinished.

In the case of *determines,* Raymond seemed to know what it would mean in the context of people making decisions or predicting outcomes, but he seemed unable to grasp the idea that existing conditions could (so to speak) do the same:

TEACHER: The passage states that environment determines the kinds of housing people choose. What does *determines* mean?

STUDENT: If they lived in a cold place, that would show that they lived in an igloo. If it was hot, that would say that they would live in a hut maybe.

TEACHER: Okay. Then what would *determine* the kind of shelter people choose?

STUDENT: Well, like the people who run the city, they can choose if they wanted brick or wood.

TEACHER: Yes.. But what does *determine* mean?

STUDENT: They . . . say it, predict.

TEACHER: Can you use the word *determines* in a sentence?

STUDENT: He determined that the house was gonna be wood.

Thus, it was not so much the meaning of the word itself that gave Raymond difficulty; it was rather the underlying concept, that environmental conditions could set limits on people's choices, that escaped him. His failure to grasp this concept could explain his inability to give generalized answers to the questions, "What determines the kind of shelter people choose?" and "Where do we usually get the materials we build houses from?"

To explore further the possibility that vocabulary knowledge was a limiting factor in Raymond's comprehension, the teacher asked him to define several other words. He knew that *plentiful* meant "there is a lot." However, for *readily,* he said, "that it's done, finished, used . . . I'm not sure." And for *insulator,* he understood that it was related to keeping warm but thought it was "a type of machine, a heater." Further, he could not pick out any clue sentences in the selection (such as, "The snow acts as an insulator") to suggest whether or not his idea of a machine made sense. The teacher continued to probe context use. Raymond knew the word *igloo* but couldn't define *nomad* or *adobe.* When he reinspected the passage, he was able to locate their meanings, which were explicitly cued by the context. Although unfamiliarity with these words did not interfere directly with overall passage comprehension, they provided additional evidence that vocabulary knowledge was somewhat inadequate. With respect to context use strategies, when Raymond was allowed to look back, he could locate and use contextual information that was quite explicit, but he had a harder time picking up contextual clues that were given less explicitly and located across the selection.

INTERPRETATION

Raymond's responses to the vocabulary knowledge and comprehension questions are summarized in Figure 5.5. The summary indicates that Raymond's comprehension (67 percent) is somewhat below the instructional range (75–89 percent comprehension) but not at his frustration level (less than 50 percent; see Table 8.1, p. 209). When comprehension falls within the borderline range between instructional and frustration levels, it is appropriate to consider whether additional instructional support, directly in the major area of reading difficulty, may enable Raymond to read passages similar to this one with adequate comprehension.

Raymond's performance on the initial administration of the questions and during the probe indicates that his major difficulty is in the area of vocabulary knowledge. Generally, he is able to process text with good understanding. However, when the text and/or the questions used to assess comprehension involve terms that are unfamiliar to him, his comprehension is not entirely adequate. For example, he

Figure 5.5 Summary of responses to comprehension and vocabulary knowledge questions: Raymond.

COMPREHENSION–VOCABULARY
KNOWLEDGE SUMMARY

Name _Raymond_ Grade _7_ Date _2/84_
Book/Page _Exploring Paths 82-83_ Level _13_

COMPREHENSION

_6_ / _9_ _67_ % Correct

Level: Independent   Instructional
(Borderline)   Frustration

A. RETELLING: Complete   Main Idea   Partial   (Inadequate)

Comments: _Missed main idea_

B. TEXT-RELATED COMPREHENSION

Item #	Response	Probe (Comments)	Item #	Response	Probe (Comments)
1	½	Examples rather than general idea	6	✗	
2	✓		7	✓	
3	✓		8	✗	
4	✓		9	½	
5	✓				

C. BEYOND-TEXT GENERALIZATION

Item #	Response	Probe (Comments)	Item #	Response	Probe (Comments)
10	½		12	✗	
11	✓				

VOCABULARY KNOWLEDGE

_5_ / _10_ _50_ % Correct

Item Tested	Response	Comments	Item Tested	Response	Comments
environment	✓		crude (P)*	✗	never heard of word before
determines	✗	"predict"	plentiful (P)	✓	"a lot"
available	✓		readily (P)	✗	defined "ready"
temporary	✓		insulator (P)	✗	knew relation to warmth
permanent	✓		adobe (P)	✓	could use context to find.
sophisticated	✗		nomads (P)	✓	

*Prefers to probe items

EVALUATION

A. COMPREHENSION: _Remembered examples and details but did not grasp the main idea of the passage; problems are directly related to unknown words._

B. VOCABULARY KNOWLEDGE: _Deficiencies in word knowledge currently interfere with comprehension; prereading activities focused on vocabulary development should improve comprehension._

misconstrued the difference between "crude" and "sophisticated" housing. Similarly, although he understood the use of available materials in the specific instances cited in the passage, he did not grasp the general principle or concept that these instances exemplified. In both these failures of comprehension, unknown words were directly implicated. This evidence suggests that Raymond should be able to cope with passages similar to this one in difficulty if special instruction focuses on developing his knowledge of the words they contain.

INSTRUCTIONAL PLAN
In conclusion, the passage represents an appropriate level of difficulty for instructional purposes as long as important word meanings are discussed before the material is read. Raymond's instruction should focus on two major areas. First, using procedures discussed earlier in this chapter, the development of word meanings should be emphasized during prereading. Second, systematic instruction should be developed in the area of using text information to infer word meanings by reasoning across the context.

CASE 2: Tanya

Tanya is a seventh grader assigned to a seventh-grade basal text. Her performance in class was erratic, and she was generally reluctant to participate in group discussions. The teacher decided to use diagnostic procedures to investigate the appropriateness of her basal assignment as well as the nature of her difficulty.

PREPARATION
Tanya's teacher selected a passage entitled "And Then There Were None" from the Bookmark Reading Program, which was being used for class instruction. The passage, 342 words in length, is shown in Figure 5.6. The reader should examine the passage in order to select words that would appear to be central to the understanding of this passage.

Tanya's teacher prepared both word meaning and comprehension questions to be administered following the reading of the passage. Before proceeding, the reader should compare the words that he or she selected with those chosen by the teacher: *specimens, slaughtered, surviving, refuge, prospective, immense,* and *extinct.*

ADMINISTRATION
Tanya read the passage in 3½ minutes, a rate of 98 words per minute. The record of her oral reading is given in Figure 5.7. Examine the evidence in order to decide whether print translation represents an area of reading difficulty for her.

Her comprehension and word knowledge responses are shown in Figure 5.8. The reader should examine this evidence in order to formulate tentative answers to the following three questions. First, is Tanya experiencing difficulty with reading comprehension? Second, is her knowledge of word meanings limited? Third, if she is experiencing difficulty with both comprehension and word knowledge, is there evidence that her inadequate knowledge of word meanings accounts for her comprehension difficulty?

Figure 5.6   Diagnostic reading passage: Tanya.

And Then There Were None

In 1534, a French sea captain reported that his men had killed more than a thousand "northern penguins" in a single day. But the bird to which the captain referred was not a penguin at all. It was the great auk, which at one time nested safely by the millions from Newfoundland to Scandinavia. Today the only specimens are in museums.

Like the penguin, the great auk could not fly but was a powerful swimmer. Each season, a female laid only one enormous egg, measuring about five inches long. Fully grown, a great auk stood three feet tall.

Originally, the great auk's largest nesting ground was an island off the eastern coast of Newfoundland. But by the early 1800's, fishermen had completely destroyed them. They used the birds' bodies for food or rendered them into cooking oil.

While the Napoleonic wars were raging across Europe, ships were sailing from Reykjavik, Iceland, to nearby Penguin Island, the second largest great-auk nesting colony, to kill the birds for food. There, using only large sticks, sailors slaughtered the proud birds by the thousands. Then, in the spring of 1830, another terrible blow struck the few great auks still at Penguin Island. The island just disappeared beneath the frigid ocean waters. Most of the surviving great auks took refuge on the small island of Eldey. This island was not far from where their home had been.

But Eldey was not to remain their home for long. The birds had become famous in Europe. Collectors paid immense sums for great auk skins throughout the 1830's. In 1884, Carl Siemson of Reykjavik, an agent for prospective buyers, offered a large cash reward in hopes of getting just a few more skins of the almost extinct bird. A daring Icelandic fisherman answered the challenge and went to Eldey with a small crew. There, he looked for and finally discovered two great auks. He promptly killed them both. Soon after, he returned to Reykjavik to collect his reward; 100 crowns ($60) for the last two great auks on earth.

(From *Exploring Paths: Skills Reader,* HBJ Handbook Reading Program, by Margaret Early, Donald Gallo, and Gwendolyn Kerr, published by Harcourt Brace Jovanovich, Inc., 1979. Passage by Mark Wexler, copyright 1974 by the National Wildlife Federation. Reprinted from the April–May issue of National Wildlife Magazine.)

PRELIMINARY ANALYSIS

Print Skill.   The results from Tanya's oral reading are summarized in Figure 5.9. A total of 18 oral reading errors were tabulated. Of these, 5 were sight word errors, mainly insertions and omissions. A few of the sight word errors seemed to result when a difficult name was being attempted; the others are typical of mature readers and do little harm to meaning. The majority of miscues were in response to content words, and almost half of these were responses to somewhat unusual names. The

Figure 5.7 Record of oral reading: Tanya.

And Then There Were None

18

In 1534, a French sea captain reported that his men had killed more than

a thousand "northern penguins" in a single day. But the bird to which the

captain referred was not a penguin at all. It was the great auk, [*est*] which at one

time nested safely by the millions from Newfoundland to Scandinavia.

Today the only specimens are in museums.

Like the penguin, the great auk could not fly but was a powerful swim-

mer. Each season, a female laid only one enormous egg, measuring about five

inches long. Fully grown, a great auk stood [*at*] three feet tall.

Originally, the great auk's largest nesting ground was an island off the

eastern coast of Newfoundland. But by the early 1800's, fishermen had com-

pletely destroyed them. They used the birds' bodies for food or ~~rendered~~ [*reneered*] them *1*

into cooking oil.

While ~~the~~ ~~Napoleonic~~ [*Nupolentic*] wars (were) raging across Europe, ships were sail- *3*

ing from ~~Reykjavik~~ [*Reja*], Iceland, to nearby Penguin Island, the second largest *1*

great-auk nesting colony, to kill the birds for food. There, using only large

sticks, sailors slaughtered the proud birds by the thousands. Then, in the

spring of 1830, another terrible blow struck the few great auks still at Pen-

guin Island. The island just disappeared beneath the frigid ocean waters.

Most of the surviving great auks took ~~refuge~~ [*rē-uge*] on the small island ~~of Eldey~~ [*at Italy*]. *3*

This island was not far from where their home had been.

But ~~Eldey~~ [*Italy*] was not to remain their home for long. The birds had become *1*

famous in Europe. Collectors paid immense sums for great auk skins

through ~~out~~ the 1830's. In 1884, Carl ~~Siemson~~ [*Simmons*] of ~~Reykjavik~~ [*Reja*], an agent for *3*

prospec ~~tive~~ buyers, offered a large cash reward in hopes of getting just a few *1*

130

Figure 5.7 *(continued)*

more skins of the almost ~~extinct~~ bird. A daring Icelandic fisherman answered   /

the challenge and went to Eldey with a small crew. There, he looked for and
<u>found</u>

~~finally~~ (discovered) two great auks. He promptly killed them both. Soon after,   2
    Reja

he returned to ~~Reykjavik~~ to collect his reward; 100 crowns ($60) for the last *kO* *

two great auks on earth.
* *Miscues occurring more than twice were not counted.*

(From *Exploring Paths: Skills Reader,* HBJ Bookmark Reading Program, by Margaret Early, Donald Gallo, and Gwendolyn Kerr, published by Harcourt Brace Jovanovich, Inc., 1979. Passage by Mark Wexler, copyright 1974 by the National Wildlife Federation. Reprinted from the April–May issue of National Wildlife Magazine.)

Figure 5.8 Responses to comprehension and vocabulary knowledge questions: Tanya.

Comprehension

½ **1.** What is this passage about? (the great auk; its extinction)
    RESPONSE: About two auks.

× **2.** In what part of the world did the great auks live? (Newfoundland, Scandinavia, Iceland, etc.)
    RESPONSE: On an island. [Do you know where it was?] No.

× **3.** When did the events in the story take place? (1500–1800)
    RESPONSE: Don't know.

½ **4.** × a. What did the great auks look like? (penguins)
    RESPONSE: Like hawks; big birds.
    ✓ b. How big were they? (3 feet)
    RESPONSE: Three feet.

½ **5.** What problem did these birds have? (hunted and killed)
    RESPONSE: They couldn't stay in one place. The place where they were at would disappear under the ocean.

½ **6.** Why were the birds hunted and killed? (for food, cooking oil, skins)
    RESPONSE: For the money. If they caught two hawks, they get $50 worth, get 50 coins each. So they got 100 coins, they got $60.

½ **7.** What happened to Penguin Island in 1830 and what did the birds do? (it sank into the ocean; the birds swam to another island)
    RESPONSE: It disappeared under the ocean. [What did the auks do when this happened?] They flew away.

Figure 5.8 *(continued)*

½ **8.**   Why did Carl Siemson offer a large sum of money for the birds? (he was an agent for prospective buyers of skins)
RESPONSE: He wanted to get some money for himself for the birds. So if he got 'em, then he would kill them. Then he would get some money for them and they both would have been even about the money.

✓ **9.**   How much were the hunters paid for the last two great auks? ($60)
RESPONSE: (not asked; answered in response to Item 6)

✗ **10.**   What happens when animals are hunted and killed with no protection from the law? (extinction)
RESPONSE: They'd be kind of scared. They'd be dead. Men would go to jail.

Vocabulary Knowledge

✗ **1.**   *specimens*
RESPONSE: Leaves. [Tell me more about it.] Not sure.

✓ **2.**   *slaughtered*
RESPONSE: Kill someone.

✓ **3.**   *surviving*
RESPONSE: They lived on.

✗ **4.**   *refuge*
RESPONSE: Don't know.

✗ **5.**   *prospective*
RESPONSE: You're looking at it . . . thinking about it.
TEACHER: Can you use it in a sentence?
RESPONSE: The prospective was easy.

✗ **6.**   *immense*
RESPONSE: Clever.

✗ **7.**   *extinct*
RESPONSE: Don't know.

others involved important content words (e.g., *extinct, rendered, refuge, prospective*). These errors may indicate some difficulty with the pronunciation of multisyllabic words. On the other hand, there were many difficult content words that she pronounced accurately (e.g., *Scandinavia, specimens, slaughtered, frigid*). Thus, the hypothesis that her apparent print translation difficulty may actually reflect unfamiliarity with these words should be considered.

Figure 5.9 Analysis of oral reading responses: Tanya.

ORAL READING ANALYSIS

Name _Tanya_ Grade _7_ Date _10/83_
Book/Page _Exploring Paths_ Level _13_

A. DIFFICULTY

_18_ / _342_   _95_ % Correct

Level: Independent (Instructional)
Borderline   Frustration

B. WORD LEARNING: Sight Word Errors

Printed Word	Oral Response	Probe	Evaluation
of	at		No problem.
finally	found		
the	[omitted]		
were	[omitted]		
at	[inserted]		

C. WORD IDENTIFICATION: Content Word Errors

Printed Word	Oral Response	Probe	Evaluation
great	greatest	✓	generally little difficulty
throughout	through	✓	with word identification
prospective	prospect	✓	when meanings and
			pronunciation of
refuge	rē-uge	re-fuge	words are known.
rendered	reneered	✓	
Napoleonic	Nupolentic	Nā-pol-e-nic	
② Reykjavik	Reja	Rē-ka-vik	
② Eldey	Italy	✓	
Siemson	Simmons	Simson	
extinct	estic	✓	
discovered	[omitted]	✓	

D. INTEGRATION – FLUENCY

Integration: _Most sight word and affixed word errors are contextually appropriate. No use of correction strategies._

Fluency: Rate _342_ / _3.5_ = _98_ wpm Evaluation _Slower than average_

Phrasing _Fluent except when she encountered unknown words_

Comprehension   The results from the comprehension questions are summarized in Figure 5.10. Of the 9 text-related comprehension questions that were asked, only one (Item 9) was correctly answered and 6 were only partially correct, yielding a comprehension score of 44 percent. Tanya showed some understanding of the destruction of the last two great auks but seemed unaware that this was the culmination of a series of destructive events. Her grasp of the details of time and place and the auks' resemblance to penguins was also quite limited.

It is not always possible to identify specific words that might be implicated in failures of comprehension. And so it was in this case. An examination of the passage in relation to incorrectly answered questions provided few good "leads" regarding specific words that might be sources of difficulty. There were, however, two words central to the general topic or theme of the passage that could have interfered with overall comprehension. The word *specimens* in the first paragraph provided an important clue to the fact that the birds were now extinct; unfamiliarity with this word would certainly make the rest of the passage more difficult to understand. Similarly, the word *extinct* in the last paragraph, if unknown, would represent a significant loss of information about the topic at large. In addition, there were a number of place names mentioned in the passage that could have been unfamiliar; and the auks' resemblance to penguins would have little meaning without some knowledge of the latter. The teacher planned to explore these items during the informal probe. In the meantime, she examined the results of the vocabulary assessment.

Vocabulary Knowledge
As is summarized in Figure 5.10, Tanya was able to define or use in a sentence only two of the seven words she was asked about. On this basis, vocabulary knowledge was definitely an area of weakness. However, the unknown words alone could not fully account for her low comprehension score, since they were not directly related to incorrectly answered questions. Further questioning was undertaken, therefore, during the informal probe which followed, to determine whether Tanya's general information and conceptual knowledge were adequate for this passage.

Probe
The probe focused on Tanya's knowledge of a few key terms (e.g., *penguins* and *extinct*) and on her knowledge of the places mentioned in the passage. When asked if she knew anything about penguins, Tanya replied that they were tiny creatures, but she did not know what they looked like. With regard to the problem of extinction, Tanya did not know of any other animals that were hunted and killed until there were none left on earth; and she was unaware that anything was currently being done to protect wildlife from extinction. For example, she assumed that hunting and fishing licenses were primarily for the purpose of raising money and that wildlife preserves were designed to make it easy for people to see the animals. Finally, she did not know where Newfoundland, Scandinavia, or Iceland could be found on the globe. Further, she could not use context to suggest clues to the meanings of *sums* or *agent*.

Figure 5.10 Summary of responses to comprehension and vocabulary knowledge questions: Tanya.

COMPREHENSION–VOCABULARY KNOWLEDGE SUMMARY

Name _Tanya_ Grade _7_ Date _10/83_
Book/Page _Exploring Paths_ Level _1³_
_334-335_

COMPREHENSION

_4_ / _9_ _44_ % Correct

Level: Independent Instructional
Borderline (Frustration)

A. RETELLING: Complete Main Idea Partial (Inadequate)

Comments: _Remembered only minor details._

B. TEXT-RELATED COMPREHENSION

Item #	Response	Probe (Comments)	Item #	Response	Probe (Comments)
1	1/2		6	1/2	
2	X		7	1/2	
3	X		8	1/2	
4	1/2		9	✓	
5	1/2				

C. BEYOND-TEXT GENERALIZATION

Item #	Response	Probe (Comments)	Item #	Response	Probe (Comments)
10	X				

VOCABULARY KNOWLEDGE

_2_ / _8_ _25_ % Correct

Item Tested	Response	Comments	Item Tested	Response	Comments
specimens	X		extinct	X	unknown concept
slaughtered	X		penguins(P)*	X	"tiny creatures"; unfamiliar
surviving	✓				
refuge	X		sums (P)	X	could not
prospective	X		reward (P)	✓	use context
immense	X		agent (P)	X	to find clues.

* P indicates a probe item

EVALUATION

A. COMPREHENSION: _Not probed because basic concepts were unfamiliar._

B. VOCABULARY KNOWLEDGE: _Lacks much background knowledge presumed by this material (e.g., didn't know what penguins looked like; could not locate Newfoundland, Scandinavia, or Iceland on a globe; completely unfamiliar with concept of animal extinction._

INTERPRETATION AND INSTRUCTION
Tanya's comprehension of the diagnostic passage was extremely limited, as was her knowledge of important words in it. But lack of vocabulary knowledge was only part of the problem. She lacked, as well, the basic concepts necessary for understanding the significance of the events described. The teacher decided that passages at this level of difficulty were inappropriate for Tanya and that she should be assigned to an easier basal text. The teacher also planned to focus on important concepts and background knowledge during prereading instruction.

INSTRUCTIONAL TECHNIQUES

Within the framework of effective instruction outlined above, a wide variety of techniques and activities are possible. In most instructional situations, teachers negotiate among various objectives and constraints and make a variety of instructional choices based on variables such as the student's initial knowledge level, the importance of the word to the study at hand, and the time available for instruction, all those things making up what have been called the cost and benefits of instruction (Graves & Prenn, 1986). Both the nature of the vocabulary words chosen for instruction and the teacher's purpose, as well as the student's prior knowledge about the words and their base concepts, can inform the decision to choose one technique over another.

The teacher's purpose in working with vocabulary is twofold. A first consideration is enlarging the student's recognition vocabulary so that impediments to effective comprehension are removed. If this is a primary objective, thorough prereading instruction on key concepts is called for, especially for those terms that are not well developed by context in the body of the reading, such as those chosen as assessment words in the case studies of Raymond and Tanya.

A second goal is the development of independent word-learning strategies, such as use of context, references, and word structure. This goal suggests an alternative instructional decision. Words can be highlighted before readings and predictive activities generating tentative meanings can be emphasized so that the reader has a focus for contextual learning. Postreading monitoring, evaluation, refinement, and verification of meaning then become essential elements in the instructional cycle. The words that have well-developed contextual references in a reading selection lend themselves to this focus.

Further, for either of these choices, the need to internalize the word and make it one's own requires numerous opportunities to use the word in discussion, writing, word play, and other reading situations. Students also need to begin to build habits of self-reflection and monitoring of vocabulary and concept knowledge. "Do I know anything about this?" and "Is my definition adequate for this context?" become important questions for the student to ask.

The teacher's task is to help the students "contextualize" the word in a relevant way. The context created should be drawn from, or relevant to, that provided by the text and should draw on what the student already knows to mediate the new learning. For example, when discussing equipment for the unfamiliar game of pelota that is the subject of a reading selection, the teacher may wish to contextualize the words by using the student's knowledge of racquetball or other racquet sports. In a situation where a concept is completely unfamiliar, the teacher may choose to build knowledge firsthand before teaching by analogy. In creating these contexts, students can "hypothesize" the meanings of unknown words from sentence or paragraph contexts before reading the selection or consulting a reference. Alternatively, the concept underlying each unknown word can be discussed before the word itself is introduced. For example, to introduce *assassination,* discussion would begin with the idea of "kill" or "murder" and lead toward the murder of a political figure (Vaughan, Castle, Gilbert, & Love, 1982). Described below are a number of additional strategies for introducing, hypothesizing about, and helping students manipulate words and relate them to real-word contexts. They are designed primarily for showing the interrelationships among word meanings and include opportunities for self-questioning and monitoring.

Learning Word Meanings from Context

Many of the words we know—perhaps most—have probably been learned spontaneously in the course of general reading and listening experience (Nagy & Herman, 1987). Yet research suggests that this is a slow and gradual process (Eller, Pappas & Brown, 1988; Gray & Holmes, 1938). This is not really surprising. When we encounter unfamiliar words in a text, we are not, in general, inclined to develop and commit to memory precise meanings for them. Because we are attending to passage meaning rather than to individual words, we are more likely to infer vague meanings consistent with the text, or else read around unknown words as long as the passage remains comprehensible. In unusual circumstances we may consult a dictionary or a friend.

McKeown (1985) has documented some of the steps involved in effectively learning from context and the difficulty some at-risk students have in becoming independent contextual learners. Some variations of the cloze procedure (Blachowicz, 1977) may be employed to make the process more transparent; or direct instruction with teacher-prepared sentences may be used, such as in the following instructional approach (Cunningham, Cunningham, & Arthur, 1981).

1. The teacher prepares for the lesson by creating one or two sentences for each word that will be taught before a passage is read. The sentences should provide clues to word meaning.
2. The words alone are listed on the chalkboard, and students are asked to write a meaning for each word. If a word is completely unknown, as many will be, students are told to make a guess.

3. The teacher elicits a few meanings for each word and writes them on the chalkboard.
4. The sentences prepared by the teacher are displayed and students again write a meaning for each word. This enables them to see the difference between pulling a meaning "out of thin air" and using contextual information.
5. Students now volunteer their context-based guesses, explaining how other words provided clues. These explanations enable "the students who do not know how to use context clues to 'look into the minds' of those students who do know how [p. 27]."
6. Each word is looked up in the dictionary; context-based guesses are verified or revised as necessary. In this way, students "discover that while the context does not 'tell the whole story' about a word, it does give important clues to its meaning [p. 27]."
7. Students read the passage that contains the words taught.

As students gain insight into the use of context for deriving word meaning, the teacher may omit the specially prepared sentences designed to illustrate the variety of such clues found in texts. Instead, the teacher identifies the words in students' texts whose meanings can readily be inferred from text information. These are written on the chalkboard along with the page numbers where they will be found, and students are directed to derive meanings for them, as in Step 4. Steps 5, 6, and 7 follow.

Schwartz and his colleagues (Schwartz & Raphael, 1985) have suggested that employing a "concept-of-definition" template can provide a framework for approaching and evaluating contextual learning. His instructional methodology focuses on having students develop expectations for adequate definitions through the process of filling out a concept-of-definition frame (see Figure 5.11) and models a step-by-step approach to achieving and utilizing such frameworks. Such processes appear productive for the development of context-sensitive independent learning strategies.

Relating New Words to What Is Already Known

Along with becoming effective independent users of context, readers must be encouraged to retain new words by connecting them to concepts and words they already know. Methods to help them activate what they already know, establish connections, organize their knowledge, and manipulate it are suggested below. Many of these can also be incorporated into a metacognitive approach to instruction, one that asks students to evaluate what they know before reading, make tentative connections to new words, establish predicitions about words they know something about, and construct questions about those that are unfamiliar. Then, after reading, students can go back and evaluate their earlier predictions about word meaning and establish or refine

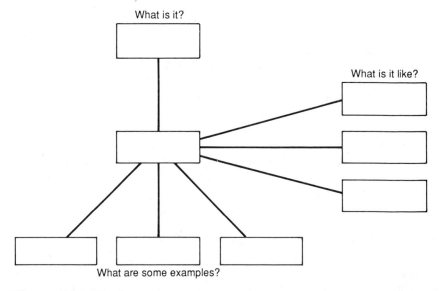

Figure 5.11 Word map. (R. Schwartz and T. Raphael, "Concept of Definition: A Key to Improving Students' Vocabulary." *The Reading Teacher, 39,* 1985. Reprinted by permission of the International Reading Association.

meanings for words that generated questions. It is important to note that all these examples are intended to be applied within the context of a selection being read or a content area being studied. It is this connection to the topic of their reading that provides the contextualization necessary for true vocabulary development.

1. *Using Graphic Organizers.* Structured overviews (Barron, 1969), semantic maps and webs (Johnson & Pearson, 1978), and vocab-o-grams (Blachowicz, 1986) all utilize a graphic model to present new words and make explicit the connections among new and already known concepts and structures. The teacher identifies the words to be taught and shows how they are related to each other in a diagram. The teacher does not present a finished diagram to the students, however. Rather, the diagram is built *with* the students as the teacher explains and discusses each new word. Students participate by recalling prior knowledge, relevant experiences, examples, and so on. The diagram then remains on display as a reference point and an aid to memory while instruction proceeds. Thus the structured overview is actually an "advance organizer" for the key concepts, as represented by the technical vocabulary, to be taught in a content area lesson or unit. As such, it may contain familiar as well as unfamiliar words, relating what is to be taught to what is already known about a particular topic.

2. *Capsule Words.* (Crist, 1975). Like the structured overview, this techniques involves the introduction of a set of words related to a single topic or idea (the capsule). However, the relationship is not graphically displayed. Instead, words are listed on the board and the teacher discusses the meaning of each word in relation to the topic, giving examples of how it is used in speaking and writing. One capsule suggested by Crist (1975) consists of words related to money: *affluent, austerity, avarice, fiscal, indigent, lucrative,* and so on. After the words are discussed, their meanings are reviewed and briefly noted in writing. Then, for practice, working in pairs, the students attempt to use the words in conversation. They are given a limited amount of time (five minutes, say) in which to use as many words as they can, each member of the pair keeping track of the words used by the other. For additional practice, students are directed to incorporate the words into a written story or essay.

3. *Brainstorming and Classification (Vacca, 1981).* In this activity students create what might be called a "concept map," a representation of what they already know in relation to a given word. Working in small groups, students are given a limited amount of time to list as many related words as they can. The teacher then combines the students' contributions into a master list, and the students group the words on the list into categories. The categories may be provided by the teacher, or the students may derive their own. This technique is often recommended as an interesting way of introducing a major concept related to a unit of study. Concepts associated with terms such as *propaganda, pollution, nutrition,* and *revolution* lend themselves to this technique, since students are likely to have a degree of knowledge in these areas.

Many other options such as exclusion brainstorming, knowledge rating (Blachowicz, 1986), and concept ladders (Gillet & Temple, 1982) are useful as formats for prereading presentation of new vocabulary. The teacher can design all these with a cognitive monitoring component by focusing on some works for prereading prediction and some for postreading evaluation and refinement.

Extending Word Meaning

Once words have been introduced and discussed, students need opportunities to relate them to real-world contexts. The following postreading follow-ups are suggested.

1. *Insult or Compliment? (Lake, 1971).* This activity works well with adjectives, since it deals with the favorable or unfavorable connotations of words. A list of words is prepared by the teacher and given to the students. The words may be unfamiliar, in which case the use of the dictionary will be involved, or they may be words that have already been defined and discussed, in which case the activity may be considered an application of word meanings. The students' task is to decide whether the use of these words to describe them personally would be a compliment or an insult. A teacher-led discussion follows.

2. *Sentence Meaning Exercises*. These can be in the form of yes–no questions, true–false statements, or fill-in-the-blank sentences. The following examples are from Hafner (1977):

> Few people make favorable impressions by making _____ remarks.
> Would a *motley* group be interesting?
> Are street urchins likely to be *squalid?* [pp. 118–19].

3. *Word Sorts*. In this activity students organize words into categories. The teacher can provide the categories, or the students may be required to search for the relationships among word concepts in order to derive their own.

4. *Post-structured Overviews*. This activity is somewhat similar to a word sort, but it allows greater freedom in portraying relationships. Students must be familiar with structured overviews or various diagram formats, however, before they can exploit this freedom. Small groups are each given a list of words and a set of 3 × 5 cards; each word on the list is written on a card. The students then "work together to decide upon a spatial arrangement among the cards which depicts the major relationships among the words [Vacca, 1981, p. 251]." Discussion of each group's solution follows, the teacher recognizing that more than one solution is possible.

A Mnemonic Device for Learning Definitions.

Acquiring word knowledge may be seen as a twofold task. It involves an initial mastery of a word's core or basic meaning—in the form of a brief definition— and it involves elaboration of that core into a full-bodied concept. We have, up to this point, emphasized the latter part of the process, because it is complex and often overlooked in the design of vocabulary instruction. Here we are concerned with the simpler task of associating words with brief definitions.

We are all familiar with mnemonic devices. We use rhymes, alphabetic and numerical sequences, and well-known dates to help us remember names, lists, telephone numbers, and the like. They involve the use of extrinsic cues to facilitate rote learning. A mnemonic for vocabulary learning has been found more effective than simple drill or contextual reading (Pressley, Levin, & Miller, 1981). Students generate a "keyword," which will serve as a mnemonic for the definition of the word to be learned. The keyword is a familiar word that is in some way similar in sound to the target word. It may, for example, rhyme with it or begin with the same syllable. The keyword is then used to construct an image (or verbal cue) that represents the meaning of the target word. For example, to remember the definition of *carlin* (an old woman), one might select *car* as the keyword and visualize an old woman riding in (or atop) a car. Then, the word *carlin* would bring to mind *car,* and this in turn would bring to mind the image of the old woman and, hence, the meaning of *carlin.* Keywords and images are sometimes difficult to create, especially for abstract words. However, the activity is likely to be interesting as well as useful to students, at least for some words or in some learning situations. It should be introduced to students accordingly—as one possible strategy for remembering definitions.

SUMMARY

We have described procedures for investigating the influence of unknown words on reading comprehension. We have also illustrated the application of those procedures in two case studies. The studies demonstrate how the assessment of word knowledge is related to the diagnostic process as a whole; they also highlight the way in which unknown words may underlie incorrect responses to comprehension questions. It was seen, in the first case study, that specific words may lead directly to incorrect answers. In the second case study, however, the relationship was less direct, and unknown words took their toll in fragmentation of overall comprehension. This latter phenomenon reflects the important principles discussed in the first part of the chapter regarding the nature of word knowledge. It reflects the fact that we ordinarily know much more about word referents than just their definitional attributes and that it is this sum total of knowledge that "drives" the comprehension process. If this knowledge is inadequate with respect to the major theme of a passage, overall comprehension is likely to be disrupted. (In other words, had Tanya been aware of the *problem* of extinction, even though she did not know the word itself, she might have been able to recognize the events described in the passage as instances of that problem.) This view of word knowledge has clear implications—supported by recent research—for the design of instruction. In general, instruction in word meanings must go beyond definitions and include experiences in which the learner constructs relationships between new words and what he or she knows. The process must be one of active learning in which self-monitoring of word knowledge and relating this knowledge to real-world situations and events are important components.

CHAPTER 6

Comprehension: Its Nature and Development

We assess comprehension by asking students questions about what they have read, by having them retell the passage or by listening to them introspect as they read. If they perform well on these tasks, we assume that reading skills are adequate for the passage in question and for others like it. If performance is poor, we hypothesize a deficiency in either vocabulary knowledge or print skill—possibly both—and explore further as discussed in earlier chapters. If further examination reveals that these two aspects of reading are not deficient, we assume that the difficulty is specific to the process of comprehension itself—to the process of integrating and organizing information across a text and connecting it with what we already know.

In other words, a diagnosis of specific difficulty in the area of comprehension is made when word identification and vocabulary knowledge have been ruled out as major factors. Thus, the assessment of comprehension plays a central role in the diagnostic process. It enables the teacher to estimate the level of materials that would be appropriate for instruction and sets a possible direction for that instruction and it also serves as a backdrop against which word-level skills and knowledge may be evaluated.

Diagnosis must be theory based; however, it is beyond the scope of this book to provide a comprehensive description of the research and theory underpinning current perspectives on comprehension. Rather, the purpose of this chapter is to focus on those aspects of comprehension which most directly affect the diagnostic process: the nature of comprehension as revealed by the behaviors of effective comprehenders; factors with the reader and within the text that affect comprehension; a framework for instructional questions that develop and assess readers' comprehension.

THE NATURE OF COMPREHENSION: WHAT GOOD READERS DO

There are many ways to view comprehension. It is "thought-getting and thought manipulating" (Huey, 1968, originally published, 1908); it is "reasoning" (Thorndike, 1917); it is the "construction . . . and progressive refinement of hypotheses in order to comprehend, interpret, or evaluate text information" (Mason et al., 1984, p. 31). These are all apt descriptions of reading and they share the characteristic of being process oriented. This redefinition of reading as an active, constructive process has stimulated a major strand of reading research over the last two decades (Pearson & Gallagher, 1983). Central to this redefinition has been the emphasis on reading as a process by which the reader interacts, or "transacts" (Rosenblatt, 1985), with the text being read. There appear to be several strategies characteristic of good readers.

Good and poor readers have been observed and compared in many situations: on experimental and school tasks (Spiro, 1980); while thinking aloud during reading (Lytle, 1982); when faced with reading difficulty that they must repair (Garner, 1987). While terminology and research methods differ, there is an emerging consensus about several behaviors that seem characteristic of skilled comprehension:

1. Good readers use what they know. They realize that reading is more than remembering exact wording from the text, it also involves reasoning, and adding their own knowledge is a critical component of the comprehension process.
2. Good readers self-question to establish what they *don't* know and what they want and need to know. For many things read, their knowledge is limited. Asking good questions helps them make hypotheses, draw analogies from experience, and set some purposes and guidelines for reading.
3. Just as good readers read with purpose, to answer their questions, to fill in knowledge, or to confirm a hunch, they integrate information across the text, add information by making inferences to build cohesion, and use structure to organize their comprehension.
4. Good readers monitor their reading. They keep track of their hunches, change them, reread, look for more evidence, but generally keep a sense of, "How am I doing? Do I understand this?" as an ongoing evaluative standard. This process is called *metacognition,* the idea that good readers are aware of their own cognitive behavior while reading and know how to use and control their strategies to read, learn, and remember ideas and information. Metacognitive theory suggests that good readers have some awareness of these processes and can call on a repertoire of strategies when something goes wrong with their comprehension. How explicit or tacit this awareness may be, however, is still a subject of debate.

WHAT INFLUENCES COMPREHENSION?

Given the model we have shared above, it is clear that influences on this process can come from many places, from the reader's knowledge and experience, from instructional input, from ways in which the author chooses to write and structure the text. Let's look, briefly, at a few of these.

The Language of the Reader

We noted earlier in this text the importance of experience for the development of the conceptual knowledge on which all comprehension is based. In Chapter 2 the significance of early literacy experiences, such as dramatic play and storytelling, being read to, and early experimentation with writing and reading, were noted. All these help develop an awareness of the transactional nature of reading and writing and give pleasure that motivates one to become an independent reader and a capable user of language, for it is this intertwining of all language functions that is a major developmental influence on reading performance.

Certainly reading is intimately related to language at many levels. Words that look alike tend to sound alike, and words and sentences have the same meaning when they are written as when they are spoken. Indeed, reading is commonly characterized as "a language process." But what is language? Is it the words we use when we speak? Or the sounds that make up the words? Or is it the organization of words in sentences? The very fact that we can ask these different questions suggests something about the answer: language involves all of these—sounds, words, and sentences.

Words, of course, have both sound (i.e., phonemes) and meaning. Thus we can say that language is a system of sounds that conveys meaning. To know a language is to know that system, its *phonology*.

But the sequence of sounds that make up a word conveys meaning only to those who already know what thing, or action, or quality of things or actions the word stands for. Knowing a language, then, involves some knowledge of its *lexicon* as well as its phonological workings.

Finally, the sequence of words that make up a phrase or sentence is meaningful only if one knows the third component of language, its *syntax*. Language, then, is not speaking or listening—these are language *behaviors*. It is, rather, a three-level system of *knowledge* that we use when we speak or listen (and when we write or read as well). It is this knowledge that enables us to express our thoughts and feelings (in speech or writing) and to understand others (in listening and reading). In other words, we use our *knowledge* of language in reading and writing just as we do in speaking and listening. And it is in this sense that we can say, "Reading is a language process."

The fact that reading and language are so closely related is sometimes taken to mean that reading comprehension—the comprehension of written language—is neither more nor less than the comprehension of spoken language. That is, it is assumed that a student need have no difficulty understanding a written passage so long as the words and sentence structures in it are familiar and express ideas that are within his or her cognitive grasp. But this is only partly true. Reading differs from listening in a number of important ways, and accommodating to these differences is part of the process of learning to read. For one thing, except in the special case of oral reading in the classroom, reading is a solitary activity whereas spoken language generally involves the presence of another human being. This may be one reason many children find it difficult to concentrate during independent (silent) reading. For another thing, written language provides less information: the stress, pause, and intonation of spoken language are absent in reading, as are the relevant social and physical contexts, which supply important nonlinguistic clues. Thus, reading places the burden of comprehension more squarely on language alone. Finally, children must become aware that written language is processed in much the same way as spoken language—that it relates to real-world situations and can be understood by reference to prior knowledge and experience. A primary purpose of language experience stories, it may be noted, is to help children develop this awareness.

For the child in the primary grades, then, the transition from spoken to written language entails a major adjustment over and above the adjustment to the print translation task. This adjustment is facilitated by the traditional practice of simulating in beginning reading materials the language of ordinary conversation. Later on, in the intermediate grades and beyond, students must adjust to written language that is more precise and tightly organized, more closely reasoned, and more complex in style and content than the language they are likely to hear in ordinary discourse. At all stages of learning to read, therefore, students need language and literacy experiences that will help them make the necessary adjustments and develop skill in reading comprehension.

The Language of the Author

Not only the language of the reader but also the language of the author—the author's lexical, linguistic, and structural decisions—affects the processes a reader must call into play to understand a selection. That what we read should make sense seems self-evident. What is not so evident, perhaps, is the fact that coherence comes about through the cooperative effort of reader and writer. Some recent investigations into the nature of comprehension make this clear. These investigations indicate that understanding connected prose is both an integrative and an inferential process. It is integrative in the sense that the reader must combine information from one sentence with that of another. For example, in reading the following lines:

(1) Father said, "Happy birthday!" as he handed Jimmy a box. (2) Jimmy opened the box, and (3) there he saw a small brown puppy.

the reader must *integrate* the information in sentences (2) and (3) in order to understand that the puppy was in the box. The reading process is inferential in the sense that the reader must often *infer* the nature of the relationship that obtains between information in two different sentences. In the sample above, the fact that the puppy was in the box must be inferred from the anaphoric referent *there* and from the fact that the puppy must *be* in the box in order to be *seen* there. In addition, the reader can infer from sentence (1) that the puppy is Jimmy's birthday present. Inferences like these are so natural that we are seldom aware of them as such. Here is another example.

> (1) He placed the big cheese carefully in a wheelbarrow. (2) His wife draped it over with a snowy white linen napkin. (3) And the farmer went down the road, pushing the cheese before him [Schlein, 1966, p. 79].

We understand, although it is not directly stated, that the farmer is not really pushing the *cheese* but pushing the wheelbarrow in which the cheese has been placed. Thus, only with the information in sentence (1) in mind can sentence (3) be correctly interpreted.

In general, the integrative process enables the reader to store information more efficiently (in condensed form), and the inferential process determines the particular way in which information is interrelated (and thus the form in which it can be condensed). In the examples given above, we saw that inferences involved linguistic elements, spatial relations, and cultural knowledge. But inferences may also involve temporal and causal relations, not to mention many others. In fact, in each of the examples, the actions in sentences (1), (2), and (3) are readily understood, through inference, as following each other in close temporal succession. And two sentences occurring together, such as *The boy was scared. This was his first race,* lead equally readily to an inference of causality.

As the examples all show, integrative and inferential processes are by no means unique to written language. Linguistic linkages and spatial, temporal, and causal relations all inhere among statements in ordinary conversation as well as in connected text. And these relations are inferred on much the same basis in both cases—on the basis of general knowledge and previous experiences with the contextual situation. Perhaps it is because these processes are so much a part of the ordinary flow of everyday language that they have so long been taken for granted and only recently become the object of serious study. In any event, like other aspects of spoken language that are important to reading progress (e.g., vocabulary knowledge and knowledge of sentence structure), it is largely through reading that these processes develop; and it is through their development that a student is able to understand more and more "difficult" prose.

The processes of integration and inference, are, as was noted, highly dependent on the reader's store of general knowledge and personal experience. There are, however, certain linguistic devices used by authors, most notably those related to text structure and coherence, that appear to facilitate the integration of information. A few of these devices are described below. The teacher will find that some familiarity with them is useful in examining instructional materials either to determine their general appropriateness or to pinpoint possible sources of difficulty for students. Comprehension is most likely to break down at those points in a text where these devices have not been used effectively by the reader (or writer).

1. *Topic Sentences.* A well-known technique for assisting the reader in integrating information involves placing a topic sentence at the beginning of a paragraph. This "points" the reader's attention to the topic of the paragraph and also to certain concepts in his or her knowledge store. The concepts thus activated serve as sources of information for making inferences (to the extent necessary) about how subsequent sentences are related to the first and to each other. For example, consider an opening sentence that reads as follows: "Tom slammed the door as he came out of the house wearing old clothes and carrying a bucket of paint." This points the reader to the idea that someone was or will be painting something (as suggested by the old clothes and, of course, the bucket of paint) and that he may be angry, possibly about having to paint. With these ideas in mind, the next sentence—"The barn was a long way off"—can be understood as (probably) telling what was to be painted. Then, if the paragraph is well structured, subsequent sentences will relate back to the slamming of the door as well as expand on the significance of the location of the barn. Thus, the opening sentence establishes a situational or conceptual context within which each sentence may be related to what has gone before. "Determining these relationships is part of the integrative process [Carpenter & Just, 1977, p. 218]."

2. *Pronouns.* Another linguistic device that signals how a sentence is related to the previous discourse is the pronoun. Typically, an author will make repeated references to the same object, event, or idea. The use of a pronoun in such instances alerts the reader to the commonality of reference and thus facilitates (at least for adults) the integration of incoming information with prior information.[1] The pronoun in effect signals that something is related to "old" information and directs the reader to search his or her memory (or the text) for the previous mention of its referent in order that he or she might integrate the new information with that already given. For example, in the paragraph:

It was a perfect *day* for flying. The air was still and there wasn't a cloud in the sky. He couldn't have asked for a better *one.*

---

[1] The unifying effect of pronouns has been demonstrated with adult subjects (Lesgold, 1972b) but not with children; apparently children (ages 8–11) can identify the antecedents of personal pronouns with a high degree of accuracy but they do not derive any advantage from them in remembering information (Lesgold, 1972a).

the pronoun *one* facilitates integration of the information in the final sentence with the "old" information about *day.*

3. *Synonyms and Synonymous Expressions.* Repeated reference to a topic that has already been introduced in discourse may also be made through synonyms. This device is a more difficult one for the reader than the pronoun. Although the antecedent of a pronoun may be ambiguous at times, the pronoun itself always clearly signals that the referent has been mentioned before. A synonym, on the other hand, is not marked as yet another word or expression for something previously mentioned and hence does not instruct the reader to search for its previous mention. If the reader does not recognize, from the referential context, that a word or expression refers to an aforementioned item, the integrative process will be disrupted and there will be some loss in comprehension. For example, notice the word *victims* in the second sentence below.

> During the past century nearly one hundred kinds of living creatures have disappeared from the face of the earth. . . . Some of the better known victims have been the European wild ox, . . . [Gilbert, 1959, p. 97].

The reader must grasp the fact that the word *victims* is coreferential with "living creatures [that] have disappeared from the face of the earth." This understanding requires an awareness that extinction comes at the hands of others, so that extinct creatures can be termed "victims." Thus familiarity with the important facets of a referential situation is often required in order for the reader to recognize coreferents.

4. *Definite Article.* The use of the definite article *the* in a text also marks a distinction between old and new information and thus facilitates comprehension. "*The* implies that the item now mentioned has a unique and specific referent that has previously been established, and therefore cues the listener/reader to match this item with only already in memory [Gourley, 1978, p. 177]." The following pairs of sentences illustrate how dependent we are on this device:

1. Yesterday Beth sold her Ford to a dealer. Jack bought *the* car [the one Beth sold] today.
2. Yesterday Beth sold her old Ford to a dealer. Jack bought *a* car [*not* the one Beth sold] today.

5. *Syntactic Structure.* The structure of a sentence is itself a device by which information may be tagged as new. In general, the information at the end of a sentence is assumed to be the new information. Thus, in the simple active sentence *John loves Mary,* "the fact that John loves someone is interpreted as old information and the identity of that someone is interpreted as new [Carpenter & Just, 1977, p. 232]." Similarly, in the passive counterpart of that sentence (i.e., *Mary is loved by John*), Mary's being loved by someone is marked as old information and the identity of that someone, John, which appears in the last part of the sentence, is the new information being conveyed. When new information is given at the beginning of a sentence, it is often marked as such in the syntactic structure, for example, through "*it* clefts": *It was Mary that John loved; It was John that loved Mary.*

    6. *Connective Terms.* The vast majority of words in a language—the nouns, verbs, adjectives, and adverbs, or so-called content words—are *referential* in nature. That is, they refer directly to particular objects, actions, attributes, and qualities. Every language includes, as well, a small set of words that are *relational*, sometimes called "function words." Unlike the linguistic devices described above, which simply signal the *advent* of new information that is related to what has gone before, relational words specify the *way* in which new information is related to the old:

> Causal relations, for instance, are typically marked by causal conjunction (e.g., "since," "because," "due to"). The description of a process may often include such temporal inter-unit links as "first," "next," and "then." Contrastive elaborations may be marked by adversative conjunctions (e.g., "however," "on the other hand"). List-like elaborations are marked by additive conjunctions such as "in addition," "likewise," and "furthermore." Conclusions are typically preceded by temporal conjunctions such as "in conclusion" or "to sum up." Finally, examples are signaled by the additive conjunctions "for example" and "for instance" [Geva, 1983, p. 385].

Thus, while nouns, verbs, adjectives, and adverbs represent the propositional content of a passage, the relational words express its structure, the connections between propositions.

The Need to Make Inferences

The linguistic devices described above help the reader relate incoming information to information previously given, and inferential processes play an important role in this aspect of comprehension. There are, however, certain types of inferences required for text coherence that are not directly motivated by linguistic cues. These might be considered "high-level" inferences. High-level inferences require the reader to add information to a text—to make certain connections that are implicit not so much in the language as in the ideation. They are necessitated by the fact that a text does not contain all the information that is needed to fully understand it. Writers—like speakers—must make assumptions about the range of knowledge and social sophistication their readers—or listeners—already possess in order not to burden them with unnecessary detail. Thus, matters of common knowledge or shared cultural values and experiences tend not to be made explicit. This means that there is almost always an implicit as well as an explicit text; understanding the implicit text is what is sometimes referred to as "reading between the lines."

The implicit text, however, does not consist of *all* inferences that *can* be made; it consists of those that must or should be made for purposes of coherence. For example, if we read that "Mike's brother took Mike to a quiet street to teach him to ride his new bike," we may infer that Mike's brother is kind and helpful and that a quiet street in this context is one with little traffic. But these inferences may not be required for text coherence; they may be only incidental, in the same way that certain details found in the explicit text—the color of the bike, perhaps—may be incidental to the story. Only if inferences are connected in some way to what has gone before or what is to come after can they be considered part of the implicit text and necessary for text coherence.

Crothers (1978) has described two general types of inferences the reader must typically make in constructing a coherent text. Both types involve adding information that relates to more than one proposition in the explicit text. In one, the information added is a connective showing how one proposition in the text is related to another. In the other, the information added is itself a proposition linking two other propositions in the text.

1. *Making Connective Inferences.* These specify the temporal, causal, or other connections between sentences, connections that are frequently left implicit in discourse text. They are equivalent to, and can usually be made explicit by, familiar terms such as *and, but, or, since/because, so/therefore/that is why, for example, this means,* and *namely.* Note how this type of inference (shown in brackets above the line of actual text) clarifies the information in the following paragraph.

Most people believe that earthworms are of little use except for fish
                                                          [for example]
bait. But scientists have found that they are very important. /Earth-
          [In this way]
worms eat soil./They make the soil better by grinding it up as it passes
              [For another example]
through their bodies./The holes that earthworms make as they burrow

in the earth make it easier for the roots of plants to enter the soil.
[For still another example]
/Earthworms use leaves to line their underground homes. These leaves
                      [Thus]
make the soil richer./Scientists have found that earthworms are the
                  [because]
earth's plowmen. /They keep stirring up the soil which helps to raise
better crops.[2]

Additional examples follow:

> Ken Baxter, who was 15 years old, wore a costume that was far too
> [since]
> young for him./He came as a bunny rabbit.
> [therefore]
> It was early Monday morning, and/the bank was nearly empty.

2. *Making Propositional Inferences.* These are "additions of new propositions to the text base [Crothers, 1978, p. 63]." They add the information and ideas that are plausible as "reasons, causes, effects, and the like [p. 63]." In the preceding paragraph on earthworms, it is stated that the leaves the earthworms use to line their underground homes "make the soil richer." Since this information represents an example of how earthworms make the soil better, the propositional inference may be drawn that "richer soil is better soil."

The Organization of Information

Beyond the processes of integration and inference, reading also involves the organization of information (both stated and implied) across many sentences—that is, at a more global level, such as that of whole paragraphs or even passages. This type of organization is made possible by what are called internal frameworks or *schemata.* Internal to the individual, these schemata are built up over relatively long periods of time out of acquired knowledge, experience, and understanding. But they are more than a simple store of information and ideas. They represent the high-level order an individual has imposed on his or her experiences (including school experiences), and at the same time, they represent the order an individual can *bring* to new experiences. New experiences are "assimilated" into existing schemata, and schemata are always in the process of changing as a result of new experiences. It may be that certain kinds of new knowledge take a long time to acquire because they require the development or rearrangement of whole systems or networks of knowledge.

Schemata are hypothetical constructs that help us understand and explain many of the cognitive behaviors we observe. In terms of reading comprehension, they help us understand why (or how) people remember certain things and forget others, or why certain things are distorted in memory. Since people tend to remember the information in a text that is important or relevant to the central theme, it is assumed that they have available some internal mechanisms for sorting and organizing incoming information. These mechanisms can be thought of as generalized ideas about the high-level organization of information. Thus, we probably have a schema that guides our reading of news stories in the daily newspapers and a different schema for reading editorials, still a different one for mystery stories, for romantic fiction, and so forth.

Educational experiences are surely an important factor in the development of an individual's schemata—in the way an individual comes to organize and understand social and natural phenomena. At present, it is by no means clear how educational practices should be modified, if at all, to facilitate this development. It seems reasonable, however, that the high-level organization of knowledge in a text should be reflected in the questions we ask if these questions are to develop and assess the ability to understand discourse.

Narrative Structure. In general, research has shown, the parts of a story that are remembered best are those that seem to "make up" the story; they are the "structurally important units." What are these "structurally important units"? Basically, they represent the kinds of information commonly found in most stories, and this commonality is probably the reason they tend to be remembered so well. What we call a story is normally made up of certain basic elements, and when people are asked to recall a story, they usually remember something about each of these elements. Apparently, through the experience of reading (or hearing) many stories, people develop a set of expectations about them. These expectations are like "slots," which people fill as they read. A story that conforms to these expectations, and thus permits the reader to find the information for each slot with relative ease, is easier to follow than one that does not. We can say that such a story is well formed (Mandler & Johnson, 1977).

The idea that stories are made up of certain common elements and that these elements are represented in the mature reader's system of knowledge is an unimportant one. It is part of the more general theory of comprehension discussed in the preceding section—the theory that organized systems of knowledge, called schemata, play a central role in discourse comprehension by serving as "advance organizers" for incoming information. Schemata are akin to the background knowledge and experience a reader brings to the reading task; in schema theory, knowledge and experience are further conceptualized as highly organized and abstract. A story schema, it is theorized, represents the reader's generalized knowledge of the elements common to most stories.

A number of investigators in the field of cognitive psychology have attempted to describe the basic elements of a well-formed story. Such descriptions are called "story grammars." These grammars categorize story events in much the same way that traditional grammar categorizes words (nouns, verbs, adjectives, etc.) and sentence parts (subject, predicate, complement, etc.). The grammars that have been developed thus far apply only to very simple stories and are often highly complex, so a detailed study of them would not be useful for our purposes. However, we will describe a simplified version of one such grammar (Rumelhart, 1975) in the belief that it may prove useful to teachers in charting the main line of a story and writing questions that pertain to it.

In Rumelhart's (1975) grammar, a story consists of a setting and one or more episodes. The *setting* includes the time and place in which the events occurred, the introduction of the main characters, and any additional information that might be necessary to make the ensuing events understandable. An *episode* consists of (1) an initiating event, (2) the reaction of the main character to that event, (3) an action on the part of the main character that is motivated by his reaction, and (4) a consequence that is a direct outcome of the action. The *initiating event* is what sets the story in motion. It may be a sudden change in the external environment (e.g., "Mary heard a strange noise in the kitchen"; "Bob came to Jill with the news that the ice was too thin for skating") or it may be some internal event (e.g., "Joe remembered that today was Lisa's birthday"; "Bill remembered he hadn't seen Joe in a long time") In either case, the initiating event sets up a situation to which the main character responds. His response is both internal and external. More specifically, the character's internal *reaction* involves some feeling, thought, desire, or goal ("Joe knew she wanted a gold necklace") and this in turn motivates him to take some external *action.* The action itself may be simple and direct ("He told his secretary to pick out a gift at Tiffany's"), or it may involve some subsidiary goals, plans, and attempts to carry them out (canceling a luncheon engagement, borrowing money from a friend, etc.). The action is likely to be the most elaborated part of the story. Finally, the action is responsible for (i.e., initiates, causes, or allows) some *consequence,* and that ends the episode. The consequence (or any other part of the episode) may then serve as the initiating event of another episode.

This story grammar, then, identifies five broad categories of story information—setting, initiating event, internal reaction, external action, and consequence. The amount of detail in each category will naturally vary from story to story, and certain categories may be omitted. Setting information may involve only a simple introduction of the protagonist (e.g., "Jenny was on her way to the library"). This is often the case in stories concerning the routines of daily life. Internal reactions are also sometimes expressed only vaguely, or not at all. A character may simply take some action in response to an external (initiating) event, as in the following example: "Mary heard a loud crash outside. [initiating event] She hurried to the window. [action]" In this example we may infer that the internal reaction was one of curiosity or, perhaps, fear. When, as here, the internal reaction is obvious given the nature of the initiating event, its omission does not interfere with comprehension. The consequence of an action may be self-evident as well (e.g., "He threw the glass across the room [and it broke]"). Finally, there may be no overt initiating event; a story may begin with a desire or goal of the protagonist, for example, "Sara was determined to win the race." In this example, the initiating event (the announcement of the race, perhaps) occurs prior to the beginning of the story and is not mentioned in the story.

In addition, the order in which story information is given may deviate from that described above. Setting information may be postponed and introduced in an episode at the point at which it is relevant; or a consequence may be described before its antecedent action: "They couldn't find the ball anywhere. Judy had hit it as hard as she could."

What story grammars do is describe in general terms the basic outline of a simple, well-formed story in Western societies. They suggest that the reader not only expects a story to be about some action or series of actions taken by a main character, but the reader also expects those actions to be purposeful. In other words, an action is expected to have both an antecedent (in the form of some initiating event and/or internal reaction) and a consequence. We believe that this view of stories can serve as a guide in the process of writing questions. If the basic outline of a story typically involves five broad categories of information, then we can think of a story as providing the answers to five categorical or generic questions, somewhat like the following:

[Setting]	1. Where and when did the story take place? Who were the main characters in the story?
[Initiating event]	2. How did it all begin? [What was the predicament of the main character(s)?]
[Action]	3. What did the main character(s) do?
[Internal reaction]	4. Why did he (she, they) do it?
[Consequence]	5. What happened as a result?

These generic questions reflect the idea of a story as a progression of related events—one thing leads to another, which leads to still another, and so on. With these questions in mind, following the initial reading of the story, the teacher should be able to derive a set of questions that reflects the main story line. There may, of course, be more than one question in any category, and some categories may be too sparsely represented in the story—too vague or nonspecific—to be questioned. Thus the generic questions should make us sensitive to any ambiguities, missing information, or other weaknesses of the story structure.

Expository Structure. While the structures of stories are familiar to most school-age readers, the structures of expository text, such as those of social studies and science textbooks, are much less predictable. Not only is there greater variation in expository structures, but many differing structures can be used and intermixed within a single article or chapter.

As is true with narrative structure, familiarity with expository structures enhances comprehension (McGee & Richgels, 1985) and can also form the basis for asking sensible, structurally coherent questions. When one is analyzing expository structures, it is sometimes useful to ask three basic questions:

1. What is the topic?
2. How does the author organize the information about the topic?
3. How could I summarize the author's message?

A conventional or informal outline or map of selection content can help isolate the topic and the organizational pattern (See Figure 6.3 for an example.) The most common patterns of overall expository organization, sometimes called macrostructures, are the following:

1. Chronological order—shows a sequential pattern of ideas as they happened in time.
2. Cause and effect—indicates interaction of at least two aspects of a situation, one of which causes the other to come about.
3. Comparison and contrast—looks at the similarities and differences of at least two items.
4. Problem and solution—indicates an interaction of at least two aspects of a situation, one of which is the problem and the others of which provide a solution.
5. Argument—presents the positive and negative aspects of a situation.
6. Category and example—presents a superordinate category with subordinate members; sometimes linked with description.
7. Simple listing—gives a list in which order is not relevant. Can be descriptive.

Looking at the topic, at the information presented, and at its organization is essential to making a clear summary of the author's message and is a prerequisite for the critical thinking necessary to evaluate that message. As we will see later in this chapter, it is also essential for developing good diagnostic questions or retelling formats.

QUESTIONS AND THE DEVELOPMENT OF COMPREHENSION

There is ample documentation showing that the use of questions in instruction has a profound effect on the development of comprehension strategies. Instructional programs focusing on the extraction of literal information engender strategies in the readers to help them note details; programs stressing critical, evaluative and other higher level tasks produce in the reader strategies for higher level thinking (Davis & Hunkins, 1966; Gallagher & Aschner, 1963; Wixson, 1984). The teacher's ability to formulate good questions is critical to the development of pupil comprehension strategies and is also essential for effective assessment.

We come now to the heart of the matter. What is a good set of comprehension questions? Of the many questions that may be asked about any given selection of text, which ones will assess fairly the comprehension skill of the student who reads it?

This question has engaged the attention of experts in reading, and in education generally, for a very long time; much has been written about the kinds of questions teachers should ask. In general, teachers are urged to ask a variety of questions, in order to give students the opportunity to respond in a variety of ways to the materials they read. Teachers are also advised, more specifically, to avoid overemphasizing questions that require only memory for directly stated information. They are encouraged, above all, to focus on questions that require high-level thinking, in order to develop high-level cognitive processes. In short, questions have traditionally been approached from the standpoint of the mental processes required to answer them.

A major problem with this approach is that it is difficult to implement. A number of question-classification schemes based on this approach have been developed over the years (e.g., Barrett, 1976; Bloom, Engelhardt, Furst, Hill, & Krathwohl, 1956), but even the simpler ones require distinctions between levels or types of thought that are both difficult to make and "not warranted by the current state of our knowledge about language and cognition [Anderson, 1972, p. 149]." Moreover, questions that appear to elicit high-level thinking because they cannot be answered from directly stated information may actually be quite trivial. Sanders (1966) points out that "thinking" questions cannot really be derived from insignificant subject matter, and he gives the following examples to illustrate:

TEXT: This little pig went to market.
QUESTIONS: Why? Did he go to buy or to be bought? . . . If to buy, what and for whom? Is he an informed buyer, the sort who would study the Buyers' Index and Consumers' Guide? . . . If he is to be sold, what price will he bring? What will be the effect on the market price . . . ?
TEXT: This little pig had roast beef.
QUESTIONS: Would you consider roast beef proper food for a pig? Which is better, nutritionally speaking, rare or well-done meat? (p. 171).

Sander's caution is particularly relevant for the field of reading, where the "instructional diet" of simple story materials may provide little "food for thought." That is to say, the stories designed for developing basic reading skills do not always lend themselves to thoughtful discussion, and attempts to use them for this purpose may be unproductive.

Another problem with the mental-process or levels-of-thinking approach to questions is that it does not recognize a distinction between literal questions that pertain to important information and those that pertain to incidental detail, a point more recently raised by Beck and McKeown (1981). Guszak (1967) alluded to this problem several years ago in his now-classic study of the kinds of questions teachers actually ask. He found that approximately 70 percent of the questions were of a literal nature, requiring only recognition (locating information in the passage) or recall (answering from memory) of factual information. While this result is frequently cited as evidence that teachers ask too many literal questions, Guszak himself was more critical of the quality of the questions. That is, he did not feel that a 7-out-of-10 proportion of literal questions was necessarily objectional; he objected, rather, to the fact that many of the questions involved "retrieval of the trivial factual makeup of stories." It appeared to him that students were likely to miss "literal understanding" of story plots, events, and sequences "in their effort to satisfy the trivial fact questions of the teacher [p. 233]." But Guszak recognized, at the same time, that teachers could not employ more appropriate questioning patterns without clearer guidelines.

In sum, the traditional focus on levels of thinking in the design of questions does not effectively guard against trivialization of either nonliteral or literal questions. We believe, therefore, that questions should be approached from the standpoint of their relationship to the text as a whole rather than from the standpoint of the mental processes they elicit. Accordingly, we shall consider questions as either *related* to the text or *beyond* the text, according to whether or not they pertain to the information and ideas set down by the author. We shall also recommend that text-related questions be designed to follow the author's train of thought—that text-related questions as a whole reflect the story as a coherent whole. Beyond-text questions, on the other hand, will be those that take off where the author left off, so to speak. They will go "beyond the lines" and generalize about the author's ideas, extending them to other contexts or relating them to other ideas and issues. In a sense, these questions will relate to the ultimate purposes of reading—the enjoyment and appreciation of literature and the acquisition of knowledge and insight into human affairs. They will consist largely of the types of questions generally categorized and valued as thought provoking.

The rationale for our approach to questions is not just that mental process taxonomies are difficult to work with or that good thinking questions are difficult to derive from simple story materials. It lies also in recent insights into comprehension as a discourse process. These insights (described more fully in a later section) suggest that understanding "what it says" is not a trivial matter. In order to understand the communicative intent of a passage, readers must engage in levels of thought that are as simple or complex as the ideas communicated. They must select, combine, and integrate passage information, including information that is not explicitly stated. This means that text-related questions will generally require both literal and nonliteral (inferential) comprehension and that they must reflect the author's general intent as expressed in the passage as a whole.

In addition, our approach preserves the basic distinction between the ideas of the author (text related) and those of the reader (beyond text), thereby emphasizing that what is written must be understood in its own right before it can be explored in greater depth. The beyond-text questions will stimulate the reader to use the text as a springboard for reflection and conjecture. These questions will also draw on information and ideas that, while peripheral to the text, may be important to the reader.

A good set of questions, then, will consist of at least two basic parts or distinct types. One part will be text related, in the sense that it will adhere closely to the significant content of the text, including the inferences directly motivated by text coherence. The other will go beyond the text as a communicative entity and explore its general implications and incidental detail. (Sadow, 1982) The first part will assess the student's comprehension of the passage as a whole—of the story told therein or the aspect of human knowledge conveyed—and will be a major factor in determining the suitability of like materials for instruction. The second part will assess the student's ability to use textual detail to broaden his or her knowledge and understanding of physical and social phenomena. The difference between these two parts is illustrated by the following example.

In the opening of *Charlotte's Web* (E. B. White, 1952), Fern learns that her father is on his way to the barn, carrying an ax, with the intent of "doing away" with the runt pig that was born the night before. Fern's mother explains that the pig would probably die anyway. Outraged at the "unfairness" of killing the pig "just because it is weak and little," Fern runs after her father and pleads for the pig's life. He gives in to her plea, saying, "I'll let you start it on a bottle, like a baby. Then you'll see what trouble a pig can be [p. 3]." The text-related questions on this passage would establish the facts of the story qua story—who did what, why they did it, and what happened as a result:

1. What is a runt pig? Who is Fern? Where does she live?
2. What was Fern's father going to do?
3. Why was Fern's father going to "do away" with the pig?
4. How did Fern feel when she learned that her father was going to kill the pig?
5. What did Fern do about it?
6. How did her father respond to her?

Notice that the questions follow the sequence of the story and that they are relatively independent of each other. That is, inability to answer (2), for example, does not preclude the possibility of answering (3) and (4). In fact, (3) and (4) give the answer to (2).

The beyond-text questions, on the other hand, might take up the conflict between Fern's point of view and her father's in terms of the more universal conflict between a child's point of view and an adult's. They might also (or alternatively) take up the conflict between the father's point of view as a farmer and as a father. For example:

1. Why did Fern's father "give in" to her plea? (Was he convinced that it would be unjust to kill a runt pig or was he merely being kind to his daughter?)
2. Why would Fern's father believe that it was all right to kill the pig?

It is clear that these questions cannot be answered from a reading of the passage, and it is in this sense that they are beyond the text or reader based. It is also clear that they represent what might be called "literary analysis." If the students have read another story in which there is a similar conflict between young and old or between the dual roles and responsibilities of an individual, the teacher may ask that it be recalled and contrasted with this one. Other beyond-text questions that might be asked include:

3. What was Fern's mother's reaction to the father's intention to kill the pig?
4. Fern's mother said, "It will probably die anyway." Why would that be likely to happen?
5. Fern's father said, "A weakling makes trouble." What is a weakling? In what way would it make trouble?
6. If you were Fern, would you be willing to take care of the pig?

Text-Related and Beyond-Text Questions

The insights discussed above are important for several reasons. They highlight the reading process as a global one, in which the reader is actively engaged in constructing a unified representation of text information, and they heighten our sensitivity to the "connectedness" of written prose. They strongly imply that there can be no substitute for "real" reading experiences, that is, for experiences with a variety of types of discourse text. Another important implication is that materials may be difficult to understand if they require inferences that are beyond the reader's experiential or knowledge base. Finally, these insights provide a rational basis for the design of text-related questions. They help us recognize that while such questions do not pertain to the deepest levels of meaning or the ultimate purposes of reading in the way that beyond-text questions do, they are an important intermediary step.

Recent insights emphasize, further, that text-related questions should pertain to the ideas and information that contribute in some way to the text as a whole, for it is a mistake to confuse comprehension with memory for incidental detail or even for incidental inferences. In fact, these insights suggest that such details are frequently forgotten because they bear so little connection to other textual information and, therefore, are only superficially processed. For example, it may make no difference, in terms of other events in a story, whether a certain incident took place in the morning or afternoon, last week or this week, or whether it was first noticed by one story character or by another. If it does not, the reader has no opportunity to relate these items of information to subsequent events nor any need to relate them to earlier ones. Similarly, in an adventure tale about a series of incidents, if it makes little difference whether the incidents occurred in one order or another, there will be minimal processing of, and little memory for, the sequence of events.

In short, the process of following the main story line or thread of an argument does not tend to reinforce or "activate" nonessential facts, and memory for them is likely to be spotty and idiosyncratic. Such facts may or may not be remembered, but good comprehension of discourse does not imply that they are likely to be. Rather, good comprehension means grasping the vital information in the text and the train of thought (the low-level and high-level inferences) that binds this information together.

If text-related quesitons involve both "reading the lines" and "reading between the lines," then beyond-text questions may be conceived as "reading beyond the lines." These questions also involve inferential processes, but the inferences are more in the nature of "grand conclusion[s] from a number of explicit and implicit propositions combined [Crothers, 1978, p. 55]." That is, they are not cued by specific liguistic devices nor by any specific inferences that are motivated by text coherence—they do not "connect" specific statements in the text with each other. It is in this sense that beyond-text questions may be said to involve the "deeper" levels of meaning. And as with text-related inferences, the reader must draw on his or her fund of general knowledge to arrive at these deeper meanings.

In the case of story materials, beyond-text questions generally call on the reader to apply his or her knowledge of human events, actions, and feelings to a given situation. For example, in a story about a young boy whose father and brothers are all fishermen, we learn that the thing the boy wanted most was to go fishing with his father. We can understand this desire in terms of boys in general—most boys would think going fishing is fun. But we can also understand it, with reference to this boy in particular, in terms of boys' desires to do what their fathers and older brothers do, to be like them, to feel grown-up, and so on. In other words, we understand the story character's feelings and appreciate the story more fully because we recognize those feelings as consistent with what we know about little boys in general. Beyond-text questions should assess this application of knowledge.

Another example is provided by Miriam Schlein's (1966) story, "The Big Cheese." In this story a farmer decides to give his finest cheese to the king. Here we recognize the farmer's pride in his work, and it is through knowledge of this type of pride that we understand why the farmer would elect to give his cheese to the king instead of selling it in the open market and allowing "just anyone" to eat it. Also involved, of course, is the special feeling that citizens may have toward their leaders. And parallel to the farmer's pride is the pride shown by a goatherd, who insists that cheese made from goats' milk is better than that made from cows' milk. For this story, too, then, beyond-text questions require an examination of the actions and reactions of story characters from the point of view of their consistency with certain general ideas about human events. As we ask such questions, we help students develop these ideas, and we help them see the relevance of these stories to the "human condition."

It should be noted that a particular question may be either text related or beyond the text, depending on the answer that is expected (or given) (Pearson & Johnson, 1978). A text-related answer can be justified with specific reference to the text. A beyond-text answer is one that is based on insights or logical reasoning that is not clearly implied in the text. Consider the following question and some possible answers concerning "The Big Cheese" (Schlein, 1966).

QUESTION: Why did the goatherd suggest that he and the farmer taste the cheese?

ANSWER A: Because it was lunchtime and he was hungry.

ANSWER B: Because he didn't believe it was the best cheese (because it was not made from goats' milk).

ANSWER C: Because he thought the farmer should be sure it was the best cheese before he gave it to the king.

Answers B and C pertain directly to the goatherd's own statements: "Then how can it be the best cheese ever made? The finest . . . cheeses are always made from goats' milk [p. 80]," and "How can you present the king with a cheese you do not know tastes best? [p. 81]." So answers B and C are text related and, as such, show good comprehension of the story line. Answer A goes beyond the text, since there is no clear implication in the text that the goatherd's motives are not as he represents them. This answer, then, is ambiguous with respect to the student's comprehension of the text itself. It could represent good insight into the fact that people sometimes have ulterior motives. On the other hand, it could be that the student simply failed to understand the persuasive arguments of the goatherd, as given in the text, and that his or her answer is really a "stab in the dark."

However, beyond-text questions need not be confined to issues involving human goals, desires, and feelings. There is much information of a factual nature to be gained from stories. Teachers' questions should help students "pull" this information out and make it part of their general fund of knowledge—part of the background knowledge they will be able to bring to subsequent stories. For purposes of assessment, these questions may help the teacher evaluate the adequacy of the student's background knowledge in relation to story content. This is important, since it is often a lack of some specific information that leads to misunderstanding of story events. In "The Big Cheese" (Schlein, 1966), for example, students must understand that farmers *sell* their products at a "market" (many city children may think of "markets" only as places where families buy food). They must also grasp the fact that cheese may be made of milk from goats as well as from cows and that in "olden" days a farmer might transport his products by wheelbarrow.

Constructing Comprehension Questions

In general, as was explained above, text-related questions recapitulate the main story line or central ideas in a text. Unfortunately, there are no simple prescriptions or rules to follow in constructing these questions, no objective methods for determining that one idea or piece of information is essential or more important than another. Here teachers must rely on their own clear understanding of the text to be used, based on a careful reading, rereading, and analysis of it. One way to proceed, though not necessarily the only way, is as follows.

The teacher should first read the text for an overview of its content and organization, much as would be done for any other material of its kind. On this reading, the teacher will also gain insight into what the passage is like, which parts stand out in memory, and which are readily lost. The teacher should then try to construct a set of questions such that the answers will represent a broad outline of its significant content. A second reading of the text will enable the teacher to "fill in" the outline. A third and final reading will suggest some beyond-text questions. These are described more fully below, then illustrated with the questions that would result with a typical passage. Because of their differences in form, content, and purpose, story materials and nonfiction will be treated separately.

Story Materials. On the first reading the teacher should simply follow the story line (i.e., find out who did what, why they did it, and how it all came out). This reading will form the intuitive base for the group of questions that will reflect the causal essence of the story and assess story comprehension. Highly relevant to this step are the results of some recent investigations into story structure and story recall.

The derivation of text-related questions based on story structure constitutes the first step in the process of writing questions. For the second step, a second reading of the story will usually be necessary. In this step, the story outline constructed in step 1 will be rounded out with important details. With very short stories, all or most of the details may be important for the story line. In fact, the shorter the story, the less likely it is to include incidental detail. With longer stories, however, many details are likely to be forgotten, particularly if they do not carry the story forward.

This process of question construction will be illustrated for the third-grade story, *The Restless Kangaroo*, shown in Figure 6.1. The reader is encouraged to study the story and derive a set of questions that reflect the important content and structure of the story.

Figure 6.1 Narrative passage.

The Restless Kangaroo

The zoo had a problem. The problem was Tanga who was the mother kangaroo.

She had begun to take her joey, as kangaroo babies are called, out of her pouch in the night. For two mornings Pete, who is the head keeper at the zoo, had found the cold little joey on the dirt floor of the kangaroo pen.

Each time Pete rubbed the joey with a towel until he was warm. Then he tucked him back into Tanga's pouch. And Tanga stood still because she was a gentle kangaroo.

But on the third morning the joey was found on the floor again.

"This is a problem," the zoo director said. "The joey is too young to be out of Tanga's pouch."

"It is a new problem," said Pete. "Tanga has been a good mother. She always kept her other joeys safe until they were older."

"We must find out why she does this now," said the director. "If this goes on the joey might catch a chill. He may even die."

"Tonight I will stand watch at Tanga's pen," said Pete. "Perhaps I can learn why she puts her joey on the floor."

"That is a good idea," said the director.

When night came to the zoo, Pete went to the animal barn where Tanga lived. He sat down on a chair in front of her low gate.

In the next pen the great elk, with its wide antlers, snorted. On the other side of Tanga's pen a zebra stamped its feet and then a deer sneezed.

The llamas and camels and the buffalo gazed over their gates at Pete for a long time. It was plain that they were surprised to see him there at that time of night.

But at last they all became used to him and, one by one, they went to sleep.

And Tanga lay down on her side in her own pen on her clean straw bed and went to sleep also.

The big barn was quiet and dark but for the soft glow of one light up near the roof.

Pete yawned and leaned back in his chair. He had worked hard all day. He was sleepy and it was hard to keep awake. But he did keep awake.

After a while he heard a "scritch-scratch" in the stillness. He stood up and looked into the shadows of Tanga's pen.

Tanga was sound asleep. But something was moving. It was the joey's tiny paw.

It waved back and forth, back and forth, out of the opening of Tanga's

Figure 6.1 *(continued)*

pouch. Then it dug down into the straw and Pete could hear the same "scritch-scratch" that he had heard before.

When the joey pulled a pawful of straw into her pouch, Tanga kicked her long back feet. But she did not wake up.

Soon the joey pulled another pawful of straw into the pouch. This time Tanga gave a loud sigh.

Without opening her eyes she turned on her back. She lifted the joey with her front paws and dropped him into the straw. Then she turned over on her side and was still again. And she hadn't waked up at all.

The joey scratched around a bit and then he too was still.

"I have found the answer to our problem." Pete whispered to himself. "Tanga's joey is a naughty baby."

He tip-toed into the pen and picked up the shivering joey and tucked him in his jacket. Then he felt inside Tanga's pouch with gentle hands. Besides the straw, he found sharp pebbles from the dirt floor of the pen.

"Poor Tanga!" Pete said. "No wonder you put your joey out in the cold! No kangaroo likes to be scratched by straw and pebbles!"

He cleaned her pouch and Tanga opened her eyes and blinked her long lashes as if she were saying "Thank you."

"There, Tanga," said Pete when he was through. "Go back to sleep. Things will be better from now on."

He took the joey to the zoo office. There he rolled him in a towel and put him in a box to keep warm.

When morning came Pete told the zoo director what happened.

"You see," he said, "when Tanga's joey wakes up he likes to play with the straw and pebbles. Then he takes them into his own pouch-bed. He is a naughty little kangaroo."

The director smiled. "I don't think he is naughty," he said. "He is just a restless little kangaroo. But we will fix it so this will not happen again."

As soon as all the other zoo keepers heard the story about Tanga and her restless kangaroo, they went right to work.

They moved Tanga and her joey away from the animal barn and into a big cage in the zoo's main building. The cage had a smooth floor with no pebbles. And instead of straw for a bed Pete gave Tanga a blanket.

From then on there was no more trouble. When the restless joey awoke at night he pulled and tugged on the blanket until he was tired. Then he went back to sleep.

The zoo's problem was solved. The joey was not found out of Tanga's pouch again until he was old enough to climb in and out by himself — which he did, over and over again, until he finally grew so big that he could no longer fit.

(From *With Skies and Wings,* Level 9, pp. 207–213. In *Reading 360,* published by Ginn and Company, 1969. Story by Edythe R. Warner, reprinted by permission.)

A typical set of questions that might result from the first and second steps of question writing is shown in Figure 6.2. While the questions derived during step 1 are quite predictable, those written during step 2 result from a less systematic process. There are no hard and fast rules regarding questions of detail; teachers must be guided by their own sense of story cohesiveness.

In examining the questions generated for *The Restless Kangaroo,* it is interesting to note the relationship between step-1 and step-2 questions. That is, there is usually only one correct answer to a step-2 question, whereas step-1 questions give the student more latitude in framing his or her answer. More importantly, step-2 questions are often implicit in one or another step-1 question, so that step-2 questions will often be answered in response to a step-1 question. Thus, step-2 questions often serve as clarifying "probes" where the answer to a step-1 question is incomplete or vague or suggests a slight misunderstanding of the question. For example, in response to question S10 (Figure 6.2), one child said, "They put him in a box," suggesting that he did not understand the zoo's final solution to the problem. However, in answering question D4, this child said, "There was no straw to put in the pouch," showing clear understanding of the solution.

The third and final step in the question-writing process is the creation of beyond-text items. As was already explained, these deal with the story as an exemplar of something interesting and important about the way people live, work, play, and otherwise conduct their affairs, or with some thematic issue or communicative intent of the author. In searching out ideas for these questions, it is useful to look to each of the five story elements for suggestions. The zookeeper's internal reaction (worry) upon finding the joey on the floor of the cage suggests that he is knowledgeable regarding the care of animals. A good question would be, "From this story, can you tell what a good zookeeper must know or be able to do?" The zookeeper's knowledge and devotion to duty, evident in the action he took to find out about the problem, suggests the following question: "If you were in charge of a zoo, would you hire Pete as a zookeeper? Why (or why not)?"

Expository Materials. Questions concerning expository texts are constructed on the same principle as narrative questions, but here it is the traditional outline form that guides the procedure. An outline shows the relative importance of text ideas and ideally, it also specifies how ideas a related to one another. That is, it depicts, in graphic form (the indentation and letter–number system), the superordinate–subordinate structure of passages and expresses, in words, the particular kind of superordinate–subordinate relationship that inheres between each topic and its subtopics.

For example, Figure 6.3 gives three possible outlines of an expository passage on trees. Outline 1 shows only the superordinate–subordinate relationships. There are, however, two different *kinds* of relationship between the subtopics (A, B, C, and D) and the major topic, trees. Clearly, subtopics A and B

Figure 6.2 Questions based on narrative passage.[a]

Story structure category	Story structure questions (step 1)	Detail questions (step 2)
Setting	S1. Where did this story take place? S2. Who is Pete? S3. Who is Tanga?	D1. What is a joey? [What is a baby kangaroo called?]
Initiating event/problem	S4. What was the problem that the zoo was having with the kangaroos?	D2. What did Pete do with the joey each time he found him on the floor of the pen?
Internal reaction	S5. Why was that a problem? [Why were the zookeepers worried about the baby kangaroo being out of the mother's pouch during the night?]	
Action	S6. What did Pete, the zookeeper, do to find out about the problem? [Why did Pete stay up all night watching the kangaroo pen?]	
Consequence	S7. What did Pete find out when he watched the kangaroos all night? [What did the joey do in the middle of the night?] S8. Why did Tanga take the joey out of her pouch at night? S9. Why did the joey put the straw in the mother's pouch? S10. What did Pete do to solve the problem for the kangaroos?	D3. What did Pete find when he felt inside the mother kangaroo's pouch? D4. How did the new pen solve the problem? [How was the new pen different from the old one?] D5. What did the joey do in the new pen when he woke up in the middle of the night?

[a] The questions shown in brackets suggest some alternatives in terms of wording and/or emphasis that seem to be equally appropriate.

Figure 6.3 Possible outlines of an expository passage on trees.

OUTLINE 1	OUTLINE 2	OUTLINE 3

Main Topic: Trees

A. Deciduous
  1. Maple
  2. Birch
B. Evergreen
  1. Spruce
  2. Fir
C. Shade
  1. Maple
  2. Oak
D. Ornamental
  1. Dogwood
  2. Hawthorn

Main Topic: Trees

A. Kinds
  1. Deciduous
    a. Maple
    b. Birch   } Examples
  2. Evergreen
    a. Spruce
    b. Fir   } Examples
B. Uses
  1. Shade
    a. Maple
    b. Oak   } Examples
  2. Ornamental
    a. Dogwood
    b. Hawthorn   } Examples

Main Topic: Trees

Kinds [
A. Deciduous
  1. Maple
  2. Birch   } Examples
B. Evergreen
  1. Spruce
  2. Fir   } Examples
]

Uses [
C. Shade
  1. Maple
  2. Oak   } Examples
D. Ornamental
  1. Dogwood
  2. Hawthorn   } Examples
]

are *kinds* of trees whereas C and D are *uses* of trees. A third type of relationship inheres between each set of minor subtopics, that is, each (1) and (2), and their superordinates, A, B, C, and D: subtopics (1) and (2) are *examples* of their superordinate topics. Thus, the subtopics of an outline are always elaborations of a topic, but there are many different kinds of elaborations. A good outline makes these explicit in some way or other. Two possible ways are shown in outlines 2 and 3 in Figure 6.3.

In addition to the relationships exemplified here—kinds, uses, and examples—subtopics may be related to their topics as causes, effects, functions, parts, characteristics, procedural steps, chronological sequence, and so on.

The first step, then, in formulating expository questions is the preparation of a complete outline. This is a relatively easy step with well-organized, clearly written passages, such as the one on forest fires in Figure 6.4. The reader should study this passage and develop an outline showing the relationships among the different pieces of information it contains.

Next, the reader should compare the outline developed with that shown in Figure 6.5. Note that there is little, if any, extraneous detail; most of the information in the passage can be subsumed under a few topics.

The next step is to derive questions from the outline using procedures similar to those described for the questions based on narrative selections. Typically, one question may be written to focus on the main topic and one or two questions may be developed to explore each of the subtopics in the

Figure 6.4 Expository passage about forest fires.

Forest Fires

An important problem for forest rangers is how to protect forests from being ruined by fire. Each year thousands of trees are destroyed by fire. Careless campers do not put their fires completely out. Cigarettes are left to burn on the dry ground. These small fires in dry forests can burn thousands of trees. One solution to the forest fire problem is to man lookout stations and use helicopters to spot fires. Fires that are spotted right away can be put out before they get too big to handle. Then fires will cause less damage to the forest. A second solution to the problem is to have experts and bulldozers ready to move in quickly to fight the fire. Bulldozers can throw huge amounts of dirt on a fire in a short time. The dirt helps put the fire out quicker. A third solution is to build fire lanes in the forests. Fire lanes are long breaks in the forest where there are no trees. These breaks prevent the fire from spreading and getting too large.

(From "The Influence of Metacognitive Knowledge of Expository Text Structure on Discourse Recall" by L. M. McGee, in J. A. Niles and L. A. Harris (Eds.) *New Inquiries in Reading Research and Instruction* [Thirty-first Yearbook of the National Reading Conference. Rochester, NY: National Reading Conference, 1982].)

Figure 6.5 Outline based on expository passage about forest fires.

MAIN TOPIC: **How forest rangers protect
forests from fire damage**

   A. Causes of fire
     1. Camp fires
     2. Cigarettes

   B. Solutions to Problem
     1. Early detection
       a. Lookout stations
       b. Helicopters
     2. Quick extinction
       a. Bulldozers — throw dirt on fire
       b. Experts
     3. Preventing spread of fires
       a. Fire lanes

outline. The reader should develop questions based on the passage outline and compare them with those shown in Figure 6.6.

Free and Elicited Recall

As an alternative to direct questioning, the teacher might consider an aided recall procedure. The student is instructed to recount everything he or she can remember about the passage. The free, or unprompted, retelling reflects the student's assessment of the important story elements, and the order in which they are told gives the teacher a clue to the organization the reader has abstracted from or imposed upon the passage. It is also possible to make an evaluation of the reader's oral language and vocabulary use based on the language he or she uses to retell the selection.

Then the teacher helps the student fill in missing information by asking specific questions about important ideas or events that were not mentioned. This means the teacher must be prepared with a list or outline of the main passage content against which the student's retelling can be checked and evaluated. It would be much the same kind of outline as was recommended for the preliminary step in constructing questions. Open-ended questions (e.g., "Tell me more about _____"; "Explain what you meant by _____") can be used to elicit more information following free recall, or the questions can be more directive. It is important to include this step since several investigations have found that much more information is normally stored than is produced in a free recall task, particularly among poorer readers (e.g., Bridge & Tierney, 1981).

Figure 6.6   Questions based on outline of expository passage about forest fires.

1. What is the important problem that forest rangers must deal with? (protect trees from fire damage; forest fires)

2. How do many forest fires get started? (cigarettes and campfires)

3. How are lookout stations and helicopters used in solving the problem of forest fires? (spot fires in early stages)

4. How are bulldozers used in fighting fires? (throw dirt on fire)

5. What are fire lanes? (areas that are bare of trees)

6. How do fire lanes prevent fire damage to forest? (prevent spread of fires)

*7. The passage mentioned that "experts" are needed in fighting fires. What sort of thing might experts know that would be helpful in fighting fires? (wind conditions; how and where to approach fires; methods of fighting fires)

*8. What might be done to prevent fires from getting started in the first place? (punish wrongdoers; supervise campgrounds; educate people)

* Beyond-text question

SUMMARY

In this chapter we have presented a theoretical overview of current conceptualizations of comprehension, emphasizing that it is an active, constructive process. We have also examined some reader and textual variables that affect this process. Last, we have applied this knowledge to the issue of what makes good questions, stressing both their connection to the text (the story map and the central story issue of the author) and the need for questions to go beyond the text to foster inference and develop literary appreciation.

CHAPTER 7

Reading Comprehension: Diagnosis and Instruction

An assessment of reading comprehension serves a twofold purpose. It enables the teacher to make an informed decision regarding the level of materials that would be appropriate for instruction, and it alerts the teacher to a student's specific instructional needs. Such an assessment is generally undertaken when there is some question concerning a student's current placement in instructional materials or the type of instructional emphasis that would enable the student to make better progress. For the most part these questions arise when a student is not performing well during daily lessons. However, they should arise when a student is performing extremely well, for instructional materials should be neither so difficult that the student can have little success with them nor so easy as to require little thought or attentional effort. Thus, the student who is always able to answer the teacher's questions may need more challenging materials, while the student who can seldom answer questions correctly may need less demanding ones. Teachers must make every effort to see that instructional materials are optimal from this point of view.

In addition, the teacher must be aware of the area(s) of reading in which a student is relatively weak and, consequently, requires special attention. A student is considered to require special attention in the area of comprehension when his or her performance on a comprehension test is inadequate (below a certain level) *and* the assessment and probe procedures described in preceding chapters indicate that print skills and vocabulary knowledge are not prime sources of difficulty. That is, a diagnosis of comprehension difficulty is made when poor comprehension cannot be attributed to the areas of reading underlying comprehension.

In this chapter we will consider the instructional level and special needs of students with relative weakness in the area of comprehension. We will discuss, first, criteria for establishing whether materials are at an appropriate level of difficulty for use in reading instruction. Then we will describe the general types of comprehension problems that students may encounter and a procedure for diagnosing an individual student's major problem along with alternative diagnostic possibilities. Finally, we will suggest some instructional techniques for helping students gain proficiency in comprehension and for carrying out further diagnostic teaching.

INSTRUCTIONAL LEVEL

In general, materials are considered suitable for instruction when the student can answer correctly a certain proportion of the questions asked. Unfortunately, there is no firm agreement among reading authorities regarding the exact proportion. Recommendations range from 60 to 75 percent. Harris and Sipay (1980) suggest that 60 percent is "marginal." They also note that a 50–60 percent criterion may be used with students of limited experiential background if "more time than usual will be spent developing the concepts and vocabulary necessary for understanding the stories [p. 185]." Betts (1954), on the other hand, recommends 75 percent comprehension for oral reading and a substantially higher percentage for "silent reading to locate specific information." In the procedures recommended by Betts, however, the oral reading of a passage is *not* the student's first encounter with the text; it is a rereading after silent reading. (Betts is a strong advocate of the principle that silent reading should precede oral reading, although he acknowledges that oral reading at sight provides valuable information regarding word recognition skills.) Nevertheless, we believe that, with well-designed questions, a criterion of 75 percent is not unreasonable even for a first reading. We also believe, with Harris and Sipay, that this criterion should be applied flexibly. There are certain conditions under which a student who scores below 75 percent on a diagnostic passage may benefit from instruction in materials at the same level of difficulty. In general, such conditions obtain when a student is relatively strong in vocabulary knowledge and, if given an opportunity to reinspect the passage, is able to answer correctly several questions that were initially missed. That is, the student would be proficient in basic language skills but lacking in the ability to interrelate and organize passage information. In addition, the teacher must be in a position to provide instruction that would take account of the student's relative difficulty with this aspect of comprehension.

It was noted earlier that diagnosis is usually undertaken to shed light on difficulties observed during classroom activities in reading. It is therefore, puzzling when students who have been selected for diagnosis perform well on a diagnostic passage that is at the same level of difficulty as their classroom materials. In such cases, the teacher will want to consider, first of all, whether the reading selection used in the diagnosis is in fact typical of classroom materials. It could be considerably easier in style, structure, and content, even if it came from the same reader level. If the passage appears to be typical, then classroom difficulties could be due to inattention, disinterest, difficulty in working in a group setting, differences in topic and type of reading material, and the like. It must also be recognized that the student has probably put forth a higher level of effort during the diagnosis that can reasonably be expected during daily classroom routines. Still, the diagnostic performance gives evidence of available strength. The teacher should therefore discuss the results of the diagnosis with the student and elicit his or her interpretation or views on the matter. The teacher's expression of interest and concern will undoubtedly be important to the student and may, in itself, help the student become more deeply involved in reading activities. Alternatively, the student may have some insights into his or her own difficulty that will be useful to the teacher in planning and implementing classroom activities.

If a student selected for diagnosis scores extremely well in comprehension—90 percent or better—the passage should be considered at a level appropriate for independent reading. The teacher may then administer a more difficult passage to determine the student's instructional level; or the student may simply be assigned to more difficult materials on a trial basis.

A 75 percent level of comprehension, then, indicates that the reader is gathering enough of the important information in a text for reading to be a satisfying and productive experience: the reader not only is successful but has a sense of accomplishment as well. At a much higher level of comprehension, say 90 percent or above, particularly if the answers to questions are full and unhesitating, the reader is processing information so efficiently that there is little to be gained from the instructional efforts of the teacher; materials that present so little difficulty can be read independently.

On the other hand, when comprehension is below 75 percent, the student is gaining too little of the information in the text for reading to be a comfortable experience under ordinary instructional conditions. It is often possible, however, to adjust instruction to accommodate a student who scores at least 50 percent in comprehension. A student who scores below 50 percent is following the text so poorly that even with strong instructional support in the form of extensive prereading discussion and activities, he or she will find reading a frustrating experience. Thus, comprehension scores between 50 and 75 percent represent borderline situations in which the teacher must consider the nature of the student's problem and decide whether instructional support would increase comprehension to a level that would be acceptable (75 percent or greater). For example, instructional support focused on the identification and/or meaning of words contained in reading selections may solve enough problems for the student to enable him or her to read with adequate comprehension.

Word recognition proficiency must also be taken into account in determining the instructional level. A student who performs well in comprehension and poorly in word recognition may need to work with easier materials for a time while developing greater skill in print skill. Easier materials may facilitate progress in this aspect of reading. On the other hand, there may be psychological or social advantages to be derived from working with the higher-level materials that would outweigh the student's difficulty with word recognition. An important consideration in this regard is the type of word recognition difficulty involved. If sight word fluency and accuracy is a major problem in addition to content word difficulties, the easier materials are likely to be the better solution. If, however, identification of unfamiliar content words constitutes the prime difficulty, then the higher-level materials can probably be used. In the latter case, of course, the teacher must plan to provide the student (along with other members of the reading group) with prereading assistance by identifying difficult words. In addition, some provision must be made for the student to receive help with specific word identification skills.

The way in which diagnostic information regarding vocabulary knowledge and print skill is used in making instructional decisions will be described more fully in the next chapter. In this chapter we will examine more closely the implications of a specific difficulty in the area of comprehension.

DIAGNOSIS OF
COMPREHENSION DIFFICULTY

It was noted in Chapter 1 that poor comprehension is often related to inadequate print skills and/or vocabulary knowledge. Sometimes, however, comprehension is poor (below 75 percent) even though the important words in a passage can be identified and their meanings are reasonably familiar. In such cases, the reading difficulty is considered to be specific to comprehension. In general, this means that the reader fails to see how ideas fit together—how one idea builds on another or is constrained by it. Often it is causal chains that go unrecognized, but other types of relationships give rise to difficulty as well. For instance, the reader might not recognize that one statement is an amplification of another, or that it is a summary of a series of preceding statements, or an example in support of a general statement.

A more precise formulation of the nature of individual problems in comprehension is not yet within diagnostic reach. In the past, it was commonly recommended that teachers attempt to determine which subskills of comprehension were weak in individual cases by analyzing comprehension test performance. It was felt that the types of questions frequently missed would indicate the specific areas of comprehension that were deficient. However, we believe, with Spache (1976), that this procedure is not really defensible. For one thing, no one passage, or even a series of passages such as is found in a standardized test or informal reading inventory, can provide a sufficient number of questions of each type to yield reliable results. Moreover, even if there were sufficient questions of each type, there is little evidence that the question types represent distinct and independent subskills. Analyses of responses to standardized test items have generally found that the ability (or inability) to answer one type of question tends to be correlated with the ability (or inability) to answer other types (Davis, 1944, 1968; Thorndike, 1973–74; Thurstone, 1946). That is, there is little tendency for students to show strength (or weakness) in one aspect of comprehension independently of strength (or weakness) in most other aspects.

More recent research tends to corroborate the view that specific difficulties in comprehension cannot be identified through analysis of question types. In a study of sixth graders, the poorer readers, as was expected, answered fewer questions correctly than the good readers; but they were similar to the good readers in that they answered more main idea questions than detail questions (Meyer, 1977). A similar result was observed with good and poor readers at the college level (Marshall & Glock, 1978–79). With regard to inferences, Bridge and Tierney (1981) found that the proportion of total information recalled that was inferential in nature was the same (approximately 40 percent) for poor readers as for good readers at the third-grade level. And, among a group of poor comprehenders at the seventh-grade level, Palinscar and Brown (1983) found no tendency for questions about implicit information to be more difficult than questions about explicit information.

At the same time, there is a growing body of evidence, consistent with the view of comprehension presented in the preceding chapter, that poor comprehension revolves around difficulty with the integrative processes involved in understanding discourse. For instance, Marshall and Glock (1978–79) found that intersentence relationships were a major stumbling block for poor readers at the college level. These relationships may be made explicit through various signaling devices (*however, because, in contrast, instead, in other words, for example, first, second,* etc.) or they may be implicit. Whereas the better readers did equally well under both circumstances, the poor readers suffered a significant reduction in recall of passage information when these relationships were implied rather than directly stated. Moreover, the poorer readers tended to include fewer interpropositional relations in their written recalls. Some further evidence that the absence of signaling devices can be detrimental to poor readers was obtained in a study of ninth graders (Meyer, Brandt, & Bluth, 1980).

In addition, research indicates that poor readers are generally insensitive to the high-level organization of passage information. That is, in recalling information after reading, poor readers are much less likely than good readers to follow the overall argument or pattern of discourse used by the author. While awareness of textual organization at the discourse level is rarely directly relevant to classroom comprehension tasks, it evidently facilitates the processing of lower-level information, for there is a high correlation between a student's ability to use the top-level structure of text in organizing his or her recall and the total amount of information recalled (Meyer et al., 1980). In addition, it has been found that instruction in the main types of expository discourse (e.g., main idea—supporting details; problem—solution; comparison—contrast) leads to marked increases in the amount of information students recall (Bartlett, 1978; McDonald, 1978; both cited in Meyer et al., 1980).

Finally, there is considerable evidence that poor readers have difficulty monitoring their mental processes while reading and that they do not make appropriate adjustments when obstacles to comprehension are encountered (Kimmell & MacGinitie, 1985). For example, poor readers often fail to recognize that something does not make sense or that they do not know the answer to a question. Nor do they regularly reread portions of text in an attempt to gain clarification. In an investigation of the question-answering strategies of good and poor readers in grades 4–10, a passage was used that required the student to look back to the text for the answers to certain questions. It was found that the good readers in grades 6 and 7 (although not in the lower grades) showed some awareness of comprehension difficulty on at least 50 percent of the questions that required lookbacks. That is, they indicated uncertainty of dissatisfaction with a response by shrugs, grunts, hesitations, and the like, and by such verbal expressions as ". . . I think"; ". . . or something"; and "that's a hard one." By contrast, the poor readers in these grades showed such behaviors on less than 7 percent of the questions. However, contrary to expectation, the sixth- and seventh-grade good readers did *not* look back to the text with great frequency for the answers to the targeted questions. It was only among the good readers in eighth grade and beyond that this strategy was observed with considerable frequency (79 percent of the questions that required lookbacks). Thus, while poor readers at all grade levels tend to be unaware when they do not understand or know the answer to a question, even good readers do not employ lookbacks to resolve difficulties until they reach the upper grades (Garner & Reis, 1981).

Given this evidence, we think it useful to view poor comprehension as arising in relation to difficulty with the integration of text information, both at the intersentence level and at higher levels of text structure. Underlying this difficulty are poorly developed strategies for utilizing background knowledge and recognizing and responding to failures of comprehension as they occur.

However, for some students, poorly developed strategies for interacting with text and organizing information represent only part of the problem. Instruction in such strategies can be effective only if students already possess the basic capacity for understanding the ideas and information with which they must interact. Therefore, in order to provide appropriate instruction once it has been determined that a student's difficulty is in comprehension, it is necessary to determine whether the student has this basic capacity. A probe of comprehension is conducted for this purpose. The teacher provides the student with an opportunity to reread relevant portions of the diagnostic passage and answer the questions that were incorrectly answered on the initial administration of the comprehension test. If the student can correct several answers on this second trial, it can be concluded that he or she has the ability to acquire basic text information and can profit from instruction in interactive and organizational strategies. On the other hand, if the student is essentially unable to correct his or her answers, then the difficulty is either at a conceptual level or at the level of acquiring basic text information, necessitating instruction in intersentence and intrasentence relationships. This latter type of instruction focuses on the anaphoric relations and linguistic devices that interrelate sentence information. It also involves the modeling of certain thought processes or interactive strategies believed to be second nature to proficient readers.

In reading the above statements which suggest distinctions among comprehenders, it is necessary to consider what information becomes available to the teacher early in his or her investigation. While the print skills required across a variety of reading situations are fairly stable and determinable by a thorough initial diagnosis, comprehension skills are not. Differences in content, organization, style, and length can make dramatically different demands on the reader, making initial diagnosis of comprehension problems more tentative and qualified (Wixson, Peters, Weber, & Roeber, 1987). It is therefore less possible to make what is called a differential diagnosis with respect to comprehension from one or two diagnostic encounters. Rather, ongoing diagnostic instruction manipulating the type and complexity of material used and degree and mode of teacher support can both pinpoint a student's abilities and disabilities and guide the appropriate sequence of instruction. We will discuss these variables in our later section on instruction.

Data Gathering

Assessment of comprehension takes place in the context of observing students in the act of comprehending; the teacher can gather information by interacting with readers in postreading discussion, by having them recall what they have read (a retelling) or by involving them in oral or written instrospection and retrospection as they read. Whatever the initial data-gathering choice, all comprehension assessment techniques call on the examiner to respond to the reader through direct, indirect, or probing questions at some point in the diagnostic cycle. Questioning is essential to all diagnosis, either as an initial stimulus or for later probes of what is spontaneously presented in a retelling, in an introspection, or in a guided reading lesson. Further, the guidelines for designing a set of questions to accurately represent the content of a selection, presented in Chapter 6, also provide the standard for analyzing a student's free recall, introspection, or instructional contribution.

Therefore the first model presented in this section will be of postreading questioning, the most common diagnostic format, followed by an explanation and example of the use of retelling. A third approach, introspective think-alouds, will be included as a promising new option for assessment.

Preparation

In constructing questions or a retelling protocol, the teacher quite naturally has specific responses in mind. These should be recorded in parentheses next to each question on the prepared question list or as entries on the retelling protocol (See Figures 7.2 and 7.3) for easy reference during testing. Then the teacher can make a quick judgment regarding the quality of the student's response and probe further when doing so seems appropriate. Often an answer is correct under a slightly different interpretation of the question. For example, in connection with the story of *The Restless Kangaroo,* one of the questions is "What did the zookeeper do to find out about the problem [that the zoo was having with the kangaroos]?" The expected answer is that the zookeeper stood watch over the kangaroo's pen one night while the animals slept. If a child answered, "He gave them a different pen," one must allow for the possibility that the child did not quite catch the words *to find out* and for this reason answered as if the question pertained to what was done *about* the problem. In such a case, it seems reasonable to clarify the question, for example, by saying, "Yes, he did that in the end. But how did he find out what the problem was?"

In other cases, the answer given might relate to an aspect of the story problem that is different from the one the teacher had in mind. In response to the question, "What was the problem the zoo was having with the kangaroos?" a student might answer, "The baby kangaroo kept putting straw into the pouch." This is, of course, the "ultimate" or underlying problem in the story, but the initial problem, in terms of the story structure, is that the baby kangaroo was found on the floor of the pen on several occasions. Again, the question should be clarified: "Yes. But they noticed a problem before they found out about that. What was the problem they noticed?" Then, if necessary, further clarification might be given: "What kept happening to the baby kangaroo because it kept putting straw into the pouch?" In general, answers that give information that is correct in terms of the story but slightly oblique in relation to the question should be probed further, either at the time of the initial response or after all the questions have been asked.

Another type of problematic response is one that is too broad or narrow. In Chapter 5 we saw that Raymond gave too narrow an answer (namely, specific examples in response to the question of what determines the kinds of housing people build), apparently because he did not fully grasp the idea that external conditions can determine what people do. He was given partial credit, however, for recognizing the examples as relevant to the question. An answer that is too broad should also be given partial credit if it represents a reasonable generalization from the evidence.

In addition, we believe it is good practice to give students an opportunity to sharpen their answers. For answers that are too narrow, the teacher may ask for a general statement about the specific facts or examples given (e.g., "What does the use of logs from a nearby forest show about the housing people build?"). For answers that are too broad, the teacher should ask for more precise information. Take as an example a passage about the problem of oil spills on the ocean, which discusses the fact that the oil kills animals, birds, and microscopic plant life. A student who says, in response to the question of why oil spills must be prevented, that they "cause pollution" should be asked for some specification of the harmful effects of this pollution.

Administration

A basic principle of instruction in reading is that the reader should be given some general purpose or guiding statement before reading. This principle should be followed in assessing reading as well. We want the assessment to be based on a task that is as much like a "normal" reading situation as possible. Therefore, the teacher should prepare a brief "warm up" or motivating statement to be read to the student before reading. For a selection dealing with the feeding of dogs, for example, the following would be appropriate: "Do you have a dog? What do you feed your dog? Let's read this to find out what a dog should be fed [Betts, 1954, p. 465]."

The questions are asked or retelling requested immediately following the oral (or silent) reading. As the procedure is basically informal, questions can, whenever advisable, be repeated, reworded, and clarified. The teacher must take account of the fact that the questions may be ambiguous, permitting of more than one interpretation, or they may elicit unanticipated (but correct) responses (as discussed above).

Evaluation

Once these questions (or the retelling task) have been administered following the reading of a passage, the following procedure is used to identify comprehension problems.

1. The number of text-related questions that were correctly answered is determined and expressed as a percentage of the total number of such questions. A retelling score is similarly obtained as a percentage of the total number of elements in the scoring checklist. If this score is 75 percent or above, comprehension is considered satisfactory and the passage is considered to represent a level of difficulty that is appropriate for instruction unless word recognition problems dictate otherwise, as explained earlier in this chapter.
2. If the comprehension score is less than 75 percent, the teacher determines, from the results of the examination of print skill and

vocabulary knowledge proficiency, whether these areas of reading interfere with comprehension. If so, further diagnosis must focus on these areas. If poor comprehension is *not* attributable to either of these underlying areas then a diagnosis of comprehension difficulty is made. It should be recognized, however, that vocabulary knowledge has a subtle, pervasive influence on comprehension, and its role in poor comprehension cannot always be singled out. Therefore, students for whom a comprehension difficulty is diagnosed may also have some degree of vocabulary knowledge difficulty.

3. If comprehension has been judged to be the main area of reading difficulty, a comprehension probe is conducted. For each question that was answered incorrectly on the comprehension test, the student is directed to reread the portion of the passage in which the answer can be found and given a second opportunity to answer the question. The purpose is to gain insight into the student's thinking and text-processing strategies in order to provide appropriate instruction.

4. When a student can generally correct his or her answers upon rereading the text, it is assumed that the difficulty on the initial trial was relatively superficial—the student is able to grasp basic text information but has difficulty combining that information into coherent units. In some cases, of course, the student will simply have misunderstood the question or failed to link an important piece of information to it. Also, students are sometimes aware of the information that would answer a question correctly but do not give this information because they have little confidence in it or it runs counter to their expectations. In general, a student's ability to answer questions correctly upon rereading the text indicates basic skill in understanding text information. At the same time, the student's inability to answer those same questions correctly on the initial trial, without the motivation and assistance provided during the probe, suggests ineffective strategies for interacting with text and sensing the organization or structure of text information and using this structure as a framework for remembering information.

5. When students are unable to respond correctly after reexamining the text, the difficulty is considered to be more severe. In such cases instruction should focus on the "flow" and cohesive elements of written discourse, as described in this chapter.

Thus, the initial administration of the comprehension test provides a measure of the student's general level of comprehension, whereas the probe enables the teacher to determine the severity of the problem, based on the level of text organization with which the student encounters difficulty, and gives suggestions for initial instructional intervention.

CASE 1: Paul—Questioning

Paul, a seventh-grader, read a story from his seventh-grade basal reader. This story was about an Eskimo boy, Noni, who was marooned with his dog on an ice island. Since there was no wildlife or vegetation on the island, within a few days the two were near starvation. With much anguish, the boy concluded that he must kill the dog for food. The story is shown in Figure 7.1. In order to understand the diagnostic techniques described in what follows, the reader should be familiar with the content and sequence of the story.

Paul showed excellent print skill when he read the story aloud. Further, the vocabulary knowledge assessment, shown in Figure 7.2, indicated that he was familiar with the key words in the story (e.g., *marooned, essential, wary, descended, intention*). The questions that Paul's teacher developed to measure his understanding of the story are also shown in the figure, along with his responses. As can be seen, Paul's comprehension score was only 60 percent. Thus, because his print skill and vocabulary knowledge were both highly satisfactory, his main difficulty was considered to be in the area of comprehension. The reader should examine the questions that Paul answered incorrectly in order to identify possible reasons for his comprehension failure.

COMPREHENSION PROBE

The first question that Paul missed in the comprehension test was drawn from the following paragraph:

> He could not kill the dog with his bare hands. Nimuk was powerful and much fresher than he. A weapon, then, was essential.

Figure 7.1   Diagnostic reading passage: Paul.

Two Were Left

On the third night of hunger, Noni thought of the dog. Nothing of flesh and blood lived upon the floating ice island with its towering berg except those two.

In the breakup Noni had lost his sled, his food, his fur, even his knife. He had saved only Nimuk, his devoted husky. And now the two marooned on the ice eyed each other warily—each keeping his distance.

Noni's love for Nimuk was real, very real—as real as the hunger and cold nights and the gnawing pain of his injured leg. But the men of his village killed their dogs when food was scarce, didn't they? And without thinking twice about it.

And Nimuk, he told himself, when hungry enough would seek food. One of us will soon be eating the other, Noni thought. So . . .

He could not kill the dog with his bare hands. Nimuk was powerful and much fresher than he. A weapon, then, was essential.

Figure 7.1 (*continued*)

Removing his mittens, he unstrapped the brace from his leg. When he had hurt his leg a few weeks before, he had made the brace from bits of harness and two thin strips of iron.

Kneeling now, he stuck one of the iron strips into a crack in the ice and began to rub the other against it with firm, slow strokes.

Nimuk watched him intently, and it seemed to Noni that the dog's eyes glowed more brightly as night came.

He worked on, trying not to remember why. The slab of iron had an edge now. It had begun to take shape. Daylight found his task completed.

Noni pulled the finished knife from the ice and thumbed its edge. The sun's glare, reflected from it, stabbed at his eyes and for a moment blinded him.

Noni steeled himself.

"Here, Nimuk!" he called softly.

The dog watched him suspiciously.

"Come here," Noni called.

Nimuk came closer. Nomi read fear in the animal's gaze. He read hunger and suffering in the dog's labored breathing and awkward, dragging crouch. His heart wept. He hated himself and fought against it.

Closer Nimuk came, wary of his intentions. Now Noni felt a thickening in his throat. He saw the dog's eyes and they were wells of suffering.

Now! Now was the time to strike!

A great sob shook Noni's kneeling body. He cursed the knife. He swayed blindly; flung the weapon far from him. With empty hands outstretched he stumbled toward the dog, and fell.

The dog growled. He warily circled the boy's body. Noni was sick with fear.

In flinging away his knife he had left himself defenseless. He was too weak to crawl after it now. He was at Nimuk's mercy, and Nimuk was hungry.

The dog circled him and was creeping up from behind. Noni heard the rattle of saliva in the savage throat.

He shut his eyes, praying that the attack might be swift. He felt the dog's feet against his leg, the hot rush of Nimuk's breath against his neck. A scream gathered in the boy's throat.

Then he felt the dog's hot tongue licking his face.

Noni's eyes opened, staring, not yet believing. Crying softly, he put out his arm and drew the dog's head down against his own. . . .

The plane came out of the south an hour later. Its pilot, a young man of the coastal patrol, looked down and saw the large, floating ice island with the berg rising from its center. And he saw something flashing.

It was the sun gleaming on something shiny which moved. His curiosity aroused, the pilot banked his ship and descended, circling the ice. Now he saw, in the shadow of the peak of ice, a dark, still shape that appeared to be human. Or were there two shapes?

Figure 7.1 *(continued)*

He set his ship down in a water lane and investigated. There were two shapes, boy and dog. The boy was unconscious but alive. The dog whined feebly but was too weak to move.

The gleaming object which had trapped the pilot's attention was a hand-made knife stuck point first into the ice a little distance away and quivering in the wind.

(From *New Worlds Ahead* by I. Willis and R. E. Willis, pp. 409–411, published by Harcourt, Brace, and World, 1969. Copyright 1942 by the Crowell-Collier Publishing Co. Reprinted by permission of the author, Hugh B. Cave.)

Figure 7.2 Responses to comprehension and vocabulary knowledge questions: Paul.

Comprehension

✓ 1. Where were Noni and Nimuk marooned? (on an ice island)
   RESPONSE: Ice island.

✓ 2. How did Noni feel about Nimuk? (loved him very much)
   RESPONSE: Liked him.

✗ 3. Why did Noni think a weapon was essential? (Nimuk was too powerful to kill with his bare hands)
   RESPONSE: To kill wild animals for food.

✗ 4. From what did Noni make a weapon? (strips of iron from his brace)
   RESPONSE: Knife.

✓ 5. Why were they wary of each other? (they were both starving — might kill the other for food)
   RESPONSE: 'Cause one might eat the other.

✓ 6. Why was Noni unable to attack the dog? (loved him too much)
   RESPONSE: Noni liked the dog; did not want to kill him.

✗ 7. What did Noni do with the knife? (threw it away — "far from him")
   RESPONSE: Tried to kill Nimuk and left it there.

✗ 8. When did Noni know that the dog would not attack him? (when he felt the dog licking his face)
   RESPONSE: The dog came closer and closer.

✓ 9. Who rescued them? (a pilot in a plane)
   RESPONSE: A plane.

✓ 10. What was quivering in the wind which caught the pilot's attention? (the knife)
   RESPONSE: Knife.

Figure 7.2 (*continued*)

Vocabulary Knowledge

✓ 1. What is a *husky?*
RESPONSE: An Eskimo sled dog.

✓ 2. What does *marooned* mean?
RESPONSE: Deserted on an island.

✓ 3. What does *gnawing* mean?
RESPONSE: A dull pain that doesn't stop.

✓ 4. What does *essential* mean?
RESPONSE: Necessary.

✓ 5. In the story, it says that Noni "steeled" himself. What does *steeled* mean?
RESPONSE: Got his nerve up.

✓ 6. What does *wary* mean?
RESPONSE: Careful-cautious.

✓ 7. What does *descended* mean?
RESPONSE: Go down.

✓ 8. What does *feebly* mean?
RESPONSE: Weakly.

✓ 9. What does *quivering* mean?
RESPONSE: Shaking.

✓ 10. What does *intention* mean?
RESPONSE: Going to do something.

The question was "Why did Noni think a weapon was essential?" Paul had initially answered, "To kill wild animals for food." (The correct answer would refer to the fact that the dog was too powerful to be killed barehanded; partial credit could be given for referring to the need to kill the dog for food.) The probe with regard to this question was as follows:

TEACHER: I'd like you to read this paragraph again and see if you can tell why Noni thought a weapon was essential.

PAUL: (after reading): To kill the dog, for food.

TEACHER: Yes, but why did he need a *weapon?*

PAUL: Can't kill a dog without a weapon, with bare hands.

TEACHER: And why not?

PAUL: It could kill you, too big.

One interpretation of this result is that Paul had initially answered as he did—"to kill wild animals for food"—because he conceived of the question as a generic one—as pertaining to weapons in general, rather than to the story in particular. Another possibility is that he had forgotten—or was never really certain—that there were no wild animals on the ice island. (That information appears in the second sentence of the story, several paragraphs before the one under discussion.) Nevertheless, the fact that he was able to answer the question correctly upon rereading showed that he could, at least, understand the intersentence relationships in the paragraph.

The probe was continued with another question that Paul had initially missed. This related to the part of the story that described how the Eskimo boy made a knife with two strips of metal taken from a brace he was wearing on this wounded knee. The relevant paragraphs read as follows:

> Removing his mittens, he unstrapped the brace from his leg. When he had hurt his leg a few weeks before, he had made the brace from bits of harness and two thin strips of iron.
>
> Kneeling now, he stuck one of the iron strips into a crack in the ice and began to rub the other against it with firm, slow strokes.
>
> Nimuk watched him intently, and it seemd to Noni that the dog's eyes glowed more brightly as night came.
>
> He worked on, trying not to remember why. The slab of iron had an edge now. It had begun to take shape. Daylight found his task completed.

In answer to the question "From what did Noni make a weapon?" Paul had responded, "a knife." After rereading, he responded as follows:

PAUL: Oh. A slab of iron.

TEACHER: And where did he get the iron?

PAUL: His brace for his knee.

TEACHER: Can you explain how he made a knife out of the iron?

PAUL: He rubbed it until it had an edge.

TEACHER: What did he rub it with?

PAUL: Not sure . . . on the ice?

This was a rather difficult sequence of text. It required the reader to visualize a step-by-step procedure, and Paul was evidently unable to do this. Still, upon a second reading he had gleaned the essential idea that the knife was made from a part of the brace.

The third question that Paul missed involved a crucial element of the story. Just as the boy was about to strike the dog, he was overcome with grief and "flung the weapon far from him." Paul evidently understood the boy's reluctance to kill the dog; in answer to the question, "Why was Noni unable to attack the dog?" he had replied, "Noni liked the dog; did not want to kill him." Yet, in answering the next question, "What did Noni do with the knife?" Paul had stated that Noni "tried to kill Nimuk and left it there." Thus, Paul seemed to have two conflicting ideas about a dramatic story event. His teacher explored further by having him reread the following segment.

> Now? Now was the time to strike!
>
> A great sob shook Noni's kneeling body. He cursed the knife. He swayed blindly; flung the weapon far from him. With empty hands outstretched he stumbled toward the dog, and fell.

Then she asked the question again, "What did Noni do with the knife?"

> PAUL: Tried to kill Nimuk. Threw it far.
>
> TEACHER: Did he throw it at the dog?
>
> PAUL: Yeah. But he missed him.

Since the student did not answer correctly on this second trial, the probe then took the form of a detailed analysis of the text.

> TEACHER: Show me the part that tells what Noni did; read it aloud.
>
> PAUL: [from passage]: "Flung the weapon far from him."
>
> TEACHER: Yes, I suppose that could mean that he threw it at the dog and missed. But I think it means something else. Do you know how I know?
>
> PAUL: No.
>
> TEACHER: Well, let's look at what happened before that, right after Noni finished making the knife. [The teacher points to the preceding paragraph and the student reads it aloud: "Closer Nimuk came, wary of his intentions. Now Noni felt a thickening in his throat. He saw the dog's eyes and they were wells of sufering."] Okay, so where was Nimuk when Noni threw the knife?
>
> PAUL: [No response.]
>
> TEACHER: [clarifying]: Where was Nimuk in relation to Noni? How close was he?
>
> PAUL: Well, he came closer . . . Oh, he saw the dog's eyes.
>
> TEACHER: Yes, so the dog had to be pretty close to Noni. Do you see now what it means that Noni "flung the weapon far from him"?
>
> PAUL: He wasn't trying to kill the dog?
>
> TEACHER: Right. We have to assume that he wasn't trying to kill the dog—that he changed his mind at the last minute and threw the knife "far from him"—far from himself and the dog.

There was, then, some plausibility to the student's interpretation of the story character's action, at least when that action is taken by itself, out of context. It only becomes implausible that the boy meant to kill the dog when he "flung the weapon far from him" when one takes into account the fact that the dog was in close proximity. Thus, as may have occurred with the first question, the student had failed to keep one fact in mind while considering another. And, as with the first question, the student did seem able to understand the language of the text at both the sentence and intersentence levels.

The fourth and final question that Paul missed involved the next event in the story. After the Eskimo boy threw the knife "far from him" he lay on the ground in fear that the dog would now attack him:

> He shut his eyes, praying that the attack might be swift. He felt the dog's feet against his leg, the hot rush of Nimuk's breath against his neck. A scream gathered in the boy's throat.
>
> Then he felt the dog's hot tongue licking his face.

In response to the question, "When did the boy know the dog would not attack him?" Paul had answered, "The dog came closer and closer." After rereading, he was able to answer correctly, "When he felt him licking his face."

Taken together, Paul's responses on the probe suggest that his main comprehension difficulty is in integrating story events. He seemed to consider each event an isolated phenomenon. As a result, his grasp of the story line was initially vague and impressionistic. Nevertheless, the fact that he was able to correct three out of four responses indicates that he had the capacity to grasp the basic information in the text. Therefore, Paul's comprehension problem was judged as involving poorly developed strategies for interacting with information and recognizing its overall structure. We will comment on instruction for Paul later in this chapter.

Retelling

Free recall, more commonly called *retelling,* is a process whereby the student is asked to retell the story or reproduce information in his or her own words. Following a prereading orientation, the examiner does not ask specific questions but rather asks the reader to retell the selection. Working with a prepared checklist (see Figure 7.3 for an example for the selection "Two Were Left," which was introduced earlier), the examiner records the information supplied by the reader in the order in which it is presented. Following the student's unprompted recall, the examiner uses quesions to probe for any information not supplied. During or after the retelling, anecdotal notes on oral language can also be made.

Scoring of aided recall need present no problem if the checklist of information prepared in advance is precise and well ordered. The student is simply given points for each idea or fact recalled, as would be the case with questions. One advantage of this procedure is that it gives the teacher some idea of the student's verbal clarity and fluency. It is more time-consuming than direct questioning, however, at least at the point of administration, and the added information may be superfluous for a teacher who has many other opportunities to observe students' verbal proficiency.

Retellings have been used extensively as a research tool and less frequently for assessment and intruction (Gambrell, Pfeiffer, & Wilson, 1985; Irwin & Mitchell, 1983; Morrow, 1985). They have the advantage of providing for the examiner a look at what the student sees as important without the prompt of teacher questions. Further, the sequence in which the information is retold and the language used to express it also provide more diagnostic information.

Diagnostic use of the retelling procedure also carries with it certain problems that can arise. Morrow (1985) found that students often have trouble with the process if it is unfamiliar but that repeated attempts produce more elaborated retellings. Further, children respond differently to different directions. For example, if both the reader and the examiner have read the story, students will often omit important information, assuming the examiner already knows it (Golden & Pappas, 1987). Moreover, the quality of the retelling or reproduction may reflect the student's verbal and expository skills as much as his or her comprehension. Students vary widely in their ability to organize and verbalize information. Like other integrative and language skills, this one depends a great deal on practice. Since questions serve as "cues" or "prompts," much more can usually be remembered about a passage in response to questioning than can be reproduced in a free recall. For example, Stein and Glenn (1979) report that, in retelling a story, young children tended to omit information about the goals and motives of story characters and yet they were able to answer questions about these story elements.

More significantly for our purposes, the tendency to provide additional information in response to questioning is much more pronounced among poor readers than among good readers. Bridge and Tierney (1981) found that of the total number of items of information that were ultimately remembered by a group of low-achieving third graders, over 40 percent were given during the probe task which followed free recall. Therefore, while it may be well to give students an opportunity to retell the story in order to assess their ability to do so, a good set of questions will be needed in order to obtain a valid estimate of comprehension skill.

CASE 2: Andrea—A Retelling

Andrea, a seventh grader with good print and fluency skills, read the same story introduced earlier, "Two Were Left," about the dilemma of an Eskimo boy marooned with his dog. The teacher began the retelling process.

TEACHER: Can you tell me the story as if you were telling it to someone who hadn't read it.

ANDREA: There was a kid and his dog and because nobody could live in the cold they had to keep going. So he was going to kill his dog because the dog was creeping around him. But a plane saved them in time.

TEACHER: Anything else you'd like to tell someone who hadn't read it.

ANDREA: (Pausing a long time) Well, the kid wanted to use his knife to kill the dog.

TEACHER: Why was that?

ANDREA: Well, it's a good weapon for killing.

TEACHER: Where did he get the knife?

ANDREA: He carried it in his leg pocket.

TEACHER: Do you have any idea where this is happening?

ANDREA: In the winter someplace.

TEACHER:	How did Noni and Nimuk feel on the ice.
ANDREA:	Cold and hungry.
TEACHER:	Was this a problem?
ANDREA:	Sure, they'd starve or freeze.
TEACHER:	Any other problems?
ANDREA:	Well, that would be enough.
TEACHER:	Why do you think he didn't kill Nimuk?
ANDREA:	He'd need his dog for pulling his sled later.
TEACHER:	What happened to the knife.
ANDREA:	He threw it away.
TEACHER:	Why?
ANDREA:	He wasn't going to use it.
TEACHER:	How did the pilot find them.
ANDREA:	He must have looked around a long time and then saw two little black dots on the ice.

Following the first retelling and questioning, the teacher asked Andrea to reexamine the selection to probe further. Simple reexamination did not help Andrea do a better job of answering some of the questions. For example, the issue of the knife is an

Figure 7.3 Retelling response checklist for "Two were Left"—Andrea.

Information	Spontaneous	Prompted
1. Noni and Nimuk	✓ (no names)	½
2. marooned on ice island		
3. Both were becoming hungry	✓	
4. Noni considers killing Nimuk	✓	
5. Nimuk too strong to kill with bare hands		—
6. Noni began to make a knife from knee brace		—
7. Both were wary because each might harm other		—
8. Noni unable to kill Nimuk because he loved him		—
9. Noni threw knife far from him		✓
10. Nimuk approached Noni		—
11. Noni feared Nimuk would attack him	(whole sequence missing)	—
12. Nimuk licked Noni, didn't harm		—
13. Pilot found boy and dog	✓	
14. because of blade's reflection		—
Percentage of comprehension:	$\frac{5.5}{14}$ = 39%	

important one for the selection. The teacher led Andrea through this series of questions:

1. Did Noni have his knife at the beginning of the story? What does the author tell us? (the knife was lost in the breakup of the ice)
2. Why did he need a knife? (Nimuk too big to kill with bare hands)
3. How did he get the knife? (made it from knee brace)
4. What happened to the knife? (he threw it far away)

and then related the knife's reflection in the sun to the pilot's discovery of the two survivors. In doing this, the teacher needed to go paragraph by paragraph, and sometimes sentence by sentence, through this short selection helping Andrea identify important information, sequence it, and make connections.

Unlike Paul, Andrea seemed to grasp only the most obvious information provided by the author and was unable to improve performance without considerable support and breaking down of the selection by the teacher. The reader should examine the summary in Figure 7.3. Andrea's problem could be judged to be much more severe and requires attention to extraction of basic information as well as its integration across the text. We will comment on her instructional plan later in the chapter.

Think-Alouds

In the *think-aloud* procedure (Lytle, 1982) the student is asked to introspect and verbalize before, during, and after reading a selection. The teacher asks the student to reflect and comment on what is being read as the text is exposed line by line. In the introspection process, Lytle has noted that students comment on what they understand (signaling understanding), indicate what is causing them problems (monitoring of doubts), analyze parts of the text (analyzing) or verbally try to figure things out (reasoning), relate the author's ideas to their own knowledge (elaborating), and evaluate aspects of the author's message and style (judging).

Readers exhibit strategies when they combine the "moves" noted in parentheses above for a particular purpose, such as to remove a doubt. Characteristic strategies in certain situations may define a student's style, which Lytle suggests may be consistent across various texts. Though this process is still an exploratory one, having a student "talk through" a selection may provide diagnostic insights and instructional leads.

CASE 3: Jake—Think-Aloud

We will consider an excerpt from a think-aloud protocol of Jake, a seventh-grade student, reading "Two Were Left." Jake's teacher noted that he is very inconsistent in his reading group. Sometimes he seems to have a good grasp of what is being read; at other times he is very confused or seems to have very different interpretations from those of the rest of the group. The teacher decided to try to think-aloud with her next lesson.

TEACHER: Jake, I'm going to show you this story sentence by sentence and I want you to think out loud as you read it.

JAKE: What do you mean.

TEACHER: You can tell me about what you think the author is saying, what it makes you think of, where you think the author is going, what puzzles you, how you figure things out, anything that comes into your head.

JAKE: Okay.

TEXT: "Two Were Left."

JAKE: It must tell about two people left off somewhere. I don't know where.

TEXT: On the third night of hunger, Noni thought of the dog.

JAKE: One person is Noni and he's probably worried that no one will take care of his dog while he is stuck somewhere.

TEXT: Nothing of flesh and blood lived upon the floating ice island with its towering berg except those two.

JAKE: They're somewhere near an island but nobody lives there. They're left.

TEXT: In the breakup, Noni had lost his sled, his food, his fur, even his knife.

JAKE: He's really stuck but I still don't know who the other guy is. Maybe the other guy wants to kill this guy. But he's got a knife.

TEXT: He had saved only Nimuk, his devoted husky.

JAKE: Well, his dog's okay. I'll bet the dog will find the other guy first and get him and save Noni.

TEXT: And now the two marooned on the ice eyed each other warily—each keeping his distance.

JAKE: Well, the other guy is near enough to see him. I'm sure the dog will save him.

It is clear from the think-aloud protocol that Jake has made a conclusion from the title concerning who the "two" were and is retaining this schema, causing himself a bit of confusion as he reads on in the selection. He keeps waiting for the other person to attack and interprets each of the sentences in light of this overriding schema. Also he has not attended to some essential signal words in the selection: *except,* indicating they are on the island; *even,* signifying his knife is gone.

After the protocol is finished, he said, "This is a really crazy story and I don't understand it at all." The teacher took him back to the beginning and worked through the first paragraph again. In their repeating the protocol, the selection now makes sense. Jake does not have much difficulty with narratives if he begins by clearly establishing the characters and their problems or goals. Diagnostically, working through a selection in this manner can give a teacher insight into strategy use, misuse, and overuse that can help pupils better approach a reading assignment. We will comment on his instruction later.

Besides its obvious diagnostic implications, teacher can use think-aloud protocols for intervention. If a student's style is nonfunctional, teachers can provide the types of responses *they* would make as modeling and feedback (Bird, 1980; Palincsar & Brown, 1983), can interrupt the reader and focus them on the teacher's own processes (Brown, 1986), or can have students write their responses in a reading journal (Mayers, 1988) for later reflection, comparison, and discussion. Students can do a rereading of a selection along with an earlier audiotape to reflect on an earlier reading. Further, teachers can structure group think-alouds by using an overhead projector on which a selection is revealed chunk by chunk for group analysis and discussion.

COMPREHENSION INSTRUCTION

We turn now to instruction in comprehension. How can we improve instruction for students with comprehension difficulties? Some years ago the answer would have been that we must identify areas of specific weakness and strengthen those areas through direct instruction. That is, it was believed that comprehension was made up of a number of subskills and that remedial efforts should be directed toward improving one or another of them. Thus some students might need help in noting and recalling details while others might need help in following sequences of events or grasping main ideas. As was already discussed, this approach is now generally perceived as unduly limited and not entirely consistent with what we know about the nature of comprehension and the research on its development. Therefore we recommend a somewhat different approach.

We noted earlier the difficulty in making a differential diagnosis for comprehension. What frequently can be determined for each reader is the degree of teacher support, the explicitness of instruction, and the length and complexity of material used in the instruction for productive comprehension. If comprehension problems are severe, adjustment may be needed in all of these conditions; if problems are minimal, fewer changes may be needed. For example, some students, like Paul, require a small degree of teaching intervention and guidance to discover ways to interact better with whole texts. Others, like Jake, need heavy intervention at the start of a new selection to help them develop a schema for completing the selection unaided. Still others, like Andrea, need to be focused on very small units of text with explicit instructional demands to develop their strategies. Therefore what differentiates comprehension instruction at the beginning of diagnosis are these three dimensions: length of the unit of text used for instruction, degree of teacher intervention, and explicitness of teacher direction.

Given these differing dimensions, we recommend two types of instructional procedures for helping all students with poor comprehension. The first introduces the students to various strategies, such as self-questioning, predicting, and self-monitoring, which foster an interactive approach to reading. Presented in this section are four techniques representing varying degrees of teacher intervention, instructional explicitness, and length of text units (though it should be noted that this last can obviously be varied within each model). The Directed Reading-Thinking Activity (Stauffer, 1969) and K-W-L (Ogle, 1986) combine implicit modeling and low to moderate teacher directness in consideration of larger chunks of text. The ReQuest Procedure (Manzo, 1969) combines a gradually increasing text size with implicit modeling and high directiveness. Reciprocal Teaching (Palincsar & Brown, 1983) is the most intensive of the four, combining small text chunks with high directedness and explicit modeling.

A second type of instruction examines relationships within a text, the structure and organization of material, the connections within and across sentences, and the relationships between questions and the text from which they are derived. The need for this focusing on organization and relationships is often revealed during some of the text interaction instruction noted above. For example, with Jake's think-aloud, which in our model would be characterized as focusing on small text units with low teacher directiveness and low modeling, revealed a problem with signal words such as *except* and *even,* suggesting some greater attention to the words that make connections within sentences.

Developing Interactive Strategies

The directed reading lesson format common to basal reading materials has a familiar and predictable structure. The teacher prepares concepts and vocabulary, sets a prereading purpose, has the student read part or all of the selection, and asks the students questions in discussion after reading. Skills are introduced and practiced at one or more places in the lesson and reteaching, extension, and enrichment activities complete the cycle. While this is a sensible and legitimate structure, there are many reasons to modify it for comprehension enhancement.

At the core of interactive reading is the active use of what the reader already knows to learn something new. Analyses of classroom instruction (Beck, McKeown, McCaslin, & Burkes, 1979; Durkin, 1978–79) have suggested that too little time before reading is devoted to developing and activating the prereading schemata necessary for effective comprehension. A second concern about the directed reading lesson is that the major part of the "work" is done by the teacher, relegating the students to the role of passive responders, not building those strategies needed to approach text independently (Stauffer, 1969). We will present several instructional alternatives to the directed reading lesson, all of which view the teacher's role as that of expert guide in leading students through a strategic approach to text. Both tacitly and explicitly these procedures call on the reader to control and monitor the reading situation.

The Directed Reading-Thinking Activity. The directed reading-thinking activity approach models the comprehension process by participants' walking through a selection bit by bit rather than locating all discussion after reading. In this way the teacher helps the student experience the thinking processes that an expert reader uses in comprehending a text (Davidson & Wilkerson, 1988; Stauffer, 1969). The basic processes to be modeled are as follows:

1. Before I read a section of text, I use clues to make predictions about what the author will tell me.
2. I stop as I read to refine or reformulate my predictions.
3. I repeat steps 1 and 2 throughout the selection.

To plan a DR-TA the teacher selects an appropriate reading selection, one that lends itself to making predictions and that is at an appropriate instructional level. After analyzing the selection, the teacher chooses several points at which the reader might be stopped and asked for a prediction about subsequent content. The title, picture, caption, first paragraph, or some combination of these often serve as the basis for the first prediction.

After each chunk is read, the teacher and student discuss their prediction in the light of the clues the author has given them. Probing questions are the norm for the teacher in the DR-TA, questions such as, "What makes you think so?" "What did the author say that confirms (or disconfirms that)?" "What will _____ do about _____?" "Why do you think the author said that?" Students go back to the selection to find more information, to clarify a point, and to resolve conflicts, and oral reading is used to substantiate opinions.

Through the process of reasoning through the text with the author, the reader comes to a full construction of the message so that the final discussion can focus on evaluating the author's message and craft. Writing also fits naturally into the DR-TA in that students can write predictions and evidence at various points, and they frequently want to rewrite sections of narratives that they find unsatisfactory.

The K-W-L. The K-W-L (Ogle, 1986) is a predictive approach to expository material. Like the DR-TA, it asks students to become active readers by specifying a purpose for reading. It has three basic strategies:

1. **Brainstorm.** Before reading, ask myself; What do I *K*now?
2. **Set purpose.** What do I *W*ant to know after I read?
3. **Consolidate after reading.** What did I *L*earn?

The teacher leads the students through brainstorming on the topic before reading, then has students list what they would like to find out. At this point the teacher can also participate as a contributor of relevant questions. After reading, students go back to see which questions were answered by the selection, refine their knowledge, and frequently set reference goals for themselves to search out information that interests them and that is not provided by the author.

ReQuest Procedure. In Manzo's (1969) ReQuest Procedure, the teacher not only models questions but also provides some feedback on the quality of students' questions by praising those that are good and withholding comment on those that are not. The procedure is one of turn taking, which gives it an attractive gamelike quality. After a sentence is read, first the student asks the teacher questions and then the teacher asks the student questions. All questions must be answered without their referring to the passage, though the responder may ask for clarification or rephrasing of the question. (Students are told to try to ask questions that a teacher might ask.) Teacher and students continue in this fashion with succeeding sentences until the teacher feels that enough information has been established for students to make reasonable predictions about the remainder of the story. At that point, predictions are made and students read to verify them.

Reciprocal Teaching/Modeling. In this procedure, developed by Palincsar and Brown (1983), students and teacher take turns leading a dialogue. The "leader" asks an important question about a small segment of text—no more than a paragraph—and is also responsible for (1) *summarizing* what has been read, (2) *predicting* what might be discussed next, and (3) offering *clarification* of anything that seemed confusing. The teacher guides students in these activities by a variety of prompting and modeling techniques (e.g."Remember that a summary doesn't include a lot of detail"; "What question would a teacher ask?"). The help and participation of other students in the group may also be solicited upon occasion. In addition to prompting the student leader, the teacher provides praise and feedback specific to the student's conduct of the dialogue. A teacher might offer corrective feedback by saying, "That was interesting information. It was information that I would call detail in the passage. Can you find the most important information? [Palincsar & Brown, 1983, p. 14]." Then, at the conclusion of each student-led discussion, the teacher models any portion of the discussion that he or she feels needs improvement (e.g., "I would summarize by saying . . .").

An important element of this instructional procedure is informing students of its self-monitoring purpose: "being able to say in your own words what one has just read, and being able to guess what the questions will be a on test, are sure ways of testing oneself to see if one has understood [p. 14]." The role of self-questioning, predicting, summarizing, and clarifying in enhancing comprehension, and the need for using these strategies during independent reading, must also be made explicit. Palincsar and Brown report that although seventh-grade students had considerable difficulty with the role of dialogue leader during the first few instructional sessions, by the end of 10 sessions they were able to produce questions and summaries of "some sophistication." Therefore, a teacher who wishes to use this procedure should plan to use it regularly for several weeks.

An attractive feature of the reciprocal teaching format is that it emphasizes certain processes of reading while focusing on the *meaning* of segments of text. That is, instruction is provided within the context of "real reading," and it is provided through repeated modeling. This is in sharp contrast to the more traditional "skills" method of helping students with comprehension difficulty. Typically, in the more traditional method, specific aspects of text processing (e.g., sequencing events, recognizing causal relations) are isolated, directly taught through explanation and illustration, and then practiced by students on specially prepared materials and exercises. Students' performance on these materials is then evaluated as correct or incorrect. A major weakness of this method, aside from the isolation of particular aspects of meaning from the holistic process of reading, is that students are not *shown how* to arrive at correct solutions to the problem of meaning. Reciprocal teaching, as we have seen, coordinates students' attention to specific elements of text with a general focus on meaning. Therefore, we believe the method may be adapted to instruction in other features of text, particularly connective terms, as noted below.

Developing Ability to Reorganize Information

Recognizing that text information is interrelated is fundamental to comprehension. We have already discussed the role of postreading questions in this connection, arguing that they should recapitulate the orderly progression of events and ideas that make up the story line. Similarly, students can be focused on overall selection organization, sentential connectedness, or the relationships between questions and the text that generates them. Again the length of textual units to which the strategies are applied, the amount of teacher directedness, and explicitness of instruction are significant variables.

In this section we will not try to present a comprehensive range of these techniques but rather offer a selection reflecting the dimensions of teacher support and intervention discussed earlier. For example, the strategy fostered in the Question-Answer Relationship procedure (Raphael, 1986) requires explicit instruction, as does the Guided Reading Procedure (Manzo, 1975) and the instruction on connective terms. In contrast, graphic organizers can be used as the basis for implicit instruction utilizing discovery techniques, but direct instruction of text structures is also possible. The ultimate goal of all these methods, however, is to pass the control of the process from teacher to learner.

Question-Answer Relationships. Students need to respond to questions throughout their school careers yet Durkin (1978–79) noted that little if any instruction focuses on the strategic processes needed to answer questions. Raphael's Question-Answer Relationship method (1986) focuses students on the different strategies that can be employed in answering a question. Her work is based on the notion that there are several definable relationships questions have with the selections from which they are drawn (Pearson & Johnson, 1978) and that each of these relationships suggests a different strategy for responding.

Some questions ask you merely to locate information that an author has given you explicitly and all in one place. Raphael (1986) terms these "Right There" questions; the author has answered them right there in the text for you. Other questions can be answered by looking for clues, implicit and explicit, scattered across a text; for these you must "Think and Search." A third type of question necessitates that you add your own knowledge to what the author tells you; these are "Author and You" questions, calling for analysis, synthesis, and evaluation. A fourth type of question can be answered by you alone; these are "On My Own" questions.

For example, for the selection, "Two Were Left," some possible QAR's would be:

QUESTION: Where were Noni and Nimuk when the selection began?

ANSWER 1: Marooned on an ice flow. (Right There: The student just searched for an answer given directly by the author.)

ANSWER 2: Maybe in Alaska (Author and You: The student used the clues of climate, terrain, sled, and husky to connect with what he knew about various locales)

The above is a good example of two possible correct answers for the same question, each with a different procedure for answering.

QUESTION: Would you say Noni loved Nimuk? Support your answer.

ANSWER: Yes, because he worried about him but he couldn't kill him. (Think and search: The reader had to collect clues across the text.)

QUESTION: Have you ever had to make a hard decision that scared you?

ANSWER: (Varies) (On Your Own: The student doesn't need to refer back to the story to answer this one.)

Raphael suggests making these categories and strategies explicit to students and having them classify and answer questions as a group. Teachers can structure this activity as a game in which students gather evidence for a set of questions and discuss how they answered the questions (Sentell & Blachowicz, 1989).

Guided Reading Procedure. As originally developed by Manzo (1975), this procedure is designed to enhance students' recall of expository materials. It also increases the level of student participation in class and provides challenge as well as variety. It consists of the following steps:

1. A passage of appropriate length is selected. The length is best judged in terms of the reading speed and attention span of the average reader in the group. As a rule of thumb, primary grade students might be expected to read for 3 minutes and to read a 90-word passage in that time (30 words per minute); intermediate grade students might read for 5 minutes at approximately 100 words per minute—a 500-word passage; junior high students might read for 7 minutes at 125 words per minute—a 900-word passage; and high school students could probably read for 10-minutes at 200 words per minute—a 2,000 word passage.

2. The teacher prepares students for the selection by introducing the general topic; relating it to previous classroom instruction as well as to students' personal experiences, and by introducing vocabulary, new concepts, and so on. A general purpose for reading is established, and students are directed to remember as much of the passage as they can.

3. After reading, students tell whatever they remember, and all information is recorded on the chalkboard by the teacher in the order in which it is recalled. (It may be abbreviated in form to save time.) One teacher found that having students write the information in their notebooks while the teacher recorded it on the chalkboard helped sustain students' attention and interest.

4. After students have contributed all the information they can remember, the teacher directs their attention to any inconsistencies, inaccuracies, or inadequacies that may be present. Students are encouraged to consult the text for necessary corrections and additions.

5. The group is then asked to organize the information they have compiled. This may take any form that is familiar to the students—a diagram, an outline, a chronological sequence, or even a semantic web. The teacher guides this process by raising questions, making suggestions, and so on.

6. The teacher then raises some final questions to help students gain full understanding of the passage.

7. For the final step, a conventional, teacher-made comprehension test is administered. The test items can be of any kind, but they should reflect the ideas and information that were brought out during class discussion. Manzo cautions against omitting this step: "it is important to the

overall design because it provides an opportunity for evaluation, feedback, and reinforcement." He also notes that "students . . . come to look forward to these tests as opportunities to show what they have learned—a just reward for effort."[1]

Although Manzo's procedure was originally designed to be used following silent reading of an entire passage, it may also be used as a prereading activity (Bean & Pardi, 1979). In this case, students first survey the passage by reading the title, headings, pictures, charts, introductory and summary paragraphs, and so on. Then they recall as much as they can, organize their recall, and check it for accuracy and completeness (as in Steps 3, 4, and 5 above). They then read the entire passage and take the final comprehension test (Step 7). When used as a prereading activity, the procedure demonstrates the value of surveying materials before reading and thus serves to combine the teaching of surveying skills with the teaching of specific content. After reading, the students contribute ideas while the teacher records them on a chalkboard. Each idea is enclosed in a circle, and lines are drawn to connect the circles as appropriate. Students are permitted to refer to the text to refresh their memories or resolve conflicts.

For example, for a story about triplets, the teacher wrote the name of each triplet in a separate circle and the names of all three in a fourth circle. The four circles radiated from a central circle, the core of the web, which was left blank. The students were directed to "remember important things about each sister [p. 645]." After the story was read (by the teacher in this case, as a listening activity), the children recalled information on how each sister differed from the others as well as on the characteristics they all shared. The core of the web, representing the central idea, was filled in after the four strands had been completed; an appropriate statement of the central idea was arrived at through brainstorming; "sisters who do same and different things [p. 645]." The completed web then served as a springboard for a group discussion of individuality, family relationships, and the like.

Direct Instruction in Text Structure. Evidence that understanding text structure plays an important role in comprehension was cited earlier. When ninth graders were given instruction in the main types of expository discourse (e.g., comparison–contrast, problem–solution, main idea–supporting details), they nearly doubled the amount of information recalled (McDonald, 1978; cited in Meyer, Brandt, & Bluth, 1980). Similar results have been obtained with poor comprehenders in the primary grades (Bartlett, 1978; cited in Meyer et al., 1980). Taylor and Beach (1984) recently showed that training in text structure is helpful to seventh graders in learning relatively unfamiliar

---

[1] From Guided reading procedure by A. V. Manzo, 1975, in *Journal of Reading, 18,* 291. Reprinted by permission of the author.

materials (drawn from social studies textbooks). However, Taylor and Beach's instruction did not so much pertain to discourse patterns as to the use of headings and subheadings. The students transferred the headings to their notebooks and organized the information under each heading in terms of main ideas and details. They also made note of relationships between headings where appropriate.

Using text structure to help students in writing is a productive approach to applying and sharpening one's knowledge about prose organization in the act of moving from reader to writer. Such techniques as writing for prereading (McGee & Richgels, 1985), Predict-o-Grams (Blachowicz, 1986), story frames (Gordon & Braun, 1983), and exposition frames (Slater, Graves, & Piche, 1985) may be useful for fostering knowledge of text structure and integrating reading and writing instruction.

Graphic Representation. Semantic maps, webs, or overviews involve the teacher and students in charting the relationships of the ideas in a selection. For example, the teacher can provide the high-level organization of a text and direct the students to read in order to find the supporting information (Cleland, 1981)

Sentence-Level Comprehension. While most instructional intervention is carried out with whole selections or large segments of text, some instruction may need to focus on sentence-level comprehension and instruction. Though children come to school with fairly sophisticated knowledge of the syntactic system of their language, this competence continues to develop over the elementary school years with exposure through reading, writing, speaking, and listening as the prime avenues of this development. Therefore, we do not suggest that extensive instruction with isolated sentences be included in the instructional program. Rather, the following techniques may be tried with sentences that proved difficult within the context of reading a larger selection.

Highlighting Anaphoric Relations. Anaphoric relations refer to the way in which certain words can be used as substitutes for words or groups of words that occurred previously in the text. In addition to personal pronouns, anaphoric devices include pronouns that substitute for places (*here, there*) and for things and ideas (*it, this, that*). One of the more difficult types of anaphora involves the substitution of pro-verbs (*does, can, will*) for previously mentioned verbs or verb phrases: *Mary* **skates well.** *John* does *too. Mary* **does figure eights.** *So* **can** *John.*

An experienced clinician (Daskal, 1983) reports that students with poor comprehension are generally responsive to instruction in anaphora. Not only do they become proficient in identifying the antecedents of anaphoric words, but they learn to attend more closely to the succession or "flow" of ideas in written materials. The procedure she follows begins with oral discussion. The student is simply asked questions that require the identification of pronoun or pro-verb antecedents. For example, given the following text:

> Harry and Josh went to the store to buy hot dogs, potato chips, and soft drinks for the picnic. But *they* were so expensive that the boy's didn't have enough money to pay for *them.*

the student would be asked "What was expensive?" or "What couldn't they pay for?" Next, the student learns to draw lines between pronouns and their antecedents. (With nonconsumable materials, a sheet of acetate is clipped to the page of print and the student uses a china marker.) This enables the teacher to monitor the student's accuracy in identifying antecedents, and it helps the student develop awareness of these cohesive text elements. After several weeks of this type of instruction, students automatically relate anaphoric terms to their antecedents.

Focusing on Connective Terms. Daskal's procedure can also be applied to connective terms. Connective terms specify how ideas are related to one another. Geva (1983) provides a useful four-way classification of these terms. She points out that some of them simply *add* ideas to other ideas (e.g., *and, also, as well,* and *in addition*) whereas others express contrastive or adversative relations (e.g., *but, however,* and *on the other hand*). A third type signals causal relations (*because, so, therefore, as a result, consequently*), and the final type pertains to temporal sequence (*before, after, first, next, then*). The relationships signaled by these terms can, of course, apply to information in any unit of text—to information contained in individual clauses or sentences, in a series of sentences within a paragraph, or in several paragraphs or even larger stretches of text.

Instruction in these relationships must be conducted, quite obviously, in the context of the kinds of situations to which they refer. For example, to show students what specific temporal words mean, it is necessary to look at situations that can be temporally sequenced. It is for this reason that reciprocal teaching appears to be a promising format for highlighting connectives and the relationships they signal. A series of sessions could incorporate specific emphasis on these relationships into the procedure; each time a signal word occurred in a passage segment, the dialogue leader would be expected to discuss its informational value. The particular signal words that students should be on the lookout for would be introduced beforehand and displayed in a prominent place for quick reference.

Signal words can also be systematically highlighted during the course or regular basal reader lessons. The teacher simply examines the lesson materials to locate these terms and then plans interesting and appropriate ways to call attention to them during postreading discussion. The purpose is to help students become aware of these terms and attend to them without external guidance.

Sentence Combining. Another type of exercise, one that can be presented as a game, is sentence combining. This process can be used to engage students in the construction of complex sentences from two or more simple sentences (Froese & Kurushima, 1979; Straw & Schreiner, 1982). Another alternative is a sentence anagram task (Weaver, 1979) whereby students learn to organize words into groups within a sentence and then into complete sentences.

Instructional Recommendations

Surveying the range of instructional possibilities, we can now design our initial instructional plans for the students whose diagnoses made up the first part of this chapter.

For Paul, who was able to improve his comprehension with some general rereading directions by the teacher, the DR-TA would be a good choice, helping him to break a selection into slightly more manageable chunks and focusing him on monitoring his own reading more closely.

For Jake, who formed an early, unproductive schema about reading that colored the rest of his comprehension, the ReQuest technique might provide a good starting point. He needs to be held closely to the text at the beginning of a reading selection to help him get on the right track. Within this process the teacher needs to help him attend to small signal words to help build an appropriate initial schema to guide the rest of his reading.

Andrea had greater difficulty with her comprehension; Reciprocal Teaching could be a good starting point, focusing on sentences or short paragraphs. Because she also has great difficulty with vocabulary and using contextual information, much of the questioning and clarification could focus on these needs. Having Andrea work with graphic organizers might help her organize her concepts more effectively.

Like all initial instructional recommendations, these are tentative, to be modified as the teacher observes the lessons and learns more about the student's abilities and problems. This is the nature of diagnostic instruction.

SUMMARY

We have argued that a diagnosis of difficulty in the area of comprehension can generally be made once it has been determined that print skill and vocabulary knowledge are not underlying sources of poor comprehension. Once such a decision has been made, it is useful to explore further to identify the nature of the comprehension problem. That is, in order to provide appropriate instruction, it is necessary to determine whether a student's difficulty stems from poorly developed strategies for interacting with text and organizing text information or from the student's inability to understand the information the text contains.

Case studies utilizing postreading questioning, retelling, and the think-aloud procedure were presented along with a framework for specifying instruction. Variables such as level of teacher support, explicitness of instruction, and the length of the instructional text unit were identified and used to construct a framework for describing instructional strategies and for selecting the type of intervention that would be appropriate for the comprehension problems of the three cases.

CHAPTER 8

Diagnosis Based on an Instructional Passage

The previous seven chapters have introduced ways of thinking about and investigating the development of reading proficiency. Chapter 1 described a model for diagnosis that focuses on the relations among print skill, vocabulary knowledge, and discourse comprehension. Chapters 2, 3, and 4 discussed ways to understand and diagnose students' print strategies. Chapter 5 focused on the development of vocabulary knowledge and described procedures for assessing students' knowledge of concepts and terms included in their reading materials. Chapters 6 and 7 discussed ways of thinking about reading comprehension and described procedures for developing questions and diagnosing comprehension problems. These various topics and diagnostic procedures were developed in separate chapters because of their complexity. In this chapter, the procedures are combined into a comprehensive diagnosis of reading proficiency in accord with the basic model described in the first chapter.

Although we do not expect teachers to perform a comprehensive diagnosis of the reading strategies of each of their students, conducting intensive case studies is a useful way to consolidate the diagnostic knowledge that was presented in previous chapters and to learn to think about reading development in terms of the diagnostic model. After conducting several case studies, teachers can begin to use the procedures more informally, during the course of daily instruction. The training procedures increase sensitivity to the pattern of oral reading responses and to the demands of comprehension questions as well as the appropriateness of student answers. There will always be students whose reading difficulties are extremely perplexing and for whom it may be useful to undertake an extensive diagnosis. But for most students informal observations during daily instruction over a period of time will suggest ways in which instruction can be more effective.

One of the more important instructional issues confronting teachers is whether the instructional materials being used in the classroom are of appropriate difficulty for their students. Betts (1954) suggested that it is useful to characterize the appropriateness of the match between students and materials in terms of levels (see earlier discussion on page 174). The *independent* reading level is the highest level at which students can read fluently with good comprehension without instructional assistance. The *instructional* level is the highest level at which students are able to read with adequate comprehension once they are provided with appropriate instructional support. Finally, the *frustration* level is that level at which the text is so difficult that even with appropriate support, students may be unable to comprehend. In this last case, faulty comprehension may reflect problems with print processing, vocabulary knowledge, or discourse processing. Figure 8.1 presents a graphic representation of the difficulty levels of reading materials.

Reading that is assigned as homework or as independent seatwork should pose almost no print-processing or comprehension problems for students. That is, students should be able to read the material orally with good intonation and phrasing or silently with ease and comprehend the main ideas and important facts. When students have difficulty correctly identifying 2 or more words in every 100, they may well have problems in focusing on the meaning and these problems may hinder them from developing mature

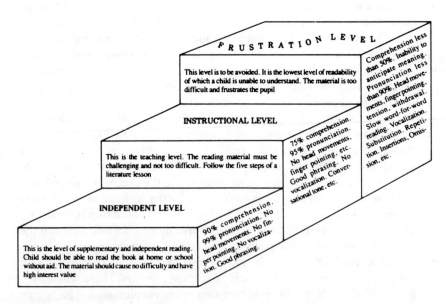

Figure 8.1 Betts's levels of reading. (From E. A. Betts, *Foundations of Reading Instruction* [p. 448], New York: American Book Company, 1954. Reprinted by permission.)

reading strategies. Failure to answer more than 1 question in every 10 is another indication that the material is probably too difficult for independent reading. It is important that the questions used in making this assessment be appropriate and nontrivial. There are some disabled readers for whom no reading material is easy and who therefore should not read unless the teacher has prepared them for the passage or provides direct support.

Given the range in reading proficiency in most classes, teachers should have for homework and independent reading assignments materials that represent a comparable range in difficulty. Students can best develop their reading strategies through contextual materials that they can read fluently with good comprehension. Unfortunately, some students never experience the pleasure of problem-free reading and are thereby deprived of appropriate reading practice.

When students read under the direct supervision of their teacher, more problems in print skill and comprehension can be tolerated. As a rule of thumb, if a student is reading aloud, he or she should have difficulty with no more than 1 word in every 20. Comprehension should be good, with at least 3 out of every 4 questions answered correctly.

Teachers need to keep in mind not only the average performance of the group with which they are working but also the performance of individuals in the group. When individual students are missing more than half the questions posed or having difficulty with more than 1 word in every 10, the materials are inappropriate, representing frustration-level work. Instructional support can rarely help a student who is reading frustration-level material enough to permit him or her to perform at acceptable levels of print processing and/or comprehension.

By contrast, students who perform in the borderline region between frustration level and acceptable instructional level may be helped by instruction that has been developed with their particular problems in mind. This borderline region is characterized by an accuracy of 90 to 94 percent on oral reading and 50 to 74 percent on comprehension questions. The criteria for determining the reading level of materials are summarized in Table 8.1.

TABLE 8.1. CRITERIA FOR DETERMINING READING LEVELS

Level	Passage reading	
	Oral reading accuracy (%)	Comprehension accuracy (%)
Independent	98–100	90–100
Instructional	95–97	75–89
Borderline	90–94	50–74
Frustration	below 90	below 50

Consider the case of Eva, discussed in Chapter 4. Eva's teacher had her read the next story in her basal reader with little instructional support. Her oral reading accuracy score of 91 percent indicates performance in the borderline range. However, her comprehension was quite good at the instructional level, with 8 out of 10 questions answered correctly. Eva was in the lowest reading group and her teacher wanted her to remain in the group. However, the analysis of her print skill difficulties indicated that her problems were severe. The teacher's alternatives were either to have her receive reading instruction on an individual basis with easier materials or to try to eliminate some of the print-processing problems posed by her current basal reader through increased instructional support.

The teacher decided to try the second alternative, spending more time on word identification and discussion of key story terms prior to reading. After providing such preparation, she listened to the quality of Eva's oral reading and found that it was more fluent than it had been, with less than 5 percent of the words causing problems. She then proceeded to offer this increased support to Eva's reading group as part of their regular instruction. Other students in the group seemed to profit as well. At the same time, the teacher helped Eva select easy reading material for independent reading. If Eva's comprehension of the story had not been so complete, her teacher might not have found it possible to keep her with the reading group.

For most teachers, the students who cause most concern are those for whom the reading materials are too difficult. When frustration-level reading is indicated, in terms of either oral reading accuracy or level of comprehension, the teacher must find more appropriate materials. If the student's performance is in the borderline region, it may be possible to make the materials accessible through appropriate instruction. Usually, further diagnosis of the student's reading strengths and difficulties must be undertaken in order to pinpoint the nature of the problem and to experiment with instructional support.

In the next section of this chapter, specific procedures for diagnosing reading strengths and difficulties are described. As was mentioned earlier, it is important to undertake individual case studies in order to consolidate the diagnostic strategies that were introduced in prior chapters.

DIAGNOSTIC PROCEDURES

In order to judge the appropriateness of instructional materials and the reading development of students, the following steps should be taken. As these steps were described in previous chapters, they are presented in summary form here.

Preparation

The teacher should select from the student's instructional materials a passage that seems to pose some difficulty for the student and that is similar in length to those typically used for instruction. A photocopy or double-spaced typewritten copy should be prepared.

Next, the teacher should study the passage and create a set of vocabulary knowledge and comprehension questions according to the procedures described in Chapters 5 and 6. The comprehension questions should be ordered according to the sequence of the story, and typed or written with sufficient space between them to record the student's responses. The vocabulary knowledge questions should follow the comprehension questions.

A system such as that described in Chapter 4 should be used to record the student's oral reading responses. The student should also be tape-recorded, so that it is possible to check the time it took to read the passage and the accuracy of the handwritten oral reading record.

Administration

The teacher should make sure that the student is comfortable and relaxed. The reason for the diagnosis should be discussed with the student (e.g., to learn more about how to work with him or her on reading). In addition, the procedures to be followed should be described. The student should be told that he or she will be asked to read a passage and answer some questions about it and that next time, his or her reading strategies will be explored more informally. When the student is asked to read the selection aloud, some version of the following directions should be given:

> This is a story in which . . . [theme-related preparatory statement]. Please read this story aloud for me. If you come to a word you don't know, try to figure it out, or skip it. I will not be able to help you, so do the best you can. After you finish, I will ask you some questions.

Before the student begins reading, the tape recorder should be tested. The student may wish to record his or her voice and then listen to the replay. The student's oral reading should be recorded on the photocopy or typed version of the story as well as on tape. The tape recorder should be kept running while the comprehension questions are being asked, so that the responses won't be lost if the student proceeds more rapidly than the teacher can write. And, as mentioned, the tape recorder can be used to check the amount of time the student took to read the passage.

Analysis

Performance on the first part of the diagnosis is studied to determine the area(s) of reading that should be probed. If print skill accuracy is below 95 percent, sight words and/or content words are selected and procedures developed for examining the student's underlying resources for identifying words. If comprehension is below 75 percent, the teacher should examine the questions that were incorrectly answered and plan questions that may facilitate the probe. At the same time, the influence of vocabulary knowledge on comprehension and print skill should be considered and, when appropriate, additional words or phrases should be selected for presentation during the probe.

Probe

During a second session with the student, the teacher administers the probe items according to the procedures summarized in Figure 8.2. If difficulty with print skill is suspected, regardless of the adequacy of comprehension performance, the probe should focus first on content word identification and then on content word meaning. The reason for this order is that presenting the vocabulary knowledge items first would invalidate the exploration of word identification. If sight words are also a problem, these shoud be explored after the content word probe. The student's responses to the print skill probe should be recorded in writing as well as on tape. It is important that complete notes be made, since it is often difficult on the basis of a tape recording to reconstruct the questions or word parts to which the student was responding.

Vocabulary knowledge items selected for obtaining further evidence regarding knowledge should be presented next if they were not already presented in exploring print skill. The probe of comprehension is conducted last. In this way, the final probe may be omitted if convincing evidence has already been obtained that print skill and vocabulary knowledge are interfering with comprehension.

Interpretation

In analyzing a student's performance on a diagnostic passage, we find it useful to focus first on print skill, then on vocabulary knowledge, and finally on comprehension. Then, when we have achieved an understanding of the student's strategies in each of these areas, we examine his or her relative strength in these areas using the model presented in the first chapter.

Print Skill. The evidence concerning a student's print skill strategies comes from two sources: oral reading of contextual materials and identification of isolated words and word parts. Specifically, the first source provides evidence

Figure 8.2 Summary of procedures for the probe.

These procedures may be used after the student has read a passage and responded to comprehension questions.

If Student Demonstrates Difficulty Identifying Content Words
1. Select content words that the student missed during the oral reading. Write them on a blank page in list form. For each word, first see if the student can pronounce it without help. If not, use the procedures described in Chapter 4: See if the student can divide the word into syllables and pronounce them. If not, see if the student can pronounce just the first syllable (cover the remainder of the word with a finger). If not, see if the student knows the sound corresponding to the first consonant or consonant cluster, then the vowel and final consonant(s). For syllables that lend themselves to visual analogy, test to see if the student can think of a word that ends the same and on that basis identify the syllable; if not, provide such a word and see if the student can use it to identify the syllable. Test a sample of consonants, consonant clusters, vowels, word endings, and word families. Continue with successive words on the list as long as the procedure yields new information and the student is responsive.

2. Ask the student to define the words missed, using the procedures described in Chapter 5.

If Student Demonstrates Difficulty with Sight Words:
1. Select sight words that the student misread during oral reading. Write them on a blank page in list form. See if the student can pronounce each word. Note whether the response is immediate or delayed. Continue the probe only as long as it yields new information and the student is able to respond attentively.

If Student Demonstrates Inadequate Comprehension:
1. Probe the student's knowledge of word meanings and/or concepts that may be interfering with comprehension, as described in Chapter 5. If vocabulary knowledge is adequate, probe comprehension further as described in the next two steps.

2. Note those questions that were answered incorrectly. Have the student reread the portion of the passage on which the question is based and reask the question. Continue this procedure for the remaining incorrectly answered questions.

3. If a question is not answered correctly after rereading, explore further using the informal interview technique illustrated in Chapter 7. Note intersentence and sentence-level problems of the text that may interfere with comprehension, and use informal procedures to explore these areas.

concerning the integrated approach to print that the student has developed; the second yields evidence concerning underlying knowledge about print. Though the two sources of evidence complement each other, the analyses are undertaken separately.

The analysis of contextual reading involves four steps. First, the student's response to the entire passage is examined in order to characterize his or her general proficiency. Analysis then focuses on responses to high-frequency sight words and, subsequently, on responses to content words in order to determine how the student identified words that were unfamiliar. Finally, the student's reading integration and fluency are assessed. The results of this four-step analysis should be recorded on the oral reading analysis form.

The analysis of performance on isolated words—the probe—may focus on sight words, content words, or both. The probe of sight words should reveal whether they are recognized on sight when other problems involved in contextual reading are removed. The probe of content words provides answers to the following questions: Can the student divide multisyllabic words into syllables? Can the student identify simple syllables and more complex syllables (those containing blends, digraphs)? Can the student identify word endings (*-ing, -es, -ed,* . . .)? Does the student know vowel pronunciation and markers? Can the student blend letter sounds?

The results obtained from the oral reading analysis and the probe are then consolidated on the oral reading analysis form in order to answer the following questions:

1. Is the passage of appropriate difficulty in terms of the student's print skills and instructional needs?
2. What is the student's strength in rapid sight-word recognition?
3. What resources does the student possess for identifying unknown words?
4. Are the student's print-processing skills integrated and fluent?
5. What, if any, aspect of print skills should be the focus of instruction?

In answering these and subsequent questions the teacher should note any supporting evidence.

Vocabulary Knowledge. Informal questioning and discussion can be used to ascertain whether the student has the background experiences that are needed to understand the passage. However, word knowledge questions and probes will be needed to assess the student's knowledge of the specific words that pertain to these experiences. They also provide evidence on whether the student is able to select the particular meaning of a word that is appropriate to the sense of the passage. This evidence concerning vocabulary knowledge should answer three questions:

1. Does the student have command of the concepts used in the passage?
2. Is this knowledge explicit and clear (definitions) or implicit and somewhat vague (sentence use)?
3. Can the student use context to select the appropriate word meaning?

Comprehension. The interpretation should begin with the evidence concerning the student's ability to respond correctly to text-related comprehension questions. In completing the comprehension–vocabulary knowledge summary form, answers to the following questions are sought:

1. Did the student understand the essential information contained in the passage and the import of the message? Is the passage at an appropriate level for the student for instructional purposes?
2. If not, what are the student's strengths and weaknesses in comprehension?
3. Is the problem mainly in the area of comprehension, or do difficulties with print skill or vocabulary knowledge underlie and account for comprehension difficulties?
4. On the basis of the comprehension probe, what, if any, instruction in comprehension is needed?

Summary/Integration. First, conclusions about the student's print skill, vocabulary knowledge, and comprehension should be summarized. Then, it should be determined whether vocabulary knowledge or print skill difficulties interfere with comprehension. Finally, the student's major strengths and difficulties in reading should be discussed.

Instructional Plan

On the basis of the summary and final integration of diagnostic information, the following questions can be answered:

1. Is the instructional material of appropriate difficulty for this student under ordinary conditions? Would certain forms of instructional intervention help the student to cope with the material?
2. What forms of instruction will help this student further refine his or her reading strategies?

Recommendations for instruction should follow directly from the final summary/integration of results and should be listed in order of priority.

It is extremely important that the diagnosis and recommendations be discussed with the student. It is also important to ascertain how the student feels about the recommendations. The instruction can be successful only to the extent that the student becomes a part of the planning and implementation.

CASE STUDY APPLICATION

The two case studies described in the remaining sections of this chapter demonstrate how these procedures can be applied. A teacher using this form of diagnosis may wish to prepare the student for reading the passage in the manner he or she normally follows in the classroom, rather than, as we have suggested, to have the student read with only a brief introduction.

CASE 1:   Sharon

Sharon is 12 years old and in seventh grade. She has difficulty in reading and is in a remedial reading class. She works hard and is very cooperative in school. She is a shy student with very little experience outside of her lower-class neighborhood. Her mother is dead, and she lives with an older sister, who is her guardian, and other sisters and brothers. She does not have many interests—"just likes to stay home and watch TV or play outside with her younger sister." Her teacher noticed that she often had difficulty comprehending assigned materials and decided to learn more about her reading strategies.

PREPARATION
Sharon's teacher selected a passage that she thought might be of interest to her. It was entitled "Bring Light to the Blind" and was taken from a high fourth-grade reading workbook called *Adventure Trail* (Charles E. Merrill). The teacher's first step was to study the passage in order to derive comprehension and word knowledge questions. The reader should examine the passage shown in Figure 8.3 and try to develop appropriate comprehension and word knowledge questions.

Before proceeding, the reader should compare his or her questions with those developed by the teacher. Figure 8.4 shows the teacher's comprehension and vocabulary knowledge questions and the responses that she expected. The first six comprehension questions involve text-related comprehension, while question 7 encourages the student to generalize beyond the text.

ADMINISTRATION
Sharon was quite relaxed when she read the passage orally and responded to the prepared questions. The record of her oral reading is shown in Figure 8.5. The reader should study the pattern of her responses in order to determine whether she has difficulty in any area of print skill.

Following the oral reading, Sharon was asked to retell as much of the selection as she could remember. Here is what she said: ". . . about blind people . . . reading and stuff. About this boy . . . he was doing something and something hurt his eye.

Figure 8.3   Diagnostic reading passage: Sharon.

Bringing Light to the Blind

Only about one-fourth of the blind people in our country can read. They read Braille (brāl). As you know, Braille is a way of printing by raised dots. The blind run their fingers over the raised dots.

Did you ever shut your eyes and run your fingers over a page of Braille printing? All the little raised dots seemed to run together. Even if you knew the Braille alphabet, your fingers could not pick out each separate dot. But the boys and girls who cannot see read stories in Braille. Their fingers are trained to be their eyes.

A Frenchman, Louis Braille, made it possible for those who cannot see, to read. When he was a small boy, he used to play around his father's harness shop. One day, he was trying to punch holes in a piece of leather with a big awl. The tool slipped and hurt Louis' eye. Before long, he became blind.

When Louis was ten years old, he was sent to a school for the blind in Paris. There he began to study music and learned to play the organ. He became a very fine musician.

Louis did not just want to become famous. He wanted to help all those who could not see. So he set to work to find an alphabet which could be read with the fingers. Today that system of writing is known as Braille.

Some books and magazines are printed in Braille for boys and girls. "My Weekly Reader Number Four" is one of them. Every week, the American Printing House for the Blind prints Braille copies of this newspaper.

There are even books that "talk." The books are like phonograph records that talk to the blind. When a blind person wants to read, he turns a key and then listens. It is as if someone were reading a book aloud to him. Our government sends the talking books free to blind people in all parts of our country.

(From *Adventure Trail,* Diagnostic Reading Workbook, Grade 4, by E. M. Johnson, p. 46. In *New Diagnostic Reading Series.* Columbus, Ohio: Charles E. Merrill Publishing Co., 1969. Reprinted by permission.)

That's all I remember." Because her retelling was so incomplete, it was necessary to administer the questions that had been prepared. Her responses are shown in Figure 8.6. The reader should study her answers in order to decide whether she is experiencing difficulty with vocabulary knowledge and/or comprehension.

ANALYSIS

On the basis of Sharon's oral reading of the passage and her responses to the comprehension questions, it was decided that the probe should focus on two areas: exploration of her content word errors, in order better to assess her word identification skill, and assessment of her vocabulary knowledge in areas pertinent to the passage.

Figure 8.4 Comprehension and vocabulary knowledge questions: Sharon.

Comprehension

1. How do blind people read? (They run their fingers over raised dots, or by Braille.)

2. What do blind people train to be their eyes? (fingers)

3. How did Louis Braille become blind? (He was hit in the eye with a tool [awl] while punching holes in leather in his father's harness shop.)

4. When Louis Braille was at school, what did he study? (music; playing the organ)

5. What did Louis Braille do for the blind? (made it possible for blind people to read by inventing an alphabet which could be read with the fingers, etc.)

6. What are books that "talk"? (like records that talk to the blind)

*7. Do you think that Louis Braille was a brave person? Why?

* Beyond-text question

Vocabulary Knowledge

1. What is *Braille*? (printing by small raised dots that can be read by touch)

2. What is an *awl*? (a tool for punching holes)

3. What does *raised* mean? (higher; above)

4. What is a *system*? (a method)

Figure 8.5 Record of oral reading: Sharon.

Bringing Light to the Blind

Only about one-fourth of the blind people in our country can read. They $\frac{20}{0}$

read Braille (brāl). As you know, Braille is a way of printing by raised dots.

The blind run their fingers over the raised dots.

Did you ever shut your eyes and run your fingers over a page of Braille

printing? All the little raised dots seemed to run together. Even if you knew

218

Figure 8.5 *(Continued)*

the ~~Braille~~ *Brāley* alphabet, your finger⑤ could not pick out each ~~separate~~ *sep-per-* dot. But **#2**

the boys and girls who cannot see read stories in ~~Braille~~ *Brāley*. Their fingers are **✗0**

trained to be their eyes.

A Frenchman, Louis ~~Braille~~ *Brāley*, made it possible for those who cannot see, **✗0**

to read. When he was a small boy, he used to play around his father'⑤ harness **✗0**

shop. One day, he was trying to punch ᴀ hole⑤ in a piece of leather with a big **2 1**

awl. The tool slipped and hurt Louis' eye. Before long, he became blind.

When Louis was ten years old, he was ~~sent~~ ©*sēen* to a school for the blind in **1**

Paris. There he ~~began~~ *begin* to study music and learned *ing* to play the organ. He **2**

could become ᴧ ~~became~~ a very fine musician. **2**

Louis did not just want to become ᴀ *a* famous. He wanted to help all those **1**

who could not see. So he set to work to find an alphabet ⟨which could be read **1**

simple ⁷ with the fingers⟩ Today that ~~system~~ it of writing is known⓪ as ~~Braille~~ s *Brāley*. **#3**

Skipped entire line in passage

Some books and magazines are printed in ~~Braille~~ *Brāley* for boys and girls. "My **✗0**

Weekly Reader Number Four" is one of them. Every week, the American⓪ **1**

Printing House for the Blind prints ~~Braille~~ *Brāley* copies of this newspaper. **✗0**

There are even books that "talk ᴀ." s ⟨The⟩ books are like phonograph **2 1**

records that talk ᴀ s to ⟨the⟩ blind. When a blind person want⑤ to read, he turn⑤ a **#1**

key and then listens. It is as if someone were reading a book aloud to him. Our

Government sends ⟨the⟩ talking books free to blind people in all parts of ~~our~~ *a* **2 1**

country.

*Dialect-based miscues occurring more than twice were not counted.

(From *Adventure Trail*, Diagnostic Reading Workbook, Grade 4, by E. M. Johnson, p. 46. In *New Diagnostic Reading Series*. Columbus, Ohio: Charles E. Merrill Publishing Co., 1969. Reprinted by permission.)

Figure 8.6 Responses to comprehension and vocabulary knowledge questions: Sharon.

Retelling

> . . . about blind people . . . reading and stuff. About this boy — he was doing something and something hurt his eye. That's all I remember.

Comprehension

✓ 1. How do blind people read? (They run their fingers over raised dots, or by Braille.)
RESPONSE: They read from Brā-ley.

✓ 2. What do blind people train to be their eyes? (fingers)
RESPONSE: They use their hands, don't they?

½ 3. How did Louis Braille become blind? (He was hit in the eye with a tool (awl) while punching holes in leather in his father's harness shop.)
RESPONSE: He was doing something and he knocked something over and it made him blind. [Q.: What hit him in the eye?] That harness stuff.

✓ 4. When Louis Braille was at school, what did he study? (music; playing the organ)
RESPONSE: Music.

✗ 5. What did Louis Braille do for the blind? (made it possible for blind people to read by inventing an alphabet which could be read with the fingers, etc.)
RESPONSE: He helped them learn to read and put up this thing about blind.

✗ 6. What are books that "talk"? (like records that talk to the blind)
RESPONSE: Don't know.

✗ *7. Do you think that Louis Braille was a brave person? Why?
RESPONSE: Yes, he was brave. He helped people that were blind to read and write.

* Beyond-text question

Vocabulary Knowledge

✗ 1. What is *Braille*? (printing by small raised dots that can be read by touch)
RESPONSE: Like a thing that goes through a line or something. [Q.: can you explain that?] Well . . . not sure.

✗ 2. What is an *awl*? (a tool for punching holes)
RESPONSE: Don't know.

✓ 3. What does *raised* mean? (higher; above)
RESPONSE: You raise it . . . raise it up.

✗ 4. What is a *system*? (a method)
RESPONSE: Don't know.

PROBE

The results from the oral reading analysis and probe are summarized on the oral reading analysis form in Figure 8.7. The probe indicates that Sharon has good knowledge of basic phonics concepts but has difficulty applying this knowledge during contextual reading.

The summary of Sharon's comprehension performance and the results from the vocabulary knowledge probe are presented on the comprehension—vocabulary knowledge summary in Figure 8.8. Because her word knowledge was so limited, there was no point in probing her comprehension skills further.

Before reading the interpretations made by the teacher, the reader should think for a moment about Sharon's reading. What are Sharon's strengths and difficulties?

INTERPRETATION

Print Skill. Sight words do not seem to be a problem for Sharon, and she possesses good phonics and structural skills. It is difficult to know whether her failure to apply these skills during contextual reading occurred because of the large number of unfamiliar words in the passage or because the general meaning of the passage was difficult for her to grasp. Most of the substitutions that did not make sense occurred in sentences that were too technical for her. While it is clear that Sharon's reading of this passage was neither integrated nor fluent, the number of problems posed may simply have overwhelmed her. It will be important to have Sharon read an easier passage with fewer unfamiliar words in order to have a more valid test of her integration and fluency.

Some affixed words and verb forms posed problems for Sharon. Dialect substitutions where the final s was either omitted or inserted were eliminated from consideration. But Sharon's problem seems to extend beyond that of pluralization and possession to other affixes. Her oral language differs in certain respects from standard English; further, at times she appears to be overcorrecting for dialect. It is important to determine the extent to which Sharon's problems with affixes arise from dialect influence as opposed to lack of knowledge. The probe results suggest that she understands affixes but during difficult oral reading becomes confused about their pronunciation.

Vocabulary Knowledge. Sharon's vocabulary and understanding of words seems to be quite limited for a seventh grader. She does not know some words typically known by students her age (*harness, system, volume*) and has vague or limited concepts of others (*separate, raised*). The possibility that she is in command of more knowledge than she is able to express was not supported by the probe, but further observation of her vocabulary knowledge should be undertaken.

Comprehension. The results from the retelling and the text-related questions are consistent, and they reveal that Sharon had difficulty understanding this selection. Even when her responses were correct or partially correct, they indicated serious limitations. She seemed to have particular difficulty describing major concepts explained in the passage. The main underlying problem seemed to be her failure to understand the technical concepts (raised dots, awl) necessary for

Figure 8.7 Analysis of oral reading responses: Sharon.

ORAL READING ANALYSIS

Name Sharon Grade 7 Date 2/84
Book/Page Adventure Trail Level 4th Grade

A. DIFFICULTY

20 / 329   94 % Correct

Level: Independent Instructional
(Borderline) Frustration

B. WORD LEARNING: Sight Word Errors

Printed Word	Oral Response	Probe	Evaluation
is	it	✓	Immediate and correct
our	a	✓	recognition of sight words.
② the	[omitted]	✓	Sight words are probably
② a	[inserted]	✓	not a problem with easier
could	[inserted]	✓	materials.
[a line]	[omitted]		

C. WORD IDENTIFICATION: Content Word Errors

Printed Word	Oral Response	Probe	Evaluation
② Braille	Brā/Brăly/Brăley Brāley		Good knowledge of phonics.
page	paget	✓	Application may be more of
known	knows	✓	a problem.
sent	seen ©	✓	Has some knowledge about
seemed	seems	✓	affixes and syllabication.
learned	learning	✓	Well developed word identification
separate	sē per ©	✓	skill; need to check
began	begin	✓	application during
became	become	✓	easier contextual
system	simple	✓	reading.
American	America	✓	

D. INTEGRATION – FLUENCY

Integration: Errors are generally not contextually appropriate; infrequent correction of errors; highly dependent on graphic cues.

Fluency: Rate 329 / 6.1 = 54 wpm Evaluation Slow, even for a fourth grader.
Phrasing Choppy-does not read with appropriate phrasing

Figure 8.8 Summary of responses to comprehension and vocabulary knowledge questions: Sharon.

COMPREHENSION–VOCABULARY   Name _Sharon_ Grade _7_ Date _2/84_
KNOWLEDGE SUMMARY   Book/Page _Adventure Trail_ Level _High 4th_

COMPREHENSION   Level: Independent Instructional

_3½_ / _6_   _58_ % Correct   (Borderline) Frustration

A. RETELLING: Complete   Main Idea   Partial   (Inadequate)

Comments: _She had a difficult time expressing herself – limited vocabulary, problems with sentence structure._

B. TEXT-RELATED COMPREHENSION

Item #	Response	Probe (Comments)	Item #	Response	Probe (Comments)
1	✓		6	NR *	
2	✓	(Mentioned "hands" not fingers)			
3	½				
4	✓				
5	X				

* NR = no response

C. BEYOND-TEXT GENERALIZATION

Item #	Response	Probe (Comments)	Item #	Response	Probe (Comments)
7	X				

VOCABULARY KNOWLEDGE

_1½_ / _6_   _25_ % Correct

Item Tested	Response	Comments	Item Tested	Response	Comments
Braille	X				
awl	X				
raised	✓	Knows verb form			
system	X				
separate dot (P)*	½				
harness (P)	X				

* P indicates a probe item

EVALUATION

A. COMPREHENSION: _Vague understanding of ideas in passage. Her comprehension is inadequate – the materials are inappropriate._

B. VOCABULARY KNOWLEDGE: _Very limited word knowledge – even unable to use words in a sentence._

understanding the central concepts (Braille) and events (the eye injury). However, print-processing problems may have also interfered with her understanding of *books that "talk."*

Summary/Integration.   The analysis shows that Sharon's sight recognition and her phonics and structural skills are strong even though she sometimes fails to apply this knowledge during contextual reading. Given the difficulty of the passage for her, it was not possible to evaluate her reading integration (use of context) and her fluency. On this fourth-grade selection, she showed poorly integrated strategies and extremely slow reading

Sharon's main problem is that her vocabulary knowledge is extremely limited. It is assumed that poor reading comprehension is a direct reflection of her limited vocabulary knowledge.

INSTRUCTIONAL PLAN

Materials.   High fourth-grade level material is too difficult for Sharon unless the reading is preceded by extensive instructional support focused on the development of word meanings. Sharon should be reading from easier material (level to be determined) to enable her to attend to meaning, use context, and increase her reading rate.

Instructional Priorities.   The major focus of instructional support should be on the development of Sharon's vocabulary and her reading integration and fluency. This instruction can be provided in a group that includes other students with similar problems.

1. Before Sharon reads a selection, the teacher should identify concepts that may be unfamiliar and encourage Sharon to speculate about their meaning and relationship to the theme of the selection. Unfamiliar or partially known concepts should be explained. Because the goal of vocabulary development is the improvement of comprehension, thorough discussion should follow the reading of each selection in order to develop comprehension and establish its importance.

   Other procedures can also be used to expand Sharon's vocabulary knowledge. For example, stories should be read to her (along with other students) and new concepts should be discussed with suggestions for their use in alternative contexts. Sharon may also profit from working with another student or synonym, antonym, and root word—affix activities.

2. To improve Sharon's reading rate, integration, and fluency, she should be given short selections that are easy for her. She should be encouraged to concentrate on gaining meaning from everything she reads.

CASE 2: Patricia

Patricia is in ninth grade. Like 80 percent of her freshman class, she is in a double-period basic English class for students reading on a second-to-fifth-grade level. On this year's California Achievement Test, she scored a grade equivalent of 5.2 on vocabulary and 3.2 on comprehension. In contrast to many other students in her class, Patricia attends regularly and does all the assigned work. She understands and enjoys the mysteries that she reads on her own but has difficulty with most of her school reading. Because Patricia's teacher is able to spend some extra time with her, she decided to undertake a more systematic diagnosis of her reading strategies in order to determine which should be the areas of instructional focus.

In the testing situation, Patricia was relaxed, friendly, and eager to proceed. She was asked to read a fifth-grade-level passage entitled "Rescue in a Burning Building." The record of Patricia's oral reading is shown in Figure 8.9.

She was then asked to retell the selection and to respond to the questions that the teacher had prepared. Patricia's responses to the comprehension and vocabulary knowledge questions are shown in Figure 8.10. The reader should study the records in Figures 8.9 and 8.10 to decide what should be probed further.

ANALYSIS AND PROBE

On the basis of Patricia's responses to the passage and the comprehension and vocabulary knowledge questions, it was decided that the probe should further examine her comprehension responses and her word knowledge. In addition, the teacher decided to have Patricia respond to several of the content words that she had had difficulty pronouncing in order to confirm that print skill was not an area of difficulty. When probed, Patricia responded quickly and accurately to words such as

Figure 8.9   Record of oral reading: Patricia.

Rescue in a Burning Building

<u>6</u>

NEW YORK, June 17 — A fireman rescued a 76 year old woman from a

burning apartment building yesterday by tossing her off a fire escape. The

woman, Mrs. Mary Rogers, lan(ded) safely in the arms of another fireman   I

waiting on the roof of an adjoi(ning) building.   I

Fireman Edward Lane had risked his life to reach the woman, who was

trapped in her smoke-~~filled~~ ^{fired} top floor apartment in the five-story building.   I

The fire was blazing out of control as Lane carried the almost unconscious

woman onto a fire escape.

Figure 8.9   *(Continued)*

As flames threatened them, Lane tried without success to first climb to
the roof and then to go below the height of the flames. He could not do ~~so~~ *such* |
while carrying the dead weight of the helpless 115-pound woman.

Then he saw another fireman, Mike Mays, ~~motioning~~ *motion* to him with his |
arms held out. Mays was on the roof of the next building, which was level
with the fire escape. A space of only four feet separated the two buildings, but   ✗ O
there was a fifty-foot drop to the ground. Lane tried to pass Mrs. Rogers over
to Mays, but the gap was too wide.

Then the two men decided that the only chance to save the woman was
to try something very dangerous. Lane reached back and threw Mrs. Rogers
across the space between the buildings. For a moment the woman was not
supported above the ground. Then Mays caught her by the neck and
shoulders, and pulled her safely onto the roof. Mrs. Rogers was uninjured.

Lane then climbed to the roof of the burning building, went down an-
other fire escape and back to fighting the fire. |

(From *Real Stories*, Book 1, pp. 200–202, Milton Katz, Michael Chakeres, and Murray Bromberg
(Eds.), New York: Globe Book, 1969. [Originally published in *Newsday;* reprinted by permission of
the publisher, Newsday, Inc., Melville, NY])

adjoining, escape, and *motioning.* Thus, no further analysis was made of her oral
reading responses.

Comprehension and vocabulary knowledge responses and the results of the
probe are given in the comprehension—vocabulary knowledge summary form in
Figure 8.11.

Before learning how the teacher made sense of the evidence, the reader should
make some tentative interpretations. In what area or areas is Patricia experiencing
major difficulty? What are the implications of this diagnosis for Patricia's instruction?

INTERPRETATION

Print Skill. Patricia seems to have almost no problems with sight word
recognition and word identification. Most of her errors on content words involved
word endings (*-ed, -ing, -s*). Examination of the passage shows that typically she

Figure 8.10 Responses to comprehension and vocabulary knowledge questions: Patricia.

Retelling

RESPONSE: It was a fire. He had to get this lady out of the building. They had to use the fire escape to get the lady out of the building.

Comprehension

✓ 1. Where did Fireman Lane find the woman? (in her smoke-filled apartment, on the top floor of the building)
   RESPONSE: In the building, in the house (house means apartment).

✓ 2. How serious was the fire? (It was blazing, out of control)
   RESPONSE: Real serious.

✗ 3. Why couldn't Fireman Lane carry the woman up or down the fire escape? (She was too heavy in her unconscious state —"dead weight.")
   RESPONSE: Because it was too hard. [Q.: Explain how.] Just too hard.

✗ 4. Where was the other fireman, Mike Mays? (on the roof of the next building, level with the fire escape)
   RESPONSE: Trying to get the fire out.

✗ 5. Why couldn't Fireman Lane pass the woman to the other fireman? (The gap between buildings was too wide — four feet.)
   RESPONSE: (Could not answer.)

✗ 6. What did Fireman Lane finally do with the woman? (threw her across the space between the two buildings; Mays caught her)
   RESPONSE: (Could not answer.)

✓ *7. Why do you think the woman was "almost unconscious"?
   RESPONSE: Because of the smoke.

   * Beyond-text question

Vocabulary Knowledge

✓ 1. What does *risked* mean, as in "He risked his life"?
   RESPONSE: Took a chance.

✓ 2. What does *unconscious* mean?
   RESPONSE: Knocked out.

✓ 3. What does *tossing* mean?
   RESPONSE: You throw it.

✗ 4. What does *adjoining* mean?
   RESPONSE: Like you join a club.

Figure 8.11 Summary of responses to comprehension and vocabulary knowledge questions: Patricia.

COMPREHENSION–VOCABULARY KNOWLEDGE SUMMARY

Name _Patricia_ Grade _9_ Date _11/82_
Book/Page _Real Stories_ Level _5th gr_
_200 – 202_

COMPREHENSION

_2_ / _6_ ___33___ % Correct

Level: Independent Instructional
Borderline (Frustration)

A. RETELLING: Complete Main Idea Partial (Inadequate)

Comments: _Incomplete and inaccurate retelling; she had only the barest_

B. TEXT-RELATED COMPREHENSION _understanding of story_

Item #	Response	Probe (Comments)	Item #	Response	Probe (Comments)
1	✓		6	X	
2	✓				
3	X				
4	X				
5	X				

C. BEYOND-TEXT GENERALIZATION

Item #	Response	Probe (Comments)	Item #	Response	Probe (Comments)
7	✓	_possesses some background knowledge about fires._			

VOCABULARY KNOWLEDGE

_6_ / _8_ ___75___ % Correct

Item Tested	Response	Comments	Item Tested	Response	Comments
risked	✓		motioning (P)	✓	
unconscious	✓		gap (P)	X	
tossing	✓				
adjoining	X				
blazing (P) *	✓				
dead weight (P)	✓				

* P indicates a probe item

EVALUATION

A. COMPREHENSION: _Does not seem to understand the situation — e.g., where the second fireman was and what the problem was. May need to work on visualizing situations. Dense prose and expository materials may be particularly difficult for her._

B. VOCABULARY KNOWLEDGE: _Some concepts are unknown, but generally she shows good strength in word knowledge._

does pronounce these endings. In fact, she often pronounces endings that she drops during oral conversation. When words were presented in isolation during the probe, she pronounced the affixes according to standard English. Thus, it is clear that she possesses knowledge about word endings. Print processing does not appear to be a problem area that interferes with comprehension. Nevertheless, her reading rate is slower than the average range for fifth graders, so some improvement in integration and fluency may be needed. It is difficult to evaluate her use of context since her word attack skills are strong but comprehension is low.

Vocabulary Knowledge. Patricia knew three-quarters of the vocabulary items tested. The two she missed, while not key words, would definitely have aided her comprehension. They also indicate that Patricia probably does not know many words typically known by ninth graders. Verbal knowledge is a possible area of weakness that may contribute to Patricia's comprehension difficulties. Nevertheless, as is also suggested by the results from the standardized reading test, her comprehension is lower than might be expected on the basis of her vocabulary knowledge.

Comprehension.   Patricia's retelling (incomplete and inaccurate) showed that she had only the barest understanding of the situation in the story. Her answers to the factual questions (two correct out of six) support this. Even her two correct answers were not specific. In the probe, where she had an opportunity to reread most of the text orally and silently, she still did not grasp the point of the story. She reread the key paragraph many times before she comprehended it.

Summary/Integration.   Patricia's main area of reading difficulty lies in comprehension. Since she could not answer the questions upon rereading, her problem appears to be at the sentence and intersentence level. Her vocabulary knowledge is relatively strong and does not seem to account for the comprehension difficulty. Print processing represents an area of strength, although work may be needed to improve integration and fluency.

INSTRUCTIONAL PLAN

Materials.   While the currently used fifth-grade-level material is appropriate for instructional purposes with respect to print-processing demands, it represents frustration level (below 50 percent) with respect to comprehension. Given the test results, instruction should begin with material with very familiar concepts or with a lower level selection.

Instructional Priorities.   Instruction should focus directly on the development of basic text-processing strategies, particularly those that are useful for expository materials. Key terms should be discussed as needed.

1. Patricia's comprehension may be improved through individual work. Instructional materials (on a third- or fourth-grade level) that ask specific questions about information presented and provide corrective feedback should be used. At least once a week Patricia's teacher should

review her work with her. At this time, the teacher may wish to engage in reciprocal teaching of comprehension strategies (as described on page 197). Patricia should then be encouraged to concentrate on comprehending what she reads, paraphrasing sentences to herself, and interacting with the text as described in Chapter 7. Work on anaphora and connectives is also appropriate.

2. Students with comprehension problems similar to Patricia's should be brought together into a group. The group should learn to speculate on the basis of titles, headings, and initial paragraphs what a selection may be about. Discussion should follow each main segment of the article, to check the accuracy of group predictions. For both expository and narrative selections, the group should be given help in organizing information as described in Chapter 7.

3. Patricia should be encouraged to read on her own and to expand her reading interests. She could be given mysteries or exciting biographies that are slightly harder than the ones she presently reads. Her integration fluency should be checked on these high-interest materials.

SUMMARY

We have shown, through detailed presentation of two case studies, how the procedures introduced in preceding chapters may be used to diagnose reading problems and modify instruction in accordance with students' needs. While the process of acquiring expertise in using these procedures may be time consuming, it leads to deeper understanding of the various facets of reading and provides the teacher with a framework for making sense of students' successes and failures and for refining instructional approaches.

CHAPTER 9

Diagnosis with Standardized IRIs

There are a number of informal reading inventories that have been commercially developed and published. These standardized inventories are comprehensive in that they usually include two or more equivalent passages (plus comprehension questions) per grade level and range from first grade to junior or senior high in difficulty. In addition, they often include a series of graded word lists for determining the appropriate level at which to begin testing and a manual describing procedures for test administration and interpretation. Some inventories also provide a series of tests for assessing word identification skills. Table 9.1 briefly characterizes some of the published IRIs (see Richek, List, & Lerner, 1983, for a detailed discussion).

As was mentioned, one of the useful features of IRIs is that they specify the criteria for passage success. These criteria are based on the actual performance of representative samples of students at various grade levels. For each passage there is an indication of the number of oral reading errors allowable and the number of comprehension questions that must be answered correctly. As with teacher-prepared inventories, the comprehension and oral reading accuracy a student obtains on a passage serves as the basis for determining subsequent passages to be read.

ADMINISTRATION

The following describes the general method for administering a standardized IRI. First, the word recognition test is administered and scored according to the instructions in the test manual. This provides the basis for determining the

TABLE 9.1. SELECTED LIST OF PUBLISHED IRIs

Inventory (publisher and date)	Word lists grade range	Passages grade range	Number of forms
Analytical Reading Inventory Charles E. Merrill, 1985	P-6	1-9	3
Bader Reading and Language Inventory Macmillan, 1983	PP-12	PP-12	3
Basic Reading Inventory Kendall/Hunt, 1988	PP-8	PP-8	3
Contemporary Classroom Inventory Gorsuch, Scarisbrick, 1980	PP-8	PP-8	3
Diagnostic Reading Scales CTB/McGraw-Hill, 1981	1-6	P-8	2
Ekwall Reading Inventory Allyn and Bacon, 1986	PP-9	PP-9	4
Sucher-Allred Reading Placement Inventory Economy, 1985	PP-9	PP-9	2

level of the first passage to be read orally by the student. The student then reads progressively more difficult passages aloud until his or her performance falls below the oral reading accuracy and comprehension criterion levels. Next, the student begins reading silently a passage at the instructional level established through oral reading. He or she then reads progressively more difficult passages, until comprehension falls below the criterion level. For silent reading, it is also important to establish the independent reading level; thus, the student must also read progressively easier passages until he or she achieves 90 percent comprehension or higher. On some tests, this standard may be unrealistic, since if there are nine questions or fewer, it means that no questions can be missed. Finally, beginning one level above the student's instructional level established during oral or silent reading, the teacher reads progressively more difficult passages aloud to the student until the student's comprehension falls below the specified criterion. Figure 9.1 summarizes these steps in administering an IRI and the general considerations for starting and discontinuing each task.

The administration of the IRI allows the teacher to identify the level of material that can be read easily by the student at his or her independent level, the levels that may be appropriate for alternative instructional purposes, and the levels that are too difficult for the student. Testing usually continues until each of these levels has been established. There may be times, however, when a teacher wishes to use the IRI to answer a more limited question (e.g., to determine a student's independent level of silent reading or instructional level for print processing). Obviously, in such cases, the procedures described here for the systematic use of the IRI would not be followed; only the relevant portion of the IRI would be used. This is an important point, since diagnostic

Figure 9.1 Criteria for administering informal reading inventory tasks.

Word Lists

Begin with the easiest list.

Discontinue when the student scores below 75% correct on the untimed administration.

Oral Reading Task

Begin with a passage at the highest level where the student achieved 90% correct on the flash administration of the Word Lists.

Discontinue when the instructional and frustration levels are established.

Silent Reading Task

Begin with a passage at the highest level where the student met the criteria for instructional level in oral reading accuracy and comprehension on the Oral Reading Task.

Discontinue when the independent, instructional, and frustration levels are established.

Listening Task

Begin with a passage one level above the highest level where the student met the criterion for instructional level in comprehension on the Oral Reading or the Silent Reading Task.

Discontinue when the frustration level is established.

---

work should never blindly follow an established set of procedures. Although it is necessary to be familiar with the procedures involved in a comprehensive approach, it is equally necessary to know when to follow only a portion of these procedures.

CASE 1: Chuck

To illustrate the comprehensive procedures, we will consider the case of Chuck, a fourth grader, tested with the Ekwall Reading Inventory (1979). Chuck was first administered the preprimary-level word recognition list. Words were exposed for a half-second interval (flash), and if not recognized, they were shown in an untimed fashion. As is shown in Figure 9.2, Chuck quickly recognized all words on the preprimer list, but he failed to recognize 1 word (out of 10) on the primer list. He was able to identify that one when it was presented without the pressure of time. Administration of the lists continued until the fifth-grade list, on which Chuck's untimed score fell below 75 percent.

Second, Chuck was asked to read a passage aloud and answer comprehension

Figure 9.2 Summary of performance on an IRI: Chuck.

INFORMAL READING INVENTORY SUMMARY

Test _Ekwall R.I._ Child _Chuck_ Age _9_ Grade _4_ Date _1/82_

| Level | Recognition test | | Informal reading inventory | | | | | |
| | | | Oral reading task | | | Silent reading | | |
	Flash (%)	Untimed (%)	Accuracy (%)	Comprehension (%)	Rate (wpm)	Comprehension (%)	Rate (wpm)	Listening comprehension (%)
Preprimer	100	100						
Primer	90	100						
First	90	100	97	100	95	100	105	
Second	80	90	95	100	81	85	84	
Third	80	90	95	75	73	50	87	
Fourth	40	80	89	50	62			75
Fifth	—	60						50
Sixth								
Seventh								
Eighth								
Ninth								

234

questions. The passage selected was at the highest level at which Chuck recognized 90 percent of the flashed words, the first-grade level. Chuck's oral reading and comprehension on the first-grade passage were good, and he was then asked to read the second-, the third-, and finally the fourth-grade passages. Oral reading was discontinued after the fourth-grade passage because both his oral reading accuracy and comprehension dropped below the test criteria.

Third, Chuck's silent reading comprehension was assessed by having him read a passage at the third-grade level, his instructional level on the oral reading task. His comprehension of this passage fell below the criterion. Thus, easier passages were administered. Testing proceeded down to the first-grade passage in order to establish Chuck's independent level for silent reading comprehension.

Finally, the passages were administered as a listening test. That is, the teacher read the passage aloud to Chuck and then asked him to answer comprehension questions. Testing began at the fourth-grade level, the level where Chuck's oral reading comprehension fell below the instructional level. Because he demonstrated adequate listening comprehension (75 percent) on the fourth-grade passage, the fifth-grade passage was administered. Since his comprehension was not acceptable at this level (50 percent), the listening task was discontinued.

These procedures work well for younger disabled readers and older disabled readers suspected of having print skill problems. However, for some older readers for whom silent reading proficiency is of particular concern, it is useful to test silent reading comprehension first and to sample oral reading second in order to obtain a more valid measure of silent comprehension. For most readers the complete IRI can be administered at one time, but for younger readers the silent reading tests when administered last may not valid because of fatigue. Therefore, it is advisable to break the testing into two sessions if fatigue is noted.

Procedures for Administering the Word Recognition Test

The word lists measure the instantaneous sight vocabulary of the student (flash presentation) and his or her word identification skills (untimed presentation). In Chapter 4, procedures were described for assessing the "basic" sight vocabulary of students through oral reading analysis. While the primary and first-grade word lists provide a similar measure of basic sight vocabulary, the subsequent lists show how well students are incorporating other words into their store of words that are quickly recognized. Proficient readers are in command of a large store of sight words, and students during the elementary grades expand their set of sight words beyond the basic set to include most other words, that they encounter frequently during contextual reading. Flash performance on the more advanced word lists shows whether the development of this larger sight vocabulary is grade appropriate.

The procedures for flash administration consist of using two rectangular cards, one placed just above the word to be flashed and the other covering the word. When the student is ready, the teacher quickly moves the bottom card down, exposing the word. After a half-second exposure, the top card is moved down to cover the word. Correct responses are marked on the student record form with a check (✔) whereas incorrect responses are recorded phonetically. When the student fails to respond, this is recorded as "NR" (no response), "DK" (don't know), or "x."

Words that are not recognized during the flash presentation are reexposed immediately, with no time limitation, in order to see if the student can identify the word. The probe procedures described in Chapter 4 for determining the knowledge a student possesses about phonics and structural analysis can be used with words incorrectly read on an IRI as well as on a diagnostic passage.

Procedures for Administering the Oral Reading Task

The first passage the student reads is determined by his or her performance on the word lists. If the student's performance on this first passage is at or above the prescribed criteria, he or she reads progressively more difficult passages until performance falls below the criteria. If, on the other hand, his or her performance falls below the criterion for either accuracy or comprehension, this level represents the borderline or frustration level. In this case, the student reads increasingly easier passages until the instructional level is established (acceptable comprehension and oral reading accuracy).

As the student reads each passage aloud, the teacher records any errors made, using the procedures described in Chapter 4. A count should be made of the number of errors. When the student finishes reading a passage, the comprehension questions are asked, answers are recorded, and a comprehension score is determined. On occasion the teacher may wish to assess comprehension by having the student retell the passage prior to asking the comprehension questions, as described in Chapter 7.

Procedures for Administering the Silent Reading Task

Following the oral reading task, the student is asked to read certain passages silently. The point of this task is to determine whether the student is at least as proficient in silent reading as in oral reading. Although many normal readers are able to read with greater comprehension when they read silently than when they read aloud, this is not the case with most disabled readers. Therefore, the first silent reading passage administered is at the *same* level of difficulty as the one the student was able to read orally with good comprehension (the instructional level). After the student reads the passage silently, the comprehension questions are asked and answers are recorded and scored. If the student's comprehension is below the criterion, successively easier passages are administered until the student achieves adequate comprehension when reading silently. On the other hand, if the student's comprehension score on the first silent reading passage is at or above the criterion, progressively more difficult passages are administered until the frustration level is established. It is also particularly important during silent reading assessment to establish the level at which comprehension is extremely high (about 90 percent) for independent reading.

Procedures for Administering the Listening Task

The listening task measures a student's comprehension and underlying verbal knowledge when print skill difficulties (if any) are eliminated. As a rule, a listening task is administered only with passages that are more difficult than those the student is able to comprehend through his or her own reading. It is unnecessary to administer as a listening task passages that represent a level of difficulty the student can read and understand through reading.

Thus the listening task usually begins with a passage one step higher in difficulty than the most difficult passage the student was able to read orally or silently with adequate comprehension. The passage is read aloud to the student, the comprehension questions asked, and the student's answers recorded and scored. If the student's comprehension score is below the criterion, the listening task is discontinued. The reason for discontinuing at this point is that under normal circumstances the next lower level passages will have been read by the student with adequate comprehension during oral or silent reading. If the student's listening comprehension score on the first passage is adequate, the next higher level passage is read to him or her, the questions asked, and the answers recorded and scored. Progressively more difficult passages are read until comprehension falls below the criterion. The listening task is then discontinued.

If the particular IRI materials being used provide only two passages at each level of difficulty, it may happen that both passages at the level that would be appropriate for the listening task have already been administered, one for oral reading and the other for silent reading. In this case, the listening task should proceed to the next higher level.

INTERPRETATION OF RESULTS

For the teacher-constructed series of graded passages, consisting usually of a single passage per level, the interpretation was similar to that for diagnoses made with individual reading passages. In contrast, the standardized inventories allow for a variety of comparisons, which provide a comprehensive basis for understanding a student's reading strength and difficulty. For example, in addition to comparing a student's performance from level to level, as was possible with the teacher-constructed inventory, it is now possible to compare oral and silent comprehension and reading rates. The student's identification of isolated words on the graded lists can be compared with his or her print processing during oral reading. Further, a student's level of vocabulary knowledge as estimated from the vocabulary questions following each passage can be compared with his or her listening comprehension. This variety of comparisons is complicated, but it does increase the precision of the diagnosis. As was discussed earlier, such a comprehensive diagnosis should be unnecessary for most students in a class. Occasionally, however, there is a particularly perplexing problem that requires a comprehensive reading inventory.

Like teacher-constructed inventories, comprehensive IRIs are interpreted in two stages. First, judgments are made about the level of materials appropriate for reading instruction and independent reading. Then the evidence concerning print skill, vocabulary knowledge, and comprehension is examined in order to determine relative strengths and weaknesses. Recommendations concerning the appropriateness of alternative materials are based on the first analysis; the establishment of instructional priorities is based on the second.

Level of Materials

Instructional Reading Level. The level of instructional materials selected depends on the nature of instruction. For example, the level of material that is sufficiently challenging to foster the further development of word identification skills may be higher than the level of materials appropriate for the development of silent comprehension strategies. The instructional level for word identification is based on oral reading accuracy, whereas the selection of instructional material for group-based comprehension instruction is based on oral reading comprehension. For instruction that emphasizes the monitoring of silent reading comprehension, material selection is based on silent reading comprehension.

Independent Reading Level. The silent reading task determines the highest level of materials the student can read silently with good comprehension. This will normally be the student's independent reading level. It represents the level at which the student can recognize and identify words without pronouncing them aloud and at which he or she can concentrate on meaning without instructional support.

Areas of Reading Difficulty

Print Skill. As was previously mentioned, the listening task provides a measure of the strength of the student's comprehension skills unconfounded by his or her ability to process print. In general, if a student can, through listening, understand materials that are too difficult for him or her to read, we may infer that print skill difficulty interfered with reading comprehension. A detailed analysis of oral reading of one or two passages at the instructional or borderline level (as outlined in Chapter 4) should confirm this inference and reveal the specific nature of the difficulty and appropriate instructional emphasis. Evidence from the word lists (flash and untimed), the oral reading, and the reading rate scores (silent versus oral) should all be considered in drawing conclusions about a student's print-processing skill.

Vocabulary Knowledge. Information about a student's vocabulary knowledge comes from two sources. First, specific questions about vocabulary and phrases provide information on whether the student understands the key terms of a passage. Vocabulary knowledge performance on any of the three tasks (oral reading, silent reading, listening) that were administered at any one level should be combined to determine the percentage of terms correctly defined or described at that level. Second, the listening comprehension score reflects a student's underlying vocabulary knowledge. A high score indicates good verbal development, whereas a low score is ambiguous since it may reflect limited vocabulary knowledge, poor discourse comprehension strategies, or both.

Comprehension. Evaluation of reading comprehension begins with a comparison of oral versus silent reading comprehension. If silent reading comprehension is a grade or more lower, this indicates that the student has not yet internalized strategies to monitor comprehension during silent reading. That is, the student is able to comprehend but, because of limited practice or for some reason, has not learned to attend to meaning without the added support of pronouncing words aloud. Once a reader becomes proficient, it is not unusual for silent comprehension to exceed oral comprehension; a discrepancy in this direction is not viewed as a problem.

Next, the highest level of reading comprehension (oral or silent) should be compared with listening comprehension. A discrepancy here indicates the existence of print-processing problems. At the same time, the higher listening comprehension score suggests that once the print problems are solved, comprehension will be similar to listening comprehension.

Finally, an analysis should be made of the student's responses to the reading comprehension questions. When it is determined that the student's major problem is in comprehension, further probe should be made of his or her strategies, using the procedures described in Chapter 7.

CASE STUDY APPLICATIONS

The two cases described in the remaining sections of this chapter show how diagnosis using an informal reading inventory can be undertaken. The first case provides an overview of the diagnostic thinking involved in the interpretation of the inventory. The second case goes into much greater detail, presenting passage-by-passage evidence from an informal reading inventory.

CASE 2: Sara

Sara is in the middle reading group in a second-grade class. The basal program being used in her class is the Houghton Mifflin series, and her group currently reads from the second-grade reader. Her teacher decided to take a closer look at her reading because of her poor comprehension of stories in the reading group in contrast to her relatively good performance on seatwork assignments. She decided to administer the Basic Reading Inventory by Johns (Kendall/Hunt Publishing Co., 1978) to gain a better understanding of Sara's reading strategies. The word lists and the oral reading passages were administered on the first day, and the silent reading and listening passages on the second day. Sara worked hard and was involved in these reading activities.

The results from the administration of the word lists are shown in Figure 9.3. The reader should study these results to determine what level passage should be administered first as an oral reading task.

Administration of the oral reading passage should begin at the highest level at which the student obtained at least 90 percent correct on the flash administration of the word lists. Thus, for Sara, oral reading should begin on the primer-level passage. When given this passage, she made only 1 oral reading error and got all the comprehension questions correct. She was then given the first-grade

Figure 9.3 Summary of performance on the word recognition tests: Sara.

	Recognition test	
Level	Flash (%)	Untimed (%)
Preprimer	95	100
Primer	95	95
First	80	90
Second	70	95
Third	55	70
Fourth		
Fifth		
Sixth		
Seventh		
Eighth		
Ninth		

passage. On this she made 4 oral reading errors on the 100-word passage; and she missed 2½ out of 10 passage questions. Given these results, what should the teacher do next? Should testing be discontinued or proceed to the next higher level?

According to the scoring guide of the test, up to 5 oral reading errors and up to 2½ comprehension errors represent the instructional level. Thus, oral reading should continue at the next higher level. On the second-grade passage, Sara made 8 oral reading errors (8 percent of the words) and missed 6 of the 10 questions. Because the comprehension score shows that the second-grade passage is in the frustration range for Sara, oral reading was discontinued.

When Sara's teacher worked with her again on the next day, she had her read the passages silently. Given Sara's performance the previous day, on what level should her teacher have her begin reading?

Sara's teacher had her read at the highest level where she last demonstrated instruction-level oral reading and comprehension. This was the first-grade level. She read this passage and knew the answers to all of the passage questions. Given this performance, what passage should Sara be asked to read next?

Her teacher had her read the next more difficult passage, which was at the second-grade level. On this passage she read with good comprehension, missing only 1 of 10 questions. Consequently, her teacher asked her to read the third-grade-level passage. On this passage she knew the answers to only 3 of 10 questions. Since this performance indicated the material was at the frustration level, her teacher discontinued the silent reading and instead had her listen to a passage. On what level should the listening task begin?

The administration of the listening task should begin at the level above the highest level successfully comprehended when the child read either orally or silently. For Sara, this means the third-grade level. (Since Sara could comprehend at the second-grade level when reading silently, there was no need to test listening comprehension at that level or below.) When her teacher read the third-grade passage aloud, Sara missed only 1 question. Thus, the teacher proceeded to the next more difficult passage. On the fourth-grade passage, Sara missed only 3 of 10 questions. Therefore, her teacher read the fifth-grade passage to her. On this passage she was able to answer only 4 of the 10 comprehension questions. The results from the inventory was summarized in Figure 9.4.

Scores in the vocabulary column are based on answers to passage questions. Since for each passage there were two questions about word meaning, it was possible to tabulate the total number of correct answers on these questions at each level. For example, on the second-grade level, the vocabulary knowledge percentage was based on the results from the passage read orally and that read silently. On the third-grade level, it was based on the passage read silently and the one read to Sara by her teacher.

Given these results, what tentative conclusions can be drawn about the nature of Sara's reading difficulty? Further, given these conclusions, what level material should Sara be reading and should she remain in her current reading group? It is not our intention here to undertake a complete diagnosis, but rather to show how the evidence contained in the summary form may be used to draw some tentative conclusions and focus further diagnostic efforts.

Figure 9.4 Summary of performance on an IRI: Sara.

INFORMAL READING INVENTORY SUMMARY

Test J. Johns' BRI   Child Sara   Age 8   Grade 2   Date 12/83

| | Recognition test | | Informal reading inventory | | | | | | | |
| | | | Oral reading task | | | Silent reading | | Listening comprehension (%) | Vocabulary | |
Level	Flash (%)	Untimed (%)	Accuracy (%)	Comprehension (%)	Rate (wpm)	Comprehension (%)	Rate (wpm)		N	%
Preprimer	95	100								
Primer	95	95	99	100	111				2/2	100
First	80	90	96	75	91	100	100		4/4	100
Second	70	95	92	40	67	90	77		3/4	75
Third	55	65				30	71	90	4/4	100
Fourth								70	1/2	50
Fifth								40	0/2	0
Sixth										
Seventh										
Eighth										
Ninth										

242

TENTATIVE INSTRUCTIONAL CONCLUSIONS

Areas of Reading Difficulty.   The diagnosis of Sara's reading is complicated in several ways. Because her reading profile does not conform to typical patterns, it is important to come to terms with the nature of her reading strengths and difficulties before specifying the levels of materials that she should read.

With respect to reading comprehension, Sara's silent reading comprehension is better than her oral comprehension by one grade level. It is not unusual for silent reading to be better than oral reading comprehension when a reader is proficient. But other evidence from the word lists and the oral reading accuracy indicates that Sara is not a proficient reader. For example, on second-grade-level materials, where her silent reading comprehension was good, she is in the borderline region for oral reading accuracy, and the flash presentation of second-grade words indicates some problems with sight recognition. The discrepancy between oral and silent comprehension would seem to indicate that Sara can compensate for poorly developed print skills when she reads silently, but when faced with the additional demands of oral reading, she is not able to process print accuractely and also comprehend at the same time.

Sara's listening comprehension shows that she possesses the necessary background knowledge to understand third- and even fourth-grade-level material. The vocabulary knowledge evidence confirms her strength in this area, at least through the third-grade level. We can conclude that Sara's difficulty in oral reading comprehension is not a reflection of poorly developed word knowledge.

It is in the area of print skill that Sara's difficulties appear to lie. The results for the word lists, for example, indicate that she had difficulty with immediate recognition of some first-grade-level words. While a single error (95 percent) may occur by chance, the 4 errors (80 percent) on the first-grade-level list suggest that some first-grade words are not familiar to her. Even when given more time, Sara was able to correct only 2 of the 4 errors. She had even more difficulty with the flash administration of the second-grade list, although here she was able to correct all but one of her errors with time. Her performance on the third-grade list is at the frustration level.

In addition to her problems reading isolated words, Sara made 4 errors on the first-grade passage and 8 on the second-grade passage (each 100 words in length), and her reading rate diminished from a relatively fast rate on the first-grade passage to a slow-average rate on the second-grade passage.

These results point to print processing as the area in need of further study. Sara's teacher should analyze the errors that she made on the second-grade passage and probe some of her responses to the passage and word lists. We can tentatively conclude, given the discrepancy between her flash and untimed scores on both the first- and second-grade lists, that she possesses knowledge about word identification but has not done enough easy reading to consolidate this knowledge and expand her sight vocabulary. Because of this lack of experience, she is able to read orally with a high degree of accuracy only when she focuses mainly on print and somewhat superficially on meaning. And as materials become more difficult (second grade), she is no longer able to avoid errors. When reading silently, primary focus on meaning and probably less stringent monitoring of print allow her to comprehend second-grade material. However, this strategy is no longer functional at the third-grade level, where she encounters many more print problems. Thus, on the basis of the evidence, we conclude that Sara's major problem is in the area of print skill. Further, we speculate that the problem pertains to the consolidation and application of her existing knowledge about print as well as to the development of new knowledge about word identification.

Levels of Materials.   If taken alone, Sara's silent reading comprehension might suggest that her independent reading should be at the second-grade level. However, her difficulty processing print at this level suggests that it might not be the appropriate place to begin if Sara is to develop good reading strategies. Indeed, even first-grade-level material may pose print problems that require her undivided attention. The level of material that appears to pose no print skill or comprehension problems is the primer level. Although she may soon progress to first-grade-level materials, at the present time primer is her independent reading level and the level that will be effective in helping her consolidate good reading strategies.

To determine Sara's instructional level, we focus on the area of her greatest need and then ask what level material would best serve to develop this area. We have tentatively concluded that Sara's main reading problem involves print skill. Not only does she need to consolidate and expand her sight vocabulary through extensive reading at her independent reading level (primer and then first grade), but she also needs further to develop her word identification strategies. Whereas first-grade materials may be appropriate for instructional purposes, second-grade materials may be too difficult. Following further study of her print-processing strategies (oral reading analysis for the second-grade passage and probe of responses), the teacher should examine her response to second-grade-level materials when instruction is specially designed to prepare her for the reading. If Sara shows better print strategies with instructional preparation, it is appropriate to keep her with her present reading group, which is working with second-grade material, and to offer appropriate instructional support that will further develop Sara's word identification skills and permit her to focus on comprehension.

Sara's performance on the third-grade-level passage indicates that this is her frustration level. Even though she is able to understand materials at this level when they are read to her, her print-processing problems are so great that she cannot comprehend them when reading.

CASE 3: James

James is a freshman in high school and is in an intensive reading program. He is ranked 31st among 50 disabled readers. He was referred to the class on the basis of teacher recommendations and diagnostic reading test results. On the most recent standardized reading test, he scored a grade equivalent of 5.3 in comprehension and 6.8 in vocabulary. These scores reflect an average gain of 2.5 grade equivalents over the prior year's test. This achievement is a result of his desire to improve his reading so that he might go to college. Because of his extremely high motivation, his teacher asked him if he would like to have an inventory made of his reading skills so that she could better advise him as to how he might improve his reading even further. He agreed that this would be of interest to him.

During the testing with the Analytical Reading Inventory by Woods and Moe (Charles E. Merrill, 1981), James was pleasant and responsive. Between passages he talked about the books he likes to read, the movies he has seen, and one of his favorite authors, Edgar Allan Poe.

ADMINISTRATION

First James read all of the word recognition lists. He achieved 90 percent accuracy on flash administration at the fifth-grade level but 95 percent at the sixth-grade level (the highest level list). He then read the sixth-grade passage orally, followed by the passages for grades 7 through 9. Next he read the seventh-grade passage silently. This level was selected because it corresponded to the highest oral reading passage for which his comprehension score was at the instructional level. Because of his low comprehension on this passage, he next read the sixth-, and then the fifth-grade passages silently. Finally, he was administered the eighth-grade listening passage, on which he correctly answered 7 out of 8 questions. Although James scored 81 percent on the next higher passage (grade 9), the testing was discontinued because there are no higher level passages on this IRI. The IRI records from James's performance are shown in Appendix C.

ANALYSIS AND PROBE

The first step in the analysis is to examine the test records and score them (see Appendix C). On the word lists it is necessary to determine the percentage of words correctly recognized for the flash and the untimed administrations.

The next step is to score the passages. It is useful to keep the passages in the order in which they were administered and to identify them as "oral," "silent," or "listening." For orally read passages, the number of errors should be recorded line by line and then the total determined. The total number of errors in relation to the total number of words read and the percentage of errors are then recorded following the passage. On the sixth-grade passage (see Appendix C) James made 3 percent errors and thus read with 97 percent accuracy. In this example, it would also be important to note that the problems were concentrated in the first three sentences, with few occurring thereafter.

Next, the comprehension questions must be scored, using the expected answers as a guide. When ambiguous responses occur, it is important to ask the student to "explain further" during the administration of the test so that credit may be given if the information has been comprehended. The total number of questions answered correctly out of the total asked and the corresponding percentage figure should be recorded on the passage next to the number of oral reading errors. For example, as shown for the Level 6 passage, James correctly answered 8 out of 8 questions, for 100 percent comprehension.

Finally, the student's rate of reading needs to be determined. For example, James read the Level 6 passage in 1 minute and 36 seconds, which is equivalent to 96 seconds or 1.6 minutes (96 divided by 60). Because the passage is 192 words in length, 192 is divided by 1.6 to yield a reading rate of 120 words per minute. This information should be recorded next to the comprehension percentage score.

After all the orally read passages have been scored, comprehension and rate scores are determined for the silently read passages. These scores are also recorded following the passage. The comprehension of the passages administered as listening tasks should then be scored and recorded. The final step is to transfer all accuracy percentages, comprehension percentages, and reading rates to the summary sheet, as shown in Figure 9.5.

Once the results have been summarized, the next step is to consider each area of James's reading to determine whether any of his responses should be probed further. The results pertaining to oral reading accuracy, reading rate, and isolated word recognition accuracy suggest that James is experiencing some difficulty with word identification. The Level 7 passage was selected for further analysis, and further probe was undertaken to explore his recognition of sight words and content words presented in isolation.

The comparison of oral reading comprehension with silent reading comprehension suggests a problem in silent reading. Since James is able to comprehend, but not without the support of oral reinforcement, the interactive and monitorial strategies described in Chapter 7 represent appropriate instructional approaches.

The results from the listening task suggest that James's vocabulary knowledge is sufficiently well developed for the comprehension of ninth-grade material. However, the vocabulary-related comprehension questions suggest otherwise. These results, summarized in Figure 9.5, show that many terms from the seventh-grade level and up are unknown to him. Thus, the probe of the Level 7 content words needs to focus on word meaning as well as recognition.

The analysis of miscues made on the seventh-grade-level passage and the probe based on this analysis are shown in Figure 9.6. The results show that James's knowledge of sight words and word identification is strong but that his application of this knowledge is inconsistent. Further exploration of his knowledge of word meaning revealed inconsistent understanding of vocabulary items (for example, he knew the meanings of such words as *terrifying, miserable, wretched,* and *vaguely* but he did not know the meaning of *independent* and *belligerent*).

INTERPRETATION

Print Skill. The analysis and probe based on the seventh-grade passage reveal that James possesses considerable knowledge about phonic and structural analysis and that his basic sight vocabulary is well developed. Whether the larger stock of sight words that he recognizes instantaneously is grade appropriate cannot be determined from the evidence because lists beyond the sixth-grade level are not included in the text. But the fact that he experienced some difficulty with the flash presentation beginning at the third-grade level suggests that his broader sight recognition vocabulary is not as large as it should be. Indeed, some of the difficulty he experienced during passage reading may have been based on the unfamiliarity of many words that are typically recognized by students his age.

Though James is able to apply his knowledge about print effectively when he is not under the time pressure of contextual oral reading or flash presentation, he does not do so easily when he *is* under pressure. If he were more proficient reading

Figure 9.5 Summary of performance on an IRI: James.

INFORMAL READING INVENTORY SUMMARY

Test **Woods-Moe** Child **James** Age **14** Grade **9** Date **3/83**

Level	Recognition test Flash (%)	Recognition test Untimed (%)	Oral reading task Accuracy (%)	Oral reading task Comprehension (%)	Oral reading task Rate (wpm)	Silent reading Comprehension (%)	Silent reading Rate (wpm)	Listening comprehension (%)	Vocabulary (%)
Primer	100	100							
First	100	100							
Second	100	100							
Third	95	100							
Fourth	95	100							
Fifth	90	100				100	109		100
Sixth	95	100	97	100	120	81	97		100
Seventh			95	88	105	56	111		25
Eighth			92	63	91			88	50
Ninth			93	25	87			81	25

Figure 9.6 Analysis of oral reading responses, Level 7: James.

ORAL READING ANALYSIS

Name _James_ Grade _9_ Date _3/83_

Book/Page _IRI Woods Moe_ Level _7_

A. DIFFICULTY

_13_ / _262_   _95_ % Correct

Level: Independent (Instructional)
Borderline   Frustration

B. WORD LEARNING: Sight Word Errors

Printed Word	Oral Response	Probe	Evaluation
run	return	✓	_Sight words are known when presented in isolation. Given the number of such errors, James should be encouraged to do more easy reading to consolidate his sight recognition_
did	had ©	✓	
had	[omitted]	✓	
from	[omitted]	✓	
a	[omitted] ©	✓	
the	[insertion]	✓	

C. WORD IDENTIFICATION: Content Word Errors

Printed Word	Oral Response	Probe	Evaluation
turn	to ©	✓	_Ability to correct miscues indicates strong knowledge of phonics and structural analysis. Systematic syllable-by-syllable word attack, but slowness of process indicates little reading practice._
friend	friends	✓	
terrifying	terrific ©	✓	
miserable	miserably ©	✓	
wretched	wretcher ©	✓	
picnic	band ©	✓	
vaguely	vă/vā-galy ©	✓	

D. INTEGRATION – FLUENCY

Integration: _Good use of content – both graphic cues and context serve as a basis for correction._

Fluency: Rate _262_ / _2.5_ = _105_ wpm Evaluation _Below norms for seventh grade_

Phrasing _Many repetitions and pauses for word ident. and perhaps comprehension_ silently than orally, these difficulties might be attributed to nervousness and be overlooked. However, because his comprehension is less adequate during silent than oral reading, we can infer that his silent print-processing strategies are no more efficient, and probably less efficient, than his oral reading strategies.

The probe indicates that James does not need special instruction to learn about print but, rather, needs considerable practice with easy materials in order to consolidate and apply what he already knows. His slow reading rate reflects his current difficulty in application and should improve once he does more reading; if reading rate does not improve spontaneously, then it may need to be the focus of special instructional intervention.

However, James's print skill difficulties may not simply be a function of too little practice. Recently, James has seen several eye doctors because of blurred vision. The conclusion from the examination is that the blurred vision stems from eyestrain and that James must learn to relax while reading. Glasses were not recommended. The eyestrain may actually be the result of his difficulty in reading print fluently rather than the cause, but in any case, James's visual difficulties should be kept in mind.

Vocabulary Knowledge.   James's listening comprehension is good at the ninth-grade level (81 percent comprehension). This passage 'about Pygmies develops a topic with which James is unfamiliar and contains many difficult words (e.g., *equatorial, Ituru Forest, Zaire, contagious, blasphemy*). It would seem that when James is not faced with the task of print skill, he may be better able to compensate for not knowing the meaning of some key terms. His listening comprehension is better than might be expected on the basis of his knowledge of specific terms.

Comprehension.   James's retelling of selected passages is comprehensive: he reported the sequence of events accurately and related many details. While his comprehension following oral reading is adequate through the seventh-grade level and borderline at the eighth-grade level, his silent reading comprehension is near frustration on the seventh-grade level. These results indicate that he will have considerable difficulty reading grade-appropriate (i.e., ninth-grade) materials, particularly when he is reading silently. Within the area of comprehension, silent reading should be the focus of instruction.

Summary/Integration.   On the basis of the listening test results, James should be able to read ninth-grade-level materials with comprehension. Currently, however, he experiences problems with eighth-grade materials and even seventh-grade material that he reads silently. Two separate problems contribute to his reading comprehension difficulties. First, his print-processing strategies are not adequately developed and thus he reads slowly with many repetitions and corrections of miscues. Second, his knowledge of key terms is limited. While he is able to compensate for this limited knowledge when materials are read to him, when he is faced with print-processing problems as well, his comprehension fails. The fact that comprehension failure is more severe under silent reading conditions suggests that in addition to developing his vocabulary and refining his print-processing strategies, he must learn to monitor comprehension during silent reading.

INSTRUCTIONAL PLAN

Materials.   Materials above the seventh-grade level yielded borderline or poor comprehension results on the IRI. With instructional preparation (discussion of the meaning and pronunciation of key vocabulary), James should be able to comprehend course materials that he reads at the seventh-grade level and perhaps at the eighth-grade level when topics are familiar.

Special reading instruction should focus on three areas: consolidation of print-processing skill, development of vocabulary, and development of silent reading comprehension. For the first, the material should be easy for James when he reads silently. Thus, fifth- (and somewhat later, sixth-) grade materials should be used. The selections should be about topics of high interest to James. Vocabulary development may be undertaken along with content area instruction and should reinforce the concepts being presented in his course materials. Silent reading of short passages followed by comprehension questions should begin on sixth-grade-level material and, as rapidly as comprehension warrants, proceed to seventh- and then eighth-grade-level passages.

Instructional Priorities.   James's content area teachers should be advised that James will have difficulty reading materials independently above the sixth-grade level but that if appropriate instructional support is provided, including the discussion of the meaning and pronunciation of key terms, James can cope with seventh- and perhaps even eighth-grade-level materials.

James also needs help in improving his vocabulary. He should be taught how to prepare vocabulary cards for words from his courses that are unfamiliar and how to review and use these words orally. If possible, he should be paired with another student who could profit from vocabulary instruction so that they can discuss words together.

For James, the development of print-processing skills will be a major priority. James needs to learn to apply his good knowledge efficiently and to enlarge the set of words that he recognizes instantaneously. His fluency can best be developed by extensive reading of easy and highly interesting materials. These materials should initially be at the fifth-grade level although James may soon progress to more difficult material. In conjunction with this reading, James should be taught a system for recording and evaluating his reading rate. Charts should be kept of the number of pages read to provide a tangible record of his accomplishments.

Finally, James should be taught study strategies, such as those described in Chapter 7, for monitoring his comprehension during silent reading. It is important that the passages for this purpose be limited to several pages at most and be followed by comprehension questions so that James can have immediate feedback on the effectiveness of his comprehension strategies.

SUMMARY

The standardized informal reading inventory has many advantages over a diagnosis based on oral reading of a single passage. It allows for the comparison of silent and oral reading and for an assessment of fluency and word recognition proficiency at various levels of difficulty. These comparisons make it possible to determine more precisely the level of materials that a student should read under various conditions. Perhaps its greatest strength lies in the assessment of listening comprehension, which allows a more definitive conclusion to be drawn regarding the influence of word recognition on a student's comprehension. However, many of these comparisons are available to the classroom teacher on a more informal basis. For instance, the teacher will note that many students have greater difficulty with silent than oral reading. What is important is that the teacher understand the significance of these comparisons in relation to the kinds of problems students encounter in becoming proficient readers.

CHAPTER 10

Organizing Students for Instruction and Interpreting Standardized Test Results

In this final chapter we will consider how curriculum-based assessment by teachers fits within the testing program of the school and district. First we will examine strategies for assessing students' reading at the beginning of the year and grouping them for instruction. Because standardized reading tests are particularly useful for making decisions at the beginning of the school year, and because they are routinely administered in most schools, we believe that it is important for teachers to be knowledgeable about them. Next, we will describe the kinds of standardized tests available, characterize their strengths and limitations, and discuss how to evaluate them and interpret results from them. Finally we will describe diagnostic procedures to be followed with standardized tests to make sound decisions about classes and individuals.

BEGINNING-OF-THE-YEAR ASSESSMENT AND GROUPING

As is clear from the prior chapters in this book, we strongly believe that for teachers to obtain information that is directly relevant to planning instruction for their students, they must learn to undertake curriculum-based assessment. That is, they must learn to observe and interpret oral reading responses and to construct vocabulary and comprehension questions and interpret student's responses to them, ideally with existing materials and instructional tasks. Such evidence provides a valid basis for shaping instruction to better meet the needs of students.

When such observation is conducted over time, it provides a reliable basis for planning instruction. However, if this information is gained through teachers' interaction with students over a period of time, how can teachers make good decisions about grouping and instruction at the beginning of the school year? Some teachers undertake reading assessment of all their students at the beginning of the school year, using such instruments as informal reading inventories, oral reading of selected passages, word lists, and phonics inventories. Others prefer to rely on recommendations of teachers from the prior year. Some use the results from standardized tests. Still others wish to see none of this evidence, relying on the information that they derive from their interaction with students during the first weeks of instruction.

Comparison of Alternative Approaches

Is there a "right" way? Each of the solutions that are traditionally followed has advantages and limitations. The first approach, assessing all students at the beginning of the school year, has the advantage of providing a wealth of information about students' reading, but there are also several disadvantages. The evidence is derived from specially contrived testing situations which are not closely related to instructional tasks. Further, some of the evidence gathered early in the school year may not be valid or accurate, because students at that time are more interested in solving other problems such as figuring out what their teacher is like and who the other students in the class are. Finally, because individual testing takes an enormous amount of time during school hours, the students not being tested must undertake much work without the direct supervision of the teacher.

The second approach, relying on the recommendations of the previous year's teachers, also has several advantages and disadvantages. Information concerning where students were reading in the basal at the finish of the school year is useful, particularly for students in the primary grades. However, successful progress in the primary grades, which is heavily dependent on the development of print skills, may not be closely related to later progress in the middle and upper grades, which is highly dependent on background knowledge and comprehension proficiency. Thus, for teachers to perpetuate the basal group structure of the previous year may hinder the progress of students who had difficulty learning print skills but who are good comprehenders. Further, there can be changes in reading proficiency over the summer, as well as changes in the instructional materials and approach from one year to the next. Thus, while we believe that the basal placement from the prior year should be considered, it should not be the only information used.

Third, some teachers use the results from standardized reading tests, administered the prior year or at the beginning of the current year, as the basis for grouping and planning instruction. This approach has the advantage of being efficient in that students are usually tested for less than an hour or two and tests are easily scored. At the same time, the tests yield relatively little evidence: single scores in such areas as word recognition, vocabulary, comprehension, and/or reading rate. Careful interpretation of patterns of test results, however, can indicate areas of a student's reading that need further exploration; these procedures are discussed later in this chapter.

Finally, some teachers prefer not to use existing information from standardized tests and prior teachers, but instead to gather information during instruction that enables them to learn more about their students' reading. Indeed, this book has emphasized such strategies. We believe that such an approach is most effective when teachers have developed observational and interpretative skill and work within a model of reading that serves to guide the diagnosis. We do not agree, however, that information from standardized tests and other teachers must distort the judgment of the teacher. That is, we believe that it is possible for teachers to treat standardized test results and teacher reports as additional sources of information, important but not definitive. However, the results from standardized measures should not be allowed to override the conclusions of teachers based on curriculum-based measures of reading.

We recommend an approach in which the teacher is the central decision maker who considers information from several different sources. At the beginning of the school year, information from standardized tests, teacher recommendations, and student records will tend to be more important than later in the year, when the teacher has had the opportunity to collect information on an ongoing basis during instruction. We do not recommend massive testing of individuals at the beginning of the school year with such measures as informal reading tests or other informal measures. Individual testing should be necessary for only a few students who are experiencing extreme difficulty or who are particularly perplexing to the teacher. Time during the beginning weeks of school should be devoted to instruction rather than assessment, though good instruction is always diagnostic to a certain degree.

Given this perspective, how does a teacher begin reading instruction? Our answer to this question differs somewhat according to grade level and whether the teacher or school is committed to some form of grouping on the basis of reading achievement.

Grouping Students for Reading Instruction

Elementary school students are almost always grouped on the basis of achievement for reading instruction. By contrast, students are only sometimes grouped for math instruction and rarely grouped for social studies and science instruction. Why is this so? It is difficult to find a definitive explanation for this tradition, but the "preferential" treatment of reading may reflect the extent to which reading is necessary for academic work in other subject areas and for life in our society. In addition, the tendency may arise from the nature of the subject matter. Reading is often described as developmentally organized, with one area of learning building directly on prior learning. Yet some aspects of reading, such as print skill, fit this characterization better than others, such as vocabulary and comprehension.

Most reading researchers agree that the beginning stages of reading differ in certain fundamental ways from subsequent stages. Most important, beginning readers must learn about the nature of print and how print relates to their spoken language. As is discussed in Chapter 2, Chall (1983) describes the initial stages of reading as learning to decode and then learning to read fluently. Typically, this focus on reading occurs in the first two or three grades of elementary school. The developmental nature of learning to read during this period becomes obvious in several ways. Children who are able to read beginning first-grade-level materials have extreme difficulty reading second- or third-grade-level materials because they have not yet acquired the needed sight vocabulary nor the skill to identify unknown words. Further, as was discussed in Chapter 3, studies of reading development show that the learning of first graders is closely tied to instructional content, the printed words, and phonics concepts in the materials they read, and this knowledge accurately predicts their ability to read graded passages and to perform well on standardized reading tests (Barr, 1974; Barr & Dreeben, 1983).

As we described in Chapter 4, once children have learned a substantial number of words and can identify them easily, they consolidate this learning to become fluent readers. For most children, this integration occurs sometime during the second or third grade. Learning about print is no longer a major emphasis of instruction; instead reading instruction focuses on the strategies that children must acquire in order to comprehend effectively and critically. The materials that children encounter in the intermediate grades pose many new problems for them: often the vocabulary is unfamiliar; the structure of reading in science and social studies differs from the narrative forms experienced in the basal series; children are expected to read longer selections silently.

Most important to our discussion here, what children need to learn to become effective readers is no longer developmentally organized. Whereas in the early stages, skill with print relates directly to the level of the material that children will be able to read, in later stages interest in and prior knowledge about the topic are highly determinant (Anderson & Davison, 1989). Accordingly, in the intermediate grades and above it becomes more difficult to predict whether or not a child can comprehend a particular story or article. As was discussed in Chapter 5, prereading discussions encourage students to share their knowledge about the topic of a selection and thereby better prepare students to comprehend the selection. Several useful teaching strategies, developed to encourage students to think about what they may learn from the text and what they already know about the topic, were described in Chapters 6 and 7. It must be remembered, however, that word identification and fluency will still be having a bearing on the reading of low-achieving students; special instructional provisions may need to be made to accommodate deficiencies in these areas.

In sum, while learning to read print fluently in the primary grades, reading can be described as developmental in nature, once students have achieved fluency, reading cannot be easily characterized in this way. Given this change in the nature of reading instruction and learning, grouping children in the primary grades so as to achieve a closer match between their ability to deal with print and the demands of printed material would seem to be desirable. In contrast, ability grouping in the intermediate grades once fluency has been achieved finds little support because of the difficulty we encounter in accurately predicting what will be easy or difficult for students to comprehend. The principle being developed here is that grouping may be justified when subject matter is developmental in nature and a close match between learner proficiency and task demands facilitates learning. It is not appropriate to group students on the basis of achievement, however, when the variety of different prerequisite experiences can enhance comprehension. In short, grouping students on the basis of their reading proficiency may be useful in the primary grades, but not in the intermediate grades.

Unfortunately, group assignments in the primary grades often determine those in the intermediate grades. That is, the level where groups read in the basal at the end of the school year determines their group placement and basal level at the beginning of the subsequent grade (Gamoran, 1984). One consequence of this practice is that groups formed on the basis of print skill may be homogeneous in the primary grades but these same groups in the intermediate grades may be quite diverse in reading comprehension. For example, Barr (1989) examined the degree to which fourth-grade reading groups overlapped in reading comprehension as measured by a standardized test. With the exception of a single disabled reader in some classes, the low and high groups were extremely similar in their range of comprehension. That is, there were many strong comprehenders in the low groups and many poor comprehenders in the high groups. Such stability in grouping would not be as inappropriate if the nature of reading stayed the same. However, as we previously discussed, the nature of reading in the primary grades differs in emphasis from that in the intermediate. Consequently, we believe that primary-grade group placement is an inappropriate basis for establishing intermediate-grade groups.

Furthermore, studies of classroom instruction indicate that students working individually or in very small groups achieve less than those instructed in larger groups or as a total class (see Rosenshine & Stevens, 1984, for a discussion of this literature). In conflict with the prevailing wisdom that individual instruction is best, these findings show that in the context of a classroom where the teacher is simultaneously responsible for the instruction of many students, grouped or total class instruction is more effective than individual or very small group instruction. The results also indicate why this might be the case. Students working under the supervision of a teacher attend to the task at hand at a higher rate than when they work independently. The more groups a teacher supervises simultaneously, while working directly with only one, the greater amount of time that students must spend working independently. Not only should the number of groups formed be limited for this reason, but alternative forms of organization such as total class or small-group instruction followed by heterogeneous cooperative group work lend themselves to strategy development and are effective in increasing comprehension (Barr, 1987; Stevens, Madden, Slavin, & Farnish, 1987). At the same time, special instructional provisions may need to be made for students who are experiencing extreme difficulty learning to read.

Implications for Beginning-of-the-Year Assessment

In making recommendations for beginning-of-the-year assessment by classroom teachers, we distinguish between kindergarten instruction, primary-grade instruction, and middle- and upper-grade instruction. Relevant information includes that previously discussed: teacher testing, recommendations of previous teachers, standardized test results, and observation during instruction.

Kindergarten Instruction. When children begin kindergarten, there is much they have to learn about getting along in the complex social settings of classes. Children must learn class routines and how to follow them, when it is permissible to talk and when not, how to get needed help, and how to interact appropriately with other children. Typically, structured language arts activites involving new learning do not begin immediately. As we discussed in Chapter 2, the nature of literacy activities in kindergarten should be broad-gauged, permitting children to participate at whatever level is meaningful to them. Given this type of activity, however, some children will have developed concept of word and learned how to represent some sounds when they write, whereas others will still be learning about the nature of stories and the ways in which book language differs from natural language. Diagnostic activities in kindergarten should generally be informal, occurring as part of instruction. The procedure developed by Morris (1980) for teaching and assessing concept of word, for example, is appropriate.

There are occasions, however, when a teacher may wish to have more systematic information about student knowledge. For example, children in most kindergarten classes are expected to know or to learn to identify letters and their names; it is sometimes useful for a teacher to test this knowledge using informal means or an inventory such as that included in the first part of the *Blachowicz Informal Phonics Survey* (Appendix B), once the children have adjusted to school. In the spring of the year, teachers may wish to examine the phonics knowledge of their students through an inventory or spelling task. Such information, coupled with observational evidence, can then serve as the basis for recommendations concerning student grouping for the first-grade teacher.

Primary-Grade Instruction. We believe that it is useful for first-grade teachers to begin the year with total class instruction, similar to that occurring during the final several months of kindergarten (Language Experience Stories, Guided Big Book Reading, Writing Activities). This allows the teacher an opportunity to observe children receiving broad-gauged instruction to which all students can relate on some level. As part of this total class instruction, children who have not yet formed a concept of word can be identified as needing extremely supportive instruction. For example, total class instruction in the morning can be followed by small-group instruction in the afternoon for these children to reinforce their earlier learning through rereading and writing activities. When the teacher works with individuals following class story reading (LEA, Big Book), she is able to identify those who learn words easily and have already established a beginning sight vocabulary. These are children who are ready to engage in more formal reading instruction. Reading groups composed of children at similar stages of reading development are easily formed in this manner.

Once all children are receiving formal reading instruction, it is important for teachers to identify those children who learn printed words and phonics concepts easily and who read contextual selections confidently; they should be moved to a more rapidly paced group. One way to make the change is to have the child be a member of his or her old group as well as the new group while the change is being made. Alternatively, the support of a parent or reading teacher might enable the child to read some of the stories that would be missed in order to master the new sight vocabulary. While moving children from more slowly to more rapidly paced groups seems to enhance motivation, not only of the child in question but also of other class members, moving children from a rapidly paced group to a more slowly paced one seems to be counterproductive. Instead, the teacher should provide additional reinforcement for the child and any other group members needing help through an extra afternoon reading session. The result of this grouping strategy is the creation of large rapidly paced groups and small slowly paced ones.

At the beginning of second and third grades, teachers should consider recommendations from the prior teacher and information concerning where the children were reading in the basal at the end of the year. In second and third grade, several different grouping arrangements are effective: one approach is to group on the basis of progress but to provide extra instructional time for the most slowly paced group, either by meeting with the most rapidly paced group three times a week, the moderately paced group five times, and the slowly paced group seven times, or by providing the most slowly paced group with an extra instructional session in the afternoon. An alternative approach, more feasible in third grade than second, is to have all children read the same stories but to provide supplementary small-group instruction for students needing more support.

As in first grade, the teacher should obtain informal diagnostic evidence on children's reading in an ongoing fashion, identifying those who are able to move to a more rapidly paced group and those who need greater support. When a teacher is undertaking informal reading assessment during instruction, it is often useful to focus on a particular child for a day, gathering as much information about his or her reading as possible, and then focusing on other children on subsequent days. During the third grade, all but a few students with print skill problems will achieve reading fluency, and most will be able to read the same stories if instructional support is provided prior to reading.

Middle- and Upper-Grade Instruction. As previously noted, it is common for most students to be grouped on the basis of reading progress at most grade levels. However, although such achievement grouping may be justified in the primary grades, we question its usefulness in the intermediate and upper grades. If one teaches in a school that groups students on the basis of achievement for reading instruction, either within classes or between classes (departmentalization), then it is particularly important that group placement from the previous year not be the only basis for assigning children to groups. In addition, evidence from both standardized reading measures and informal measures should be used in adjusting the group assignments from the prior year.

As an alternative to grouping on the basis of reading achievement, teachers may wish to instruct the class as a whole for reading. This arrangement enables students with considerable knowledge on a topic to share their understanding with their classmates. Once students have engaged in discussion to prepare them for reading selections (see Chapter 7), it is often necessary for teachers to allow different amounts of time for story reading. Students completing the assigned reading quickly should be allowed to undertake alternative reading and writing activities of their own choosing. Those students who have more difficulty with longer selections can work through the reading with the teacher using one of the instructional strategies described in Chapter 7. Following reading, discussion can be undertaken as a total class under the guidance of the teacher or in cooperative peer groups, where more children will have an opportunity to discuss their ideas and feelings. Supplementary small-group instruction should be planned for any students still experiencing print skill, vocabulary, or organizational problems.

It is particularly important, once students achieve reading fluency, to consider their reading comprehension and vocabulary in a systematic manner. Curriculum-based ways to gather such information were discussed in earlier chapters. Informal reading inventories were described in Chapter 9. We will now examine standardized reading tests in some detail in order to determine how they can be used effectively by classroom teachers.

STANDARDIZED TESTING

In this book we have proposed a framework for curriculum-based assessment in which teachers use instructional materials and curriculum tasks to structure classroom diagnosis. The term "testing," however, refers to a much larger realm of school assessment. In this section we will describe the types of formal measures with which a teacher must be familiar, will explain some concepts basic to these measures, and will give examples of how teachers might adapt more formalized assessment instruments to provide instructional information.

What Kinds of Tests Are There?

Formal measures are basically of two types: criterion-referenced and norm-referenced, the latter frequently referred to as "standardized" tests. It is important to understand the ways in which these two types of tests differ.

Criterion-Referenced Tests. The goal of criterion-referenced measures is to compare a particular student's performance with goals set by a curriculum or program. These instruments provide qualitative information on the skills and knowledge felt to be basic for progressing in a particular curriculum. For example, a curriculum goal might be that students should be able to divide compound words into their constituents. Figure 10.1 shows a criterion-referenced test item designed to assess achievement of this goal.

Figure 10.1 Criteria referenced test item: Division of compound words.

Goal: Students will divide compound words into their constituent words.
Direction: Give each student a duplicated sheet with the following words.
Say: These words are all made up of two or more words. Draw a line between the words that make up the compound.
Example: mail/man
Items:

truckload	icecream
dishpan	baseball
fireman	joystick

Along with the curricular goal, criterion-referenced tests (CRT) frequently indicate a performance standard to be met. While 70 to 80 percent is a common mastery standard, criteria vary by age of student and by item being tested. For example, an appropriate mastery level for naming the letters of the alphabet for first graders might be 100 percent. Though this type of testing is very much like teacher-created informal testing, many CRTs are part of larger, purchasable instruction and management systems such as the Wisconsin Design (Otto & Askov, 1972) or those provided by basal programs.

Several issues must be addressed when criterion-referenced measures are used for either assessment or placement. The user should ask:

1. Are the objectives related to essential skills, strategies, and knowledge? Frequently the items most essential to the reading task are the most difficult to conceptualize as discrete objectives, and the items most easily tested may not be essential for effective reading.
2. Is the performance required a real measure of the goal? Does circling a digraph on a worksheet, for example, measure how well a student can use graphophonic knowledge of that cluster for reading or it is just an isolated measure? How genuine is the reading in the testing situation?
3. Is the criterion level appropriate for the age and ability of the student?

All of these issues relate to the larger issues of reliability and validity, which we will discuss later in this chapter. In sum, CRTs can provide specific information about the particular skills of a particular student. However, in their use we must be sure that we are not just assessing one-time mastery of peripheral behaviors but rather focusing on knowledge, skills, and strategies important to the reading act.

Norm-Referenced Tests. The purpose of norm-referenced tests is to allow the evaluator to compare the performance of a student or group of students to a larger group for the purpose of identifying potential problems or for assessing group achievement. Most norm-referenced tests are group tests, but a small number are individually administered both for achievement estimates (e.g., the Peabody Individual Achievement Test) or for diagnostic purposes (e.g., Woodcock Reading Mastery Test, Gilmore Oral Reading Test).

A standardized test is an *objective, normed* measure of a *sample* of behavior. Let's look at each of these key words to try and understand some basic concepts about this type of test.

Objective. When we say a friend is objective in deciding arguments, we mean that that person treats each person in the same manner and does not show favoritism. The same sense of the term applies to "objective" in standardized ·tests. In order to treat each test taker alike, these tests are designed with a set of answers from which to select so that the answers can be scored impartially.

Time limits, specific directions for explaining and administering the test, answer sheets, all of these help ensure that the test taking, answering, and scoring process is as much alike as possible for all students.

Normed. Tests that are normed are developed and tested on a large group of diverse students so that the test designers are able to calculate the average performance of many students in differing age and geographic groups. Tests can have *nationwide* norms, norms that reflect a broad spectrum of geographic and ethnic diversity, or they can provide *local* norms so that the user can compare the performance of a particular group of students with closely matched peers, such as, for example, rural, Midwestern students.

Normed scores are used to place a value on the *raw score* (the number right), which, since there is no standard for comparison, cannot by itself tell the teacher how well a group has performed. For example, a raw score of 24 out of 26 might seem good. However, it becomes very clear that such a score is not good when you know the task is naming the letters of the alphabet and the test taker is applying for graduate school.

The most common normed scores are stanines, percentile scores and grade-equivalent scores. The word *stanine* is a contraction of standard-nine, because stanines represent divisions of the normal curve divided into nine equal or standard parts. Stanines place students in a broad performance band and allow comparisons across tests, with stanines 4 to 6 considered average with 5 as the mean; stanines 1 to 3 are below average, and stanines 7 to 9 are above average.

Percentiles, better called percentile ranks, are often confusing for teachers and parents, who confuse them with percentages, indicators of the number of items correct. Ranging from 1 to 99, percentile rank indicates a student's relative position in the norming group. For example, a score of 60th percentile means a student did better than 60 percent of the other students taking the test; it does not mean that the student only got 60 percent correct.

Grade scores indicate a level of achievement in terms of years and months in school; for example, 6.3 would indicate an average level of performance for a sixth grader in the third month of school. Such scores have great saliency because grade organization is most familiar to parents, children, and teacher. There are some very significant problems in the use of grade scores, however.

The first of these is the question of growth across the school years. Consider the observable changes in reading from the beginning of first grade to the beginning of second grade. Normally these are significant changes in what we would call reading performance. Then imagine the change from junior to senior year of high school. These changes would be harder to detect and harder to describe. A year's growth at earlier levels may not indicate the same amount of change as at later levels, and using grade scores to discuss growth can have similar problems of equivalence.

A second problem is typified by interpreting a high score gained by a young child. For example, a good second-grade reader may score 4.6 on a standardized test, but when placed on fourth-grade materials, the child is unable to function. Why? It is important to remember that the score of 4.6 was obtained on a test meant for second graders. That indicates that the able second grader did as well as a fourth grader in the sixth month of school would do *on second grade material.* Both the reporting and interpreting of grade scores require care.

Sample. When you have your blood tested, the technicians and doctor don't require that all the blood be removed from your body and analyzed. Rather, they work with a sample that they assume represents that quantity. In the same way, reading tests take a short sample of what you do and extrapolate to a larger estimate of your performance. Like a medical test, there are two important requirements: that this test be reliable and that it be valid.

Reliability. Reliability refers to the degree of consistency a test has. If a particular blood-testing technique is correct 9 times out of 10, it is fairly reliable; tests must also be reliable in the way they rank students who take them. Tests are also checked for consistency of items across the test and for equivalency of different forms. Every test manual describes the way or ways in which reliability is estimated, and expresses this reliability as a decimal, a coefficient of reliability; the closer to 1.0 a coefficient of reliability is, the more consistent a test is.

Along with a high reliability, look for a low standard error of measurement (SEM). This figure indicates how accurate given scores on a test are and emphasizes that no score is absolute, that each is subject to a certain degree of error. For example, with a raw score SEM of 2 points, a child whose obtained raw score is 43 can be estimated to have an actual raw score between 41 and 45 with about 70 percent surety. If we double the value of the standard error of measurement to 4, we can be 90 percent sure that the score is between 39 and 47. The smaller the standard error of measurement, the more likely that the child's obtained test score and actual score are close together. SEM can also be useful in helping report scores as ranges, often with grade level variations of .3 to .6 of a year, rather than an absolute, to give parents and others a better picture of the student's performance.

Reliability alone, however, is not sufficient to make a test good. Consider our initial metaphor of a blood test. A blood test can give us the same data each time and be highly reliable. Yet it is useless as a test for vision. It has no real connection with the trait we want to assess.

Validity. A test is valid when it measures what it is intended to measure. For a reading test to be valid, it must measure those things that we think are important to reading. For example, a test that assesses only decoding might better be called a decoding test than a reading test, since no comprehension is involved. Validity is assessed by evaluating the content of the test and comparing it with one's own definition of or curriculum for reading. Frequently tests are deemed valid by testimony of experts or by a comparison of their content with that of other, more established tests. Nothing substitutes, however, for examining and taking a test oneself.

Problems with Standardized Tests

Standardized tests are useful for gathering large-scale statistics but may often be misleading when used for analyzing a particular student. In addition to the difficulties inherent in reliability, error of measurement, and reporting, teachers are normally aware of other problems. We will discuss a few of these here.

High Floor Problem. Many teachers have received a new student into class with records suggesting that the student has a low but measurable reading level. Yet the student in question is unable to read at the primer level. How is it that a nonreader can receive a score, one that goes up each time he or she is tested? The answer lies in the way in which increasing grade forms of tests are designed. It is almost impossible for any student to receive a zero raw score. By chance a few of the answer marks will find themselves in the right space, giving the students the lowest possible score on the test. While this score will remain in stanine 1 over the years, the lowest grade possible becomes *higher* on each higher level of a test. Therefore, a student who can't read gets a score, one that goes up each year.

Test–Question Independence. In the 1970s some interesting research was done on test construction (Tuinman, 1974). Students were allowed to see the comprehension questions on some standardized tests without having read the passages to which the questions referred. They they were asked to answer the questions as best they could. What the researchers found was that many questions on tests were test independent, that is, they tested a student's knowledge and reasoning rather than the reading of the passage. For example, a question, "What did the monkey eat?" is very likely to have the answer "bananas" whether or not you have read the selection. Since the publication of Tuinman's work, test questions have undergone more stringent evaluation but it is still possible for students with specific prior knowledge to answer from their knowledge base rather than from their reading of material.

Task Validity. The formats of most standardized reading tests have undergone some major criticism. The passages are generally short and unrelated, switching from narrative to exposition, from topic to topic. Further, unlike real-life comprehension tasks, test tasks look for one right answer. Recent developments in state-based assessment (Valencia & Pearson, 1986; Wixson,

Peters, Weber, & Roeber, 1987) have recognized these as serious difficulties. The next decade will be an interesting one as test designers search for more ecologically valid assessment devices.

Specific Sources of Test Information

The Mental Measurement Yearbooks provide an invaluable aid to the practitioner. Begun by Oscar Buros in 1938, the yearbooks are issued and revised periodically and contain reviews on most standardized instruments. Their index volumes, *Tests in Print I and II* (Buros, 1961, 1974), can be used to locate initial and subsequent surveys of particular tests. Separate volumes, *Reading Tests and Reviews* (Buros, 1968, 1975, 1978) are excerpted from the Yearbooks. In addition, professional journals such as the *American Psychologist, Journal of Educational Measurement, Psychological Bulletin, The Reading Teacher,* and *The Journal of Reading* also contain regular test reviews.

USING STANDARDIZED TEST INFORMATION

Teachers typically receive standardized test results as part of the portfolio of information for an incoming class. The major purpose of such assessment is for school-wide or district-wide assessment; however, these results can also provide a starting point for a teacher to get to know a new class and can serve as a screening instrument for the initial formation of instructional groups.

Interpreting Standardized Test Scores

In order to demonstrate how teachers can use the information from standardized tests, we have selected a fourth-grade class from an inner city school in a poor neighborhood. The teacher is faced with the problem of organizing her students for reading instruction at the beginning of the year. She examines the standardized reading test results (administered the previous May when students were in the third grade) to consider how her students clustered together in reading ability and to form hunches about special problems they might be experiencing. The scores are shown in Figure 10.2.

The teacher's goal for the first month of the school year is to have two instructional groups in her class, a large group using the fourth-grade-level basal and a small group working below level. In her large group the most independent readers take part in the initial background setting and final discussion for each selection but work through the lessons more quickly, spending the extra time on a cooperative learning "book club." With the students needing most support in this larger group, she typically works through the selection using some of the guided reading techniques described

Figure 10.2 Standardized test results: Fourth grade/tested at 3.9.

Student	Reading vocabulary	Reading comprehension
Ann	3.4	3.7
Candy	4.1	3.8
Carol	3.0	4.3
Connie	4.3	4.0
Cornelia	4.1	3.9
Daniel	4.1	3.8
David	4.0	4.3
Denise	4.5	4.0
Donald	4.8	3.7
Dorothy	4.3	5.1
Dottie	3.1	3.1
Gary	3.4	3.9
Gordon	3.7	3.9
Grace	3.5	3.0
Greta	4.4	3.9
Jean	2.9	2.0
Jesse	5.7	4.9
John	3.1	2.8
Kay	4.3	4.0
Lois	3.4	3.3
Lottie	2.7	1.8
Tia	4.5	3.9
Walter	1.9	2.2
Wanda	2.2	2.7

in Chapter 7. Her small group works on a separate set of materials but, in addition, they often have a second reading period in which they listen to a tape of the selection being read by the larger reading group so they can take part in the discussion. They also have additional sessions focused on their particular needs.

Her first assessment goal, therefore, is to identify those students who might need immediate support and to identify other students about whom she is perplexed. Since comprehension is the main focus of the program, she begins by making a hypothetical classification of her class based on the standardized test comprehension scores from the previous spring. She then compares these placements with the students' end-of-third-grade placements to formulate her first diagnostic questions. The reader should also attempt to form a tentative grouping of the class for reading instruction based on the information in Figure 10.2, before looking at Figure 10.3.

Comparing her hypothetical grouping with that of last year's teacher (see Figure 10.3), the teacher identifies the names of at least five students—Dottie, John, Lottie, Walter, and Wanda—who may need special support through small-group reading instruction with easier reading materials. The reading comprehension scores of these students are at or below the 3.1 grade equivalent level and below those of the other students in the class. Jean and Grace, who also score at the third-grade level or below, were in the middle and high groups last year. Thus the teacher decides to have them read with the large group but to monitor their progress. Ann and Carol were low group members last year, but their reading comprehension scores are within the

Figure 10.3 Standardized test results: Third-grade grouping and hypothetical groups based on comprehension scores.

Student	Reading vocabulary	Reading comprehension	Third-group	Hypothetical group
Ann	3.4	3.7	L	M
Candy	4.1	3.8	M	M
Carol	3.0	4.3	L	M
Connie	4.3	4.0	M	M
Cornelia	4.1	3.9	H	M
Daniel	4.1	3.8	H	M
David	4.0	4.3	M	H
Denise	4.5	4.0	H	M
Donald	4.8	3.7	H	M
Dorothy	4.3	5.1	M	H
Dottie	3.1	3.1	L	L
Gary	3.4	3.9	M	M
Gordon	3.7	3.9	M	M
Grace	3.5	3.0	H	L
Greta	4.4	3.9	H	M
Jean	2.9	2.0	M	L
Jesse	5.7	4.9	H	H
John	3.1	2.8	L	L
Kay	4.3	4.0	H	M
Lois	3.4	3.3	M	M
Lottie	2.7	1.8	L	L
Tia	4.5	3.9	H	M
Walter	1.9	2.2	L	L
Wanda	2.2	2.7	L	L

range of the remaining students in the class; thus the teacher decides to group them with the large group and watch their progress closely. The teacher also notes the wide discrepancy between Carol's vocabulary and comprehension scores and wonders if her comprehension test score was reliable.

Studying the reading test evidence raises other questions to be addressed in the first weeks of school. Jesse appears to be a very able reader; thus the teacher makes a note to form the book club soon. She also decides to have Grace, who did poorly in her testing but ended last year in the high group, read selected passages from an informal reading inventory. Most important, she learns that she needs to find out more about the nature of the reading difficulties of the low students. The following section describes ways in which she can quickly get further information about these students.

Probe Techniques with Standardized Tests

To yield standardized results, tests must be carefully administered according to the guidelines provided in the testing manual. After these procedures have been followed, however, a teacher may go back and use the instrument in different ways to gather new information. What is important is to keep the two administrations, and the data gained from them, separate and to make sure that the standardized data are gathered *before* any probing takes place.

Extending Time for Test Completion. Most tests have strict time limits which must be carefully adhered to in order for a teacher to compare a particular group of students with the norming population who were given a predetermined amount of time. Students who are slower than average readers may consistently receive low comprehension scores because they are unable to finish enough items, even though their comprehension of the sections finished may be quite good. Often this problem is apparent when answer sheets are examined, since these students complete the beginning of the test with few errors.

If a teacher suspects that rate is causing a particular student's score to be depressed, he or she can collect the answer sheet for the standardized score at the end of the prescribed time but give a second answer sheet for the student to continue the test until finished. In this way, two raw scores can be computed, the first for the standardized comparisons, the second as a measure of power: how well that student could comprehend given extra time. Different methods of collecting the data for this double scoring can be utilized: writing the answers on a sheet of blank paper, using a different colored pencil if the tests are hand-scored, or any other method that does not "contaminate" the answers to be used for the standardized data gathering.

Probe with the Vocabulary Subtest. One basic question in the diagnostic model presented earlier is, "Do print-processing problems interfere with comprehension?" One reason a student's vocabulary or comprehension score may be depressed is that he or she had poor print skill; completing the task in a meaningful way is not possible because the words, sentences, or paragraphs were not decoded. An insight into this problem can be gained by administering the vocabulary subtest as a group listening test. This can be done with little time and effort. If a significant increase in the vocabulary score occurs when a student listens to the items rather than reading them, one can assume that poor print skill interfered with the student's reading the vocabulary items and that this problem may also interfere with comprehension.

Typically, vocabulary tests are of four types: word and synonym or definition match, pictures matched with words, analogies, and cloze tasks. To probe through a listening test, the teacher reads the items to the students and has the students respond on a sheet of paper or, if individual testing is being done, orally or by pointing to the correct answer. Students who score significantly higher when the test is administered in this way should be checked for problems with print skill. Let's assume a listening vocabulary probe has been administered to the fourth-grade class we considered earlier to see if any students are experiencing print skill problems. These scores are shown in Figure 10.4.

This new evidence suggests that the print-skill development of some students should be explored further through informal diagnosis and instruction. Dottie, John, Lottie, Walter, and Wanda all showed a significant improvement when the vocabulary subsection was administered as a listening test, with Dottie and Walter showing an especially large increase. The teacher must further assess their print skills early in the school year.

Jean, on the other hand, shows only a small gain when the load of print skill is removed, a possible explanation for her not being grouped with the low group the prior year. The teacher wonders if Grace had enough time to finish her test. When she checked her answer sheet, she found that the last twelve items were not completed. Thus the teacher had her finish the test in an untimed fashion and decided to check her reading rate at a later time. Carol's listening vocabulary score makes her comprehension score even more suspect or suggests that she has a real need for building her store of words and concepts. The teacher is still perplexed about Ann's placement and plans to work with all four girls using a DR-TA on the first reading selection to better understand their placement and to decide with whom she should undertake further diagnostic assessment.

The teacher tentatively plans to begin a small "book club" group with Jesse, Kay, Tia, David, and Daniel, based on their high listening scores and adequate comprehension. Donald and Greta are possible members of this group but the teacher wants to observe their rate of reading selections to see if slow reading speed might account for their average comprehension performance. Gary is also an interesting student with a very high listening vocabulary score. The teacher wonders if he should be placed in the book club group or if some independent work problems exist.

Figure 10.4 Listening and standardized test results: Fourth grade.

Student	Reading vocabulary	Listening vocabulary	Reading comprehension
Ann	3.4	3.7	3.7
Candy	4.1	4.3	3.8
Carol	3.0	3.1	4.3
Connie	4.3	4.7	4.0
Cornelia	4.1	4.8	3.9
Daniel	4.1	5.2	3.8
David	4.0	5.0	4.3
Denise	4.5	4.5	4.0
Donald	4.8	5.2	3.7
Dorothy	4.3	4.7	5.1
Dottie	3.1	4.5	3.1
Gary	3.4	5.0	3.9
Gordon	3.7	4.7	3.9
Grace	3.5	3.8	3.0
Greta	4.4	5.4	3.9
Jean	2.9	3.1	2.0
Jesse	5.7	5.9	4.9
John	3.1	4.1	2.8
Kay	4.3	5.0	4.0
Lois	3.4	4.5	3.3
Lottie	2.7	3.7	1.8
Tia	4.5	5.0	3.9
Walter	1.9	4.5	2.2
Wanda	2.2	3.8	2.7

Therefore, after the first weeks of school, with only a small amount of extra assessment the teacher has identified a small group for extra support and further print-skill diagnosis, chosen a small group with which to begin the book club, and identified several students about whom she has specific questions to be addressed by initial diagnosis.

SUMMARY

Standardized test results are a useful supplement to other information available to teachers about their students' reading, particularly at the beginning of the year. In order to make good use of standardized test information, a teacher must understand the advantages and problems with such tests and know how to interpret scores based on them. Standardized test information can be used effectively, along with other information available to the teacher, in establishing how students should be grouped for reading instruction at the beginning of the year. Informal probe techniques, particularly those involving listening vocabulary, expand the range of information available to the teacher. We strongly advise that initial grouping plans, once made, remain tentative, subject to further understanding based on evidence obtained during reading instruction using the informal observational procedures described earlier in the book.

CONCLUSION

Learning to diagnose the reading problems of students is not a simple process. This is so because the process of learning to read is itself extremely complex, and there are important differences from one stage of reading development to another. We believe that a teacher must understand the nature of this development in order to be an effective diagnostician. This means having an overview of the reading process and a thorough understanding of its component processes. Instead of providing a simple "cookbook" solution to problems, we have in this book attempted to build, step by step, a conceptual framework for viewing the component processes of reading development: print skill vocabulary knowledge, and discourse comprehension.

But it is not enough to understand how the three components work as separate entities. The teacher must also learn to understand how they combine to form a balanced and smoothly operating system—and to recognize when imbalances occur that interfere with effective reading development.

One way in which we attempted to show the nature of these imbalances was through detailed case studies. We carefully selected the cases to reflect major types of problems that students encounter as they attempt to establish a balance among the component processes of reading.

Just as we believe that students are active problem-solvers responding to the demands of their instructional materials, so we believe also that teachers must become active problem-solvers as they learn to diagnose reading problems. To this end, we focused on developing the observational skills that are necessary for gathering evidence about reading, and the interpretive skills that are necessary for making sense of the evidence. In our presentation of the case studies, we have encouraged the reader to assume an active role by interspersing into the text various activities, both procedural (generating questions, selecting key words) and interpretive (drawing conclusions about the component reading processes, deriving instructional recommendations).

But skill in diagnosis can be acquired only if the teacher goes beyond this book, carrying out projects that build on the concepts and skills presented. This book will have been used most effectively if such projects were undertaken while it was being read. And this is just the beginning. The development of diagnostic skill is in many ways similar to the development of reading skill. Just as students need to undertake much contextual reading, so must teachers continue to study the reading problems of their students in order to consolidate their diagnostic strategies.

Finally, it must be emphasized once again that the purpose of diagnosis is to create instruction that is responsive to the needs of students. If this last step is omitted, the diagnosis is an idle exercise. There are two prerequisites to effective instructional planning. One is to understand the strengths and difficulties of a student well enough so that instruction is "on the mark." In this book we have been attempting to provide the basis for such an understanding. The second—more difficult, perhaps, to convey in a book—is to create instruction that captures the interest and energy of students and leads them to assume an active role. Accordingly, many of the instructional procedures we have described are designed to create active learners. As in the development of diagnostic skill, teachers will become more expert in providing high-quality instruction through experimentation with these and other procedures.

APPENDIX A

Dolch Basic Sight Vocabulary[1]

a _____ big _____ down _____
about _____ black _____ draw _____
after _____ blue _____ drink _____
again _____ both _____ eat _____
all _____ bring _____ eight _____
always _____ brown _____ every _____
am _____ but _____ fall _____
an _____ buy _____ far _____
and _____ by _____ fast _____
any _____ call _____ find _____
are _____ came _____ first _____
around _____ can _____ five _____
as _____ carry _____ fly _____
ask _____ clean _____ for _____
at _____ cold _____ found _____
ate _____ come _____ four _____
away _____ could _____ from _____
be _____ cut _____ full _____
because _____ did _____ funny _____
been _____ do _____ gave _____
before _____ does _____ get _____
best _____ done _____ give _____
better _____ don't _____ go _____
goes _____ never _____ stop _____
going _____ new _____ take _____

---

[1] *Source:* E. W. Dolch, Basic Sight Vocabulary, *Elementary School Journal,* 1936, *36,* 456–560. Published by The University of Chicago Press, Copyright © 1936 by the University of Chicago. All rights reserved.

good _____	no _____	tell _____
got _____	not _____	ten _____
green _____	now _____	thank _____
grow _____	of _____	that _____
had _____	off _____	the _____
has _____	old _____	their _____
have _____	on _____	them _____
he _____	once _____	then _____
help _____	one _____	there _____
her _____	only _____	these _____
here _____	open _____	they _____
him _____	or _____	think _____
his _____	our _____	this _____
hold _____	out _____	those _____
hot _____	over _____	three _____
how _____	own _____	to _____
hurt _____	pick _____	today _____
I _____	play _____	together _____
if _____	please _____	too _____
in _____	pretty _____	try _____
into _____	pull _____	two _____
is _____	put _____	under _____
it _____	ran _____	up _____
its _____	read _____	upon _____
jump _____	red _____	us _____
just _____	ride _____	use _____
keep _____	right _____	very _____
kind _____	round _____	walk _____
know _____	run _____	want _____
laugh _____	said _____	warm _____
let _____	saw _____	was _____
light _____	say _____	wash _____
like _____	see _____	we _____
little _____	seven _____	well _____
live _____	shall _____	went _____
long _____	she _____	were _____
look _____	show _____	what _____
made _____	sing _____	when _____
make _____	sit _____	where _____
many _____	six _____	which _____
may _____	sleep _____	white _____
me _____	small _____	who _____
much _____	so _____	why _____
must _____	some _____	will _____
my _____	soon _____	wish _____
myself _____	start _____	with _____
work _____	yellow _____	your _____
would _____	yes _____	
write _____	you _____	

APPENDIX B

Blachowicz Informal Phonics Survey[1]

This informal survey gives subtests for many sound–symbol correspondence patterns. It is rarely useful or advisable to give the *whole* test to any student. It should be used after an oral reading diagnostic test to pinpoint those areas that look like possible weaknesses.

Since the test utilizes nonsense syllables, some mispronunciations will be artifacts of the test. Often a child will try to make a nonsense syllable into a real word. All conclusions from this test should be verified in real reading situations. For example, if you think a student has done badly on *bl-*, you might want him or her to read a paragraph containing words like *blue, blend, blood,* and so forth. Never lose sight of the fact that phonics used in context is the important tool.

GENERAL GUIDELINES

1. The subtests get harder. For very young children, start at subtest 1. For most students, subtest 3 is a good starting point.
2. For subtests 3 and up, always write down what the student says when he or she mispronounces a stimulus item. This is essential for final analysis.
3. Stop whenever the student shows signs of distress. If you want to give other subtests, do them another day.

[1] *Source: Blachowicz Informal Phonics Survey.* C. L. Z. Blachowicz, (Unpublished assessment device.) Evanston, IL: National College of Education, 1980. Reprinted by permission.

4. Always tell the students what you are doing and why. Be sure to tell them that THESE ARE NOT REAL WORDS and that they are not expected to know them all.
5. Give praise and encouragement whenever you can. Start a child on an easy subtest to give success. If a student flounders, you can go back to an easier subtest to end with success.
6. Try to modify the materials to make them more usable. You might want to cut and mount the subtests for the student's copy. This makes the order less obvious.
7. A most effective use of the materials is to turn it into a board game. Place the stimulus items on index cards and have the student draw cards and move spaces for each one correctly pronounced. You can put different subtests on different colored cards for easy use and sorting.

ANALYSIS

1. Look for patterns.
2. Test your conclusions with real reading materials.
3. Try to break down the task into its parts when conclusions don't add up. For example, if the student could recognize *up*, knows the consonant sound associated with *t*, but could not pronounce *tup*, perhaps he or she cannot blend sounds.
4. Keep a record of your findings to check out in the real-life reading situation. Remember, testing is always artificial.

TEST ITEMS

1. *Naming upper and lower case letters.* Circle those not known when pointed to.

a	S	q	I	R	h	k
s	J	d	A	f	O	U
l	w	z	Q	v	X	B
n	H	T	b	e	G	P
V	N	j	y	K	w	f
F	r	Z	x	L	m	O
E	o	C	D	P	g	A
i	M	t	u	c	Y	d
S	j					

2. *Sound values of isolated consonants.* Point to each letter and ask the child to tell you what sound "this letter makes" or to give you a word that starts with this letter. Circle those not known.

b   c   k   j   g   t   v   d   m   h   r
p   z   l   f   n   s   u   w   y   qu

3. *Short vowel phonograms blended with initial consonants.* Check to see if the student knows the following simple sight word phonograms: *up, it, am,* and *on.* (If they are not known, try to train the student to recognize them, or choose phonograms the child does know.) Point to each item and have the child pronounce it. If an item is mispronounced, write the mispronunciation above it for later analysis.

mup   zam   tup   sam   con   rit   gam   kon
dup   vit   hon   quam   bup   pon   wup   jam
nit   fup   lam   yup

4. *Consonant blends plus short vowel phonograms.* This and all subsequent tests follow the same procedure as test 3. Have the child pronounce each item, and write in any misprounounced words.

brup   scon   plit   skam   slup   twit   dron
gram   swis   spup   fron   blit   snam   glup
clam   trit   flon   smam   slup   cron   prit   glup

5. *Consonant digraphs plus short vowel phonograms.*

chup   shon   thup   whit   pham   shup   whon
chon   thon

6. *VC∉ pattern plus initial consonants.*

dake   mime   fole   tule   mede   tate   fope
dute   dite   sede

7. *Long vowel digraphs.*

leat   mied   boad   tay   ley   moe   teef
buel   moes   lail   bie   toat   meep   tay
lue   bain   leam

8. *R-controlled vowels.*

mer   tir   hur   dir   fer   dar   mor   tur
sar   dor   bur

9. *Ending-blend phonograms.*

selt	mext	basp	mick	dunch	mulk	tand
goft	sunch	mimp	kent	munk	jung	dulf
baft	dilk	nolt	satch	fodge	hink	disp
folt	namp	dist	gelf	mond	bant	ting
dast	holf	fask	rept	felp	nold	hent

10. *Ending-digraph phonograms.*

tath fash nich baph dith sosh tach ruph

11. *Alternate sounds of c and g.*
gap gity cot came gend cend git cim

12. *Three-letter blends.*

splan	chrin	thrup	schon	strat	scrup
squit	spron	chris	thrat	scris	spron
strup	splup	squis	schan	shrat	

13. *Diphthongs.*
dow doy dound doint doy doud doil fown

14. *Silent letters.*

talf	tamb	demn	falm	knop	wrid	gnap
knop	ghat	wrod	gnom	phot	pnip	psin

15. *Multisyllabic words.* Show division points in responses with slash marks.

buffle	hotrat	rewant	sunting	fendle
inserg	unpottle	rembat	rebark	bullingable
minkfall	refizwissing	wenkerfil	mendle	submarkable
raction	bunded	madsion		

APPENDIX C

Complete Records of Performance on an IRI[1]: James

Analytical Reading Inventory, Word Lists

Level 3	Flash	Untimed	Level 4	Flash	Untimed
1. beginning	✔		1. worm	✔	
2. thankful	✔		2. afford	afforded	✔
3. written	✔		3. player	✔	
4. reason	✔		4. scientific	✔	
5. bent	✔		5. meek	✔	
6. patient	✔		6. rodeo	✔	
7. manage	✔		7. festival	✔	
8. arithmetic	✔		8. hillside	✔	
9. burst	✔		9. coward	✔	
10. bush	✔		10. boom	✔	
11. gingerbread	✔		11. booth	✔	
12. tremble	treb—	✔	12. freeze	✔	
13. planet	✔		13. protest	✔	
14. struggle	✔		14. nervous	✔	
15. museum	✔		15. sparrow	✔	
16. grin	✔		16. level	✔	
17. ill	✔		17. underground	✔	

[1] *Source: Analytical Reading Inventory,* 2nd ed. by M. L. Woods & A. J. Moe. Columbus, OH: Charles E. Merrill, 1981. Word Lists and Questions reprinted by permission of Charles E. Merrill Publishing Co. Passages reprinted by permission of original sources.

Analytical Reading Inventory, Word Lists (*Continued*)

	Flash	Untimed		Flash	Untimed
18. alarm	✓	———	18. oxen	✓	———
19. cool	✓	———	19. eighty	✓	———
20. engine	*ing-✓*	———	20. shouldn't	✓	———

Number correct	95	100	Number correct	95	100

Level 5	Flash	Untimed	*Level 6*	Flash	Untimed
1. abandon	✓	———	1. seventeen	✓	———
2. zigzag	✓	———	2. annoy	✓	———
3. terrific	✓	———	3. dwindle	*dind-*	✓
4. terrify	✓	———	4. rival	✓	———
5. plantation	✓	———	5. hesitation	✓	———
6. loaf	✓	———	6. navigator	✓	———
7. hike	✓	———	7. gorge	✓	———
8. relative	✓	———	8. burglar	✓	———
9. available	✓	———	9. construction	✓	———
10. grief	✓	———	10. exploration	✓	———
11. physical	✓	———	11. technical	✓	———
12. commander	*commanded*	✓	12. spice	✓	———
13. error	✓	———	13. spike	✓	———
14. woodcutter	✓	———	14. prevail	*pre✓*	———
15. submarine	✓	———	15. memorial	✓	———
16. ignore	✓	———	16. initiation	✓	———
17. disappointed	✓	———	17. undergrowth	✓	———
18. wrestle	✓	———	18. ladle	*lădle✓*	———
19. vehicle	*vick*	✓	19. walnut	✓	———
20. international	*in-ter*	✓	20. tributary	*tri-✓*	———

Number correct	90	100	Number correct	95	100

Analytical Reading Inventory, Form A
Level 6 (192 words, 12 sentences)

EXAMINER'S INTRODUCTION

Dr. Charles Drew overcame many obstacles to become a remarkable black American surgeon. Dr. Drew, who died in an auto crash at the age of forty-six, lived a life of dedication and kindness. The following information was derived from a book entitled, *Black Pioneers of Science and Invention,* by Louis Haber.[2]

"Thousands of people are dying on the battlefields from loss of blood,"   *5*

said Dr. Charles Drew. "I must give my time to solving the problems of blood   *1*
transfer
transfusion."   *1*
physics
Physicians had studied blood transfusion for years. However, they had   *1*

met with many difficulties because the whole blood spoiled within days, and

the matching of blood types was time-consuming. Nevertheless, Dr. Drew
palsma
found there were fewer problems if plasma, instead of whole blood, was used   */*
palsma
in transfusion. Plasma, the liquid part of the blood without the cells, could be   */*

stored much longer and made the matching of blood types unnecessary.
palsma
Anybody could be given plasma, and this was important on the battlefields of   *X O* *

World War II.

In 1940 the Blood Transfusion Association set up a program for war-
palsma
torn France. Dr. Drew asked them to send plasma rather than whole blood.   *X O*

But, it was started too late since France had fallen into the hands of the

enemy.

Later, when Great Britain suffered heavy losses from air raids, Dr. Drew
palsma
was asked to run a program called "Plasma for Britain." He organized the   *XO*

entire project, and thousands of Americans gave blood to help the British.

* *Miscues occurring more than twice were not counted.*

[2] Excerpt from *Black Pioneers of Science and Invention* by Louis Haber, copyright © 1970 by Harcourt Brace Jovanovich, Inc., reprinted by permission of the publisher.

$$Errors: 5/192 = 3\%$$

$$Comp: 8/8 = 100\%$$

$$Rate: 96 \text{ sec} = 1.6 \text{ min}$$

$$192 \text{ words}/1.6 \text{ min} = 120 \text{ w/m}$$

COMPREHENSION QUESTIONS AND POSSIBLE ANSWERS

✓1. What was the area of Dr. Drew's major work?
   (blood transfusion)   *blood — transfusions*

✓2. What is meant by the word *difficulties*?
   (problems)   *problems*

✓3. Why did Dr. Drew decide to devote his time to solving the problems of blood transfusion?
   (Thousands were dying on the battlefields of World War II.)
   because of men dying— World War II

✓4. What is *plasma*?
   (the liquid portion of the blood without cells)
   part of blood – not cells

✓5. In 1940 what program was organized to aid war-torn France?
   (Blood Transfusion Association)
   Blood Transfusion Program — No, Association

✓6. What is meant by the phrase "fallen into the hands of the enemy"?
   (France had lost battles to the enemy.)
   You lose a battle to the enemy.

✓7. Why did Americans give blood to help their British neighbors?
   (Britain had suffered heavy losses from air raids.)
   Because air raids killed lots of them

✓8. What is said in this story that makes you think more people survived injuries on the battlefield because of Dr. Drew's work in blood transfusion?
   (Stated: Plasma could be stored longer; with plasma, blood typing was unnecessary; anybody could be given plasma.)
   There were fewer problems with plasma — it didn't spoil as easy as blood.

Retelling: This doctor, Drew was his name, discovered plasma. Because it didn't spoil as easy as blood, it was better for transfusions — and blood types didn't have to match. It was used during World War II, not in France because it was too late, but in Britain for air raid victims

Scoring Guide	
Word Rec.	Comp.
IND 2	IND 0–1
INST 10	INST 2
FRUST 20+	FRUST 4+

Analytical Reading Inventory, Form A
Level 7 (262 words, 14 sentences)

EXAMINER'S INTRODUCTION

S. E. Hinton wrote a very sensitive book called *The Outsiders,* showing the loyalties teenagers in gangs have toward one another. In this passage, Johnny is in serious trouble, and his friends, Ponyboy and Dally, prefer to stick by him until he can decide how best to solve his problem. Please read a retelling of one of the incidents from this memorable book.   *13*

While he had been hiding out for the past five days, Johnny had given

serious thought to the whole mess. He (had) decided to return home, turn   *2*

himself in to the police, and take the consequences of his crime. Being only

sixteen, he was too young to have to run away for the rest of his life. He knew   */*

the fight had been in self-defense, but the fact still remained that he had

killed another person, and the thought of that miserable night in the city   */*

park sent Johnny into a terrifying panic.   */*

He told Dally and Ponyboy of his decision, and now Dally reluctantly

began the long drive home. Dally had gone to jail before, and this was one

wretched experience he did not want his friend to have to endure.   *3*

As they reached the top of Jay Mountain, Dally slammed on the brakes!   */*

The old church where Johnny and Ponyboy had been hiding was in flames!

Ponyboy and Johnny bolted from the car to question a bystander who ex-   */*

plained that they were having a school picnic when the church began to burn.   *2*

Suddenly, the crowd was shocked to hear desperate cries from inside!

Ponyboy and Johnny ran into the burning church, and the boys lifted the

children one by one through a window to safety. Chunks of the old roof were

already beginning to fall as the last child was taken out. Ponyboy leaped

through the window, vaguely hearing the sound of falling timber. Then, as he   */*

lay coughing and exhausted on the ground, he heard Johnny's terrifying

scream!

Errors: $^{13}/_{262} = 5\%$
Comp: $^7/_8 \quad = 88\%$
Rate: 150 sec = 2.5 min
262 words/2.5 min = 105 w/m

COMPREHENSION QUESTIONS AND POSSIBLE ANSWERS

✓ 1. What difficult conflict did Johnny have to solve?
(He had committed a crime, and he had decided to turn himself in to the police or to run away.) *whether to go home and turn himself in or stay out.*

✓ 2. What is meant by the phrase, "take the consequences"?
(take the punishment for his crime) *he would take whatever punishment they gave him.*

✓ 3. Where did the crime take place?
(in the city park) *in New York. (James was familiar with the book.)*

✓ 4. Why were Dally and the boys returning home?
(Johnny had decided to return home and turn himself in.) *So Johnny could turn himself in.*

✓ 5. Why did Dally slam on the brakes?
(He saw the burning church.) *because the church was burning.*

✓ 6. How did the boys get the children out of the burning church?
(lifted them through the window) *They ran in and the roof was caving in the boy jumped out the window with the children.*

✗ 7. What is meant by the word *vaguely*?
(not clearly defined, unclear) *D. K.*

✓ 8. What is said in the story that makes you think Johnny thought he should turn himself in?
(Stated: He said that he was too young to run and hide for the rest of his life; the fact still remained that he had killed another person, and this was apparently something he felt he couldn't live with.)
He was running and hiding and things and he just didn't want to stay away from people and be afraid of everyone.

Scoring Guide	
Word Rec.	Comp.
IND 2–3	IND 0–1
INST 13	INST 2
FRUST 26+	FRUST 4+

Analytical Reading Inventory, Form A
Level 8 (286 words, 15 sentences)

EXAMINER'S INTRODUCTION

Witch-hunts took place in England back in the 1600s. The following information was derived from an article entitled, "East Anglican and Essex Witches," from *Man, Myth, and Magic: An Illustrated Encyclopedia of the Supernatural.*

Witch-hunts were common in the seventeenth-century England. The mere $\frac{22}{1}$

presence of a witch-hunter in a village caused such fear among the people

that children would even denounce their parents.

© Belee
Belief in magic was common in those days. Perhaps some of the victims   /

of these hunts did think themselves guilty of witchery, but history has proven

that the majority of men and women accused and tortured by witch-hunters

© put
were but poor, defenseless victims of the times.   /

of
One of the best-known methods for the detection of a witch was the   2

© orderly
"swimming test." In this ordeal the suspect was dragged into a pool or stream   /

suspect
after he was already tired from torture and fear. If the suspect floated to the   /

top he was found guilty, and long pins were plunged into his body in search of   /

devil
the devil's marks. If he sank to the bottom, he was presumed innocent.   /

1945
In 1645 a man who titled himself, Witchfinder General Matthew Hop-   /

© of   ragging
kins, led a severe and cruel hunt. Because a civil war was raging in England at   2

© tense
the time, tensions and fears were common among the people. The time was   /

prosecution
ripe for persecution.   /

At
In that same year Hopkins imprisoned as many as 200 persons, all   /

and
charged with witchcraft. Among eighteen of those who died by hanging was   /

© and
one John Lowes, a seventy-year-old clergyman who had been accused of   /

the   © inter
witchcraft by his congregation. After undergoing intolerable torture, the old   2

a leggled
man admitted ownership of an evil spirit which he allegedly ordered to sink a   /

ship. No one bothered to check out the existence of such a vessel or to ask

ⓒ an
ⓒ over

about ~~any~~ reported sinkings on that day, and he was hanged ~~after~~ reading his   2

own burial service.

Errors: 22/286 = 8%
Comp: 5/8 = 62.5%
Rate: 188 sec = 3.13 min
        286 words / 3.13 min = 91 w/m

COMPREHENSION QUESTIONS AND POSSIBLE ANSWERS

✓**1.** What commonly happened in seventeenth-century England?
(witch-hunts) *they had trials of bewitched*

✓**2.** According to this passage, what has history proven about witch-hunts?
(Most of the men and women accused and tortured for being witches
were but poor and defenseless people.) *that there really is no such
thing as witchcraft.*

✗ **3.** Why would children even denounce their parents as witches?
(The mere presence of a witch-finder caused such fear among the people
and children.) *if their parents got mad at them and accused
them and told.*

✓ **4.** What is meant by the phrase, "method of detection"?
(way of finding something out) *it's a test to see if a person's
a witch or evil*

✓ **5.** In seventeenth-century England, why was the time ripe for persecution?
(A civil war was raging, causing tension and fear.) *a civil war*

✗ **6.** What is meant by the word *allegedly*? *he said he would sink a ship*
(asserted to be true or exist but not proven) *and the people thought
he was a witch because they got no report.*

✗ **7.** What did John Lowes allegedly do?
(owned an evil spirit which sank a ship) *he was the guy who committed
people to death was in the witch hunts.*

✓ **8.** What is said in the story that makes you think the swimming test was
unjust?
(Stated: If the accused person sank, thus being proven innocent, he or
she was probably dead from drowning.) *If they weren't a witch, they
would die anyway. If they were innocent, they would die anyway.*

Scoring Guide	
Word Rec.	Comp.
IND 3	IND 0–1
INST 15	INST 2
FRUST 30+	FRUST 4+

Analytical Reading Inventory, Form A
Level 9 (339 words, 18 sentences)

EXAMINER'S INTRODUCTION

This selection, based upon information from two articles appearing in a 1973 issue of *Plain Truth,* entitled, "Who's That Polluting My World?" and "How One Town Solves Pollution and Saves Water," describes some interesting facts concerning pollution and its control.

"This lake is all treated sewer water," the old gentleman murmured in admiration. The old man sat on a bench as close to the bank as possible with

his elbows resting on his knees while gazing at the rippling water. The breeze sweeping across the lake caused the sailboats to glide about with amazing

ease.
    "We are making great ecological strides," he thought to himself. He knew well the story of this remarkable lake nestled in the foothills of south-

ern California. He swelled with pride to recall the wise choice the Santee citizens had made when they elected not to join the metropolitan sewage

system where the waste would have been discharged into the Pacific with

only inadequate primary treatment. Rather, the residents constructed their own sewage facility, reclaiming the sewer water, thus extending their own

supply to provide basic needs and clean recreational extras.

    "This is probably the only city park in the world which is built just yards

downstream from a sewer plant," the gentleman thought. He leaned forward

scooping up a handful of water. "This lake is more sanitary than most natu-

ral streams."
    It has taken ingenious foresight to make this unprecedented plan viable.
Its resourcefulness lay in the fact that clean water provided not only lucra-

tive recreational facilities, but the sewage waste solids furnished marketable

soil conditioners and plant fertilizers.

As the old gentleman arose he caught sight of paper trash carelessly
tossed beside the shore. His <u>contented</u>-expression <u>changed</u> to one of concern. 2

               content   © *charged*

He already knew that twenty million tons of paper are <u>discarded</u> each year in 1

               discharged

the United States representing a net loss of <u>340</u> million trees to the envi- 1

             © *thirty*

ronment. The gentleman shook his head to think of this <u>needless</u> waste. He 1

                © *needle*

knew the United States comprises only 6 percent of the world's population,

     the

yet <u>its</u> citizens consume 30 percent of the world's total energy output, only to 1

waste half of it. The old gentleman shuddered at these thoughts as he picked

up the discarded paper and placed it into the trash container.

Errors: 24/339 = 7%

Comp: 2/8 = 25%

Rate: 234 sec = 3.90 min

    339 words / 3.9 min = 87 w/m

COMPREHENSION QUESTIONS AND POSSIBLE ANSWERS

X   **1.** What is the main idea of this passage?
(We are making progress in pollution control, but still there is needless waste.) *how many people think bad thoughts about pollution.*

X   **2.** What is meant by the phrase *inadequate primary treatment*?
(insufficient water treatment) *does not give good treatment to the water*

✓   **3.** Where is this remarkable lake?
(in Santee in southern California) *in a city park — in California*

X   **4.** What happened when the Santee citizens constructed their own sewage facility?
(It provided basic needs and clean recreational extras.)
to stop pollution and sewage from going into the lake

X   **5.** What is meant by the phrase *an unprecedented plan*?
(one not done before)
it wasn't given to them — it wasn't stated to them

X   **6.** How much of the world's total energy does the United States use?
(30 percent) *350%*

✓ **7.** Why did the old gentleman's expression change when he got up from the bench?

(He caught sight of paper trash carelessly tossed beside the shore.)

He saw a piece of paper and it kills the beauty and the trees around the lake

✗ **8.** What is said in the story that makes you think the Santee plan to reclaim sewage water was an ingenious and well thought-out ecological one?

(Stated: The clean water provided not only lucrative recreational facilities, but the waste solids furnished marketable soil conditioners and plant fertilizers.)

He would stop pollution going into the lake.

Scoring Guide			
Word Rec.		Comp.	
IND	3–4	IND	0–1
INST	18	INST	2
FRUST	36+	FRUST	4+

Analytical Reading Inventory, Form B
Level 7 (234 words, 15 sentences)

EXAMINER'S INTRODUCTION

Dave's Song, a book by Robert McKay, is a very sensitive story about a young girl who finds out that she can learn to appreciate and care for someone quite different from other young adults in her class. Please read a retelling of some of the information from this memorable book.

Kate sat in her senior biology class, but she wasn't hearing a single word the teacher was saying since her mind was thoroughly preoccupied. She could only think about Dave and her date with him last Friday night.

The entire thing was so confusing and distracting that she kept glancing sideways to where he was sitting near the windows. He was by far the most handsome boy at Tylerton High. He was tall, strong, with shaggy hair, and brilliant blue eyes, but there was something very different about Dave Burdick which she found difficult to accept. She knew that he was independent, and at times he seemed actually defiant. She found this disturbing. He always neglected his appearance as if he didn't care what others thought. He was an excellent football player, probably the best in the entire school, but he quit the team. He was stubborn and belligerent, and he would argue with anyone over anything. He never hung around the other kids, so it seemed to her that he was a loner. He drove an old Ford pickup, which had chicken feathers and farm tools scattered all over the floor. Kate felt that he was more interested in raising chickens than in having friends. Yet, even knowing all of these things, there was something crazy going on in her mind. To her surprise she found Dave Burdick fascinating and quite to her liking.

Comp: 4½/8 = 56%
Rate: 126 sec = 2.1 min
234 words / 2.1 min = 111 w/m

COMPREHENSION QUESTIONS AND POSSIBLE ANSWERS

✓ **1.** Why was Kate confused and distracted?
(Dave was very different from her other friends but she still found that she liked him.) *cause she kept thinking about the last date she had with Dave*

✓ **2.** Why didn't Kate hear anything the biology teacher was saying?
(She was preoccupied.) *cause she was too interested in dreaming about Dave*

✗ **3.** What is meant by the word *independent*?
(not dependent upon others) *he's dedicated to work*

✓ **4.** What did Kate find disturbing about Dave?
(his defiant attitude) *he didn't care for other people.*

✗ **5.** What is meant by the word *belligerent*?
(hostile, waging war) *D.K.*

✓ **6.** What did Dave's truck have in it?
(chicken feathers and old farm tools) *chicken feathers and farm equipment*

✗ **7.** Why did Kate think Dave was a loner?
(because he never hung around other kids) *because he wouldn't talk at all - just sit around and think to himself.*

½ **8.** What is said in the story that makes you think Dave had a negative attitude?
(Stated: He seemed defiant, stubborn, belligerent.) *The one date he had with the girl — she said he was too much to himself. If anyone said something about him, he didn't care what they said about him.*

Retelling : It's about this one girl saying about she was in class- she was sitting there dreaming about that one last dream that she had with Dave and she felt that he was the cutest boy in school — she saw how strong he was and she said he has furry hair and he was skinny and had shaggy hair and all - he was on the football team - he was the best one on the football team and he quit the team and he drove a pick-up truck that had feathers in the back of it. She knew that he was more interested in farming than he was in school.

Scoring Guide		
Word Rec.		Comp.
IND	2–3	IND	0–1
INST	13	INST	2
FRUST	26+	(FRUST 4+)

Analytical Reading Inventory, Form B
Level 6 (186 words, 12 sentences)

EXAMINER'S INTRODUCTION

Garrett A. Morgan, a black American inventor, was born in 1877. He not only invented the first electric traffic signal but also other important inventions. The following information was derived from a book entitled, *Black Pioneers of Science and Invention,* by Louis Haber.[3]

The explosion was horrible that tragic day in Cleveland, Ohio, in 1916. Thirty-two men were trapped in a tunnel 250 feet below Lake Erie. No one could enter the smoke-filled tunnel to rescue the survivors.

"Someone get Garrett Morgan to help those men down there," shouted a man from the crowd. "Morgan and his breathing device are the only chance those men have!"

Garrett Morgan and his brother quickly came to the aid of the men trapped in the tunnel. Morgan had invented what he called a "Breathing Device," later to be known as the *gas mask.* Two years before, Morgan's invention had been tested by filling an enclosed tent with the foulest, thickest smoke possible. Placing the device over his head, a man entered this suffocating atmosphere, stayed twenty minutes, and emerged unharmed! Later, using a poisonous gas in a closed room, another test also provided the same successful results.

Although not all lived, every man was brought to the surface by the brothers. It was Morgan's concern for safer working conditions that saved lives that day and in the years to come.

Comp: 6½/8 = 81%
Rate: 115 sec = 1.92 min
  186 words/1.92 min = 97 w/m

---

[3] Excerpt from *Black Pioneers of Science and Invention* by Louis Haber, copyright © 1970 by Harcourt Brace Jovanovich, Inc., reprinted by permission of the publisher.

COMPREHENSION QUESTIONS AND POSSIBLE ANSWERS

✓ **1.** What did Garrett Morgan invent?
(gas mask — breathing device) *a gas mask*

✓ **2.** Where was the tunnel located in which the men were trapped?
(250 feet below Lake Erie) *Cleveland, Ohio - 250 feet down*

½ **3.** What happened as a result of the terrible explosion in Cleveland?
(thirty-two men were trapped) *gas filled the tunnel*

✓ **4.** What is meant by the phrase, "this suffocating atmosphere"?
(the air in the tent was without oxygen)
run out of air - can't breathe - you'll die

✓ **5.** What is meant by the word *device*?
(something intricate in design; a machine)
Something used to help someone — like a camera is a device.

✓ **6.** What happened to the man who stayed in the tent for twenty minutes?
(He emerged unharmed.) *he survived — he got out of it*
— he could breathe

✗ **7.** What was used to test the gas mask the second time?
(a poisonous gas) *smoke — I don't know*

✓ **8.** What is said in the story that makes you think Morgan cared for the safety of others?
(Stated: It was Morgan's concern for safer working conditions which saved lives that day.)

He came as fast as he could with the breathing thing —
and he invented it to save lives.

Scoring Guide	
Word Rec.	Comp.
IND 2	IND 0–1
INST 10	INST 2
FRUST 20+	FRUST 4+

Analytical Reading Inventory, Form B
Level 5 (197 words, 12 sentences)

EXAMINER'S INTRODUCTION

This is a story about Robyn Smith who left a career as a movie star to become one of the first female jockeys. The following information was derived from an article appearing in *The Lincoln Library of Sports Champions.*

"I know that I was last in the race," announced Robyn Smith, "but I am determined to be the best woman jockey! I want to ride race horses!"

It was a rainy morning in 1969, and as Robyn stood outside talking to the trainer, Frank Wright, she was so dripping wet that water came running out of the top of her boots. Many people had doubts about Robyn's riding ability, but Wright was sure she could be a successful rider. He decided to give her a first big chance.

By December of that same year she had proven herself by placing fourth in a race. Robyn not only had skill as a jockey, but she also had a way with horses which made them run fast for her.

Soon, she became accepted by others as an excellent rider. She went on to highlight her career with a surprising victory riding a horse named North Star. This horse was known for being wild on the track, but Robyn was able to handle him. Together they outran a horse named Onion. This was a special victory for Robyn because later, in another race, Onion defeated the famous horse, Secretariat!

Comp: 8/8 = 100%
Rate: 108 sec = 1.8 min
197 words/1.8 min = 109 w/m

COMPREHENSION QUESTIONS AND POSSIBLE ANSWERS

✓ 1. What was Robyn Smith determined to be?
       (the best woman jockey) *the best woman jockey*

✓ 2. Why did water run out of the top of Robyn's boots?
       (because she was standing outside in the rain)
       She was in the rain

✓ 3. What did Frank Wright do for Robyn?
       (gave her a first big chance) *gave her a chance to ride*

✓ 4. What is meant by the phrase, "proven herself"?
       (She showed that she could ride well.) *to show she could do it*

✓ 5. What did others think of Robyn when she proved her riding skill?
       (She was accepted as a good jockey.)
       thought she was a good jockey

✓ 6. What was North Star known for?
       (being wild on the track) *being wild and hard to handle*

✓ 7. Why was this a special victory for Robyn?
       (North Star defeated Onion; Onion defeated the famous horse Secretar-
       iat.) *because she beat the horse who later beat Secretariat*

✓ 8. What is said in the story that makes you think Robyn's trainer had
       confidence in her riding?
       (Stated: Wright was sure she could be a successful rider; she had a way
       with horses which made them run fast for her; she had skill as a rider.)
       Because he gave her a chance

Scoring Guide	
Word Rec.	Comp.
IND 2	IND 0–1
INST 9	INST 2
FRUST 18+	FRUST 4+

Analytical Reading Inventory, Form C
Level 8 (257 words, 15 sentences)

EXAMINER'S INTRODUCTION

The next selection you are to read is about vampires. At one time in our history vampires and other supernatural beings were believed to exist. The following information was derived from an article entitled, "Vampires," from *Man, Myth, and Magic: An Illustrated Encyclopedia of the Supernatural.*

"I am . . . Dracula," murmured a black-caped, fanged-toothed, pointed-eared monster. "I never drink . . . wine," he declared as moviegoers sat petrified in their seats.

In 1931, a novel by Irish author Bram Stoker became vividly alive on the movie screen as thousands flocked to see this re-creation of the vampire superstition which dates back to the sixteenth century.

According to the novel, a vampire looks pale, lean, and has a death-like icy touch. His eyes gleam or flash red, his ears are pointed like those of a werewolf, and his fingernails are curled and sharp. Some tales describe him as skeletal and often dressed in a black costume. His limited diet of blood gives him a foul-smelling breath. Old legends depict him with only one nostril and a barbed tongue. These creatures have the power to change their form into a cloud of mist or a bizarre nocturnal animal.

Despite modern disbelief in vampires, during the seventeenth century many thought they existed. It was believed that once a person died he could possibly return as a vampire. A corpse was often fastened in its grave with pegs or iron skewers to prevent a potential vampire from escaping.

Since the vampire was dormant during the day, graves were examined for small holes through which the monster could escape. If a grave was discovered with such holes, vampire hunters would remove the body and destroy it. This procedure took place during the daytime hours and all the

hunters returned to their homes before sunset.

Comp: $\frac{7}{8}$ = 88 %

COMPREHENSION QUESTIONS AND POSSIBLE ANSWERS

  ✓ **1.** What is the main idea of this article?
     (Belief in vampires existed in the 16th and 17th centuries.)
      they used to believe in vampires

  ✓ **2.** What are a vampire's eyes supposed to look like?
     (gleaming or flashing red) flash red

  ✓ **3.** What is meant by the phrase, "bizarre animal"?
     (unique or strange) strange

  ✓ **4.** How did old legends describe a vampire?
     (one nostril and a barbed tongue) one nostril [Anything else?]
               a funny tongue - a barb tongue

  ✗ **5.** What is meant by the phrase, "barbed tongue"?
     (a forked or pointed tongue) D.K.

  ✓ **6.** Why were iron skewers used to fasten a corpse to its grave?
     (to prevent it from escaping) to stop it from getting away

  ✓ **7.** Why were the graves examined during the day?
     (There was less danger as vampires slept during the day.)
        the vampires slept then

  ✓ **8.** What is said in this story that makes you think people in the 16th and
     17th centuries believed in and feared vampires?
     (Stated: They fastened corpses in their graves with iron skewers; they
     searched graves for perforations and if holes were found they destroyed
     the corpse.) they went hunting for them

Scoring Guide	
Word Rec.	Comp.
IND 3	IND 0–1
INST 15	INST 2
FRUST 30+	FRUST 4+

Analytical Reading Inventory, Form C
Level 9 (315 words, 17 sentences)

EXAMINER'S INTRODUCTION

Jean-Pierre Haller, a Belgian explorer and author, was born and raised in the Belgian Congo. Since his childhood playmates had been members of the Efé Pygmy society, he returned in 1957 to become an adopted member and assist them in their dramatic struggle for survival. The following information was derived from an article entitled, "To Save a People," appearing in a 1975 issues of *The Plain Truth.*

A young Pygmy stood in the parching equatorial African sun. He stood but five feet tall and his stature was bent from hard labor. His skin was golden brown and his hair was short and curled tightly to his head. His feet were bare and his clothes tattered. His eyes had the dull stare of a man once proud and free, but now deprived of the will to maintain his own gentle life-style.

The Pygmies are central Africa's oldest known surviving people and in the 1930's about 35,000 proudly lived in the Itiru Forest of the eastern Congo, now called Zaire. By 1957 their population had fallen to 25,000.

During the fifties, the Pygmies' ancestral forest was wastefully chopped down by lumber industrialists, robbing them of the vegetation and game they depended upon for survival. Consequently, the people were forced into the blistering sun to which they were unaccustomed. Large plantations closed in on their environment. National parks and game reserves were established, but no land was set aside to aid the Pygmy societies in their struggle for survival. Tourists brought contagious diseases to which the Pygmies had no immunity, and as a result their population continued to decline.

In 1960 the Belgian Congo received political independence, becoming the nation of Zaire. This political change brought civil war for which the nonaggressive Pygmies were the first to suffer and their number rapidly dwindled to 15,000. They became victims of new burdens such as paying income taxes, being drafted into the Zaire army, further loss of cultural identity, and by 1975 their size numbered some 3,800.

The Pygmies have a warm and gentle life-style with a dignified moral code which forbids killing, lying, theft, devil worship, sorcery, disrespect for elders, and blasphemy. They do not engage in cannibalism, mutilation, ritual murder, intertribal war, initiation ordeals, or other cruel customs sometimes associated with equatorial Africa.

Comp: 6½/8 = 81%

COMPREHENSION QUESTIONS AND POSSIBLE ANSWERS

✓ 1. What is the main idea of this passage?
   (This Pygmy tribe is facing near extinction.) about how Pygmies were forced to become like our society

✓ 2. Where is the Itiru Forest?
   (eastern Congo, now called Zaire) in Africa

½ 3. What happened to the Pygmy society when their forests were chopped down?
   (They were robbed of the vegetation and game they depended upon for survival.) they weren't used to the sun beating down on them

✓ 4. What is meant by the word *immunity*?
   (condition of being able to resist a particular disease) if a person isn't immune to a sickness, they'll probably get it

✓ 5. What did tourists bring to the Pygmies?
   (contagious diseases) diseases

✗ 6. What is meant by the phrase, "nonaggressive Pygmies"?
   (nonhostile, nonwarlike) you're not selfish, like someone who is crazy and always wanting something, they're nonaggressive

✓ 7. In 1960, what happened when the Belgian Congo received political independence?
   (civil war and new suffering for the Pygmies) they had to pay taxes and were drafted into the army.

✓ 8.   What is said in this story that makes you think no one cared enough to
       protect the Pygmies' rights?
       (Stated: Lumber industrialists wastefully chopped down the Pygmies'
       forests; parks and game reserves were set aside but no land was saved for
       the Pygmies.)

they had to move to the cities and countryside
with people

Scoring Guide			
Word Rec.		Comp.	
IND	3–4	IND	0–1
INST	18	INST	2
FRUST	36+	FRUST	4+

References

Allington, R. L. (1983). Fluency: The neglected reading goal. *Reading Teacher, 36,* 556–561.

Anderson, R. C. (1972). How to construct achievement tests to assess comprehension. *Review of Educational Research 42,* 145–170.

Anderson, R. D., & Davison, A. (1989). Conceptual and empirical bases of readability formulas. In G. Green & A. Davison (Eds.), *Linguistic complexity and text comprehension.* Hillsdale, NJ: Erlbaum.

Anderson, R. C., & Freebody, P. (1981). Vocabulary knowledge. In J. Guthrie (Ed.), *Comprehension and teaching: Research reviews.* Newark, DE: International Reading Association.

Anglin, J. M. (1977). *Word, object, and conceptual development.* New York: Norton.

Asch, S. E. & Nerlove, H. (1960). The development of double-function terms in children: An exploratory investigation. In B. Kaplan & S. Wapner (Eds.), *Perspectives in psychological theory: Essays in honor of Heinz Werner.* New York: International Universities Press. Cited in Gardner, H., Winner, E., Bechhofer, R., & Wolf, D. (1978). The development of figurative language. In K. E. Nelson (Ed.), *Children's language* (Vol. 1). New York: Gardner.

Baer, J. A. (1926). Case studies in reading. *Educational Research Bulletin* (Ohio State University) *5,* 319–321.

Baldwin, R. S., Luce, T. S., & Readence, J. E. (1982). The impact of subschemata on metaphorical processing. *Reading Research Quarterly 17,* 528–543.

Barr, R. (1972). The influence of instructional conditions on word recognition errors. *Reading Research Quarterly 7,* 509–579.

Barr, R. (1974a). Influence of instruction on early reading. *Interchange 5,* 13–22.

Barr, R. (1974b). Instructional pace differences and their effect on reading acquisition. *Reading Research Quarterly, 9,* 526–554.

Barr, R. (1975). The effect of instruction on pupil reading strategies. *Reading Research Quarterly 10,* 555–582.

Barr, R. (1987). Classroom interaction and curricular content. In D. Bloome (Ed.), *Literacy and schooling.* Norwood, NJ: Ablex.

Barr, R. (1989). Influence of basal programs on fourth grade reading instruction. *Reading Research Quarterly, 14,* 44–71.

Barr, R., & Dreeben, R. (1983). *How schools work.* Chicago: University of Chicago Press.

Barrett, T. C. (1976). Taxonomy of reading comprehension. In R. Smith & T. C. Barrett, *Teaching reading in the middle grades.* Reading, MA: Addison-Wesley.

Barron, R. (1969). The use of vocabulary as an advance organizer. In H. L. Herber & P. L. Sanders (Eds.), *Research in reading in the content areas: First year report.* Syracuse, NY: Syracuse University Reading and Language Arts Center.

Bartlett, B. J. (1978). *Top-level structure as an organizational strategy for recall of classroom text.* Unpublished doctoral dissertation, Arizona State University. Cited in Meyer, B. J. F., Brandt, D. M., & Bluth, G. J. (1980). Use of top-level structure in text: Key for reading comprehension of ninth-grade students. *Reading Research Quarterly 16,* 72–103.

Bean, T. W., & Pardi, R. (1979). A field test of a guided reading strategy: *Journal of Reading 23,* 144–146.

Beck, I. L., & McCaslin, E. S. (1978). *An analysis of the dimensions that affect the development of code-breaking ability in eight beginning reading programs.* (LRDC Publication 1978/6) Pittsburgh: University of Pittsburgh, Learning Research and Development Center.

Beck, I. L., & McKeown, M. G. (1981). Developing questions that promote comprehension: The story map. *Language Arts, 58,* 913–918.

Beck, I. L., McKeown, M. G., McCaslin, E. S., & Burkes, A. M. (1979). *Instructional dimensions that may affect reading comprehension: Examples from two commercial reading programs.* (LRDC Publication 1979/20). Pittsburgh: University of Pittsburgh, Learning Research and Development Center.

Beck, I. L., Omanson, R. C., & McKeown, M. G. (1982). An instructional redesign of reading lessons: Effects on comprehension. *Reading Research Quarterly 17,* 462–481.

Beck, I. L., Perfetti, C. A., & McKeown, M. G. (1982). The effects of long-term vocabulary instruction on lexical access and reading comprehension. *Journal of Edcuational Psychology 74,* 506–521.

Becker, W., Dixon, R. C., & Inman-Anderson, L. (1980). *Morphographic and root word analysis of 26,000 high-frequency words.* Eugene, OR: College of Education.

Bennett, A. (1942). An analysis of errors in word recognition made by retarded readers. *Journal of Educational Psychology 33,* 25–34.

Betts, E. A. (1934). A physiological approach to the analysis of reading disabilities. *Educational Research Bulletin 8,* 135–140, 163–164.

Betts, E. A. (1954). *Foundations of reading instruction.* (rev. ed.). New York: American Book.

Biemiller, A. (1970). The development of the use of graphic and contextual information as children learn to read. *Reading Research Quarterly 6,* 75–96.

Biemiller, A. (1979). Changes in the use of graphic and contextual information as functions of passage difficulty and reading achievement level. *Journal of Reading Behavior 11,* 307–318.

Bird, M. (1980). Reading comprehension strategies: A direct instruction approach (Doctoral dissertation, University of Toronto, 1980). *Dissertation Abstracts International, 41,* 2506A.

Blachowicz, C. L. Z. (1977). Cloze activities for primary readers. *Reading Teacher, 31,* 300–302.

Blachowicz, C. L. Z. (1985). Vocabulary development and reading: From research to instruction. *The Reading Teacher, 38,* 876–881.

Blachowicz, C. L. Z. (1986). Making connection: Alternatives to the vocabulary notebook. *Journal of Reading, 29,* 643–649.

Bloom, B. S., Engelhardt, M. D., Furst, E. J., Hill, W. H., & Krathwohl, D. R. (1956). *Taxonomy of educational objectives. The classification of educational goals. Handbook I: Cognitive domain.* New York: David McKay.

Bolinger, D. (1968). *Aspects of language.* New York: Harcourt, Brace, & World.

Bond, G. L. (1935). *The auditory and speech characteristics of poor readers.* Teachers College Contributions to Education, No. 657, Columbia University.

Bond, G. S. & Dykstra, R. (1967). The cooperative research program in first-grade reading. *Reading Research Quarterly, 2.*

Bortnick, R., & Lopardo, G. (1973). An instructional application of the cloze procedure. *Journal of Reading, 16,* 296–300.

Bradley, L., & Bryant, P. E., (1983). Categorizing sounds and learning to read: A causal connection. *Nature, 301,* 419–421.

Bridge, C. A., & Tierney, R. J. (1981). The inferential operations of children across text with narrative and expository tendencies. *Journal of Reading Behavior 13,* 201–214.

Brown, C. (1986). A tutorial procedure for enhancing the reading comprehension of college students (Doctoral dissertation). University of Pennsylvania, *Dissertation Abstracts International, 47,* 3719A.

Bruce, D. 1964. Analysis of word sounds by young children. *British Journal of Educational Psychology, 34,* 148–169.

Buros, O. K. (Ed.). (1961). *Tests in Print I.* Highland Park, NJ: Gryphon Press.

Buros, O. K. (Ed.). (1968). *Reading Tests and Reviews I.* Highland Park, NJ: Gryphon Press.

Buros, O. K. (Ed.). (1974). *Tests in Print II.* Highland Park, NJ: Gryphon Press.

Buros, O. K. (Ed.). (1975). *Reading Tests and Reviews II.* Highland Park, NJ: Gryphon Press.

Buros, O. K. (Ed.). (1978). *Eighth Mental Measurement Yearbook.* Highland Park, NJ: Gryphon Press.

Bussis, A. M., Chittenden, E. A., Amarel, M., & Klausner, E. (1985). *Inquiry into meaning: An investigation of learning to read.* Hillsdale, NJ: Erlbaum.

Calkins, L. (1986). *The art of teaching writing.* Portsmouth, NH: Heinemann Educational Books.

Carpenter, P. A., & Just, M. A. (1977). Reading comprehension as eyes see it. In M. A. Just & P. A. Carpenter (Eds.), *Cognitive processes in comprehension.* Hillsdale, NJ: Erlbaum.

Carr, E., & Wixson, K. K. (1986). Guidelines for evaluating vocabulary instruction. *Journal of Reading 29,* 588–595.

Carver, R. P. (1983). Is reading rate constant or flexible? *Reading Research Quarterly, 18,* 190–215.

Chall, J. S. (1967). *Learning to read: The great debate.* New York: McGraw-Hill.

Chall, J. S. (1983). *Stages of reading development.* New York: McGraw-Hill.

Chomsky, C. (1976). After decoding: What? *Language Arts, 53,* 288–96, 314.

Clark, E. V. (1973). What's in a word? On the child's acquisiton of semantics in his first language. In T. E. Moore (Ed.), *Cognitive development and the acquisition of language.* New York: Academic Press.

Clay, M. M. (1967). The reading behavior of five year old children: A research project. *New Zealand Journal of Educational Studies 2,* 11–31.

Clay, M. M. (1975). *What did I write?* Portsmouth, NH: Heinemann Educational Books.

Clay, M. M. (1979). *Reading: The patterning of complex behavior.* Auckland, N.Z.: Heinemann.

Cleland, C. J. (1981). Highlighting issues in children's literature through semantic webbing. *Reading Teacher, 34,* 642–646.

Clowes, H. C. (1930). A reading clinic. *Edcuational Research Bulletin* (Ohio State University) *9,* 261–268.

Cochran-Smith, M. (1984). *The making of a reader.* Norwood, NJ: Ablex.

Cocks, P. (1974). *Verification of answer categories for a definition task: A study of linguistic and cognitive processes.* Unpublished doctoral dissertation, University of Chicago.

Cohen, A. S. (1974–1975). Oral reading errors of first grade children taught by a code emphasis approach. *Reading Research Quarterly, 10,* 616–650.

Crist, B. I. (1975). One capsule a week—A painless remedy for vocabulary ills. *Journal of Reading, 19,* 147–149.

Crothers, E. J. (1978). Inference and coherence. *Discourse Processes, 1,* 51–71.

Cunningham, P. M. (1975–1976). Investigating a synthesized theory of mediated word identification. *Reading Research Quarterly, 11,* 127–143.

Cunningham, P. M. (1978). Decoding polysyllabic words: An alternative strategy. *Journal of Reading, 21,* 608–614.

Cunningham, P. M. (1979). A compare/contrast theory of mediated word identification. *Reading Teacher, 32,* 774–778.

Cunningham, J. W., Cunningham, P. M., & Arthur, S. V. (1981). *Middle and secondary school reading.* New York: Longman.

Daskal, J. (1983). *Basic strategies for improving comprehension of written materials.* Unpublished manuscript, Chicago.

Davidson, J. L. & Wilkerson, B. C. (1988). *Directed Reading-Thinking Activities.* Monore, NY: Trillium Press.

Davis, F. B. (1944). Fundamental factors of comprehension in reading. *Psychometrika, 9,* 185–197.

Davis, F. B. (1968). Research in comprehension in reading. *Reading Research Quarterly, 3,* 499–544.

Davis, O. L., Jr., & Hunkins, F. 1966. Textbook questions: What thinking processes do they foster? *Peabody Journal of Education, 43,* 285–92.

Dearborn, W. F. (1906). The psychology of reading. *Archives of Philosophy, Psychology and Scientific Methods, 1,* 71–132.

Dearborn, W. F. (1933). Structural factors which condition special disability in reading. *Proceedings of the 57th Annual Session of the American Association of Mental Deficiency, 38,* 268–283.

Dodge, R. (1905). The illusion of clear vision during eye-movement. *Psychological Bulletin, 12,* 193–199.

Dodge, R. (1907). An experimental study of visual fixation. *Psychological Review Monograph Supplements, 8,* 1–96.

Dolch, E. W. (1936). Basic sight vocabulary. *Elementary School Journal, 36,* 456–460.

Dougherty, M. L. (1929). Reading difficulty. *Johns Hopkins University Studies in Education, 11.*

Draper, A. G., & Moeller, G. H. (1971). We think with words (therefore, to improve thinking, teach vocabulary). *Phi Delta Kappan, 52,* 482–484.

Drum, P. A. (1983). Vocabulary knowledge. In J. A. Niles & L. A. Harris (Eds.), *Searches for meaning in reading/language processing and instruction* (Thirty-second Yearbook of the National Reading Conference). Rochester, NY: National Reading Conference.

Durkin, D. (1978–1979). What classroom observations reveal about reading comprehension instruction. *Reading Research Quarterly, 14,* 481–533.

Durrell, D. D. (Chairman). (1936). *Research problems in reading in the elementary school* (Fourth Annual Research Bulletin of the National Conference on Research in Elementary School English). Philadelphia: J. Conrad Seegers. Temple University.

Ehri, L. C. (1975). Word consciousness in readers and prereaders. *Journal of Educational Psychology, 67,* 204–212.

Ehri, L. C. (1979). Linguistic insight: Threshold of reading acquisition. In T. G. Waller & G. E. MacKinnon (Eds.), *Reading research: Advances in theory and practice* (Vol. 1., pp. 63–114). New York: Harcourt Brace Jovanovich.

Ehri, L. C. (1980). The development of orthographic images. In U. Frith (Ed.), *Cognitive processes in spelling.* London: Academic Press.

Ehri, L. C. (1983). How orthography alters spoken language competencies in children learning to read and spell. In J. Downing & R. Valtin (Eds.), *Language awareness and learning to read.* New York: Springer Verlag.

Ekwall, E. E. (1976). *Diagnosis and remediation of the disabled reader.* Boston: Allyn & Bacon.

Ekwall, E. E. (1979). *Ekwall Reading Inventory.* Boston: Allyn & Bacon.

Elder, R. D. (1971). Oral reading achievement of Scottish and American children. *Elementary School Journal, 71,* 216–230.

Elkonin, D. B. (1963). The psychology of mastering elements of reading. In B. Simon (Ed.). *Educational psychology in the U.S.S.R.* London: Routledge & Kegan Paul.

Eller, R. G., Pappas, C. C., & Brown, E. (1988). The lexical development of kindergarteners: Learning from written context. *Journal of Reading Behavior, 20,* 5–24.

Feifel, H., & Lorge I. 1950. Qualitative differences in the vocabulary responses of children. *Journal of Educational Psychology, 41,* 1–18.

Fernald, G. M., & Keller, H. (1926). The effect of kinesthetic factors in the development of word recognition in nonreaders, *Journal of Educational Research, 4,* 355–377.

Ferreiro, E. (1984). The underlying logic of literacy development. In H. Goelman, A. Oberg, & F. Smith (Eds.), *Awakening to literacy.* Portsmouth, NH: Heinemann Educational Books.

Ferreiro, E., & Teberosky, A. (1982). *Literacy before schooling.* Portsmouth, NH: Heinemann Educational Books.

Ferroli, L., & Shanahan, T. (1987). Kindergarten spelling: Explaining its relation to first-grade reading. In J. E. Readence & R. S. Baldwin (Eds.). *Research in literacy: Merging perspectives* (Thirty-sixth Yearbook of the National Reading Conference). Rochester, NY: National Reading Conference.

Fisher, J. H. (1905). A case of congenital word blindness. *Opthalmic Review, 24,* 315–318.

Ford, C. A. (1928). A case of congenital word blindness showing its social implications. *Psychological Clinic, 17,* 73–84.

Freebody, P., & Anderson, R. C. (1983a). Effects of differing proportions and locations of difficult vocabulary on text comprehension. *Journal of Reading Behavior, 15,* 19–39.

Freebody, P., & Anderson, R. C. (1983b). Effects of vocabulary difficulty, text cohesion, and schema availability on reading comprehension. *Readin Research Quarterly, 18,* 277–294.

Froese, V., & Kurushima, S. (1979). The effects of sentence expansion practice on the reading comprehension and writing ability of third graders. In M. L. Kamil & A. J. Moe (Eds.), *Reading research: Studies and applications* (Twenty-eighth Yearbook of the National Reading Conference). Clemson, S.C.: National Reading Conference.

Fuchs, L. S., Fuchs, D., & Deno, S. L. (1982). Reliability and validity of curriculum-based informal reading inventories. *Reading Research Quarterly, 18,* 6–26.

Gallagher, J. S., & Aschner, M. J. 1963. A preliminary report on analysis of classroom interaction. *Merrill-Palmer Quarterly of Behavior and Development, 9,* 183–194.

Gambrell, L., Pfeiffer, W., and Wilson, R. (1985). The effects of retelling upon reading comprehension and recall of text information. *Journal of Educational Research, 7,* 216–220.

Gamoran, A. (1984). *Teaching, grouping, and learning: A study of the consequences of educational stratification.* Unpublished doctoral dissertation, University of Chicago.

Gardner, H., Winner, E., Bechhofer, R., & Wolf, D. (1978). The development of figurative language. In K. E. Nelson (Ed.). *Children's language* (Vol. 1). New York: Gardner.

Garner, R. (1987). *Metacognition and reading comprehension.* Norwood, NJ: Ablex.

Garner, R., & Reis, R. (1981). Monitoring and resolving comprehension obstacles: An investigation of spontaneous lookbacks among upper-grade good and poor comprehenders. *Reading Research Quarterly, 16,* 569–582.

Gates, A. I. (1926). A series of tests for the measurement of diagnosis of reading ability in grades 3 to 8. *Teachers College Record, 28,* 1–23.

Gates, A. I. (1927). Methods of constructing and validating the Gates reading tests. *Teachers College Record, 29,* 148–159.

Gates, A. I. (1935). *Improvement of reading* (rev. ed.). New York: Macmillan.

Geva, E. (1983). Facilitating reading comprehension through flowcharting. *Reading Research Quarterly, 18,* 384–405.

Gilbert, D. W. 1959. *Breaking the reading barrier.* Englewood Cliffs, NJ: Prentice-Hall.

Gillet, J. W. & Temple, C. (1982). *Understanding reading problems: Assessment and instruction.* Boston: Little, Brown.

Golden, J. M. & Pappas, C. C. (1987). A critical review of retelling procedures in research on children's cognitive processing of written text. Paper presented at the annual meeting of the National Reading Conference. St. Petersburg, FL.

Goodman, K. S. (1965). A linguistic study of cues and miscues in reading. *Elementary English, 42,* 639–643.

Goodman, K. S. (1967). Reading: A psycholinguistic guessing game. *Journal of the Reading Specialist, 6,* 126–135.

Goodman, K. S. (1969). Analysis of reading miscues: Applied psycholinguistics. *Reading Research Quarterly, 5,* 9–30.

Goodman, K. S. (1976). Reading: A psycholinguistic guessing game. In H. Singer & R. Ruddell (Eds.), *Theoretical models and processes of reading.* Newark, DE: International Reading Association.

Gordon, C. J. & Braun, C. (1983). Using story grammar as an aid to reading and writing. *The Reading Teacher, 27,* 116–121.

Gourley, J. W. (1978). This basal is easy to read—or is it? *Reading Teacher, 32,* 174–182.

Graves, M., & Prenn, M. (1986). Costs and benefits of various methods of teaching vocabulary. *Journal of Reading, 29,* 596–602.

Gray, C. T. (1922). *Deficiencies in reading ability: Their diagnosis and remedies.* Boston: D. C. Heath.

Gray, W. S., & Holmes, E. (1938). *The development of meaning vocabularies in reading* (Publications of the Laboratory Schools, No. 6). Chicago: University of Chicago.

Gray, W. S., with Kibbe, D., Lucas, L., & Miller, L. W. (1922). *Remedial cases in reading: Their diagnosis and treatment* (Supplemental Educational Monograph). Chicago: University of Chicago Press.

Guszak, F. J. (1967). Teacher questioning and reading. *Reading Teacher, 21,* 227–234.

Hafner, L. E. (1977). *Developmental reading in middle and secondary schools: Foundations, strategies, and skills for teaching.* New York: Macmillan.

Hansen, J., & Pearson, P. D. (1983). An instructional study: Improving the inferential comprehension of good and poor fourth-grade readers. *Journal of Educational Psychology, 75,* 821–829.

Harris, A. J., & Jacobson, M. D. (1982). *Basic reading vocabularies.* New York: Macmillan.

Harris, A. J., & Sipay, E. R. (1980). *How to increase reading ability* (7th ed.). New York: Longman.

Harste, J. Woodward, V., & Burke, C. (1984). *Language stories and literacy lessons.* Portsmouth, NH: Heinemann Educational Books.

Heath, S. B. (1983). *Way with words: Language, life, and work in communities and classroom.* Norwood, NJ: Ablex.

Henderson, E. H. (1981). *Learning to read and spell.* DeKalb, IL: Northern Illinois University Press.

Henderson, E. H. (1985). *Teaching spelling.* Boston: Houghton Mifflin.

Henderson, E. H., & Beers, J. W. (Eds.). (1980). *Developmental and cognitive aspects of learning to spell: A reflection of word knowledge.* Newark, DE: International Reading Association.

Hiebert, E. H. (1981). Developmental patterns and interrelationships of preschool children's print awareness. *Reading Research Quarterly, 16,* 236–260.

Hincks, E. M. (1926). *Disability in reading and its relation to personality* (Harvard Monographs in Education, No. 7). Cambridge, MA: Harvard University Press.

Holdaway, D. (1979). *The foundations of literacy.* Sydney: Aston Scholastic.

Hood, J. (1976). Qualitative analysis of oral reading errors: The inter-judge reliability of scores. *Reading Research Quarterly, 11,* 577–598.

Huey, E. B. (1898). Preliminary experiments in the physiology and psychology of reading. *American Journal of Psychology, 9,* 575–586.

Huey, E. B. (1900). On the psychology and physiology of reading, I. *American Journal of Psychology, 11,* 283–302.

Huey, E. B. (1968). *The psychology and pedagogy of reading.* Cambridge, MA: MIT Press. (Originally published, 1908.)

Hughes, A., Bernier, S. A., & Gurren, L. (Eds.) (1979). The eagle and the baker. In *The Gold Book, The Headway Program.* LaSalle, IL: Open Court Publishing.

Irwin, P. I., & Mitchell, J. N. (1983). A procedure for assessing the richness of retellings. *Journal of Reading, 2,* 391–396.

Jackson, E. (1906). Developmental alexia (congenital word blindness). *American Journal of Medical Sciences, 81,* 843–849.

Jastak, J. (1934). Interferences in reading. *Psychological Bulletin, 21,* 244–272.

Jenkins, J. R., Pany, D., & Schreck, J. (1978). *Vocabulary and reading comprehension: Instructional effects* (Technical Report No. 100). Urbana: University of Illinois, Center for the Study of Reading. (ERIC Document Reproduction Service No. ED 160 999)

Johns, J. L. 1978. *Basic reading inventory* (3rd ed.). Dubuque, IA: Kendall/Hunt.

Johnson, D. & Pearson, P. D. (1978). *Teaching reading vocabulary.* New York: Holt, Rinehart & Winston.

Juel, C., & Roper/Schneider, D. (1985). The influence of basal readers on first grade reading. *Reading Research Quarterly, 20,* 134–152.

Kameenui, E. J., & Carnine, D. W. (1982). An investigation of fourth-graders' comprehension of pronoun constructions in ecologically valid texts. *Reading Research Quarterly, 17,* 556–580.

Kameenui, E. J., Carnine, D. W., & Freschi, R. (1982). Effects of text construction and instructional procedures for teaching word meanings on comprehension and recall. *Reading Research Quarterly, 17,* 367–388.

Karpova, S. N. (1955). Osoznanie slovesnogo sostava rechi rebenkom doshkol'nogo vozrasta (The preschooler's realization of the lexical structure of speech). *Voprosy Psikhol.,* No. 4, 43–55.

Kibby, M. W. (1979). Passage readability affects the oral reading strategies of disabled readers. *Reading Teacher, 32,* 390–396.

Kimmell, S., & MacGinitie, W. H. (1985). Helping students revise hypotheses while reading. *The Reading Teacher, 37,* 768–771.

Koskinen, P. S., & Blum, I. H. (1986). Paired repeated reading: A classroom strategy for developing fluent reading. *The Reading Teacher, 40*(1), 70–75.

LaBerge, D., & Samuels, S. J. (1974). Toward a theory of automatic information processing in reading. *Cognitive Psychology, 6,* 293–323.

Lake, M. L. (1971). Improve the dictionary's image. *Elementary English, 48,* 363–365.

Langacker, P. W. (1973). *Language and its structure: Some fundamental linguistic concepts* (2nd ed.). New York: Harcourt Brace Jovanovich.

Lesgold, A. M. (1972a). *Effects of pronouns on children's memory for sentences.* (LRDC Publication 1972/17). Pittsburgh: University of Pittsburgh, Learning Research and Development Center. (ERIC Document Reproduction Service No. ED 068 974)

Lesgold, A. M. (1972b). Pronominalization: A device for unifying sentences in memory. *Journal of Verbal Learning and Verbal Behavior, 11,* 316–323.

Lesgold, A. M. (1974). Variability in children's comprehension of syntactic structures. *Journal of Educational Psychology, 66,* 333–338.

Lesgold, A. M., & Resnick, L. B. (1982). How reading difficulties develop: Perspectives from a longitudinal study. In J. P. Das, R. F. Mulcahy, & A. E. Wall (Eds.), *Theory and research in learning disabilities.* New York: Plenum.

Liberman, I., Shankweiler, D., Fischer, F., & Carter, B. 1974. Explicit syllable and phoneme segmentation in the young child. *Journal of Experimental Child Psychology, 18,* 201–212.

Lopardo, G., & Sadow, M. W. (1982). Criteria and procedures for the method of repeated readings. *Journal of Reading, 26,* 156–160.

Lundberg, I., Frost, J., & Petersen, O. (1988). Effects of an extensive program for stimulating phonological awareness in preschool children. *Reading Research Quarterly, 23,* 263–284.

Lytle, S. L. 1982. *Exploring comprehension style: A study of twelfth grade readers transactions with text.* Unpublished Dissertation, University of Pennsylvania, Philadelphia, 317 pp.

Mandler, J. M., & Johnson, N. S. (1977). Remembrance of things parsed: Story structure and recall. *Cognitive Psychology, 9,* 111–151.

Manzo, A. V. (1969). The ReQuest procedure, *Journal of Reading, 11,* 123–126.

Manzo, A. V. (1975). Guided reading procedure. *Journal of Reading, 18,* 287–291.

Marshall, N., & Glock, M. (1978–1979). Comprehension of connected discourse: A study into the relationships between the structure of text and information recalled. *Reading Research Quarterly, 16,* 10–56.

Mason, J. (1980). When *do* children begin to read: An exploration of four-year-old children's letter and word reading competencies. *Reading Research Quarterly, 15,* 203–227.

Mason, J. M. & The Staff of The Center for the Study of Reading, University of Illinois. (1984). A schema-theoretic view of the reading process as a basis for comprehension instruction. In G. G. Duffy, L. R. Roehler, & J. Mason (Eds.), *Comprehension instruction: Perspectives and suggestions.* New York: Longman.

Masonheimer, P. E., Drum, P. A., & Ehri, L. C. (1984). Does environmental print identification lead children into word reading? *Journal of Reading Behavior, 16,* 257–271.

Mayers, P. (1988). A novel within a novel: A case study description of the interaction between a young adolescent and a novel. Paper presented at the annual meeting of the International Reading Association, Toronto.

McDonald, G. E. (1978). *The effects of instruction in the use of an abstract structural schema as an aid to comprehension and recall of written discourse.* Unpublished doctoral dissertation, Virginia Polytechnic Institute and State University. Cited in Meyer, B. J. F., Brandt, D. M., & Bluth, G. J. (1980). Use of top-level structure in text: Key for reading comprehension of ninth-grade students. *Reading Research Quarterly, 16,* 72–103.

McGee, L. M. (1982). The influence of metacognitive knowledge of expository text structure on discourse recall. In J. A. Niles & L. A. Harris (Eds.), *New inquiries in reading research and instruction* (Thirty-first Yearbook of the National Reading Conference). Rochester, NY: National Reading Conference.

McGee, L. M., & Richgels, D. J. (1985). Teaching expository text structure to elementary students. *The Reading Teacher, 38,* 739–748.

McKeown, M. G. (1985). The acquisition of word meaning from context by children of high and low ability. *Reading Research Quarterly, 20,* 482–496.

MacKinnon, A. (1959). *How DO children learn to read?* Toronto: Copp Clarke.

Meyer, B. J. F. (1977). The structure of prose: Effects on learning and memory and implications for educational practice. In R. C. Anderson, R. J. Spiro, & W. F. Montague (Eds.), *Schooling and the acquisition of knowledge.* Hillsdale, NJ: Erlbaum.

Meyer, B. J. F., Brandt, D. M., & Bluth, G. J. (1980). Use of top-level structure in text: Key for reading comprehension of ninth-grade students. *Reading Research Quarterly, 16,* 72–103.

Meyer, L. A., Greer, E. A., & Crummey, L. (1987). An analysis of decoding, comprehension, and story test comprehensibility in four first-grade reading programs. *Journal of Reading Behavior, 19,* 69–98.

Mezynski, K. (1983). Issues concerning the acquisition of knowledge: Effects of vocabulary training on reading comprehension. *Review of Educational Research, 53,* 253–279.

Miller, G. A. (1977). *Spontaneous apprentices.* New York: Seabury Press.

Monroe, M. (1928). Methods for diagnosis and treatment of cases of reading disability. *Genetic Psychology Monographs, 4,* 335–456.

Monroe, M. (1932). *Children who cannot read.* Chicago: University of Chicago Press.

Morgan, W. P. (1896). A case of congenital word blindness. *British Medical Journal, 2,* 1378.

Morris, D. (1980). Beginning readers' concept of word. In E. H. Henderson & J. W. Beers, *Developmental and cognitive aspects of learning to spell: A reflection of word knowledge.* Newark, DE: International Reading Association.

Morris, D. (1986). *Teaching reading in kindergarten: A language-experience approach.* Occasional Paper No. 13. Evanston, IL: The Reading Center, National College of Education.

Morris, D. (1988). The relationship between word awareness and phoneme awareness in learning to read. A longitudinal study in kindergarten. Occasional Paper No. 17. Evanston, IL: The Reading Center, National College of Education.

Morris, D., & Perney, J. (1984). Developmental spelling as a predictor of first-grade reading achievement. *Elementary School Journal, 84,* 441–457.

Morrow, L. M. (1985). Retelling stories: A strategy for improving young children's comprehension, concept of story structure and oral language complexity. *Elementary School Journal, 75,* 647–661.

Nagy, W. E. (1988). *Teaching Vocabulary to Improve Reading Comprehension.* Newark, DE: International Reading Association.

Nagy, W. E., & Herman, P. A. (1987). Depth and breadth of vocabulary knowledge: Implications for acquisition and instruction. In M. G. McKeown & M. E. Curtis (Eds.), *The Nature of Vocabulary Acqusition.* Hillsdale, NJ: Erlbaum.

Nelson, K. (1974). Concept, word, and sentence: Interrelations in acquisition and development. *Psychological Review, 81,* 267–285.

Nelson, L. J., & Morris, D. (1988). Echo reading with taped books. *Illinois Reading Council Journal, 16,* 39–42.

Ogle, D. M. (1986). K-W-L: A teaching model that develops active reading of expository text. *The Reading Teacher, 39,* 564–570.

Orton, S. T. (1928). A physiological theory of reading disability and stuttering in children. *New England Journal of Medicine, 99,* 1046–1052.

Otto, W. S., & Askov, E. (1972). *The Wisconson design for reading skill development.* Minneapolis: National Computer Systems.

Page, W. D., & Barr, R. C. (1975). Use of informal reading inventories. In W. D. Page

(Ed.), *Help for the reading teacher: New directions in research.* Urbana, IL: National Conference on Research in English, ERIC Clearinghouse on Reading and Communications Skills, National Institute of Education.

Palincsar, A. S., & Brown, A. L. (1983). *Reciprocal teaching of comprehension-monitoring activities* (Technical Report No. 269). Champaign: University of Illinois, Center for the Study of Reading.

Parker, S. L. (1984). *A comparison of four types of initial vocabulary instruction.* Unpublished master's thesis, University of Minnesota, Minneapolis.

Pearson, P. D., Barr, R., Kamil, M., & Mosenthal P., (Eds.). (1984). *Handbook of reading research.* White Plains, NY: Longman.

Pearson, P. D., & Gallagher, M. C. (1983). The instruction of reading comprehension. *Contemporary Educational Psychology, 8,* 317–344.

Pearson, P. D., Hansen, J., & Grodon, C. (1979). The effect of background knowledge on young children's comprehension of explicit and implicit information. *Journal of Reading Behavior, 11,* 201–210.

Pearson, P. D., & Johnson, D. D. (1978). *Teaching reading comprehension.* New York: Holt, Rinehart & Winston.

Pelosi, P. L. (1977). *The origin and development of reading diagnosis in the United States: 1896–1946.* Unpublished doctoral dissertation, State University of New York at Buffalo.

Perfetti, C. A. (1985). *Reading ability.* New York: Oxford University Press.

Pikulski, J. A. (1974). A critical review: Informal reading inventories. *Reading Teacher, 28,* 141–153.

Powell, W. R. (1970). Reappraising the criteria for interpreting informal reading inventories. In D. L. Deboer (Ed.), *Reading diagnosis and evaluation.* Newark, DE: International Reading Association.

Powell, W. R., & Dunkeld, C. G. (1971). Validity of the IRI reading levels. *Elementary English, 48,* 637–642.

Pressley, M., Levin, J. R., & Miller, G. E. (1981). How does the keyword method affect vocabulary comprehension and usage? *Reading Research Quarterly, 16,* 213–226.

Quantz, J. O. (1897). Problems in the psychology of reading. *Psychological Review Monograph Supplements, 2,* 52.

Raphael, T. (1986). Teaching question–answer relationships, revisited. *The Reading Teacher, 39,* 516–522.

Read, C. (1971). Preschool children's knowledge of English phonology. *Harvard Educational Review, 41,* 1–34.

Readence, J. E., Baldwin, R. S., & Rickelman, R. J. (1983). Instructional insights into metaphor and similes. *Journal of Reading, 27,* 109–112.

Richek, M. A., List, L. K., & Lerner, J. W. (1983). *Reading problems: Diagnosis and remediation.* Englewood Cliffs, NJ: Prentice-Hall.

Robinson, H. M. (1937). The study of disabilities in reading. *Elementary School Journal, 38,* 15–38.

Robinson, H. M. (1946). *Why children fail in reading.* Chicago: University of Chicago Press.

Rosch, E. H. (1973). On the internal structure of perceptual and semantic categories. In T. E. Moore (Ed.), *Cognitive development and the acquisition of language.* New York: Academic Press.

Rosenblatt, L. M. (1985). Viewpoints: Transaction versus interaction—A terminological rescue operation. *Research in the Teaching of English, 19,* 96–107.

Rosenshine, B., & Stevens, R. 1984. Classroom instruction in reading. In P. D. Pearson, R. Barr, M. Kamil, and P. Mosenthal (Eds.), *Handbook of reading research.* White Plains: Longman.

Roser, N. & Juel, C. (1982). Effects of vocabulary instruction on reading comprehension. In J. A. Niles & L. A. Harris (Eds.), *New inquiries in reading research and instruction* (Thirty-first Yearbook of the National Reading Conference). Rochester, NY: National Reading Conference.

Rosner, J., & Simon, D. 1971. The auditory analysis test: An initial report. *Journal of Learning Disabilities, 4,* 384–392.

Rumelhart, D. E. (1975). Notes on a schema for stories. In D. G. Bobrow & A. Collins (Eds.), *Representation and understanding: Studies in cognitive science.* New York: Academic Press.

Sadow, M. W. (1982). The use of story grammar in the design of questions. *Reading Teacher, 35,* 518–522.

Samuels, S. J. (1979). The method of repeated readings. *The Reading Teacher, 32*(4), 403–408.

Sanders, N. M. (1966). *Classroom questions: What kinds?* New York: Harper & Row.

Schlein, M. (1966). The big cheese. In B. Martin, Jr. (Ed.), *Sounds of the storyteller.* New York: Holt, Rinehart & Winston.

Schwartz, R., & Raphael, T. (1985). Concept of definition: A key to improving students' vocabulary. *Reading Teacher, 30,* 198–205.

Sentell, C., & Blachowicz, C. L. Z. (1989). Comprehension court: A process approach to inference instruction. *Reading Teacher, 42,* 347–348.

Singer, H., & Donlan, D. (1982). Active comprehension: Problem-solving schema with question generation for comprehension of complex short stories. *Reading Research Quarterly, 17,* 166–186.

Slater, W. H., Graves, M. F., & Piche, G. L. (1985). Effects of structural organizers on ninth grade students' comprehension and recall of four patterns of expository text. *Reading Research Quarterly, 20,* 189–202.

Slobin, D. (1966). English abstract of Soviet studies of child language. In F. Smith & G. Miller (Eds.), *The genesis of language.* Cambridge, MA: MIT Press.

Smith, F. (1971). *Understanding reading.* New York: Holt, Rinehart & Winston.

Spache, G. D. 1972. *Diagnostic reading scales.* Monterey, CA: CTB/McGraw-Hill.

Spache, G. D. (1976). *Diagnosing and correcting reading disabilities.* Boston: Allyn & Bacon.

Spiro, R. (1980). Constructive processes in prose comprehension and recall. In R. Spiro, B. Bruce, & W. Brewer (Eds.), *Theoretical issues in reading comprehension.* Hillsdale, NJ: Erlbaum.

Stahl, S. (1983). Differential word knowledge and reading comprehension. *Journal of Reading Behavior, 15,* 33–50.

Stahl, S., & Fairbanks, M. (1986). The effects of vocabulary instruction: A model-based meta-analysis. *Review of Educational Research, 56,* 72–110.

Stanovich, K. E. (1980). Toward an interactive-compensatory model of individual differences in the development of reading fluency. *Reading Research Quarterly, 16,* 32–71.

Stanovich, K. E. (1986). Matthew effects in reading: Some consequences of individual differences in the acquisition of literacy. *Reading Research Quarterly, 21,* 360–407.

Stauffer, R. G. (1969). *Directing reading maturity as a cognitive process.* New York: Harper & Row.

Stauffer, R. G. (1970). *The language experience approach to the teaching of reading.* New York: Harper & Row.

Stein, N. L., & Glenn, C. G. (1979). An analysis of story comprehension in elementary school children. In R. O. Freedle (Ed.), *Advances in discourse processes, Vol. 2: New directions in discourse processing.* Norwood, NJ: Ablex.

Sternberg, R. (1987). Most vocabulary is learned from context. In M. G. McKeown & M. E. Curtis (Eds.), *The nature of vocabulary acquisition.* Hillsdale, NJ: Erlbaum.

Stevens, R. J., Madden, N. A., Slavin, R. E., & Farnish, A. M. (1987). Cooperative integrated reading and composition: Two field experiments. *Reading Research Quarterly, 22,* 433–454.

Straw, S. B., & Schreiner, R. (1982). The effect of sentence manipulation on subsequent measures of reading and listening comprehension. *Reading Research Quarterly, 17,* 339–352.

Sulzby, E. (1985). Children's emergent reading of favorite storybooks: A developmental study. *Reading Research Quarterly, 20,* 458–481.

Sulzby, E., & Teale, W. H. (1987). *Emergent literacy: Writing and reading.* Norwood, NJ: Ablex.

Taylor, B. M., & Beach, R. W. (1984). The effects of text structure instruction on middle-grade students' comprehension and production of expository text. *Reading Research Quarterly, 19,* 134–146.

Taylor, D. (1983). *Family literacy: The social context of learning to read and write.* Portsmouth, NH: Heinemann Educational Books.

Taylor, D., & Dorsey-Gaines, C. (1988). *Growing up literate: Learning from inner-city families.* Portsmouth, NH: Heinemann Educational Books.

Taylor, S. E. (1965). Eye movements in reading: Facts and fallacies. *American Educational Research Journal, 2,* 187–202.

Temple, C., Nathan, R., Burris, H., & Temple, F. (1988). *The beginnings of writing* (2nd ed.). Newton, MA: Allyn & Bacon.

Thomas, C. J. (1905). Congenital word blindness and its treatment. *Opthalmoloscope, 3,* 380–385.

Thorndike, E. L. (1917). Reading as reasoning: A study of mistakes in paragraph reading. *Journal of Educational Psychology, 8,* 323–332.

Thorndike, R. L. (1973). *Reading comprehension education in fifteen countries.* New York: Wiley.

Thorndike, R. L. (1973–1974). Reading as reasoning. *Reading Research Quarterly, 9,* 135–147.

Thurstone, L. L. (1946). Note on a reanalysis of Davis's reading tests. *Psychometrika, 11,* 185–188.

Tinker, M. A. (1934). The role of eye-movements in diagnostic and remedial reading. *School and Society, 39,* 147–148.

Tuinman, J. J. (1974). Determining the passage-dependency of comprehension questions in five major tests. *Reading Research Quarterly, 9,* 207–223.

Tuinman, J. J., & Brady, M. E. (1974). How does vocabulary account for variance on reading comprehension tests? A preliminary instructional analysis. In P. L. Nacke (Ed.), *Interaction: Research and practice in college-adult reading* (Twenty-third Yearbook of the National Reading Conference). Clemson, SC: National Reading Conference.

Tunmer, W. E., Herriman, M. L., & Nesdale, A. R. (1988). Metalinguistic abilities and beginning reading. *Reading Research Quarterly, 23,* 134–158.

Uhl, W. L. (1916). The use of the results of reading tests as a basis for planning remedial work. *Elementary School Journal, 17,* 266–275.

Vacca, R. T. (1981). *Content area reading.* Boston: Little, Brown.

Valencia, S. W., & Pearson, P. D. (1986). Reading assessment: Time for a change. *Reading Teacher, 40,* 726–732.

Vaughan, J. L., Castle, G., Gilbert, K., & Love, M. (1982). Varied approaches to preteaching vocabulary. In J. A. Niles & L. A. Harris (Eds.), *New inquiries in reading research and instruction.* (Thirty-first Yearbook of the National Reading Conference). Rochester, NY: National Reading Conference.

Venezky, R. (1970) *The structure of English orthography.* The Hague: Mouton.

Walker, B. J. (1988). *Diagnostic teaching of reading.* Columbus, OH: Merrill.

Weaver, P. A. (1979). Improving reading comprehension: Effects of sentence organization instruction. *Reading Research Quarterly, 15,* 129–146.

Weber, R. (1968). The study of oral reading errors: A review of the literature. *Reading Research Quarterly, 4,* 96–119.

Whaley, J., & Kibby, M. W. (1981). The relative importance of reliance on intraword characteristics and interword constraints for beginning reading achievement. *Journal of Educational Research, 74,* 315–320.

White, E. B. (1952). *Charlotte's Web.* New York: Harper & Brothers.

Wittrock, M. C., Marks, C. B., & Doctorow, M. J. (1975). Reading as a generative process. *Journal of Educational Psychology,67,* 484–489.

Wixson, K. K. 1984. Level of importance of postquestions and children's learning from text. *American Educational Research Journal, 21,* 419–33.

Wixson, K. K., Peters, C. W., Weber, E. M., & Roeber, E. D. (1987). New directions in statewide reading assessment. *Reading Teacher, 40,* 749–754.

Wixson, K. L. (1979). Miscue analysis: A critical review. *Journal of Reading Behavior, 11,* 163–175.

Wolman, R. N., & Barker, E. N. (1965). A developmental study of word definitions. *Journal of Genetic Psychology, 107,* 159–166.

Zirbes, L. (1918). Diagnostic measurement as a basis for procedure. *Elementary School Journal, 18,* 507–523.

Index

Affixes. *See* Word identification
Allington, R. L., 43, 92
Amarel, M., 66
Analysis
  comprehension performance, 181–182, 212
  instructional passages and, 212, 217, 225–226
  IRI-standardized, 245–247
  oral reading, 71–78
Anaphoric relations, 202–203
Anderson, R. C., 112–113, 116, 157
Anderson, R. D., 256
Anglin, J. M., 102, 103, 105, 111, 112
Antonyms, 111
Arthur, S. V., 137–138
Asch, S. E., 108
Aschner, M. J., 156
Askov, E., 262
Assessment. *See also* Diagnosis
  comprehension, 143, 156–162, 170
  reading rate, 71
Auditory acuity, 33
Automaticity. *See* Integration and fluency

Baer, J. A., 2–3
Baldwin, R. S., 108–109
Barker, E. N., 103–104
Barr, R., 42, 43, 45, 69, 256, 257, 258
Barrett, T. C., 157
Barron, R., 139
Bartlett, B. J., 178, 201
Beach, R. W., 201–202

Bean, T. W., 201
Bechhofer, R., 108, 110
Beck, I. L., 42, 74, 114, 115, 158, 195
Becker, W., 115
Beers, J. W., 46
Bennett, A., 43
Bernier, S. A., 117
Betts, E. A., 3, 74–75, 174, 181, 208
Biemiller, A., 43, 65, 66, 75
Bird, M., 194
Blachowicz, C. L. Z., 91, 114, 115, 137, 139, 140, 199–200, 202
Blachowicz Informal Phonics Survey, 57, 258–259, 277–280
Blending, 62
Bloom, B. S., 157
Blum, I. H., 93
Bluth, G. J., 177–178, 201
Bolinger, D., 103
Bond, G. L., 3, 45
Borderline reading level, 74, 174
Bortnick, R., 91
Bradley, L., 24, 40, 44
Brady, M. E., 100
Brainstorming, 140
Brandt, D. M., 177–178, 201
Braun, C., 202
Bridge, C. A., 170, 177, 190
Brown, A. L., 177, 194, 195, 197–198
Brown, C., 194
Brown, E., 115, 137
Bruce, D., 44
Bryant, P. E., 24, 40, 44

Burke, C., 21
Burkes, A. M., 195
Buros, O. K., 266
Burris, H., 37
Bussis, A. M., 66

Calkins, L., 37
Capsule words, 140
Carnine, D. W., 113, 115
Carpenter, P. A., 148, 149
Carr, E., 114
Carter, B., 44
Carver, R. P., 71
Case studies
    Alex, 51–53, 57–58
    Andrea, 190–192
    Chuck, 233–235
    comprehension, 183–189, 190–194
    Eva, 84–91, 210
    instructional passages, 216–230
    IRI-standardized, 233–235, 240–244,
        244–250
    Jake, 192–194
    James, 244–250
        record of IRI performance, 283–305
    Jody, 27–28, 30–32
    John (diagnostic model), 12
    Ken, 49–50, 55–56
    Larry (diagnostic model), 13
    Mary (diagnostic model), 12
    Patricia, 225–230
    Paul, 183–189
    print awareness in, 27–28
    Raymond, 118, 119–128
    reading diagnostic model, 8, 9
    Sara, 240–244
    Sharon, 216–224
    Stan, 94–98
    Tanya, 128–136
    Tom (diagnostic model), 13–14
    word identification in, 86–98
    word learning in, 86
Castle, G., 137
Categories, words and, 100–109
Chall, J. S., 16, 19, 45, 256
Chittenden, E. A., 66
Chomsky, C., 92
Clark, E. V., 111
Clay, M. M., 21, 41, 43, 66
Cleland, C. J., 202
Clowes, H. C., 2
Cloze tasks, 91–92
Cochran-Smith, M., 19, 37
Cocks, P., 104
Code programs, 41–46
Cohen, A. S., 43
Comprehension. See also Diagnostic patterns;
        Probe techniques; Questions; Recall;
        Vocabulary knowledge

administration of tests and, 181, 239
analysis of tests and, 181–182, 212, 221,
    225
anaphoric relations and, 202–203
assessment of, 143, 179–180
case studies of, 183–189, 190–191,
    192–194
characteristics of effective, 144
diagnosis of, 176–179
exposition, patterns of, 166
expository structure, 155–156
inference and, 146–148, 150–152
influence on, 145–155
instruction and, 174–176, 194–204
instructional passage, 215, 221–224, 229
instructional recommendations, 204
integration and, 146–150
interactive strategies for, 195–198
    DR-TA, 196
    K-W-L, 196–197
    Reciprocal teaching/modeling, 197–198
    ReQuest procedure, 197
IRI-standardized and, 239, 249
narrative structure, 153–155
nature of, 144
organizing information and, 152–156
preparation of tests and, 117–119,
    180–181
probe techniques and, 181–182, 183–189
processes of, 179, 180
questions and, 156–170
reorganizing information, 198–199
    graphic representation, 202
    guided reading procedure, 200–201
    Question-Answer Relationship (QAR)
        and, 199–200
    sentence-level, 202–204
    text structure, instruction in, 201–202
retelling, 189–191
strategies for, 10–11, 195–198
think-alouds, 192–194
Concepts, meanings and. See Word meanings
        and concepts
Connective inferences, 150–151
Connective terms, 150, 203–204
Consonants. See Word identification
Content words. See Word identification
Context clues, 137. See also Errors, reading;
        Word learning
Crist, B. I., 140
Crothers, E. J., 151, 152, 161
Crummey, L., 42
Cunningham, J. W., 137–138
Cunningham, P. M., 62, 137–138

Daskal, J., 202–203
Davidson, J. L., 196
Davis, F. B., 99, 177
Davis, O. L., Jr., 156

Davison, A., 256
Dearborn, W. F., 2, 3
Definite article, 149
Definition frame. *See* Word map
Diagnosis. *See also* specific areas of difficulty,
    e.g., Comprehension; Integration and
    fluency; Print skill; Vocabulary
    knowledge; Word identification;
    Word learning; Writing
  case studies of model, 12–14
  classroom instruction, as part of, 3–5
  history of, 2–3
  instructional passage, based on, 207–230
  major decisions of, 9–11
  model
    diagnostic flexibility of, 16–17
    for reading diagnosis, 8–11, 68
  model of reading
    for integration and fluency, 68–89
    with IRI-standardized, 231–251
Diagnostic patterns, 14–16
Directed Reading-Thinking Activity (DR-TA),
    195, 196, 204
Dixon, R. C., 115
Doctorow, M. J., 100
Dodge, R., 2
Dolch, E. W., 3, 49
Dolch Word List, 86, 275–277
Dorsey-Gaines, C., 19
Dougherty, M. L., 2
Draper, A. G., 113–114
Dreeben, R., 43, 45, 256
Drum, P. A., 23, 111
Dunkeld, C. G., 75
Durkin, D., 195, 199
Durrell, D. D., 3
Dykstra, R., 45
Dyslexia, 3

Ehri, L. C., 23, 24, 39–40, 44, 46
Ekwall, E. E., 75
Elder, R. D., 42
Elkonin, D. B., 61
Eller, R. G., 115, 137
Engelhardt, M. D., 157
Errors, reading, 74–78, 79–83. *See also*
    Integration and fluency; Oral
    reading; Probe techniques; Word
    identification; Word learning
Extended word meanings, 107

Fairbanks, M., 114
Farnish, A. M., 258
Feifel, H., 103
Fernald, G. M., 2
Ferreiro, E., 22
Ferroli, L., 47, 53–54
Figurative language. *See* Meanings; Metaphors
Fischer, F., 44

Fischer, J. H., 2
Fluency. *See also* Integration and fluency
    instruction to develop, 91, 92
    modeling fluent reading, 70, 91–93
    reading practice and, 92–93
    reading rate improvement of, 71, 93
    integration and, 65–69, 78, 92, 93
Ford, C. A., 3
Freebody, P., 112–113, 116
Freschi, R., 113, 115
Froese, V., 204
Frost, J., 24, 40, 44
Frustration reading level, 208, 209
Function words. *See* Word learning
Furst, E. J., 157

Gallagher, J. S., 156
Gallagher, M. C., 144
Gambrell, L., 189
Gamoran, A., 257
Gardner, H., 108, 110
Garner, R., 144, 178
Gates, A. I., 3
Geva, E., 150, 203
Gilbert, D. W., 149
Gilbert, K., 137
Gillet, J. W., 59, 140
Gilmore Oral Reading Test, 71
Glenn, C. G., 190
Glock, M., 177
Goals
  of book, 5–6
  of reading instruction, 1–2
Golden, J. M., 190
Goodman, K. S., 66, 69
Gordon, C. J., 202
Gourley, J. W., 149
Graphemes, 23
Graphic representation, 139, 202
Graves, M., 136
Graves, M. F., 202
Gray, C. T., 2
Gray, W. S., 2, 137
Greer, E. A., 42
Guided Reading Procedure, 198, 200–201
Gurren, L., 117
Guzak, F. J., 158

Hafner, L. E., 141
Harris, A. J., 49, 71, 174
Harste, J., 21
Heath, S. B., 19
Henderson, E. H., 45, 46, 53, 63
Herman, P. A., 114, 115, 137
Herriman, M. L., 40
Hiebert, E. H., 22
Hill, W. H., 157
Hincks, E. M., 3
Holdaway, D., 34

Holmes, E., 137
Homework, 208–209
Hood, J., 73
Huey, E. B., 2, 111, 144
Hughes, A., 117
Hunkins, F., 156

Independent reading level, 146, 175, 208
Inference, 150–152. *See also* Comprehension
Informal Reading Inventories (IRI)
    standardized. *See* IRI-standardized
Inman-Anderson, L., 115
Instruction
    comprehension and, 174–176, 194–204
    error patterns and, 22–46
    instructional passages and, 215, 224,
        229–230
    integration/fluency and, 89–98
    IRI-standardized, 243, 250
    learning programs and, 41–46
    phonics and, 44–45
    reading development and, 25–27
    word identification and, 45–46, 86, 88, 90,
        97
Instructional passages
    administration of, 211, 216–217
    analysis of results of, 74–76, 212, 217,
        225–226
    case studies of, 216–230
    comprehension and, 215, 221–224,
        229
    difficulty of, 95–99, 116–117
    instruction and, 215, 224, 229–230
    integration and, 215, 224, 229
    interpretation of results of, 212, 221–226
    preparation of, 211
    print skill and, 212, 221–224, 226–229
    probe techniques and, 212, 221, 225–226
    reading levels and, 208
    vocabulary knowledge and, 214–215, 221,
        229
Instructional reading level, 174–176, 238
Integration and fluency. *See also* Errors,
        reading; Word identification
    analysis of, 74–78, 85
    areas assessed and, 68–72
    assessment of, 72–78
    case studies, 84–89, 89–91
    comprehension and, 146–150
    development of, 65–68
    diagnosis of, 68–89
    instruction and, 84, 89–98
    instructional passage and, 74–76, 215, 224,
        229
    interpretation and, 83–84
    IRI-standardized and, 249
    oral reading and, 69–72
    print knowledge and, 68–69

probe techniques and, 78–83
response characteristics and, 88, 90
Interactive strategies, 195–198
Interpretation
    comprehension and, 215, 221, 229
    instructional passage and, 212, 221–226
    IRI-standardized and, 237–238, 247
    print skill and, 212, 221–226
IRI-standardized (Informal reading
        inventories)
    administration of, 231–233, 235–237
    analysis and, 245–247
    case studies of, 233–235, 240–250
    comprehension and, 239, 249
    instruction and, 243, 250
    integration and, 249
    interpretation of results of, 237–238, 247
    list of inventories of, 232
    listening task of, 233, 237
    materials, levels of, 238
    oral reading task of, 233, 236
    print skill and, 247–249
    probe techniques and, 245–247
    silent reading task and, 233, 236–237
    vocabulary knowledge and, 239
    word recognition test, 233, 235–236
Irwin, P. I., 189

Jackson, E., 2
Jacobson, M. D., 49
Jastak, J., 3
Jenkins, J. R., 100
Johns, J. L., 51
Johnson, D. D., 139, 162, 199
Johnson, N. S., 153
Juel, C., 42, 116
Just, M. A., 148, 149

Kameenui, E. J., 113, 115
Karpova, S. N., 40
Keller, H., 2
Kibbe, D., 2
Kibby, M. W., 75
Kimmell, S., 178
Klausner, E., 66
K-W-L, 195, 196–197
Koskinen, P. S., 93
Krathwohl, D. R., 157
Kurushima, S., 204

LaBerge, D., 67
Lake, M. L., 140–141
Langacker, P. W., 101, 107
Language, reading and, 145–146
Learning, word knowledge and, 58
Lerner, J. W., 231
Lesgold, A. M., 45, 148
Letter sounds, 45–46, 57. *See also* Word
        identification

Levin, J. R., 141
Liberman, I., 44
Lieberman study, 114
List, L. K., 231
Listening task. *See* IRI-standardized
Lopardo, G., 91, 92
Lorge, I., 103
Love, M., 137
Lucas, L., 2
Luce, T. S., 109
Lundberg, I., 24, 40, 44
Lytle, S. L., 144, 192

McCaslin, E. S., 42, 195
McDonald, G. E., 178, 201
McGee, L. M., 155, 169, 202
MacGinitie, W. H., 178
McKeown, M. G., 74, 114, 115–116, 137, 158, 195
McKinnon, A., 43
Madden, N. A., 258
Mandler, J. M., 153
Manzo, A. V., 195, 197, 198, 200–201
Markers, 61, 82. *See also* Word identification
Marks, C. B., 100
Marshall, N., 177
Mason, J., 23
Mason, J. M., 144
Masonheimer, P. E., 23
Materials, instructional. *See* Instructional passages; IRI-standardized; Reading, levels
Mayers, P., 194
Meanings. *See also* Vocabulary knowledge
  concepts and, 104–106
  contextual material and learning, 59
  extended, 107–110
  metaphors and, 107–110
  multiple, 106–107
Metacognition, 144
Metaphors, 108–110
Meyer, B. J. F., 177–178, 201
Meyer, L. A., 42
Mezynski, K., 113, 114
Miller, G. A., 110
Miller, G. E., 141
Miller, L. W., 2
Miscues. *See* Errors, reading
Mitchell, J. N., 189
Mnemonic devices, 141–142
Model for reading diagnosis, 8–11
Moeller, G. H., 113–114
Monroe, M., 2, 3
Morgan, W. P., 2
Morris, D., 35–37, 39, 41, 47, 48, 53–54, 92, 258
Morrow, L. M., 189–190
Multiple meanings of words, 106–107

Nagy, W. E., 114, 115, 137
Nathan, R., 37
Nelson, K., 103, 111
Nelson, L. J., 92
Nerlove, H., 108
Nesdale, A. R., 40

Ogle, D. M., 195, 196–197
Omanson, R. C., 74
Oral reading. *See also* Integration and fluency; IRI-standardized; Reading, levels
  analysis of, 74–78, 85–88, 95–97
  assessing errors in, 68–74
  fluency and, 70, 89, 92–93
  influence of passage difficulty on, 74–76, 85–86, 95
  response characteristics and, 69–78
Oral reading task. *See* IRI-standardized
Organization of information, 152–156
Orton, S. T., 3
Otto, W. S., 262
Overgeneralization, 111–112

Page, W. D., 69
Palinscar, A. S., 177, 194, 195, 197–198
Pany, D., 100
Pappas, C. C., 115, 137, 190
Pardi, R., 201
Parker, S. L., 115
Passage, instructional. *See* Instructional passage
Pearson, P. D., 139, 144, 162, 199, 265–266
Pelosi, P. L., 2–3
Perfetti, C. A., 67, 114, 115
Perney, J., 47, 53–54
Peters, C. W., 179, 265–266
Petersen, O., 24, 40
Pfeiffer, W., 189
Phonemes, 40, 44–45
Phonemic awareness (phoneme awareness), 23–24, 44–45
Physical condition, reading and, 33
Piche, G. L., 202
Pikulski, J. A., 75
Powell, W. R., 75
Predict-o-Grams, 202
Prenn, M., 136
Preparation
  comprehension and, 180–181
  instructional passages and, 211
  oral reading assessment, 72–73, 84
  vocabulary knowledge and, 117–119
Pressley, M., 141
Print awareness
  development of, 19–25
  diagnosis of, 25–33
  instruction to support, 33–37
  writing and, 28–32, 37–38

Print knowledge, 20, 39. *See also* Word
    elements; Word identification; Word
    learning
  areas assessed and, 68–69
  diagnosis of, 47–58, 68–69
  instruction to develop, 58
  knowledge of word elements, 43–44,
    52–58
  phoneme awareness, 44–45
  printed word discrimination, 41–43
  word awareness, 40–41
  word identification, 45–46
Print skill, 10. *See also* Diagnostic patterns;
    Writing
  case studies of, 49–58
  comprehension and, 212–214
  developing strategies for, 19–38
  instruction and, 58–60
  instructional passages and, 212, 221–224,
    226–229
  integration/fluency and, 65–98
  IRI-standardized and, 247–249
  probe techniques and, 78–79, 79–83
  sight words and, 76
  stages of understanding, 19–20
  word learning and, 48–49
Probe techniques
  advanced, 79–83
  basic, 78–79
  comprehension and, 181–182, 183–189
  instructional passages and, 212, 221,
    225–226
  integration/fluency of, 88–89
  IRI-standardized and, 245–247
  print skill and, 78–79, 79–83
  vocabulary knowledge and, 88–89
  word learning and, 56–57
Pronouns, 148
Propositional inferences, 152

Quantz, J. O., 2
Question-Answer Relationship (QAR)
    procedure, 198, 199–200
Questions
  beyond-text, 158–160, 160–163
  comprehension and, 156–171
  construction of, in expository materials,
    166–171
  construction of, in story materials,
    163–166
  recall and, 171
  scoring performance on, 181–182
  self, 195, 199
  text-related, 158–160, 160–163

Raphael, T., 138, 139, 198, 199–200
Rate of reading. *See* Reading rate
Read, C., 45

Readence, J. E., 108–109
Reading. *See also* Oral reading
  difficulty areas of, 238, 243
  Directed Reading-Thinking Activity
    (DR-TA), 196
  instructional programs, 41–46, 92–94
  K-W-L, 196
  language and, 145–146
  levels
    Betts's criteria, 174, 208
    borderline, 74, 174
    frustration, 74, 208
    independent, 74, 208, 238
    instructional, 74, 174–176, 208, 238
  rate
    chart for assessing, 71
    fluency and, 70–71, 93–94
Reading assessment. *See also* IRI-standardized;
    Testing, norm referenced
  beginning-of-year, 253–255
  grouping for instruction, 255–258
    kindergarten, 258–259
    middle and upper grades, 260–261
    primary grades, 259–260
Recall, free elicited, 170
Reciprocal teaching/modeling, 195, 197–198,
    204
Reis, R., 178
ReQuest procedure, 195, 197, 204
Resnick, L. B., 45
Response characteristics
  integration/fluency and, 69–78
  interpretation of, 74–79
  oral reading and, 68–72
  word identification and, 44–46
  word learning and, 48–49
  writing conventions and, 28–29,
    37–38
Retelling, 189–191
Richek, M. A., 231
Richgels, D. J., 155, 202
Rickelman, R. J., 108–109
Robinson, H. M., 3
Roeber, E. D., 179, 265–266
Roper/Schneider, D, 42
Rosch, E. H., 105
Rosenblatt, L. M., 144
Rosenshine, B., 257
Roser, N., 116
Rosner, J., 44
Rumelhart, D. E., 153–154

Sadow, M. W., 92, 159
Samuels, S. J., 67, 92
Sanders, N. M., 157
Schemata, 152–153
Schlein, M., 147, 161–163
Schreck, J., 100

Schreiner, R., 204
Schwartz, R., 138, 139
Scott Foresman, 43
Self-monitoring, 195
Self-questioning, 199
Semantic Feature Hypothesis, 67, 111
Semantic webbing, 139, 202
Sentell, C., 199–200
Sentence
  combining, 204
  comprehension, 158–160, 202
  method, 203, 204
  topic, 120, 148
Sentence-level comprehension, 202–204
Sight vocabulary, 49, 53. See also Word
      learning
Sight word recognition, 79. See also Word
      learning
Silent reading. See Independent reading;
      IRI-standardized
Similes. See Metaphor
Sipay, E. R., 71, 174
Slater, W. H., 202
Slavin, R. E., 258
Slobin, D., 40
Smith, F., 66
Spache, G. D., 42, 176
Spelling
  developmental stages, 20
  to diagnose knowledge of word elements,
      43–44, 52
Spiro, R., 144
Stahl, S., 114, 116–117
Standardized testing. See Testing,
      norm-referenced
Stanovich, K. E., 66, 67, 68
Stauffer, R. G., 34, 59, 195–196
Stein, N. L., 190
Sternberg, R., 114
Stevens, R., 257
Stevens, R. J., 258
Story reading
  to develop print awareness, 34–37
Storybook reading
  to assess print awareness, 25–27
Straw, S. B., 204
Structural analysis. See Word identification
Sulzby, E., 21, 25, 37
Syllabication. See Word identification
Synonyms, 149. See also Meanings
Syntactic knowledge, 149–150

Taylor, B. M., 201–202
Taylor, D., 19, 20
Taylor, S. E., 71
Teale, W. H., 37
Teberosky, A, 22
Temple, C., 37, 59, 140

Temple, T., 37
Testing, criterion-referenced (CRT), 261–262
Testing, norm-referenced (or standardized).
      See also IRI-standardized
  interpreting scores, 226–269, 270–271
  probe techniques with, 269–270
  problems with, 265–266
  sources of information about, 226
Text structure, instruction in, 201–202
Think-alouds, 192–194
Thomas, C. J., 2
Thorndike, E. L., 144
Thorndike, R. L., 99, 177
Thurstone, L. L., 177
Tierney, R. J., 170, 177, 190
Tinker, M. A., 3
Tuinman, J. J., 100, 265
Tunmer, W. E., 40

Uhl, W. L., 2
Undergeneralization, 112

Vacca, R. T., 140, 141
Valencia, S. W., 265–266
Vaughan, J. L., 137
Venezky, R., 61
Verbal knowledge. See Vocabulary knowledge
Visual acuity, 33
Vocab-o-grams, 139
Vocabulary knowledge, 10, 99–142. See also
      Diagnostic patterns; Word meaning
      and concepts
  case studies of, 119–136
  comprehension and, 121, 134
  diagnosis of difficulty, 116, 239
  diagnostic procedures, 116–119
  instruction, 58–60, 112–116, 128
    brainstorming and classification, 140
    capsule words, 140
    components of, 112–116
    context, learning from, 137
    goals for, 136–137
    graphic organizers, 139
    post-reading follow-ups, 140–141
  instructional passage, 214–215, 221, 229
  IRI-standardized, 239
  learning and, 104–106
  meanings and concepts, 100–112
  preparation of tests of, 117
  print skill and, 121, 129
Vowels. See Word identification

Walker, B. J., 93
Weaver, P. A., 204
Weber, E. M., 179, 265–266
Weber, R., 66
Whaley, J., 75
White, E. B., 159–160

Wilkerson, B. C., 196
Wilson, R., 189
Winner, E., 108, 110
Wittrock, M. C., 100
Wixson, K. K., 114, 156, 179, 265–266
Wixson, K. L., 73
Wolf, D., 108, 110
Wolman, R. N., 103–104
Woodward, V., 21
Word awareness, 40–41
Word banks, 59
Word discrimination, 41–43
Word elements. *See also* Word identification
  case studies of, 49–50, 51–52, 55–56
  informal diagnostic probe and, 56–57
  instruction to develop knowledge of
    application and blending, 62–63, 81
    markers, 61
    multisyllabic words, 63–64, 83
    one-syllable words, 60, 79–82
  knowledge of, 52–58
  spelling task, 52–55
Word identification. *See also* Print
      knowledge; Word elements; Word
      learning
  affixes, 82–83
  blending, 62
  case studies of, 57–58, 84–89, 94–98
  consonants, 81
  diagnosis of difficulty in, 45–46
  markers, 82
  phoneme awareness, 40, 44–45
  phonics and, 44
  strategies, 76–78
  syllables, 61
  vowels, 81

Word learning. *See also* Word identification;
  basal program words, 48
  case studies of, 49–50, 51–53, 55–56,
    57–58
  diagnosis of difficulty in, 116–117
  graded word lists, 50–51
  instruction and, 48–49
  instruction to develop knowledge of, 58,
    112–116
    contextual reading practice, 59
    word banks, 59
    writing and spelling, 59
  word awareness, 40–41
  word discrimination, 41–43
Word lists, 48–49, 51, 275–276
Word map, 139
Word meaning and concepts
  antonyms, 111
  development of, 99–116
  extended, 107–110, 140–141
  extensive, 102
  intensive, 102
  learning of, 101–104
  metaphors and similes, 108–110,
  multiple, 106–107
  overgeneralization, 111
  synonyms, 149
  undergeneralizations, 112
Word recognition. *See* Word identification;
    Word learning
Writing
  to assess knowledge of print, 28–32
  to support print awareness, 37–38

Zirbes, L., 2